The Root Causes
of Biodiversity Loss

Edited by
Alexander Wood,
Pamela Stedman-Edwards
and Johanna Mang

Earthscan Publications Ltd, London and Sterling, VA

First published in the UK in 2000 by
Earthscan Publications Ltd

Copyright © 2000 Macroeconomics for Sustainable Development Program Office,
WWF-International

Panda symbol © 1986 WWF

A catalogue record for this book is available from the British Library

ISBN: 1 85383 699 0

Typesetting by PCS Mapping & DTP, Newcastle upon Tyne
Printed and bound by Biddles Ltd, Guildford and King's Lynn
Cover design by Susanne Harris

For a full list of publications please contact:

Earthscan Publications Ltd
120 Pentonville Road
London, N1 9JN, UK
Tel: +44 (0)20 7278 0433
Fax: +44 (0)20 7278 1142
Email: earthinfo@earthscan.co.uk
http://www.earthscan.co.uk

22883 Quicksilver Drive, Sterling, VA 20166–2012, USA

Earthscan is an editorially independent subsidiary of Kogan Page Ltd and publishes in
association with WWF-UK and the International Institute for Environment and
Development

This book is printed on elemental chlorine-free paper

Contents

Figures, Tables and Boxes

FIGURES

TABLES

BOXES

Acronyms and Abbreviations

AID	Agency for International Development (US)
APC	Agriculture Production Cooperatives (Vietnam)
CAMPPO	Brazilian Agricultural Extension Agency and Support Centre
CAR	Central African Republic
CBD	Convention on Biological Diversity
CBR	Calakmul Biosphere Reserve
CDA	Chilika Development Authority
CDC	Cameroon Development Corporation
CEDAC	Communauté Economique de l'Afrique Centrale
CFA	Central African franc
CGR	Compound Growth Rate
CITES	Convention on International Trade in Endangered Species of Wild Fauna and Flora
CRAX	Consejo Regional de Xpujil (Mexico)
cusec	28 cubic litres per second
DAR	Department of Agrarian Reform (Philippines)
DENR	Department of Environmental and Natural Resources (Philippines)
ECAN	Environmentally Critical Areas Network (Philippines)
EIA	environmental impact assessment
EMATER	Brazilian Agricultural Extension Agency
EMBRAPA	Brazilian Agricultural Research
EPA	Environmental Protection Agency (Pakistan)
ERP	Economic Recovery Programme
ESAP	Economic and Social Action Programme
EU	European Union
FAO	Food and Agriculture Organization (UN)
FEMAGO	Goiás State Environmental Agency
fob	free on board
FOMENTAR	Sociedad de Fomento Mercantil
GATT	General Agreement on Tariffs and Trade
GDP	gross domestic product
GEF	Global Environment Facility
ha	hectare
IBAMA	Brazilian Environmental Agency
IBGE	Brazilian Institute of Geography and Statistics

ICDP	Integrated Conservation and Development Programme
IMF	International Monetary Fund
INCRA	Instituto Nacional de Colonização e Reforma Agrária
INPE	National Institute of Space Research
ISPN	Institute for Society, Population and Nature (Brazil)
ITR	Rural Land Tax (Brazil)
IUCN	International Union for Conservation of Nature and Natural Resources (The World Conservation Union)
LQMS	Logging Quota Management System (China)
MAI	Multilateral Agreement on Investments
MEPZ	Mactan Export Processing Zone
MNRT	Ministry of Natural Resources and Tourism (Tanzania)
MOF	Ministry of Forestry
MP	Macroeconomics for Sustainable Development Program
nd	no date
NAFTA	North American Free Trade Agreement
NCS	National Conservation Strategy (Pakistan)
NEAP	National Environmental Action Plan
NEMC	National Environmental Management Council (Tanzania)
NEQS	National Environmental Quality Standards (Pakistan)
NESP	National Economic Survival Programme (Tanzania)
NGO	non-governmental organization
NNR	National Nature Reserves
NORAD	Norwegian Agency for Development Cooperation
NTFP	non-timber forest product
PEPA	Pakistan Environmental Protection Agency
PEPC	Pakistan Environmental Protection Council
PGPM	Minimum Price Guarantee Policy (Brazil)
PLA	Protected Landscape Area (Slovakia)
PND I	First National Development Plan (Brazil)
PND II	Second National Development Plan (Brazil)
PND III	Third National Development Plan (Brazil)
POLOCENTRO	Cerrado Development Programme
ppm	parts per million
ppt	parts per trillion
PROALCOOL	Programa Nacional do Álcool (Brazil)
PRODECER	Nipo-Brazilian Cooperation Programme for Development of the Cerrado
RUBADA	Rufiji Basin Development Authority
SAP	Structural Adjustment Programme
SEAn	Strategic Environmental Analysis (Danube Basin)
SEP	Strategic Environmental Plan (Philippines)
SFE	State Forest Enterprises (Vietnam)
SNEC	Cameroon State Water Company
SODECAO	Cameroon State Cocoa Development Agency
SONEL	Cameroon State Electric Company

spp	species
SRA	Sugar Regulatory Agency (Philippines)
TCMP	Tanzania Coastal Management Partnership
TLA	Timber Licensure Agreement (Philippines)
Tsh	Tanzanian shilling
TVE	Township and village enterprise (China)
UN	United Nations
UNDP	United Nations Development Programme
UNEP	United Nations Environment Programme
WRI	World Resources Institute
WTO	World Trade Organization
WWF	World Wide Fund For Nature
WWF	World Wildlife Fund (in the United States and Canada)

THE ROOT CAUSES PROJECT

The Root Causes project originated in a dialogue between the World Wide Fund For Nature (WWF) Macroeconomics for Sustainable Development Program Office (MPO) and the Global Environment Facility (GEF). At the heart of this dialogue was our joint conviction that the conservation of biological diversity needed to be based on an understanding of the factors and the dynamics that drive its loss (what we came to call the 'root causes'). Recognizing that there was little in the way of guidance on how to identify and analyse those root causes, and even less on what to do about them, the MPO developed the Root Causes project with the objective of understanding the root causes of biodiversity loss and effecting responses to them.

This project has conducted case studies in ten separate countries, in two separate phases carried out over two and a half years. These case studies were chosen following discussions with WWF offices and are meant to reflect a geographical and thematic diversity. It is also important to note that the project has always had, as one of its objectives, the building of local capacity to understand and address the root causes of biodiversity loss. As a result, even though local WWF offices directed most of the case studies, they usually collaborated with WWF research and project partners. The MPO in Washington DC provided overall guidance and oversight of the project, as well as programme administration. The project was structured to take advantage of the WWF's global reach and expertise on matters of biodiversity loss. This imposed certain constraints on the project, but also provided us with a ready-made constituency to test out the operational implications of the project. Indeed, in its third phase, the project will begin to move from analysis to implementation by helping WWF offices which have been involved in the analytical phase to design operational activities that draw from the conclusions and recommendations of the Root Causes project

Funding for the project was provided by the Dutch, German, and Danish bilateral aid agencies (Ministerie van Buitenlandse Zaken (DGIS) of the Netherlands, Bundesministerium für wirtschaftliche Zusammenarbeit und Entwicklung (BMZ) of Germany, Danish International Development Agency (Danida) respectively), as well as WWF Sweden. Because these agencies play a key role in the GEF and have large biodiversity portfolios of their own, and because of their early and enthusiastic support, they have always constituted, with the GEF, our most immediate audience for the project.

A Program Advisory Board, composed of leading experts in the social and natural sciences and economics, was created to help provide guidance and oversight for the project's development and implementation. The Board met twice during the course of the project's two phases to review case study reports, to discuss methodological aspects of the project, to reach general conclusions and make recommendations arising out of the project findings.

As mentioned, ten case studies were carried out. Executive summaries for each of these are found in the later chapters of the publication. The case studies are:

- Brazil: Cerrado
- Cameroon: Bushmeat and Wildlife Trade
- China: South-Western Forests
- Danube River Basin: Wetlands and Floodplains
- India: Chilika Lake
- Mexico: Calakmul Biosphere Reserve
- Pakistan: Mangroves
- Philippines: Cebu, Negros and Palawan
- Tanzania: Rufiji, Ruvu and Wami Mangroves
- Vietnam: North and Central Highlands

Foreword

How to stem the loss of our natural heritage, and the capital it represents to current and future generations, is one of the great challenges we face at the dawn of the 21st century. While much has already been done to try to address the problem, every indicator of biodiversity loss shows that the situation is getting worse, rather than better.

In this context, the Root Causes project described in this publication is an innovative programme designed and implemented by WWF's Macroeconomics Program Office to analyse and address the root causes of biodiversity loss. It makes two important contributions.

First, it develops an Analytical Approach to help identify, analyse, and organize the many complex factors that drive biodiversity loss. This new approach is based on the straightforward assumption that our success in addressing this problem depends on our ability to understand and act upon the forces driving it. These forces are growing ever more complex, and so the development of tools to understand what these factors are and how they relate to one another is especially important.

The second important contribution this publication makes is in the development of recommendations for how institutions and governments can, and should, address the root causes of biodiversity loss. These recommendations are firmly grounded in the realization that biodiversity loss is occurring because the factors that are acting to deplete it are far stronger than the forces acting to conserve it.

My previous association at the GEF, and my current responsibilities at the World Bank, have convinced me that this dynamic is at the root of the many challenges we face in implementing sustainable development. Difficult trade-offs are at the heart of these challenges, with societies having to find a balance between economic growth, social equity, and the environment, particularly the conservation of biodiversity. As policy-makers, we need to accept that the current set of incentives in the international system facilitates economic growth, often at the cost of accelerating biodiversity loss, and does not favour sustainable development.

Our challenge is therefore twofold: first, to understand what set of incentives needs to be promoted, and disincentives removed, to promote sustainable development and protect biodiversity; and second, to translate such understanding into strategic activities that involve all affected parties, from the highest levels of government to local communities.

This publication goes a long way in helping us define the first part of this equation, and WWF is to be commended for building on a growing consensus to propose this new approach to the conservation of biodiversity. It is now left to us to take up the second challenge and to find ways in which we can all work to bring about solutions.

Ian Johnson
Vice-President,
Environmentally and Socially Sustainable Development
The World Bank

Acknowledgements

This project has its origins in discussions of the MPO with management and staff of the GEF more than five years ago. During the ensuing four years of research, we received the support and input of many dedicated people around the globe. Without them this project would not have happened, and we want to express our thanks to them.

The central part of this project is its ten case studies. We would like to begin our acknowledgments by thanking our project partners, the ten research teams, for their cooperation and professionalism.

The international Program Advisory Group provided invaluable guidance on the development and implementation of this project. We would like to express our sincere appreciation for their time, effort, and wisdom. The members of the Group are Dr Jorge Soberón, Dr Katrina Brandon, Dr Kamaljit Bawa, Dr Carle Folke, Dr Peter Utting and Dr Geoff Heal.

We also want to pay special tribute to the funders of this project: DGIS of the Netherlands, BMZ of Germany, Danida of Denmark and WWF Sweden. Their financial support and ongoing interest in the project have been very much appreciated.

In particular, we want to thank the GEF Secretariat. In addition to being a project funder, the GEF, as described above, has always been one of the key audiences for this project, and its willingness to engage in a dialogue on these issues has been a major motivating factor in our work.

There are several WWF colleagues who contributed greatly to the content of this book, and to whom we owe thanks. Among them are Jenny Heap, Tim Geer, Jason Clay, Dave Olson and Charlie Arden-Clark.

We owe special thanks to our colleague, Teresa Román, who kept the project running smoothly. She managed the communications with the research teams, the day-to-day organization of the project activities, prepared the text for the publisher, and oversaw editing and production of the text. Monica Chacon-Glenn and Maria Boulos (WWF International) helped immensely in coordinating the project in its early stages. Without their input this project could not have been carried out in such a coordinated and smooth way. Sherri Alms took on the editing of the authors' texts and transformed them with precision, rigour and patience into the final text. Marilyn Worseldine is the creative centre behind the graphics of the book. In addition, our consultant, Doreen Robinson, provided valuable input into the recommendations, and thoughtful comments on the various drafts of the document. Pamela Stedman-Edwards edited the ten case study summaries found in this publication.

Our deepest gratitude goes to Dr David Reed, Director of the MPO. He was instrumental in the conceptual development of this project, and shaped it with his intellectual rigour and energy. The editors are especially thankful for his advice and guidance in how to make this publication work.

Even with all of this help, the responsibility for any lapses and errors are the editors' alone.

Alexander Wood
Pamela Stedman-Edwards
Johanna Mang
WWF Macroeconomics Program Office

Chapter 1

An Emerging Consensus on Biodiversity Loss

Alexander Wood

INTRODUCTION

Global biodiversity loss is a crisis whose importance is now well understood and widely accepted. What is also accepted is that a problem with such a global scale requires a global response. The international community's response has been to rely on a structural approach common to the resolution of international problems. The Convention on Biological Diversity (CBD) has developed a legal framework while the Global Environment Facility (GEF) has provided a financial framework. The combined framework continues to provide the rationale and standards for how the international community should address the issue of biodiversity loss. As such, it has not only played a role in maintaining the visibility of the issue on the international agenda, it has also provided the impetus for activities and programmes that have directly contributed to the conservation of biological diversity around the world. As a global organization committed to the conservation of biodiversity, WWF has been directly involved in the push for, and the development of, this global response. We have supported and encouraged the work of the multiplicity of institutional, governmental, and non-governmental responses that have emerged to address the problem.

In spite of many positive and encouraging developments that have arisen in this area over the last ten years, it is our belief that the approaches and responses have failed to stem the loss of biodiversity in any meaningful way. Indicators of loss in terrestrial and marine ecosystems continue to show that species and habitats are disappearing. A recent WWF report estimates that the world has lost 30 per cent of its natural wealth in the span of one generation from 1970 to 1995.[1]

In fact an increasing amount of research in the environmental community has focused on why biodiversity loss continues to exist as a global problem; this despite the many initiatives and innovations that have been devoted to the issue over the years, and which have pushed the geographical and conceptual boundaries of what needs to be addressed to conserve biodiversity ever-outward. The Root Causes project is our contribution to this emerging school of thought. One of the assumptions underlying our research is that biodiversity loss will continue unabated until its indirect or root causes are understood and addressed.

The Root Causes project is driven by a need to focus attention on what we believe to be the new requirements necessary to stem and halt the loss of biodiversity. Its four basic premises are that:

1. Biodiversity loss, as a global phenomenon, is accelerating in scale and scope.
2. The solutions proposed and activities undertaken to date have not been sufficient to address the problem.
3. This basic failure stems from an inability to understand and articulate the basic conflict that exists between the promotion of growth and consumption on one side, and activities and incentives promoting sustainable development and conservation of biological diversity on the other. We believe that this conflict and the large bias that continues to exist in favour of growth and consumption are the root causes of biodiversity loss.
4. New conservation approaches must begin with an understanding that conflict and be based on the expectation that the roots of that conflict must be addressed if they are to succeed in the long run.

The MPO designed the Root Causes project to test the basic validity of those premises and has generated three distinct and related outputs. First, to help us understand how to carry out a root causes analysis and what it might tell us about the nature of the conflict driving biodiversity loss, we developed an *Analytical Approach* designed to facilitate the analysis of the root causes of biodiversity loss. Second, to look at the status of biodiversity, and what the effectiveness of current approaches has been, we carried out ten case studies around the world to look at the root causes of biodiversity loss in specific instances. And third, to help define the development of new conservation approaches, we offer recommendations on how the international community can develop new ways of thinking about biodiversity loss and how it should be addressed.

To place the project in a useful context, this chapter will examine the development of an international consensus on the loss of biodiversity to illustrate how the global community has addressed the problem. We will then look at how that consensus has begun to be challenged, from both within and without its framework, and where we are left today. The chapter ends with a preview of the publication that follows.

Before we begin, however, we need to consider the term 'root causes' itself. This term is employed early and often and needs to be defined. For the sake of clarity and coherence, therefore, we use the term 'root causes' to refer to the set of factors that truly drive biodiversity loss, but whose distance from the actual incidence of loss, either in space or time, makes them a challenge to identify and remedy.

THE IMPERFECT GLOBAL CONSENSUS ON BIODIVERSITY LOSS

In the lead-up to the 1992 United Nations Conference on Environment and Development (the Rio Summit), the traditional aid donors were under pressure to provide financial resources to address what were acknowledged to be the major 'global' environmental problems: loss of biological diversity, climate change, loss of the ozone layer, and degradation of the marine environment.[2] Beginning in the 1980s, these issues were capturing increasing scientific and public attention and a fledgling consensus on how to address them was emerging by the time of this summit.[3]

These issues represented, in economic parlance, problems of the 'global commons', ie problems whose manifestation might be local or national but whose consequences would be global in scale. As Timothy Swanson has noted, describing the global nature of the biodiversity issue, 'the global stocks of biological diversity generate a flow of services to all societies on Earth' (Swanson, 1997). The particular logic that followed this definition of the problem reasoned that the costs of inaction would be global in scope so the responsibility for addressing the problems – even if its manifestation was highly localized – should be borne by the global community. Two leading environmental economists, David Pearce and Dominic Moran, used the term 'global appropriations failure' explaining that '...if the country in question received no financial or other resources to pay for these global external benefits, it will have no incentive to look after the biological resources' (Pearce and Moran, 1994). As to who would actually pay for solutions to the problems, a debate raged over claims made by developing countries and the environmental constituency that, since the dynamic driving much of this global environmental degradation originated in the industrialized Northern economies – the concept of historical responsibility – they needed to pay to mitigate its effect.

This debate was therefore defined very early on as an issue of resource transfer. It was in effect a continuation of the North–South debate on development that had begun in the 1960s. In 1987 the World Commission on Environment and Development (the Brundtland Commission) report, entitled *Our Common Future*, introduced the concept of sustainable development, explicitly bringing together environment and economic development, and in doing so '...legitimized the consideration of financing for the environment' (Sjoberg, 1994). This legitimization had as a backdrop a familiar North–South confrontational dynamic.

Developed countries believed that the South was only interested in sustainable development to guarantee itself continued resource transfers, while developing countries suspected that the North was using the environment to impose further conditions on the terms of their economic development. Facing political and scientific pressure to act on environmental problems, the developed and developing countries struck a less-than-perfect bargain: increased funding would be made available to address global environmental issues, in addition to existing development assistance, but the solutions and strategies followed would not place 'conditionalities' on economic planning in developing countries. Having agreed in theory that sustainable development would require integration of environmental concerns and development options, the political fix that emerged in effect served to separate the issues. Integrated strategic thinking about sustainable development gave way to the more expedient solution of financing strictly for the environment, deliberately leaving out the question of development. The CBD enshrined the separation of these issues in Article 20, paragraph 4:

> 'the extent to which developing country Parties will effectively implement their commitments under this Convention will depend on the effective implementation by developed country Parties of their commitments under this Convention related to financial resources and transfer of technology and will take fully into account the fact that economic and social development and eradication of poverty are the first and overriding priorities of the developing country Parties' (United Nations Environment Programme – UNEP – 1992)

What the Convention focuses on instead is the conservation of biodiversity through 'in situ' (ie protected areas) or sustainable-use strategies.

The Institutional Response

Going into the Rio Summit, the nations of the world started putting together the basic outline for what would be the institutional framework to address global biodiversity loss. As mentioned at the outset, that framework had two pillars: the legal, in the form of the CBD, and the financial, represented by the GEF. The GEF emerged from a flurry of competing proposals developed in 1989 – from the Hague Declaration in March calling for a UN financial authority to protect the atmosphere to the Belgrade Declaration in September recommending a Planet Protection Fund – whose common characteristic was to seek an institutional format through which the anticipated Rio agreements could be funded (Sjoberg, 1994). Created as an institutional response to the consensus, the GEF would be used to transfer funds from the developed nations to the developing ones as a way of mitigating historical responsibility for biodiversity loss and addressing the pressing political need for action on the subject. This response was reflected in the concept of incremental cost, the principle underlying the GEF's funding decisions. In adhering to this concept, the GEF funds the portion of a given project whose benefits accrue to the global community. This spares countries that receive GEF assistance the burden of having to use national budgets to pay for what is considered a global biodiversity benefit (Wolf, 1995).

We need to be clear that we focus on these institutions not as a way of assigning responsibility to them for the state of the world's biodiversity, but as a way of demonstrating the existence of a global consensus on how to deal with biodiversity loss. For better or worse, the Convention and the GEF represent the global community's commitment to addressing biodiversity loss.

The Operational Response

Defining the problem of biodiversity loss has from the outset been the province of natural scientists, who are most familiar with its parameters. As reflected in the most prominent literature on the subject,[4] it is generally agreed that biodiversity loss has four major categories of direct (or 'proximate') causes. These are habitat alteration and loss, over-harvesting, species and disease introduction, and pollution and climate change. Of these, habitat alteration is clearly the predominant cause and is a problem that operates at the local scale. A corollary to this definition is the assumption that behaviour that causes biodiversity loss is explained by factors operating at a defined geographical level (even if this level is national).

And while it is generally agreed, as described above, that the cost of biodiversity loss is an international concern, the focus of analysis and activity has always betrayed a bias for the local level and for activities that address the direct causes of loss. When global factors were recognized, they were either as problems as general as 'northern models of consumption' or enumerated as lists with no clear linkage either between each other or to the direct causes of biodiversity loss (Stedman-Edwards, 1998). This focus on a defined geographic site grew out of experience accrued in developed countries over the last century, which had validated an approach that focused on protecting natural resources and landscapes through a strategy of legal protection. As a result, early efforts at protecting biodiversity focused on the preservation of specific species through the use of legal mechanisms such as protected areas and endangered species legislation. By necessity and experience, this protective approach was best implemented through the protection of the ecosystems these species inhabited, leading to the creation of protected areas and national parks. From 1970 to 1990, '...more parks and reserves were created than had previously existed...' (Brandon et al, 1998). However, the limits of this approach, which had had its successes in developed countries, soon became obvious in the context of developing countries. Setting aside areas of land (or water, in some cases) as a mechanism for ensuring the conservation of biodiversity often meant ignoring long-standing human interactions with the ecosystems contained in these areas. This often resulted in protected areas whose formal designation had very little impact on the ground (so-called 'paper parks') because mechanisms for supervision and enforcement failed. In other cases the best efforts of governments to set aside critical ecosystems ran foul of local needs for natural resources, with resulting encroachment and degradation.

Reflecting once again the political accommodation that lay at its heart and the importance accorded to in situ conservation by the CBD, the GEF took up these basic approaches as the focus of its activities in the area of biodiversity. Michael Wells states that 'while GEF program areas (ie biodiversity, climate change, etc) require long-term actions, GEF operations and procedures encourage short-term measures for a 'quick-fix' approach' (Wells, 1994). He goes on to enumerate the three main operational activities supported with GEF grants as:

1. Studies and management plans for habitat protection.
2. Establishment and management of protected areas.
3. Government agencies responsible for protected area management.

In our own critique of the GEF's Pilot Phase, published in 1993, we wrote:

> '*WWF is deeply concerned that the Global Environment Facility will produce a seemingly handsome portfolio of projects that actually are only of peripheral relevance to the central development issues that threaten the viability of the biosphere. Only through a fundamental shift toward promoting sustainability, and a change in the way policies are translated into operational criteria of project design and selection by the implementing agencies, can the GEF become a dynamic vehicle for addressing the development challenges of the twenty-first century*' (Reed, 1993).

CHALLENGING THE CONSENSUS

What we call a 'consensus' was never more than a political accommodation between developed and developing countries. There have always been many schools of thought on how to define biodiversity and how best to deal with its loss. In simplified terms, the conservation of biodiversity has tended to be a

Northern concern driven by an increasingly powerful environmental constituency. In preparing his assessment of the GEF, Wells conducted a survey of over 100 non-governmental organisations (NGO) in developing countries and found that, in their opinions,

> *'the GEF was created by a few northern countries that have set the "global" environmental agenda with little consideration for southern countries' perspectives. The GEF has failed to recognize the richer countries' responsibilities for major global environmental problems and ignores fundamental questions of poverty, population, growth, debt, and access to resources'* (Wells, 1994)

While these opinions may gloss over the role Southern governments played in using the environmental agenda for their own interests (ie in securing funding), we bring it up to make the point that even if a consensus existed, it was a consensus between governments, which did not reflect the growing body of knowledge that was emerging on the nature of biodiversity loss and how to deal with it.

Starting in the early 1980s, the conservation community was beginning to 'scale up' the approaches they were employing to understand and address the loss of biodiversity, a process that continues to this day. Groups and individuals slowly began to challenge the basic consensus that biodiversity loss was best addressed through funding activities that relied almost exclusively on the creation and management of protected areas.

One of the critical milestones of this challenge to the consensus was the World Conservation Strategy, developed by the International Union for Conservation of Nature and Natural Resources (IUCN). It highlighted the need to link protected-area management with economic opportunities for adjacent communities based on the experience previously described, in which the viability of protected areas in developing countries was being directly challenged by the lack of consideration for factors such as management and enforcement capacity or economic development of local communities. It also placed a great deal more importance than had been accorded to the idea that there could be 'sustainable use' of biodiversity. The 1982 World Congress on National Parks endorsed this approach. Conservation organizations like WWF began to design 'debt-for-nature swaps' and other innovative financial instruments, to channel funding to national/local environmental authorities to ensure adequate systems for monitoring and enforcement of protected areas. Integrated conservation and development projects (ICDP) and a host of other initiatives sought to promote small-scale economic development in communities immediately adjacent to protected areas as a way of deflecting pressure away from the areas themselves.

It is beyond the scope of this publication to examine the full range of strategies and options discussed during this period.[5] What is important, though, is that this progression in approach made the consideration of economic issues an important concern, and so considerably 'scaled up' the scope of activities needed to ensure effective conservation. The fact that the CBD recognized 'sustainable use' reflected the emerging importance of these new approaches.

Strategies focusing on local economic development as a conservation tool were supported by a growing body of environmental economics, pioneered by people such as Robert Repetto of the World Resources Institute (WRI) and David Pearce of the University of London.[6] This relatively new discipline sought to explain the direct causes of biodiversity loss and focused on the failure of economic systems to properly value natural resources. One of the most important issues raised by environmental economists was the degree to which biodiversity loss occurs because markets do not adequately recognize the full and true value of biological resources and so do not adequately reflect the cost to society of exploiting them. In explaining the process of resource conversion, one of the direct causes of biodiversity loss, Swanson explains that: 'If diverse biological resources are systematically undervalued, then they will be too readily converted to their specialised substitutes' (Swanson, 1997). Strategies for conservation, such as the debt-for-nature swaps and integrated development and conservation projects, consequently sought to address that lack of economic incentive.

Even the gains achieved through these new approaches proved to be inadequate to addressing the full range of factors driving biodiversity loss.

> *'In practical terms, conservationists would like to think they are knowledgeable about how to plan and execute conservation activities. But as increasing numbers of evaluations of these activities suggest, many of today's field-based initiatives are not living up to their proclaimed potential'* (Brandon et al, 1998).

A review by WWF of its integrated development and conservation projects concluded that:

> *'the success or failure of conservation or development efforts hinges on powerful influences such as international and national policies and laws from outside the project area...Conservation organizations should be more proactive and should significantly expand their investments in promoting an enabling policy environment for ICDPs'* (Larson et al, 1998).

Growing scientific evidence was proving that activities centred on a protected area and sustainable-use approach failed to conserve biodiversity in a meaningful and long-term way. Research showed, for example, how much outside environmental pressures such as climate change or pollution might make the boundaries of a given protected area redundant as species migrated to adapt to new conditions. More significantly, biologists were beginning to believe that the objective of conservation would be better served through an approach that focused on larger geographical areas, which would allow critical ecological processes upon which biodiversity depends to be protected.

Environmental economics also evolved to include analysis of the influence and impacts of macro-economic policies and regimes on the environment. These include international trade agreements, stabilization and structural adjustment programmes as well as what the increasing integration of the global economy means for the global environment.[7]

Changes in the international institutions that concern themselves with questions of environment and development mirror the evolution in how to think and deal with the loss of biodiversity. Without overstating the degree to which this has resulted in new programmes and projects, it can be said that the World Bank has given a great deal of thought over the last five years to how it can mainstream global environmental problems into its operations. This has come about through a steady acceptance of the importance of considering sustainable development as a central pillar of its mandate. Finding practical operational applications for how development – especially development that focuses on macro-economic and macro-social conditions – can integrate environment in a more strategic fashion has proven more problematic. To be fair, the Bank is far from alone in having this problem.

The GEF has also evolved in its thinking about what approaches and strategies are required to promote the conservation of biodiversity. After its pilot phase, which ended in 1994, the GEF acted on one of the major criticisms raised in its independent evaluation and created an operational strategy to guide its activities. In its section on biodiversity, this strategy makes reference to the need to consider 'underlying causes and policies' (GEF Secretariat, 1996). While suggesting that the solutions to many of these lay beyond the institutional mandate of the GEF, this reference does show that the GEF was trying to break out of an approach that had kept its focus strictly on the direct causes and manifestations of biodiversity loss.

An Emerging Consensus

It is our belief that on the basis of the evolution in thinking that has occurred in the various organizations that are concerned with biodiversity loss, elements of a new consensus on how to address the loss of biodiversity are beginning to emerge. This emerging consensus rests on two assumptions:

1. That conservation strategies must be multi-disciplinary in nature to encompass activities that range from the creation and management of protected areas to the integration of sustainable development principles into international economic policy-making. These strategies must be based on analyses of the complexity of factors that drive biodiversity loss and must seek to involve many different actors, with their differentiated comparative advantages, in the identification and implementation of solutions.
2. The paradox of biodiversity loss is that it is considered a global problem but that its actual occurrence is a highly localized phenomenon. The conservation of biodiversity therefore needs to be an undertaking that occurs simultaneously at a variety of scales.

Perhaps the simplest way of distinguishing between the 'old' and 'emerging' consensuses is to say that the old has proven inadequate in facing up to the conflicts and difficult choices that are now understood to be critical elements in the conservation of biodiversity. But where work needs to be done in the definition of the emerging consensus is in the development of operational responses that derive from these new assumptions.

The Root Causes project places itself squarely in the context of this new consensus. While it grew out of a specific dialogue with the GEF on how to define root causes, it took on the more ambitious undertaking of investigating the four premises that are referred to earlier in this chapter. These four premises helped shape the activities undertaken in this project and the outputs that it has generated. They also provide a convenient way of structuring this book, and the chapters that follow are arranged to address the questions underlying each of these premises.

Chapter 2 deals with the need for tools to understand the nature of root causes. It provides an overview of the Analytical Approach created by the MPO to help guide the conceptual development and analysis of the case studies. Chapter 3 presents the case studies by offering a very brief summary of the main findings. Chapter 4 addresses the question of the common socio-economic causes of biodiversity loss. It does so by building on the specific findings of each case study to produce conclusions for the project as a whole. Chapter 5 deals with the need for new solutions and approaches by making recommendations on how to enhance the positive steps being taken at the local level, and how changes at the systemic level are necessary in ensuring their long-term viability. Chapters 6 to 15 are executive summaries of the reports we received for each of the ten case studies carried out in this project. They each contain specific analyses and conclusions on the root causes of biodiversity loss.

Chapter 2

A Framework for Analysing Biodiversity Loss

Pamela Stedman-Edwards

The framework for analysing socioeconomic root causes of biodiversity loss is designed as an interdisciplinary approach, which allows for analysis that integrates the varied work of social sciences. It emphasizes the links across scales from local to international to create a conceptual model – a descriptive picture using qualitative and quantitative data – of the causes of biodiversity loss for a particular site.

The rapid loss of biodiversity and habitats around the world is occurring at a local level as a result, for example, of farmers clearing new fields, timber companies opening new forests for logging and hunters producing for city markets. The explanation for these activities, however, is often found in socio-economic forces that arise not at the local level but far from the sites of biodiversity loss. As discussed in Chapter 1, conservation work has rarely understood the importance of these socioeconomic factors, with the result that biodiversity loss continues to accelerate despite years of efforts to protect habitats and species.

To provide the basis for more effective action for conservation, the framework or Analytical Approach presented here seeks to connect well-known local drivers of biodiversity loss to the broader range of socioeconomic factors, or root causes, that shape the decisions made at the local level. The framework for analysing socioeconomic root causes of biodiversity loss is designed as an interdisciplinary approach, which allows for analysis that integrates the varied work of social sciences. It emphasizes the links across scales from local to international to create a conceptual model – a descriptive picture using qualitative and quantitative data – of the causes of biodiversity loss for a particular site.

This chapter briefly explains the need for this type of framework and discusses the types of socioeconomic factors that must be considered in studies of root causes. It then outlines the approach for case studies developed for the Root Causes project and reviews an example of the application of the approach. Finally, this chapter discusses some of the methodological and data-related issues encountered in the process of carrying out the ten case studies, and considers how these studies can lead to recommendations for conservation actions.

THE NEED FOR A COMPREHENSIVE APPROACH

Habitat loss and degradation are the primary proximate causes of biodiversity loss world-wide.[1] To understand why extensive alteration and destruction of habitats is occurring, it is essential to understand what lies behind these proximate causes. Socioeconomic forces and circumstances create incentives for activities that put pressure on biodiversity and create disincentives for more sustainable behaviour. Socioeconomic institutions, including, inter alia, markets, laws, political bodies and social norms, frequently favour expansion of patterns of development that lead to biodiversity loss. Yet, the connections between social and economic structures, on the one hand, and biodiversity loss, on the other, are not well understood.

Most analyses of the economic, social, political and cultural causes of biodiversity loss have focused on proximate and root causes at the local level. This focus on the community and micro-regional level has led to an emphasis on conservation solutions at the same level, as discussed in Chapter 1. The continuing loss of biodiversity, however, points to the need to take a broader look at factors beyond the local level that are driving environmental change. Only by exploring and understanding the socioeconomic factors at various levels – local, regional, national and international – that drive people to degrade the natural environment will we be able to change this behaviour. To find more effective conservation solutions, we must step back and look at the complex set of influences on local resource use that constitute the root causes of biodiversity loss.

While individual socioeconomic factors affecting the environment, such as population growth and economic policies, have received substantial attention, a review of the existing literature turned up few examples of analyses that went beyond a single socioeconomic factor and virtually none that cut across all types of factors. The socioeconomic root causes of biodiversity loss are frequently mentioned, but there has been little empirical analysis of particular causes or cases of biodiversity loss. Lists of causes of biodiversity loss all suggest the same group of socioeconomic factors[2] but do not provide the in-depth, multi-level analysis needed to show how these factors cause biodiversity loss. Methodologies for the study of environmental problems, which must integrate knowledge and methods from a variety of social and biological sciences, are in the early stages of development.[3] However, a wide literature on the roles of human migration, population growth, economic policies and structures, poverty, cultural and social structures, and development patterns in determining resource exploitation – although generally analysing only a few factors at a time – provides a strong basis for examining the question of biodiversity loss.

This extensive literature[4] on the relationship between specific socioeconomic factors and the environment provides important background for studying the root causes of biodiversity loss and was drawn on extensively both in the development of this analytic framework and by the case studies. Most analysis has focused on the following areas:

- demographic change;
- poverty and inequality;
- public policies, markets, and politics;
- macroeconomic policies and structures; and
- social change and development.

This literature provides important knowledge and methodologies for understanding the relationship between these factors and environmental degradation and points to the key factors that must be considered in these studies. While there is extensive overlap among the five categories mentioned, they reflect common divisions and distinctions in the literature. Within each category a variety of theories, arguments, and studies from various disciplines offer diverse explanations for environmental degradation, many of which are relevant to biodiversity loss. These categories are described in greater detail in Box 2.1. What is important to remember is that these five categories provide a basic structure for categorizing root causes. Whether they are inclusive or exclusive and how they overlap is less important than the fact that they allow us to conceptualize, and so categorize root causes and therefore ensure that all possible root causes are incorporated into the analytic framework. Addressing biodiversity loss requires an understanding of how all these factors are linked together and how they operate at different scales to drive biodiversity loss. All of the issues raised by this literature must be considered within a single analytic framework for root causes rather than as distinct categories.

A framework for integrating our understanding of the role of this broad range of socioeconomic factors that are at work at any one place and time was clearly needed. In order to carry out the case studies it was essential to create an Analytical Approach that would allow the researchers to take a truly inter-disciplinary approach to the complex causes of biodiversity loss. The approach

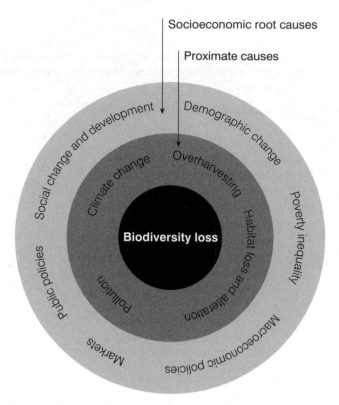

Figure 2.1 *Biodiversity Loss: Proximate and Socioeconomic Root Causes*

that was used, which is described later in this chapter, was designed to be flexible enough to be applicable to a wide range of situations and incorporate all types of socioeconomic factors, while providing a common framework that would ensure comparability of findings and conclusions across the case studies.

CONCEPTUAL BASES OF THE ANALYTICAL APPROACH

The Analytical Approach is designed to provide a framework to bring together under one umbrella the work of a variety of social science disciplines that have sought to understand the causes of biodiversity loss – from anthropology to economics to political science.[5] This framework is intended to allow a clear vision of how all the various parts of the puzzle – from local population growth to national politics to international markets – together drive biodiversity loss at a particular site. It was developed based on work that has been done in political economy, political ecology and qualitative modelling of complex systems. The approach draws from political economy and political ecology work to develop the types of questions that must be asked and the types of linkages that must be explored to understand the socioeconomic causes of biodiversity loss. From work on modelling it draws the tool of the conceptual

Box 2.1 Review of Socioeconomic Factors Driving Biodiversity Loss

The following gives a brief overview of the types of issues addressed by the existing literature relating socioeconomic factors to the environment and which must be addressed by an interdisciplinary study of the causes of environmental degradation.

Demographic Change

Population growth is associated with the growth of resource consumption and degradation, expansion and intensification of land use, increasing poverty, exploitation of marginal lands and the breakdown of traditional resource management systems.[6] High fertility rates – common in some of the world's poorest countries – and poverty are clearly linked. The location of population growth is perhaps equally important for biodiversity loss as the absolute numbers. Local population growth is often a result of displacement and migration caused by population pressure, war and social unrest, resource scarcity, political or economic insecurity, or perceived economic opportunity. Local population growth directly affects the use of resources and their degradation and often drives habitat conversion in areas important for biodiversity conservation.

Population growth, at a global level, is continually raising absolute consumption of resources. Many traditional resource-use patterns, such as shifting cultivation, that are viable at low population densities are degrading at higher densities. At the same time technology is allowing per capita consumption to rise well over basic needs in some parts of the world, meaning that population growth in the developed countries has a greater impact on biodiversity than population growth in the developing countries. In turn the expansion of commercial production is often related to population displacement, migration and the expansion of impoverished populations in marginal locales, leading to biodiversity loss.

The Mexico case study illustrates some critical issues related to population and biodiversity loss. In and around the Calakmul Biosphere Reserve in southeastern Mexico, the growth of population poses the greatest threat to biodiversity. Although the Reserve and the surrounding region remain largely forested, populated areas along the eastern boundary and in a development corridor that cuts across the middle have been cleared for subsistence and small-scale commercial agriculture. The population is growing rapidly and many communities will double in size within ten years. Population growth in the region is rooted in a number of factors. Natural growth stems from poverty, lack of education and limited access to reproductive health services. Immigration to the area stemmed from government efforts to attract migrants to the region, particularly in the 1970s and, more recently, it stems from social conflicts, poverty, landlessness and rapid population growth in other parts of rural Mexico. While overall population density in the Calakmul region is still low, every increase leads to further habitat degradation and loss.

Inequality and Poverty

Inequality of income and resource distribution has received much of the blame for environmental degradation.[7] Poverty in particular has been linked with poor management of resources. Numerous studies have illustrated the vicious cycle of poverty, resource degradation and further impoverishment. Wealth has also been closely linked with environmental degradation through high levels of consumption and short-term management of environmental resources.

Land degradation – both a result and a cause of rural poverty – has direct and indirect impacts on biodiversity as it forces changes in production patterns, migration and frontier expansion. Many authors find that the poor are disproportionately located in marginal lands and fragile ecosystems. Moreover the poor are thought to make particularly damaging use of the environment when traditional systems of resource management break down as a result of socioeconomic change. Insecurity of tenure rights and the prevalence of landlessness, lack of financial and human resources and poor access to government resources and infrastructure all promote short-term management strategies and unsustainable use of natural resources among the poor.

Wealthy resource users, such as large-scale farmers and other commercial producers, also take short-term economic and environmental views. Because they can appropriate large shares of the resource base, they use resources extensively rather than making investments in resource management. Inequality among nations has also received substantial attention. Poor countries are transforming and exporting their natural resources to rich countries. This pattern is linked with inequality within developing countries: the poor are exploiting the environment to provide exports that primarily benefit the rich.

In Tanzania's river deltas, degradation of the mangrove forests is largely driven by poverty. Agriculture, fishing and harvesting of mangrove poles, bark and logs are the main economic activities, all of which affect the mangrove ecosystem and consequently biodiversity. Fishing provides an annual income of US$300 or less per fisherman. Agriculture provides little more. Access to nearby towns is difficult and social services are limited. Given the lack of other sources of support, land is cleared for subsistence farming. Mangroves are cut both for subsistence use, including use for fuelwood, housing, boat making and fish traps, and for commercial sale, providing one of the few local sources of cash income. Mangrove habitat is being destroyed without providing any long-term relief from poverty.

Public Policies, Markets, and Politics

National laws, economic and political institutions and government policies are central to many recent explanations of biodiversity loss.[8] Most attention has focused on ways to eliminate or compensate for 'failures' in laws, policies and organizations without an examination of the underlying socioeconomic forces that produce the governance and market structures that promote biodiversity loss. Two types of policy failures are pointed out. The first are perverse government policies that provide incentives for environmental degradation. The second are government policies and market institutions that fail to incorporate environmental values, including the value of biodiversity, into decision-making.

Policy and market 'failures' are rarely accidental. Policies, laws and formal and informal institutions are products of political, social and economic forces. They are established and maintained because they benefit, or are intended to benefit, some sector or class of the economy or society. Environmentally perverse policies often serve traditional development goals, such as industrialization, export expansion, increased food production and poverty relief. In many cases natural resources provide a cheap way to support economic growth. To understand biodiversity loss, a complete model must look not only at the results of policies and market structures, but also at the reasons why those policies and market structures persist.

The Vietnam case illustrates some of the environmental problems that arise from government policies. The Vietnamese government has supported colonization in and around protected areas. Increasing populations have led to shortened fallow periods for shifting agriculture as well as increased hunting and use of timber and other forest products. Government efforts to resolve persistent food shortages included collectivization of agriculture from the 1950s to the 1970s, which actually aggravated the problem by reducing production incentives and land colonization programmes. Once the failure of the collectivization movement was recognized, it was replaced by a contract-output system, which increased producer incentives, but rice markets remained in the hands of the government and production fell once again. Yet while productivity fell, use of land for agriculture continued to expand under all these programmes, increasing habitat destruction and biodiversity loss.

Macroeconomic Policies and Structures

Biodiversity is affected by the structure and behaviour of international and national markets and related government policies that shape local resource-use decisions.[9] The role of national and international markets in shaping production patterns and resource-use patterns is enormous. Governments have often sought to mitigate some of the effects of relations with international markets and to promote development through macroeconomic policies that alter prices, including controls on trade, capital flows, exchange rates and national markets. However, the current shift toward market liberalization, often manifested through structural adjustment programmes in developing countries, has increased the role of international markets, leading to large-scale changes in production and resource-use patterns.

Adjustment has been essential to regaining macroeconomic stability and promoting economic growth in many countries. However, demand for foreign exchange needed to support imports and debt repayments and the lack of other market opportunities provide impetus to developing countries to mine their natural resources for exports. International trade agreements, such as the General Agreement on Tariffs and Trade (GATT) and the new World Trade Organization (WTO), have little to say about environmental problems created by trading patterns; nor have public or private financial institutions evinced much concern for the environmental impact of financial and investment flows.

Two broad theoretical camps that present very different models of the role of macroeconomic factors in driving resource-use patterns have emerged. Traditional neoclassical economic theory posits that improvements in a government's macroeconomic policy, such as trade liberalization and exchange-rate deregulation, will improve resource-use patterns. Political economy theory posits that changes in macroeconomic policy, without changes in the underlying power and market structures, may worsen resource-use patterns. Empirical works seem to show that both have some truth.

The case of Pakistan illustrates the wide-ranging impacts of macroeconomic policies. The mangrove forests of the Indus Delta have been affected in various ways by the country's efforts to improve its balance of payments. The greatest threat to the mangroves is the reduction in fresh water flows to the delta, a reduction caused by dams designed to provide irrigation water for agriculture. The government subsidizes agriculture with cheap irrigation water in part to provide support to industry, which produces most of the country's exports. The expansion of industry in the Karachi area, a result of a deliberate policy to increase exports to improve the balance of payments, has led to heavy pollution of the mangrove forests directly as well as indirectly, since the centralized industrialization has promoted rapid urban growth. Finally, export policies have promoted over-fishing in the region. Devaluation of the rupee greatly increased the price of fish, leading to an influx of migrants to the region and a rapid expansion of fishing. The political power of agricultural landlords and of industry has maintained policies of cheap water and support for exports in place, despite the environmental degradation caused by these policies.

Social Change and Development Biases

Development is widely considered synonymous with increases in consumption and the transformation of natural resources.[10] This understanding of development is deeply entrenched in many economic and political systems. In addition a social or cultural preference for this type of development has become widespread. Both direct and indirect linkages are apparent between a people's culture and its resource-use patterns. Culture has a direct bearing on population, economic activities, settlement patterns, political structures and other factors affecting biodiversity.

Despite great differences among the societies of the developed world, broad similarities appear in their approaches to resource exploitation and consumption. The expansion of Western culture has induced social change around the world. The bias of many developing country governments in favour of urban over rural areas and in favour of industry over agriculture reflects this understanding of development. In this process, traditional cultures that are less destructive of environmental resources are being lost. The modernization of traditional societies not only introduces these peoples to markets and rising consumption levels, it also leads to loss of traditional knowledge about sustainability and to the disruption and loss of traditional institutions for managing resources.

The role of social structures and culture in shaping environmental outcomes is illustrated by the Brazil case. Similar policies, designed to promote commercial agriculture and reflecting a belief in this 'modern' style of development as well as in the need to occupy 'vacant' lands, were applied throughout the Cerrado region. The impact of the promotion of this development model varied with the social context. In one area – Rio Verde – where the topography was conducive to mechanized agriculture, the commercial monoculture model was widely adopted. In a second area – Silvânia – where agricultural conditions also appeared favourable, the model was not widely adopted because social conditions – including a long history of settlement in the area and a well-established community – favoured the maintenance of the diversified family-run farm over the new model. In yet a third area – Alto Paraíso – the rugged terrain meant that large-scale agriculture was less viable. Added to this is the fact that new settlers in the area were attracted by the area's natural beauty and are investing in ecotourism and similar enterprises, thus reducing the likelihood that the commercial model will be accepted there.

model, which provides the means of effectively describing or illustrating the factors affecting biodiversity loss at a particular site. The benefits of these methods are explained as the approach is described more fully below.

The framework recommended here is first and foremost an interdisciplinary approach for conducting case studies.[11] It is designed to reveal socioeconomic factors working across scales from local to global and the mechanisms or processes linking socioeconomic factors to resource use and thence biodiversity loss. It is also designed to be functional within severe data limitations for both biological and socioeconomic indicators. The case study is seen as the most useful tool for understanding biodiversity loss, given the great variations in the ecological and socioeconomic conditions shaping resource use and biodiversity loss at different sites. Case studies of areas critical for biodiversity conservation serve two purposes: they provide the basis for developing effective policy changes, for protecting a particular site and for developing comparisons across regions and countries that deepen our knowledge of socioeconomic root causes. (The main findings of the case studies are presented in Chapter 3. Summaries of the individual case studies follow in Chapters 6–15.)

In recent years, a few researchers have attempted to analyse the full complexity of environmental degradation through case studies.[12] Their analytic approach, often described as political ecology, has served as the basis for some of the strongest literature on socioeconomic–environment relationships. Although there are important variations among these case studies, they are characterized by an attempt to define the international, national and regional socioeconomic conditions that shape local resource-use patterns, and to examine the varying responses of local resource-users to their context. Political ecology, like political economy, is rooted in two fundamental ideas.[13] First, political and economic factors are inextricably linked. Second, political and economic power is central in determining resource-use patterns including environmental degradation. This approach, with the addition of social and cultural factors, forms the basis of the methodological discussion developed here.

Political ecology often uses chains of explanation in order to address the questions of scale and linkages (Blaikie and Brookfield, 1987). Studies start by looking at the local level and then move up the chain of explanation through interrelationships of local resource users with regional, national and international actors. Chains of explanation provide a tool for understanding local responses to factors operating at a scale beyond the local level. Biodiversity loss occurs at the local level as the result of many individual decisions about resource use. The local actor who contributes to biodiversity loss – subsistence farmer or fisherman, commercial producer, government agent – is acting within a particular set of social, cultural, political, economic and environmental constraints (Perrings et al, 1995). To understand biodiversity loss, we must understand those limits and possibilities and how they affect resource use. This does not mean that biodiversity loss is predetermined by circumstances. Resource users make decisions not only within their particular circumstances but also affecting their circumstances. Global and regional systems generate

Temporal	Geographical	Political	Economic
Today	Farm	Agreements among neighbours	Subsistence
Agricultural cycle	Wildlife reserve	Local council	Local market
Political term	Eco-region	State government	State development funds
Timber cycle	Nation	National government	National policies
Generation	Continent	International interventions	International markets

Figure 2.2 *Examples of Scale*

both opportunities and constraints for local socioeconomic systems (Gallopin, 1991) and local conditions in turn will affect regional and global factors. The chain of explanation can be followed in both directions.

Selecting the appropriate scale or scales for analysis is crucial to determining the results of the case study (Sanderson, 1994; see also Gallopin, 1991, and Garcia, 1984). Differences in socioeconomic factors across scales imply both differences in the size or generality of their impact and differences in distance from their effect. For example, at the local level, community demand for firewood might be driving deforestation. At the national level, national forest policies allowing unrestricted logging might have more widespread impacts on forest use. At the international level, foreign demand for timber might be shaping forest policies in many countries. Differences in geographic, socioeconomic and temporal scales must all be taken into account. Political scales, for example, could run from the village council to provincial government alliances and to national government agencies. Geographic scales could run from the local park to the ecosystem and to the nation. Temporal scales could run from a snapshot of the situation to a year's agricultural cycle, to a generation or longer.

Particular variables play a larger or smaller role, depending on spatial or temporal scales, geographic location and other factors (Machlis and Forester, 1996; Roque, 1997; Stern et al, 1992). An analysis of biodiversity loss that considers only local factors will find a different range of causal factors than an analysis that looks only at global factors. Thus the Analytical Approach emphasizes taking all scales into consideration. Likewise, an analysis that looks only at the contemporary situation may ignore important historical variables that have shaped current resource use. Defining the appropriate temporal scale, given the possibility of long gaps between cause and effect, may be one of the greatest obstacles to understanding biodiversity loss. For example, historical patterns such as exploitation of natural resources by a colonizing country may continue to shape resource use through surviving patterns of land tenure, or historical use may have degraded resources to the point where new means of subsistence have been developed that bear little resemblance to historical patterns. Defining the appropriate geographic scale can also be difficult. For example, population growth is highly correlated with deforestation at a global level, but the correlation often decreases when measured at smaller geographic scales. In other words, population growth and deforestation are often occurring at different locations and so are not directly linked (Meyer and Turner, 1992). There may, however, be strong indirect linkages between population growth and deforestation, as growing urban populations demand more agricultural products from rural areas. The best analysis will consider factors across a range of scales, weigh their relative impact and examine the linkages across scales.

The *linkages* among the global, regional, and local socioeconomic and ecological systems are multidirectional. Changes in local systems contribute to political, social, cultural or economic change at various levels, just as changes at regional, national and global scales affect local systems. In such complex systems relationships are continually evolving (Gallopin, 1991). And as international socioeconomic systems expand their reach, local systems are increasingly influenced by distant processes (Gallopin, 1991). However, processes at a larger scale are not necessarily more important determinants of local resource use than processes at a local scale. For example, local markets may be more closely linked and, therefore, more important in determining hunting patterns than national or international markets. Analysis at the local level will reveal the variety of factors affecting biodiversity, whereas strictly global analysis may conceal this variety. However, global trends may explain the similarity in worldwide patterns of biodiversity loss, if not the complexity of the linkages through which they work at the local level (Sanderson, 1994).

Conceptual models, sometimes called causal maps or informal models, allow us to describe various scales and linkages among factors in one picture. A conceptual model 'is an idea of how the components of a system fit together' (Machlis and Forester, 1996). Conceptual models provide a descriptive picture, either through words or diagrams, of the chain of explanation. They are flexible, qualitative and closely linked to the kinds of data available.[14] They are not intended to be predictive or highly quantitative.

These models provide a flexible framework that can accommodate and integrate a broad range of quantitative data and qualitative information about biodiversity loss. Human causes of environmental change can be divided roughly into two broad categories: physical factors and socioeconomic factors (Robinson, 1991). Physical factors, such as population growth, consumption and extraction of resources, can be measured not only physically but quantitatively as well. Quantitative description of these factors contributes substantially to our understanding of biodiversity loss. Socioeconomic factors such as political power, markets, organizations and attitudes are the factors by and through which decisions about physical resource use are made. These factors are inherently unquantifiable, but they are essential to describing human behaviour.

The scientific community is calling for predictive, testable models of the relationship between root causes and biodiversity loss.[15] However, the nature of the data needed and of social science methodologies suggests that the development of such models will be exceedingly difficult, if not impossible, for most cases. Existing quantitative approaches to understanding resource use and biodiversity loss are inadequate to analyse the broad range of micro- and macro-level factors affecting local decisions. These approaches necessarily focus on only one or two pieces of the much larger puzzle, ignoring both cross-scale and interdisciplinary issues in favour of precise analysis of a single factor, often at the micro-level, because of the dearth of other appropriate data.

Conceptual models can describe the complexities of socioeconomic relationships that analysis of strictly quantifiable relations cannot be expected to reveal (Stern et al, 1992). These relationships can best be described with words or diagrams rather than quantitative measures. For example, mathematical models have been developed that relate deforestation to migration induced by road building. While it is important to recognize and confirm the impact of road building, solutions can only be found if we examine the reasons for road building and the reasons why people are migrating. Qualitative, intuitive thinking is the only methodological approach that can incorporate all of the relevant socioeconomic factors. Therefore, case studies can be the most important tool for explaining the root causes of biodiversity loss. By answering the question 'why?', detailed qualitative work provides a critical tool for finding solutions to socioeconomic problems.

The defining characteristics of the root causes analytic approach are the multi-level character of analysis and the development of conceptual models. Most of the case studies presented here begin at the local level, where biodiversity losses are occurring, and then move outward in scope of analysis along a chain of explanation to understand the regional, national and international forces at work. Each root causes case study describes a unique pattern of linkages between biodiversity loss and socioeconomic factors at various scales. Each creates a descriptive picture – or a 'conceptual model' – of root causes relevant to the site, based on qualitative and quantitative data about the five types of factor discussed above. Given that this analytic approach is intended to address socioeconomic issues and that many of the case studies were carried out in remote areas where data are scarce, the conceptual model was adopted as a way to incorporate both quantitative and qualitative data. The emphasis of this approach is placed on understanding how different factors driving biodiversity loss work at different scales and how they are linked to one another and to biodiversity loss.

THE ANALYTICAL APPROACH: BUILDING CONCEPTUAL MODELS

Conceptual models provide a useful tool for exploring the links between biodiversity loss and socioeconomic factors and are the central component of the case studies. Each of the studies presented here built a conceptual model to describe the primary root causes and mechanisms driving biodiversity loss at the case study site. This section describes the key steps in constructing a conceptual model. Given the diverse circumstances and the wide range of natural and socioeconomic environments in which biodiversity loss is occurring, each case study team necessarily made some modifications to the approach and drew conclusions appropriate to the particular case. Nevertheless, the basic steps for each case study were a literature review, development of a conceptual model, data collection and revision of the conceptual model.

Literature Review

Each study first reviewed the relevant general literature on the five categories of socioeconomic factors from a variety of social sciences, which is discussed in more detail in Box 2.3, along with the literature and existing data pertinent to the particular case study site and to hypothetical root causes for the site.

Development of Conceptual Model

A thorough literature review provided a set of hypotheses about root causes that served as the basis for an initial iteration of the conceptual model. Using knowledge gained from the literature review, the preliminary hypotheses are best drawn up by asking who, what and why at each step of the analysis, following a chain of explanation. This first iteration of the conceptual model allowed the researchers to make decisions about further data collection. This model was subsequently revised and amplified with information collected for the case study.

Such models will undoubtedly be complex. However, an effort was made to keep them as simple, or parsimonious, as possible without sacrificing understanding of the nature of the system. Systems are often too complex to analyse effectively in a single model, so some studies opted to break them down into subsystems to facilitate the analysis. For example, the Pakistan case study created separate models for each of four types of environmental degradation. Studies of large regions, such as the Brazilian Cerrado and the Danube Basin, needed to work down toward the local as well as out toward the macro level to get a full picture. For such studies it was also useful to divide the large site into smaller areas with distinct characteristics in order to begin a chain of explanation at the local level. Likewise, those studies that selected several sites for comparison purposes, such as several mangrove areas in the Tanzania and Pakistan case studies, initially considered each as a separate site, before generalizing about root causes across distinct sites.

Data Collection

The third step was gathering further data. Development of the initial version of the conceptual model provided a basis for organizing data, defining gaps in the existing data and setting priorities for further data collection. In most cases

BOX 2.2 THE CONCEPTUAL MODELS

A conceptual model can be effectively represented in a diagram or description that represents system components and flows between components. Such diagrams identify key variables and illustrate the relations among variables in a system (Hall and Day, 1977). In a diagram, the flows represented in the model are usually causal relations and the diagram indicates the direction and impact of the flows. Although analysis starts with the local and works out to the global, the conceptual model will not always appear as a direct chain of linkages across

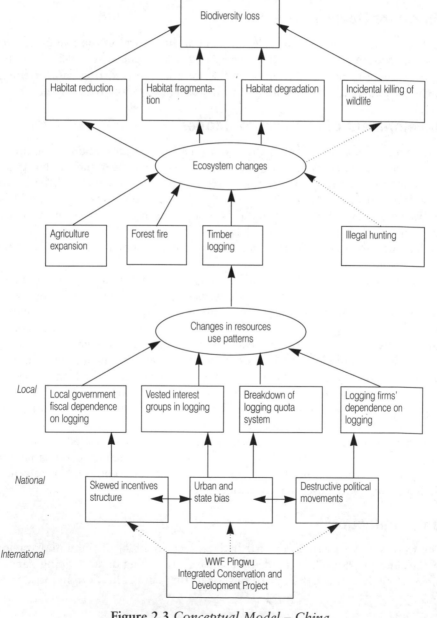

Figure 2.3 *Conceptual Model – China*

all scales. In some cases distant factors will affect local behaviour through effects at intermediate levels; in other cases distant factors will directly affect local behaviour.

The conceptual model may be represented in many different ways. Two different examples from the case studies are shown here.

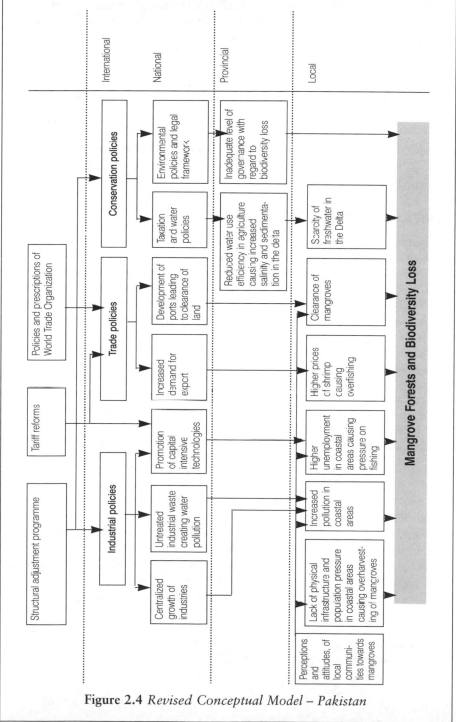

Figure 2.4 *Revised Conceptual Model – Pakistan*

this included local data gathering, such as rapid rural appraisal with surveys, participatory appraisal or other social science methods (Roque, 1997). It also included research on national and international policies and socioeconomic trends, such as policies on prices or changes in political systems that affect local decision-making about resource use. Drawing on the expertise of a variety of social scientists in each of the research teams helped ensure that appropriate methodologies were chosen and that the full range of socioeconomic causes was considered.

The case studies did not attempt to quantify the loss of biodiversity at the various sites. Sites were chosen because there was reason to believe that biodiversity was being lost or was seriously threatened. The use of proxies, such as loss of forest cover or decline in indicator species, was recommended, but it was felt that quantification of biodiversity loss within the context of these studies was not necessary. Certainly for making decisions about conservation these socioeconomic studies should be accompanied by detailed ecological or biological studies.

Revision of Conceptual Model

The fourth step was a revision of the conceptual model based on the new data. Some of the initial hypotheses were confirmed; others were disproved and new questions were raised. Revision should confirm that the model has been clearly described. A well-designed model balances qualitative and quantitative data to explain links among socioeconomic factors and links between socioeconomic factors and biodiversity loss. It will provide sufficient information about the causes of biodiversity loss to support informed decisions for the development of a sound conservation strategy. It will point to those factors that must be addressed in order to improve conservation and will allow us to find those places in the complex web of socioeconomic factors where we can successfully intervene to change patterns of resource use.

EXPERIENCE WITH THE ANALYTICAL APPROACH: STRENGTHS AND WEAKNESSES

The case studies presented in this book each had to grapple with the variety and complexity of the factors driving biodiversity loss. The sites selected for study cover a wide variety of environmental pressures – from industrial expansion threatening mangrove habitat to hunting of threatened species in tropical forests and agricultural pressures threatening frontier areas. The studies all attempted to answer the same fundamental questions about the pervasive trend toward environmental change in the context of a particular site:

- What are the underlying socioeconomic forces and circumstances driving biodiversity loss?
- How are these root causes interlinked?

BOX 2.3 USING THE APPROACH: A BRIEF EXAMPLE

The application of the Analytical Approach in the case study of biodiversity loss at the Calakmul Biosphere Reserve in south-eastern Mexico provides a practical illustration of the development of a conceptual model.

Step 1: Literature Review

For the Calakmul study, literature on the local situation, on the national context and on generally recognized causes of biodiversity loss was reviewed. This literature was drawn from a variety of fields including anthropology, economics, policy analysis and demography. Literature specific to the Calakmul site produced primarily by academic researchers and conservation groups included studies of population growth, hunting patterns, attitudes toward development, successes and failures of sustainable development programmes and resource-use patterns. Relevant literature on the national situation included government and academic reports on agriculture, forestry and protected area policies, as well as on liberalization and impacts of international markets. More general literature[16] included studies on the effects of population growth, integration into international markets and poverty. The literature review suggested the following hypotheses, among others, which contributed to the construction of the initial conceptual model.

Hypotheses specific to the Calakmul and Mexican case:
- At the local scale:
  - Expansion of chilli production is causing extensive deforestation.
  - Population growth is causing expansion of agriculture and deforestation.
- At the national scale:
  - Liberalization of agriculture, including elimination of subsidies, is causing expansion of commercial crops and a decrease in subsistence production.
  - Changes in land tenure laws are encouraging clearing and sale of land.
- At the international scale:
  - Exposure to international markets makes local production of timber and staple crops unprofitable.
  - The North America Free Trade Agreement (NAFTA) is increasing export-oriented commercial agricultural production.

General hypotheses relevant to the Calakmul and Mexican case:
- Population growth is associated with environmental degradation.
- Poverty prevents sustainable resource use.

Step 2: Development of a Conceptual Model

The initial conceptual model defines the scales and linkages believed to be most critical in determining biodiversity loss. The model necessarily includes only those factors that the initial review suggests are important. A series of questions were used to construct a chain of explanation. These questions began at the local level and moved outward to examine the layers of factors affecting biodiversity in the Calakmul region. The hypotheses found in the literature review were used to answer these questions in the initial iteration of the conceptual model. An example of the questions and answers used to construct a chain of explanation follows.

Biodiversity is being lost in Mexico's Calakmul Biosphere Reserve in large part because of the loss of forest to shifting agriculture. Who is converting the forest? Small-scale farmers, including recent migrants from other parts of Mexico. Why are they clearing forest in the protected area? Various contributing factors include poor implementation of environmental laws and government agricultural policies that promote forest clearing. Why do government policies promote agricultural expansion? To help reduce the poverty of the rural population. And so forth.

The initial model (Figure 2.5) emphasizes one local-level cause – population growth – and two national-level causes – land tenure policies and liberalization. Deforestation and agricultural land are taken as proxies for biodiversity loss.

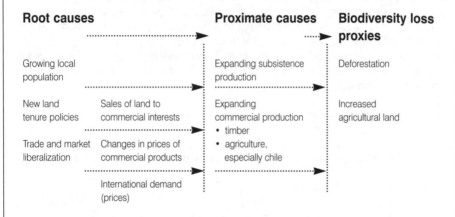

Figure 2.5 *Diagram of Initial Conceptual Model*

Step 3: Data Collection

In order to confirm or reject the hypotheses incorporated in the initial model, additional data were collected on local agricultural production for subsistence markets, local production of timber and other forest products, local prices, local income from government programmes, recent changes in land tenure, national and international markets, deforestation and impact of the protected area and sustainable development programmes. Further literature was reviewed on resource-use patterns and attitudes toward agriculture in similar regions in Mexico, the probable impact of NAFTA and liberalization and tenure policies.

Serious gaps in data on the region could only be partially filled by the case study. Physical and biological data on deforestation and species loss were lacking and, while threats to biodiversity appear to be great, the impact as yet has been small and therefore difficult to measure. Moreover, the isolation of the region, its frontier character and the rapid changes that are occurring in terms of population growth, legal status of lands and political boundaries make socioeconomic data scarce and unreliable. The clandestine nature of many local activities, such as logging and hunting, and the uncertain legality of others, such as land clearing, make it difficult to get honest responses from local people or government officials about activities in the area.

Nevertheless a number of the initial hypotheses were disproved or brought into question in this step. For example, qualitative and quantitative data on chilli production revealed that it is no longer making a significant contribution to deforestation. Information on local markets revealed that local production, even commercial production, has little relation to national or international prices and therefore little connection to liberalized national policies that emphasize market-based decision-making. The lack of links between the local level and other scales – economic, political, and temporal – emerged as one of the most pervasive characteristics of the region. As hypotheses were confirmed or disproved, and corresponding new information was gathered, a clearer picture was developed of the root causes operating in Calakmul.

Step 4: Revision of the Conceptual Model

The revision of the conceptual model based on the new data and further literature review required new answers to questions about the relevance of various scales and of the linkages across various scales to local resource use. The initial literature review suggested that national policies affecting markets and land tenure, along with international demand for forest products, were primary drivers of local resource use. However, the new data showed that the most important linkages with the regional and national scales were probably through policies and conflicts driving migration to the region rather than through markets. Because of disjunctions between national policies and local conditions, national

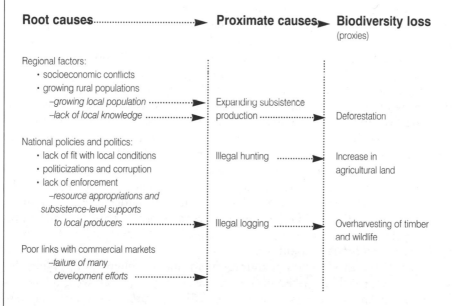

Figure 2.6 *Diagram of Revised Conceptual Model*

policies designed to improve resource use may be having perverse effects in the Calakmul region. For example, new policies intended to improve security of land tenure may be promoting deforestation since forested land is not covered by these policies. Local-level responses to external socioeconomic forces in some ways promote biodiversity loss and in others may protect it. For example, there is local opposition to the creation of the Reserve, but its creation has also led to the development of a strong grassroots organization that supports sustainable activities.

The completed case study (see Chapter 11) begins with a description of local population and resource-use patterns, which are the proximate causes of biodiversity loss. From there it moves outward or upward in scale to describe the various levels of socioeconomic factors that are shaping local resource use patterns. Figure 2.6 shows some key parts of the revised conceptual model described by the study. This revised diagram emphasizes growth of local population due to regional factors, the inappropriateness of many policies to local conditions and the marginality of the region to markets. These are factors that must be addressed if conservation is to be achieved.

Each of the case studies adapted the approach described above to the particular context of the site, thus serving as a test of its usefulness. These adaptations are described in the study summaries. The great variety of thought processes behind the studies is clearly illustrated by the variety of conceptual model diagrams that emerged. The studies reveal the flexibility of the framework but also some of its limitations as a tool for sorting out complex situations of which knowledge is limited.

Most of the studies took a comparative approach, looking at two or three sites. This approach strengthens the conclusions by illustrating how biodiversity is affected differently at similar sites because of different socioeconomic pressures. For example, the three islands studied in the Philippines case each had different development experiences in large part because of Spanish and American colonial policies, with the result that one island remains almost pristine while the others have lost much of their original biodiversity. The comparative approach can also illustrate how the same socioeconomic pressures have very different impacts at various sites because of different environmental or socioeconomic conditions. The Brazil study shows how national government policies for agricultural development were effective in promoting large-scale commercial agriculture in some parts of the Cerrado region but ineffective in others, as a result of different underlying environmental and social conditions. In other cases, the reverse proves true. In the Danube Basin, socialist policies have had similar effects on biodiversity and resource use in two very different countries.

Most of the case studies encountered similar problems in applying the Analytical Approach described in this chapter, many of which were related to data issues. Some of these issues were practical in nature, others more theoretical. These included issues of data availability and quantity, setting the appropriate limits for the research and for the conceptual models, dealing with contextual factors, determining what constitutes a root cause of biodiversity loss and assigning priority to different causes.

Data Availability

On the practical side, quantitative data were seriously lacking for many sites; this lack of quantitative data made it hard to back up qualitative assertions. Since many of the sites are remote or marginal areas in developing countries the lack of data is not surprising. Even when data are available, for example through government censuses, they are often unreliable. The case studies compensated for this lack in many instances by carrying out their own local surveys and by drawing inferences from data at the regional or national level. For example, facing a lack of data on the impact of human activities on fish populations, the Pakistan study surveyed local residents in the mangrove areas to find out what changes they had observed in local fish catches. Likewise in Tanzania local surveys were used to better understand local resource use. This type of data collection serves to support qualitative assessments, such as the assessment that fish populations have decreased, but it is insufficient to draw quantitative conclusions about the impact of human activities.

One of the most frequent quantitative problems faced in the case studies was the lack of hard data on biodiversity loss. To deal with this problem the studies had to assume that environmental changes, such as land-cover change, have direct impacts on biodiversity levels and therefore provide a useful proxy for biodiversity loss. For example, in the study of Tanzania, the loss of mangrove cover and mangrove species is taken as indicative of a more general loss of biodiversity in mangrove ecosystems. In addition, the analytic approach is not well designed for making a quantitative link between human resource use and biodiversity loss. The use of proxies such as land-use change for biodiversity loss must take into account the fact that changes in land use or habitats will have different impacts on biodiversity under different conditions. Shifting cultivation, for example, when practised on a small scale may have a minimal or even beneficial impact on biodiversity; on a more extensive scale it will have more serious impacts; and extensive commercial agriculture with heavy use of agrochemicals is likely to destroy local ecosystems. In the case of the Brazilian Cerrado, the expansion of mechanized agriculture is assumed to cause more biodiversity loss than the expansion of family farming. Similar differences exist between the impacts of small-scale selective logging and commercial clear-cutting and between artisanal fishing and large-scale commercial fishing.

Finding the proper balance between quantitative and qualitative data presented a theoretical challenge for most of the teams. In fact this issue often resolves itself, given the limited quantitative data available and the limited time and resources available for conducting these studies. Quantitative data of varying comprehensiveness and reliability are used in each of the studies to support a qualitative picture of biodiversity loss. The conceptual models themselves, however, are not quantitative.

Setting Limits to the Models

Another practical problem faced by many of the case studies was in setting the limits of the conceptual models, particularly limiting the time-frame considered in the models. This is essentially a question of deciding what scale is sufficient for the investigation. A related issue raised by several research teams is the question of how we know when we have reached the root cause. In fact this type of analysis can be extended back indefinitely, revealing different operational root causes during different historical periods. Two of the case studies, those of the Danube Basin and the Philippines, took a long historical perspective on biodiversity loss. This approach provides a very useful understanding of the context in which biodiversity loss is currently occurring. In the Danube Basin, for example, the Cold War has largely determined the conditions in Bulgaria and Slovakia that are shaping the use of river-basin resources today. This historical approach can also provide some indications of likely future developments. In the Philippines, development patterns on three islands colonized sequentially reveal the likely path of future development.

The difficulty lies in determining which of the causes of biodiversity loss revealed through this type of analysis are still operating – causes which may be subject to intervention – and which are historical factors that can no longer be changed. While understanding the immutable historical context is useful, it may go a step beyond the knowledge necessary to slow or stop current biodiversity loss. We can say that we have reached a root cause when we have found a point at which we can successfully intervene in order to alter the loss of biodiversity. In other words, our interest in root causes analysis is to uncover the socioeconomic factor or set of factors driving biodiversity loss that can be effectively changed so as to reduce or eliminate the pressure on biodiversity. Root causes may be found at the local, regional or international levels, depending on where the factors lie that determine local resource use. In many cases, as the studies clearly show, there will not be one single root cause but rather a complex network of root causes. This complexity is what the conceptual model attempts to describe. Only once we have a clear picture of the causal factors at work can we begin to think about appropriate points of intervention.

On the more theoretical side lies the concern that this approach creates an inherent bias toward the selection of distant, generally historical and international factors as the root causes of biodiversity loss. Again the conceptual models are not expected to determine an ultimate cause, but rather to present a picture of the factors and the links among those factors across various scales to provide a complete explanation of biodiversity loss as it generally occurs, at the local level, as the basis for halting biodiversity loss.

Contextual Factors

Several of the studies pointed to some causal factors that did not fit easily into the five socioeconomic categories listed above. These causal factors included the effects of war, ideology and historical context, as well as physical factors such as the accessibility of an area and natural processes. What all these factors have in common is that they are best classified as contextual elements. They may appear as root causes of biodiversity loss if we trace the chains of explanation back as far as we can go. But because they are immutable historical or physical facts they do not offer points where we can intervene to slow or halt the loss of biodiversity. If we look at the current consequences of this context, however, we may find some points for intervention. For example, in the cases of Vietnam and Cameroon, war has shaped current patterns of biodiversity loss. In Vietnam, war drove large population shifts that greatly affected land use and habitat loss. In Cameroon, guns remaining from wars in neighbouring states facilitate wildlife hunting. While the historical facts of the wars cannot be changed, the present effects, such as land-use change and over-hunting, can be affected. Likewise in the case of the Danube countries, Slovakia and Bulgaria, the socialist ideology imposed during much of this century has had an enormous impact on biodiversity. This history cannot be changed. However, the end of the Cold War has opened the possibility of changing many of the patterns of behaviour that were generated by this ideology.

Physical factors present a similar challenge to our understanding of causes of biodiversity loss. Several of the case studies pointed out the importance of the accessibility of an area in determining the fate of biodiversity. The Philippines study, looking at three different islands, found the most remote one to have sustained the least environmental damage. Likewise the study in Brazil found that the most remote region with the most difficult topography was least affected by agricultural expansion. Again, these physical conditions are largely contextual factors that do not offer points for intervention. Clearly, however, human ingenuity and the drive to obtain new resources lead to improvements in infrastructure and technologies that allow even remote and difficult areas to be exploited. The incursion of roads into the south-eastern forests of Cameroon and the Brazilian Cerrado has changed the use of resources in these regions. The question of physical access and environmental obstacles to settlement or resource use is therefore of interest. Patterns of resource use and opportunities for conservation of biodiversity are very different in areas that are readily accessible and offer easy access to markets and other facilities, from those in areas that remain remote and isolated. For example, the situation in the mangroves of Pakistan which are found near the large urban area of Karachi differs greatly from that of the mangroves in Tanzania, which remain relatively isolated.

Weighing Causal Factors

One of the greatest difficulties in every study was assigning priority to, or weighing, the various root causes. While attempts were made to weigh these causes quantitatively, none of these efforts was very satisfactory. For example, the Vietnam study assigns relative weights to each of the causes, but this does not tell us where intervention will be most effective, since some of the causes, including the consequences of several wars, cannot be altered. The India study attempted a statistical analysis, but the sheer number of variables involved, as well as the lack of data, limits the reliability of this type of analysis. Because these causes often cannot be measured quantitatively – much less be measured in a comparable way with other causal factors – the final judgements about their relative importance must be qualitative. To this end, the diagrams used to illustrate the conceptual models are useful, since they indicate not only the direct impacts of a particular factor but also how that factor is linked with other socioeconomic factors affecting biodiversity.

One reason why it is difficult both to select the root causes and to weigh various causes is because, in most cases, biodiversity loss is driven or determined by several factors. We can say that biodiversity loss at a particular site is *over-determined* in the sense that, while these factors are closely interlinked through complex relationships, each on its own may be sufficient to cause biodiversity loss. In other words, addressing one cause of biodiversity loss alone may have little impact if several others are also operating at the same site. While one cause or another may predominate in a particular set of circumstances, many factors are often pushing in the same direction: moreover they tend to reinforce each other. In the Mexico case, for example, a protected area is threatened not only by migration to the area but also by government policies in agriculture and forestry. These policies aggravate the impacts of the new population. Even in isolated areas, where much biodiversity loss is occurring, a number of causal factors both at and beyond the local level are likely to be at work. For example, in the remote forests of Cameroon, hunting is increasing not only because of increased demand in the cities and abroad for bushmeat, but also because logging, driven in part by macroeconomic policies, is facilitating access to the region. The findings from the case studies analysed in Chapter 4 provide further discussion of the problem of over-determination.

ARRIVING AT RECOMMENDATIONS

These case studies give us a very complete, if not always quantitatively measurable, picture of what is happening at each site studied. We learn about what causal factors, and how many, are driving biodiversity loss and about how they are interlinked. Once we have this complete picture it is feasible to select the appropriate points for intervention to slow or halt biodiversity loss. The conceptual models developed in the case studies provide a crucial input to any decision-making about how to address biodiversity loss at the study sites. Of course, defining the problem and the context in which we must work is only the first step. At the conclusion of the studies the research teams each made very preliminary recommendations for the next steps.

To move from these analytic studies to actions for biodiversity conservation will require another process – a political process to make decisions about how to address the problems analysed by the studies. The factors affecting biodiversity will need to be addressed at a variety of levels. Some issues will be best addressed through local projects, but many of the socioeconomic issues can only be addressed at a regional, national or sometimes international level. Many issues will need to be addressed at several levels or scales in order to effect a real change. For example, addressing poor enforcement of logging restrictions – a problem common to many of the study sites – may require improvements in the law, which must be accomplished at the national level. It may involve training of enforcement officials, which must be done at a regional level, and it may involve environmental education targeted to the local communities.

The recommendations presented in the studies here are initial, indicative suggestions that should be fed into a participatory process with the relevant stakeholders. The case studies can serve as the basis for a stakeholder analysis, providing information on who needs to be involved, where the greatest opposition to change will be found and where partners can be found for promoting conservation. Most importantly, the conceptual models developed by the studies provide the basis for selecting the target issues and target areas where intervention for conservation will be most effective. The case studies also provide the basis for educating people about the causes of biodiversity loss and for debating the best solutions to the problem. Final recommendations derived from the participatory process will provide the basis for an action plan. Although important similarities emerged from these case studies, each case is unique and solutions will always need to be carefully adapted to each site.

Chapter 3

Ten Case Studies – An Overview

Pamela Stedman-Edwards and Johanna Mang

Ten research teams applied the Analytical Approach to assess the underlying forces that drive biodiversity loss. At each site a complex interplay of the driving factors was found, some of them unique to the specific site, while other factors are common among the case studies. Short summaries of the ten case studies introduce the reader to the findings.

Conservation efforts have been in place for many years, especially in locations of high biodiversity value. The Root Causes project was looking for partners interested in conducting a truly multidisciplinary and in-depth analysis of biodiversity loss. In many instances this project provided the local teams with a first opportunity to explore the broader influences driving environmental degradation in their localities. By using the Analytical Approach, research

Figure 3.1 *World Map Indicating Countries of the Ten Case Studies*

teams were able to construct a more complete picture of the complex web of socioeconomic factors driving biodiversity loss.

The previous chapter presented the Analytical Approach. This chapter introduces readers to the case studies themselves as a way of understanding how the Analytical Approach was applied, but also to ground the project's findings and conclusions in the case study experience.

Chapter 4 provides the overall findings and conclusions of the ten case studies carried out in the course of the project. The case studies are presented in Chapters 6–15.

BRAZIL:
CERRADO

The unique mosaic of tropical grasslands and forests of Brazil's Central Plateau, known as the Cerrado, has been transformed by rapid development of commercial agriculture, particularly monoculture production of soybeans, since the 1960s. Only 35 per cent of the biome remains in its natural state and only 0.6 per cent is officially protected. The pressure for agricultural development, driven largely by government policies, elicited three different types of responses in the three counties studied, each with different consequences for the environment.

The agro-development policies that have driven the expansion of soybean production in the Cerrado have been primarily determined by Brazil's need to generate foreign exchange through exports. The main goal of agricultural policy has been to improve the balance of payments through support to large-scale, capital-intensive agriculture. As the international price of soybeans rose in the 1960s and 1970s, the Brazilian government invested in infrastructure, subsidies for inputs, selective credit promoting particular crops and price supports to promote the expansion of commercial agriculture in the region. Much of this investment was funded through international borrowing. The push was quite successful: soybeans are now Brazil's second-leading export. However, as commodity prices fell in the 1980s and the debt crisis worsened, Brazil faced an increasing need to export commodities to meet its international obligations. Despite the high costs, the government continued to protect Brazil's commercial agricultural producers with minimum price guarantees and fuel subsidies in order to allow continuing expansion of export-oriented production.

These agricultural policies also supported several other objectives. First among these was the perceived need to occupy this relatively unpopulated territory. The establishment of the new capital, Brasilia, in the centre of the Cerrado, accompanied by the construction of new roads and infrastructure, was part of the push to occupy the area. The agro-development policies also served to relieve land pressure in the south of the country and served to meet demand for agricultural products in growing urban areas. In addition the political power of large-scale commercial producers has ensured the continuing flow of benefits to the sector.

The direct impacts of commercial monocultural agriculture, namely habitat destruction, alteration of the natural fire regime and agricultural pollution, have been limited to a fairly small area of the Cerrado. However, the indirect effects have been at least as important. These have included an influx of new migrants to the area as well as the displacement of small farmers and farm labourers to urban areas and the Amazon frontier as small properties have been absorbed by large commercial enterprises.

The extent of the changes caused by these agro-development policies varies with the environmental and socioeconomic contexts found in different parts of the Cerrado. In Rio Verde County, where topography was conducive to mechanized agriculture and there were significant deposits of lime – a key input to the new agricultural technology – the commercial monocultural model was widely adopted. About 25 per cent of this county is now in annual crops. In Silvânia County, where conditions also appeared favourable, the model was not widely adopted because socioeconomic conditions – including a long history of settlement and a well-established community – favoured the maintenance of the diversified family-run farm and only 12 per cent of the county is in annual crops. In Alto Paraíso, rugged terrain and isolation meant that large-scale commercial agriculture was not very viable. Population density remains low and agriculture occupies less than 3 per cent of the county. A national park has been established and new settlers interested in the county's natural beauty are investing in ecotourism and similar enterprises.

The study concludes that the commercial agricultural model is economically viable in the most geographically favourable areas and will bring significant growth and income. There is little doubt that it will dominate such regions. The question remains whether there will also be space for the alternative models revealed by the Silvânia and Alto Paraíso cases. With careful planning and targeted investment, these models could coexist.

The primary recommendation is for a more diversified model for the Cerrado that includes intensive agriculture in the most favourable areas, a more diversified family agricultural model, with conservation as a third approach for some parts of the region. This would require regional planning and zoning in order to channel the alternative forms of development to the best-suited areas for each and incentives for the optimal implementation of each of these models.

CAMEROON:
THE BUSHMEAT AND WILDLIFE TRADE

The growing bushmeat and wildlife trade in Cameroon is causing biodiversity loss in both Mount Cameroon, an area with a long history of agricultural development, and in the relatively undisturbed south-eastern forests. Social change and development, unrestrained by environmental controls, lie behind the rising toll on wildlife in both these biodiversity 'hotspots'.

Mount Cameroon has been largely deforested by the Cameroon Development Corporation (CDC), a large government-owned agro-industrial plantation that has attracted many immigrants to the area. Habitat loss and hunting have decimated wildlife, but hunting continues in the area to meet subsistence needs and the demands of the local market. The poor wages offered by the CDC leave its workers with little choice but to clear land for subsistence agricultural plots, which must be defended from animal pests, and engage in hunting.

Wildlife is still abundant in the south-eastern forests where human population density remains low. However, as logging roads have penetrated the area and new migrants have arrived with the logging companies, traditional subsistence hunting patterns are being gradually replaced by commercial-scale hunting and wildlife collection. Loggers provide transport to markets and hunt for their own subsistence, since the logging companies pay poorly. Among the indigenous population traditional methods of hunting using snares and nets are being replaced by much more extensive trapping systems, homemade guns and even automatic weapons. Taboos on hunting certain species and during certain seasons are being abandoned. These changes are occurring because markets for wildlife products are now readily available, given improvements in transport to Cameroon's urban areas and beyond.

The development of these remote forests, most notably the expansion of logging company operations, is occurring for several reasons. Among these is the government's desire to incorporate the region more completely into the country by creating better transport links. Other factors include the macro-economic problems of recent years. A fall in the price of cacao, the traditional product of the South-East, made commercial hunting a much more attractive option for the local population. Devaluation increased the profitability of timber exports. The country's heavy reliance on primary products in the face of unstable and often falling prices for these products has meant that timber production had to increase to meet the country's need for foreign exchange. At the same time, structural adjustment measures have severely reduced the government's capacity to enforce laws limiting hunting and wildlife collection. Added to corruption and lack of political will to protect biodiversity, it has meant that most of these laws are ineffectual. International treaties governing wildlife capture, notably the Convention on International Trade in Endangered Species (CITES), have failed to reduce the markets for regulated species and may only have succeeded in increasing the profitability of illegal operations.

An understanding of the country's colonial history, in which Germans and French eliminated traditional land tenure and, as illustrated by the case of Mount Cameroon, replaced the forests with plantations, is fundamental to the changes taking place. Development has been based on the exploitation of natural resources, and the appropriation of land and resources by the government in the name of modernization has continued until the present. The 1994 Forestry Law nationalized all natural resources, leaving the inhabitants of the south-eastern forests with no claim to the region's land or resources. However, the loss of traditional patterns of resource use cannot be blamed entirely on development. Wildlife in Cameroon is traditionally seen as inexhaustible. The pidgin word for animal is 'beef', clearly indicating man's perception of wildlife. As long as the population of these forests remained low, however, and access to weapons and markets was limited, hunting served subsistence needs and posed little threat to biodiversity.

The study recommends changes at national and international levels to reduce the impact of the bushmeat and wildlife trade. At the national level recommendations include developing a secondary sector of the economy to reduce dependence on exploitation of natural resources and reducing the damage caused by private companies and their employees by imposing more effective environmental controls. At the international level, recommendations include developing better information about the value of biodiversity as the basis for improving controls on international trade in species; reforming CITES to make importing countries assume more responsibility for enforcement; and reforming structural adjustment programmes to recognize the special environmental challenges facing countries which rely heavily on primary products.

CHINA:
SOUTH-WESTERN FORESTS

Destruction of temperate forests in the two counties studied in south-west China is eliminating habitats of the giant panda and the Yunnan snub-nosed monkey, among other species. Both counties have important nature reserves, but habitat loss is extensive. In Deqin County, the poorer and more isolated of the two, forest loss is primarily driven by the expansion of agriculture. Logging also plays a role. In Pingwu County, commercial logging is the main driver of forest loss.

Population growth and lack of economic development in Deqin lead to forest clearing for agriculture despite low productivity levels. Food shortages have become chronic. Government policies – including policies on population, poverty, land reform and logging – have only aggravated the unsustainable exploitation of resources. For example, poverty-alleviation funds allocated by the central government must be matched by the local government, which routinely obtains them from logging. Political movements, notably the Food First Movement of the 1960s, the Great Leap Forward and the Cultural Revolution, promoted unsustainable resource use and reduced the government's capacity for management.

These policies and political movements have played a similar role in Pingwu. Those driving clear-cutting by state timber companies have had the greatest impact on biodiversity. Particularly striking has been the way a network of institutions and incentives has developed that promotes over-harvesting of timber. Commercial timber companies are government-owned, so revenues flow directly to the state, provincial or local government. Until recently the government controlled timber prices. Moreover, the taxes and forest fees paid by these companies also flow to the government. As a result governments at all levels have a strong interest in continuing unsustainable timber harvests. The local government in Pingwu County relies heavily on this income, which accounted for 47 per cent of county-generated revenue in 1997. Other groups have also become dependent on the continuation of logging, including villages that receive a stumpage fee, the forestry department that collects fees, timber company employees who are guaranteed life-time employment and various private concession grantees, middlemen and agents engaged in illegal trading of logging quotas.

These close ties between government and the logging industry, including heavy government dependence on logging income, have led to over-harvesting of timber. Centralization of decision-making firmly rooted in political ideology led to unsustainable use. Recently China has been moving toward a market-based economy, which could be expected to eliminate this problem by removing government from the logging business. However, new, more liberal policies have not been properly designed to promote a move toward sustainability. On the contrary, the opening of markets, including freeing timber prices, has created new incentives for logging. Communally owned lands, formerly used in a more sustainable manner, are now being used for extensive commercial logging. Timber prices have risen, but the bulk of profits still goes to the government either through government-owned companies or taxes. Rural households harvesting timber receive only 10 to 14 per cent of the final price. Moreover, the market prices do not account for the environmental services provided by forests. In Deqin County, for example, where 190,000 ha have been put aside as protected forest, people are complaining that they have lost the value of these resources, since they receive no compensation for the environmental services provided.

The China National Forest Conservation Action Programme, established as a result of severe flooding in 1998, creates new opportunities for conservation in these two counties. Commercial logging may be reduced or even halted. The Action Programme could be used as a vehicle for designating old-growth forests as nature reserves, strengthening the management of nature reserves and developing alternatives to logging. In Pingwu, halting logging will depend on the development of economic alternatives for the government and communities. In Deqin, reduction of logging will have to be complemented by population policies and improvements in agricultural productivity to reduce land clearing for agriculture.

DANUBE RIVER BASIN:
WETLANDS AND FLOODPLAINS

Alteration of habitats and biodiversity loss in the Danube Basin date back over hundreds of years. The natural habitats of the Danube River wetlands, islands and floodplains in Bulgaria and Slovakia have been substantially reduced. The Morava floodplains in Slovakia, for example, now cover only a quarter of their original extent. Remaining areas are threatened by further conversion to agriculture and plantation forestry and by water pollution, mining, hunting and fishing. These threats are driven by economic turmoil, poor land tenure definition, a long history of biodiversity exploitation and a lack of enforcement of environmental laws. Despite geographic, historic and cultural differences between the two countries, significant similarities were found in the root causes of biodiversity loss. In both, two key factors underlie these current socioeconomic threats: the legacy of the Cold War and socialist governments, and the persistent failure to recognize the value of biodiversity.

From early in this century, through the period of socialist governments, and into today's political and economic transition period, a variety of policies have had detrimental environmental effects. Before World War II both governments invested heavily in regulation of the Danube to facilitate shipping and decrease flooding, changing both the course and the depth of the river and altering flooding patterns, which resulted in the loss of wetlands and naturally flooding meadows, amongst other critical habitats. During the socialist period, draining and damming of the Danube continued as a response to population and production pressures in Bulgaria. Expansion of agriculture and plantation forestry were encouraged in the region. In Slovakia, where the river formed the Iron Curtain border, the floodplains were placed off limits. However, socialist policies in agriculture unintentionally promoted the illicit use of these lands to meet production quotas that could not be met legitimately. Environmental protection was ignored in both countries.

The current transition to capitalism has led to economic disruption and decline and created confusion over resource rights and tenure. This confusion is promoting unsustainable use of some resources. For example, an illegal gravel mining operation in Slovakia is causing considerable degradation on lands of unclear tenure. It is also leading to neglect of other resources, including the abandonment of traditional mowing practices that are critical for the maintenance of floodplain meadow habitats. The slow process of land re-privatization has been largely to blame in both cases. The economic difficulties created by the current transition have also left the governments of both countries with insufficient political will or funds to enforce environmental laws, so degradation and unsustainable use are allowed to continue unchecked.

The study attributes these repeated policy failures to a consistent failure to recognize the value of biodiversity. Whether it be pre-war progress in the form of new engineering technologies for controlling the Danube, socialist progress based on planned agricultural output to which nature provided free inputs, or current private-sector development, development has always been put before conservation of natural resources.

While many of the causes of biodiversity loss in the region are historical and cannot be reversed, the failure to value biodiversity is a key driver of current degradation and must be addressed to ensure protection of the region's biodiversity. Recommendations therefore focus on the need to determine the value of the region's biodiversity and to incorporate that knowledge into decision-making. Armed with fuller economic data on the true value of the island and floodplain ecosystems, it will be easier to convince decision-makers, the general public and local resource users such as the farming community, that these resources are worth conserving and using in a sustainable manner. Two international developments offer promise of improving environmental protection in the region. First, both Bulgaria and Slovakia are strengthening ties with the European Union (EU) and are likely to be influenced by the environmental policy climate of Western Europe. Second, the recent Danube River Protection Convention offers a promising framework for international cooperation and more integrated river basin management.

INDIA:
CHILIKA LAKE

Chilika Lake and its wetlands cover about 100,000 ha in eastern India. The area is widely known for its bird population, which includes over 150 species and about one million migratory visitors in the winter. Biodiversity of the lake, however, has been severely affected by rapid expansion of the human population, by changes in aquaculture technology and production, by ecological changes affecting the lake, and indirectly by entry into global markets.

The lake is connected to the ocean through a long narrow channel. As deforestation in the surrounding area has increased siltation, this channel has become increasingly blocked, leading to decreasing levels of salinity in the lake. At the same time eutrophication has followed the expansion of agriculture in the region, leading to rapid weed growth and a shrinkage by 1.5km^2 of the lake surface area every year. The greatest threat to biodiversity, however, has come from changes in fishing practices which have aggravated the impact of these ecological changes. Both commercially important species such as the tiger crab and the tiger prawn, as well as the fish and birds which normally prey on these species, have been affected. Crocodiles, green sea turtles, and gharials have become locally extinct and the number of fish species has fallen by about one third.

Rapid expansion of prawn culture began in the lake in the mid-1980s, boosted by India's new policies of market orientation, by growing global demand and by the development of low-cost technology. The fishermen abandoned traditional fishing techniques, which exploited a variety of species, to concentrate their efforts on prawn fishing and prawn culture. Many new people were attracted to the business who had not traditionally worked in fishing. Population growth in the region reached 4 per cent in the 1990s and the number of active fishermen rose from around 8000 in 1957 to over 27,000 in 1996. Structural adjustment in 1991 led to rising prices that made exports of prawns and crabs increasingly attractive. Middlemen, politicians and money lenders were brought into the business and production was intensified with fine-mesh nylon nets, motorized boats and larger ponds. Aquaculture was expanded further and processing and storage facilities were constructed. Very little of the catch is now consumed locally, most of it going to Calcutta or abroad.

The result of this expansion of prawn culture has been a drastic fall in fish landings, associated with the loss of food for the fish as prawns are removed from the food chain and as a direct result of over-fishing. Prawn landings have also fallen, but prawn culture persists because high and rising prices offset the decline. For example, prices for export-quality prawns rose from Rs 280/kg in 1992 to Rs 420/kg by 1996. Total catch for both fish and prawns in the 1995–96 season was just 14 per cent of the 1985–86 catch.

Local people recognize the environmental problems of the lake but, because of overwhelming poverty, see little choice but to over-exploit the fisheries, especially as they fall deeper into debt as the yields decline.

The government's approach to resolving these problems has been the restriction of licences for boats and prawn-culture ponds, for example. These restrictions have been largely unenforceable and have contributed to local social conflicts. The study recommends that local fishing traditions, such as restrictions on number of people in the industry, leasing arrangements and the use of cooperatives be respected and reinforced legally. A 1996 ruling by the Supreme Court called for the establishment of an authority to protect coastal zones based on the principles of 'precaution' and 'polluter pays'. The implementation of this ruling through environmental taxes on prawn-culture ponds, motor boats and export products, for example, with the proceeds to be used for restoration of the lake, would be a major step toward protection of the lake's biodiversity. Development of alternative activities such as ecotourism, marine fishing and small-scale businesses would also reduce the pressure to expand prawn production.

MEXICO:
CALAKMUL BIOSPHERE RESERVE

The Calakmul Biosphere Reserve on the Yucatan Peninsula covers about 725,000 ha of lowland tropical forests and remains one of the most isolated and least populated regions of Mexico. It protects many species endangered elsewhere in Mexico, provides an important refuge for migratory birds and forms a biological corridor to reserves in Guatemala and Belize. Nevertheless, expansion of shifting cultivation and logging in and around the Reserve are threatening the conservation of biodiversity.

Many of the changes are driven by socioeconomic forces, of which rapid immigration following an expanding agricultural frontier is dominant. Areas along the Reserve's eastern boundary and in a development corridor that cuts across the middle have been cleared for subsistence and small-scale commercial agriculture. The population is growing so rapidly that many communities will double in size within ten years. Poverty, lack of education, and limited access to reproductive health services contribute to this growth. Immigration to Calakmul stems from government efforts in the 1970s to attract migrants to the area and, more recently, from social conflicts, poverty, landlessness and rapid population growth in other parts of rural Mexico.

The lack of real economic alternatives to slash-and-burn subsistence agriculture is equally important in shaping resource use. The political and economic marginalization of the area has made it difficult to improve local socioeconomic conditions or support sound resource use. Government policies have failed to provide real alternatives to subsistence agriculture.

Poor agricultural land in the region, combined with frequent drought, provides little more than subsistence living. Government subsidies have provided support to *campesinos*, particularly in years of bad harvests, but the problems of lack of transport, lack of water and lack of adequate social services such as education have not been resolved. Current national policies, which support privatization of land and increased participation in markets, are largely irrelevant in Calakmul given the lack of commercial products from the region. The government, however, has encouraged settlement in the region through its continued support to subsistence agriculture even as it enacts policies promoting markets. At the same time that these supports are provided, the creation of the Reserve has theoretically placed limits on people's use of natural resources. Unresolved contradictions between laws on land tenure and use rights and the country's various environmental laws have left the legal rights of Calakmul residents unclear, but they have taken advantage of those policies that allow them to improve their living conditions, such as agricultural subsidies, and ignored those that seem to limit their options, such as the Biosphere Reserve restrictions on resource use.

The creation of the Reserve, however, has brought political attention and funds to the region. Together with valuable local efforts to exert control over resources, international conservation interventions in the area offer some hope of slowing the loss of biodiversity. If these conservation programmes are to be successful, they must move beyond efforts to improve the sustainability of agriculture and forestry and address the underlying problems of population growth and marginalization, taking into account the poverty of local agricultural resources. Communities must be convinced of the need to use resources sustainably and limit population growth. Incomes need to be increased to make these changes possible. Production of honey, certified timber and promotion of ecotourism based on local Mayan ruins offer some promising options, but only if better links with markets are established. Local communities, government agencies and conservation organizations need to work together to ensure that local development supports the Reserve and the local people.

PAKISTAN:
MANGROVES

Ninety-seven per cent of the mangrove forests are found in the Indus Delta and just 3 per cent are found in three pockets along the Baluchistan Coast. These forests have been severely degraded over the last 50 years as a result of reduced fresh water and silt supplies following upstream dam and barrage construction and marine pollution. Of eight species of mangroves that were found in Pakistan 50 years ago, all but one have become rare or extinct today. Only 15 per cent of the mangroves in the Indus Delta are considered healthy. In addition to preventing erosion and reducing flooding, mangroves support many marine species.

The reduced flow of fresh water to the delta has a severe impact on the mangroves because it both increases salinity levels and reduces the flow of nutrient-rich silt. Only one species of mangrove has fared well under these conditions. Freshwater flows have been reduced from 172,670 million m^3 to 49,334 million m^3 by the construction of three large dams and 20 barrages over the last 50 years. These dams and barrages were constructed to provide irrigation water for agriculture without any consideration given to coastal water needs.

Feudal-style agricultural landlords wield substantial political power that has allowed them not only to ensure the supply of irrigation water to agriculture, but also to maintain substantial subsidies in the provision of water. The result is that use of irrigation water is highly inefficient. Pressure from international lenders for the establishment of water markets has been ineffective. The current Water Accord guarantees only 12,333 million m^3 of fresh water to the delta, an amount barely sufficient to keep the extant mangrove forests healthy.

The national government has supported the agricultural sector not only because of the political power of landowners but also to provide support to industrialization by ensuring an adequate domestic food supply. Marine pollution, from industries in the Karachi area and from the urban areas that have expanded as a result of the centralized industrialization process, is also closely linked with the drive for exports. Over 70 per cent of Pakistan's international trade originates in the Karachi area. Recent structural reforms have reinforced the drive for exports but have not reduced the government's commitment to the centralized growth approach. Environmental laws are largely unenforced and industries take no responsibility for environmental protection.

Likewise, over-fishing can be linked with export policies. Over 90 per cent of the local population depend directly or indirectly on fishing. Devaluation of the rupee has made fishing very lucrative, attracting immigrants from other parts of Pakistan and foreign countries to the coastal areas. Immigration has directly increased pressure on marine resources, introduced the use of illegal small-mesh nets that increase the fish catch and disrupted traditional communities, thus reducing traditional controls on fishing. Household surveys conducted in the Indus Delta and the Baluchistan Coast provided strong evidence not only of reductions in overall catch but also of a reduced number of fish species. In these coastal regions poor local political representation has meant that local physical and social infrastructure such as roads and education are very limited. As a result, economic alternatives to fishing are scarce and the area is unable to attract investment for development of new activities. Fishing will remain an important activity.

Halting the loss and degradation of mangrove forests and the biodiversity they support depends first and foremost on ensuring an adequate supply of fresh water to the coast. Water use efficiency must be increased upstream both at the level of the irrigation system and at the farm level. Otherwise even the 12,333 million m^3 guaranteed in the Water Accord are likely to be reduced as agricultural land continues to expand. Control of marine pollution will require enforcement of existing environmental standards and closer involvement of industry in pollution control. To reduce the impact of over-fishing, immigration to the coastal region needs to be stopped, fishing laws need to be adequately enforced and economic alternatives to fishing need to be developed. The high levels of income generated by fishing should provide the basis for the development of local financial institutions that could support the development of alternative activities. Finally, export promotion and trade policies, which have aggravated all of these threats to the mangrove forests, need to be systematically evaluated for their environmental impact.

PHILIPPINES:
CEBU, NEGROS AND PALAWAN

Rates of biodiversity loss as high as 60 per cent among the country's numerous endemic species are being reported in the Philippines. Forest cover has fallen from 90 per cent of total land area to only 18 per cent. In the forest ecosystems, the immediate or proximate causes of this loss are logging and expansion of shifting cultivation. Among the socioeconomic root causes driving forest clearing, population pressure stands out most clearly with a ten-fold increase in population during the last century. However, population density is in turn a consequence of other historical and current socioeconomic factors, notably inequality of political and economic power.

Three islands in the archipelago provide evidence of a strong correlation between population density and biodiversity loss. Cebu, the island with the greatest population density as well as a long history of intense settlement, has lost almost all its natural habitat. Negros, which is less densely occupied, has also lost much of its natural habitat, but to plantations rather than urbanization. Palawan, which has only recently begun to attract settlers, remains relatively unscathed. While patterns of development have differed greatly on the three islands, the end results are deforestation and land degradation.

Cebu was among the first islands settled by the Spanish, who placed strict limits on emigration and thereby promoted population concentration. Much of Cebu's forests had already been lost by the beginning of the 20th century. Concentration of land ownership has pushed many poor peasants to steep slopes and marginal lands where they practise shifting agriculture. At the same time, the central location of Cebu allowed it to develop into a trading centre. While there has been substantial emigration from the island's rural areas in more recent years, urban development and industrialization have attracted migrants. Population densities have reached 518 people per km^2 and virtually no original forest cover remains.

Settlement in Negros was based on the growth of sugar plantations, beginning in the mid-19th century. These plantations attracted many farm workers from Cebu and elsewhere. While the plantations claimed the better lands, workers and landless farmers facing continued impoverishment and underemployment moved into the uplands. Under American rule, policies encouraged migration to other islands, but failed to resolve the fundamental inequalities in land tenure that had been created. More recent land reform laws have also been unsuccessful because of the power of landowners. Today little remains of the original forests on Negros.

In contrast, Palawan has a remarkable 54 per cent of its original forest cover remaining. Population density is only 35 people per km^2. In large part because of its remoteness, Palawan experienced only minimal population growth under Spanish rule. The establishment of a prison and a leper colony on the island under American rule did little to boost immigration. Following

World War II, however, government policies began to encourage settlement in order to relieve population and land pressures elsewhere, and today this island has one of the highest rates of immigration. Since Palawan has only recently begun to follow the development path of the other islands, it offers the best hope for conservation of biodiversity in the Philippines. The establishment of an island-wide legally mandated environmental plan is a very promising step.

Population density on the three islands is itself a factor of Spanish and American colonial policies, ease of access and socioeconomic structures. Spanish colonial policies not only limited migration within the Philippines, concentrating population in Cebu, but also established a rigid social structure that has created lasting inequalities in economic and political power. This social structure was replicated in Negros, where a few plantation owners have controlled the local economy and political system. The so-called 'sugar bloc' has held tremendous political sway at the national level, in large part because of the country's heavy dependence on sugar exports. American trading preferences kept the sugar bloc in power. Throughout the last two centuries government policies have actively encouraged monopolies in export crops, reinforcing economic and political inequality and provoking continued pressure on marginal, biodiversity-rich lands by the poor. Of the three islands, only Palawan has largely escaped the development of industry or plantations.

Biodiversity loss is unlikely to stop unless access to endangered ecosystems is prevented and the number of rural poor is substantially reduced. Some steps in the right direction are being taken. Family planning services, for example, are being made available for the first time and land reform is underway. Palawan provides an example of what can be done in environmental policy if civil society is given a greater voice.

Tanzania:
Rufiji, Ruvu and Wami Mangroves

The Rufiji, Ruvu and Wami Deltas of Tanzania support an extensive system of wetlands and mangrove forests. Agriculture, fishing and harvesting of mangroves for poles, fuelwood and charcoal are the main economic activities. These all affect the mangrove ecosystems and consequently threaten biodiversity, particularly macro-invertebrates (molluscs, crustaceans etc) and fish, including commercially important species.

Degradation of the mangrove forests is largely driven by poverty, which results from isolation rather than from population pressure on local resources. Isolation means that there is limited access to markets, education and other social and economic resources. Fishing provides an annual income of approximately US$304 in the Ruvu and Wami Deltas, and only US$164 in Rufiji Delta. Agriculture provides little more. Seventy per cent of the population cultivates two hectares or less. Given the lack of other sources of livelihood, land in the deltas is cleared for subsistence farming. Mangroves are cut both for subsistence use, including fuelwood, housing, boat-making and fish traps, and for commercial sale, providing one of the few local sources of cash income. Isolated as these sites are, the local people cannot subsist entirely outside of the cash economy.

The effects of poverty are aggravated first by a lack of infrastructure and social support services and second by the failure of the government to enforce existing regulations on natural resource use. Earlier in this century, when trading vessels frequented these areas, the range of products sold was much greater, including not only mangroves but also cashew, prawns, cotton, rice and coconut, and the region supported a larger population than it does now. Today, however, roads in the delta areas are poor, particularly those in the Rufiji Delta, and transportation is correspondingly expensive and unreliable. Markets for fish and agricultural products are therefore largely inaccessible. The commercial sale of prawns is particularly limited by the lack of infrastructure, which affects many people's incomes. Mangrove products are one of the few local products that can be reliably transported to market. Since taxes are almost exclusively collected by the central and district governments, local governments are left without funds for infrastructure improvements. The current dependence on mangrove exploitation is therefore an effect of poor infrastructure, which can be attributed in part to the tax structure.

At the same time, the lack of government commitment to environmental protection, reflected in numerous conflicts among policies, has meant that enforcement of restrictions on natural resource use is rare. Centralized government policies have offered local people little voice in decisions about environmental management. A variety of ministries and departments with different objectives and interests in the use of delta resources have some authority in the region. These conflicts not only prevent adequate enforcement, as for example in the case of a large-scale prawn farm approved by the government for an area where mangroves are legally protected, but they also reduce the will of local people to cooperate. The national mangrove programme, for example, is pushing local rice farmers to replant their fields with mangroves, but these farmers have not been offered an alternate livelihood. Even when environmental offenders are apprehended, their sentences are little more than token punishments. Weak sentences can be blamed on lack of commitment to environmental protection. However, the shortage of funds for monitoring and enforcement can also be blamed on macroeconomic policies, notably structural adjustment policies, which have cut government budgets for low-priority items such as environmental protection.

In the mangrove areas, better access to markets and development of economic alternatives could promote diversification of resource use and thus reduce pressure on the mangroves. A recently enacted forest policy and the national mangrove programme both offer promise of giving greater voice to the local communities in management decisions. At the same time, the conflicts among government policies need to be resolved in favour of environmental management. The establishment of a body responsible for coordinating coastal zone management could resolve many of these issues.

VIETNAM:
NORTH AND CENTRAL HIGHLANDS

Three protected areas in Vietnam, the Ba Be Park and Na Hang Nature Reserve in mountainous northern Vietnam and the Yok Don National Park in the Central Highlands, are threatened by expansion of land for agriculture, logging, fuelwood collection, hunting and harvesting of forest products. In these three areas poverty and rapid population growth, aggravated by the country's turbulent recent history and by government policies that have promoted land clearing, are driving biodiversity loss.

While natural population growth rates are high in and around all three protected areas, large landless populations, created by war and natural population growth, have been resettled through planned and spontaneous government colonization programmes. For example, a government campaign of land colonization in the 1960s brought one million migrants from the Red River delta to the northern highlands and midlands. During the Second Indochina War, bombing forced further migration from the delta to the mountains, including many thousands to the province where the Na Hang Nature Reserve is located. In 1979 border conflicts with China forced further migration to the area. Migration continues today, since there are still some fertile lands under forest cover in the region. In the Yok Don area, immigration has been more recent, with nine planned migrations leading to a rise in the provincial population from just 36,000 in 1975 to 1.6 million today.

The population in and around each of the three protected areas is composed largely of ethnic minorities who depend on shifting agriculture for subsistence. The agricultural conditions in these mountainous areas are generally poor, and the people, including the many recent migrants, are uneducated and rely on inefficient agricultural techniques. Productivity is low, food shortages have been common and the hillsides are rapidly degraded. In Ba Be it is estimated that 30 per cent of the population suffers from continuous food shortages. Likewise, in Yok Don villages are only able to produce enough rice to support themselves for a few months each year. Forest products are used heavily for subsistence purposes and for sale. Isolation of these areas leaves people with little choice but to exploit local natural resources.

Increasing populations have led to increased land clearing for shifting agriculture, shortened fallow periods and increased hunting and use of timber and other forest products. Government efforts to resolve persistent food shortages included the development of cooperatives and the collectivization of agriculture from the 1950s to the 1970s, which aggravated the food shortage problem by reducing production incentives. At the same time, the war economy demanded large quantities of food to keep soldiers in the field. Once the failure of the cooperative movement was recognized, it was replaced by a contract-output system that increased producer incentives. However, rice markets remained in the hands of the government and production fell again. A further government programme has aimed to replace shifting cultivation with settled agriculture, but this effort too has had limited success, in part because the government did not take local conditions, traditional practices or local wishes into account.

Recent economic openness, known as *doi moi*, has boosted production, especially of forest and agricultural products. Land tenure has been reformed, giving farmers incentives to invest for the long-term, and exports have been promoted. The resulting increase in logging and in land clearing for crop production for export, particularly around Yok Don, has had a serious impact on forest cover and biodiversity. Moreover, infrastructure, credit and other assistance to small farmers remain inadequate, so most remain dependent on subsistence agriculture and extraction of forest products. Also under *doi moi*, the border with China has been opened, creating new markets for forest products including a broad range of wildlife and medicinal plants. Where park protection is adequate, the effect of *doi moi* on protected habitats has been limited. In those parks where government capacity for administration and enforcement is minimal, poverty-driven encroachment on the protected area has been significant.

Reducing the population pressure on Vietnam's protected areas must entail better planning and better controls on migration, including land-use planning and prevention of settlement in protected areas. Reducing the impact of local populations must entail more effective settlement programmes and integrated conservation and development projects that will improve local incomes and reduce degradation of natural resources.

Chapter 4

Main Findings and Conclusions of the Root Causes Project

Pamela Stedman-Edwards

Each of the ten case studies tells a unique story of biodiversity loss. By integrating analysis of the multiple socioeconomic factors contributing to biodiversity loss, each case study reveals the complexity of the root causes of biodiversity loss. Comparison of the study results reveals a common pattern across the diverse range of stories they tell, a pattern that can help us understand why the loss of biodiversity has become so widespread and so rapid in recent years. Degradation of habitat and overharvesting of species is the common response to growing domestic and international pressures facing the countries studied. Environmental management efforts have been insufficient to offset the impact of this pattern of development in which many socioeconomic factors drive biodiversity loss.

Expansion of agriculture, logging, fishing and other natural resource-based activities, as well as increases in pollution, directly drive biodiversity loss. A complex array of pressures that arise at local, regional, national and international levels shapes the use of resources at the local sites examined by the case studies. In each of the cases a number of domestic factors, including population growth, migration, poverty, inequality and increased demand for consumer goods, are putting pressure on socioeconomic institutions, leading to an expanded use of natural resources. At the same time, international or global factors, such as changing trade opportunities and growing economic interdependence, also appear in many of the case studies, creating pressure for resource exploitation. While none of these pressures is new, the combination of increasing external and internal pressures is accelerating the rate of habitat and species loss in every case. The behaviour of governments and the private sector in the face of these growing pressures – including changes in policies and changes in resource use patterns – must be understood if the problem of biodiversity loss is to be adequately addressed.

This chapter first reviews the domestic and external pressures, including economic, social and political pressures, which the case studies found important to biodiversity loss. The ways in which government and society cope with these pressures are then explored in an effort to understand how and why unsustainable resource use, inappropriate public policies, market failures and lack of effective efforts at environmental management are the common response to both domestic and international pressures. The pervasiveness of biodiversity loss and the frequency with which the case studies uncover this similar set of underlying root causes strongly suggest that the value of biodiversity and the many other environmental resources upon which biodiversity depends – forests, oceans, rivers, mangroves, grasslands – are consistently ignored in the face of socioeconomic pressures that government, communities and individuals must address in the short-term.

THE CASE STUDIES

The broad range of the case studies gives us reason to believe that these general conclusions have widespread validity. The ten sites selected for the case studies represent not only a broad range of ecosystems but also a variety of socioeconomic contexts. The degree and the rate of damage from biodiversity loss also vary greatly at each site. Forest, coastal, riverine and dryland ecosystems are all covered by the studies. Socioeconomic contexts range from highly industrialized and urbanized countries to agricultural, fishing and hunting communities. Some sites were selected because they are representative of a particular ecosystem or of a particular social, political or economic situation. Others were selected because they are biodiversity 'hotspots' critical to conservation. The studies that take a comparative look at several sites focus on similarities and differences across those sites both in environmental and socioeconomic conditions.

BOX 4.1 SUMMARY OF CASE STUDIES

The Brazil study looks at the rapid expansion of large-scale agriculture in the central plateau, known as the Cerrado. Driven by government policies, agricultural development of this region has had a dramatic effect on the ecosystems where it has taken hold. However, government policies introducing this agricultural model succeeded better in some places than others, depending not only on physical conditions but also on socioeconomic conditions. In the two counties studied in China, agricultural expansion and commercial logging are destroying habitat of the giant panda and the Yunnan snub-nosed monkey. Limited economic opportunities and government policies that have led to unproductive agricultural expansion and created a heavy dependence on commercial logging have resulted in widespread deforestation. In and around a Biosphere Reserve in south-eastern Mexico, rapid population growth and persistent poverty are driving forest clearing. Failure to address the problems of poverty and social conflict underlie this threat to conservation. Government policies intended to improve the use of resources, including recent changes in tenure laws, do not have their intended impact in such a marginalized region that has only limited links to markets. Likewise in the mangrove forests of Tanzania's river deltas, poverty and isolation drive degradation of the local natural resources. Contradictory government policies, failure to enforce environmental laws, and centralized decision-making about resource management, aggravate poverty's impacts. Freshwater diversion for agriculture, industrial and urban water pollution, and over-fishing have seriously degraded coastal mangrove ecosystems in Pakistan over the last 50 years. National policies that have favoured agriculture and industry over the coastal regions and given high priority to exports have largely driven these proximate causes. In India's Chilika Lake, the rapid expansion of commercial aquaculture, particularly prawn culture, contributes directly and indirectly to the decline of the lake's fisheries and world-renowned bird population. Changes both in India's economic policies and in global markets have caused a rapid rise in the price of prawns and the abandonment of traditional fishing patterns in favour of aquaculture. In Cameroon, the bushmeat and wildlife trade presents a growing threat to biodiversity. The resulting network of commercial hunters and markets is closely linked to the country's dependence on primary export products, including agricultural products and timber, which has led to land clearing and road construction without relieving local poverty. The study of three protected areas in Vietnam illustrates how international conflicts, national policies, and ideologies shape the impact of population pressures and poverty on forests and biodiversity. Three islands in the Philippines also show the strong link between population density and biodiversity loss. Exploration of the root causes of population trends on the islands uncovers the different historical patterns of political and economic power and access to land that continue to shape resource use and biodiversity loss today. Environmental degradation of the Danube River Basin likewise reflects its long history. While historic causes of habitat alteration and biodiversity loss, such as the 40-year period of socialist government in Bulgaria and Slovakia, play a role, other causes also drive biodiversity loss in the current period of political transition and offer a place for intervention to halt the unsustainable use of resources.

The results of the case studies reflect this wide diversity of environmental and socioeconomic conditions. The institutional, social, political, economic and geophysical contexts of each site, which all play critical roles in shaping environmental outcomes, are unique in each case. For example, while historical trends in resource use are important in most of the cases, in Brazil we find that the historical context of current agricultural patterns refers only to the last 20 or 30 years. In Cameroon's forests, the shift toward over-exploitation of resources is even more recent. In contrast, the historical context that has shaped today's resource-use patterns is measured in hundreds of years in the Danube Basin and the Philippines. Each case tells its own individual story of the pressures of development and the acceleration of biodiversity loss.

The similarities among the ten cases are also striking. In reviewing the results with the research teams as they completed their studies, a list of fewer than ten socioeconomic issues emerged as the most important drivers of biodiversity loss. The issues revealed by the studies correspond closely with the lists of factors underlying biodiversity loss found in other publications[1] and fit easily into the five categories of factors described in Chapter 2. Given that these categories were intended to be comprehensive, this is perhaps not surprising. However, we should bear in mind that these studies represent a very broad range of places in Africa, Asia, Latin America and Europe, with a great variety of conditions in terms of economics, politics, state of development and degree of isolation. The types of environmental damage leading to biodiversity loss at these sites also runs the gamut from land-use change to destruction of wetlands, hunting and industrial expansion.

The innovative contribution of these studies lies in the way they integrate the analysis of multiple socioeconomic and environmental factors to tell a complete story about biodiversity loss and their ability to analyse both the linkages among various diverse factors – demographic change, inequality, government policies, market forces, macroeconomic conditions, cultural change – and how they interact across local, national and international levels. These studies provide a complete picture of what is happening to biodiversity at each site because, unlike single-discipline studies, they focus on the chains of causality that cross the boundaries of different academic categories and cross the boundaries of different temporal, geographic, economic and political scales. From this complexity we learn that addressing biodiversity loss in any site, region or country will require a detailed understanding of the specific factors at work.

The process of carrying out the case studies, working with multidisciplinary teams and using the framework described in Chapter 2, made the complexity of each case very clear. Conservation problems that were initially hypothesized to be driven by one socioeconomic factor often turned out to be driven by several factors. In the Philippines, for example, population stands out as the primary driver of biodiversity loss. On closer study, complications arising from the fact that population density on the three studied islands is a consequence of government policies, colonial rule and a social structure

Table 4.1 Common Causes of Biodiversity Loss

● Cause of Biodiversity Loss
■ Very Important Cause of Biodiversity Loss

	Vietnam	Tanzania	Philippines	Pakistan	Mexico	India	Danube Basin	China	Cameroon	Brazil
Domestic Pressure										
Population growth	■	■		■	■	■	●		●	●
Poverty	■	■	■	■	●	■	■	●	■	■
Immigration	■	■		■	■	■	●	●	●	●
Inequality				■	■	●				■
Isolation/marginalization			■		●	■		●	●	
Cultural changes	●	●	●	●	■	●	●			■
International Pressure										
Macroeconomic policies	●	●		■	●		■	■		■
International trade factors	●	●			●		■			■
Policy Responses										
Policy failures	■	■	●	■	●	●	●	■	■	■
Domestic market factors	■	■	■				●	●	■	●
Poor environmental law/weak enforcement	■	■	●	●	■	●	●	●	●	●
Unsustainable development projects			●		■	■	■			●
Lack of local control over resources	●	●	●		●	●	■		●	●

marked by strong inequalities become apparent. In India, biodiversity loss in Chilika Lake, which appeared initially to be driven by deforestation and agricultural land use outside the immediate area, was found to be driven primarily by aquaculture practices in the lake itself, which in turn are driven in part by government domestic and macroeconomic policies. While the ten studies sought to be comprehensive and to avoid bias for or against any particular factors, undoubtedly some aspects of each story have been neglected and others have been over-emphasized. In all of the cases, however, a complex array of socioeconomic factors was found to be at work. Reading the individual case studies is the best way to gain a knowledge of the complicated linkages among social, economic and political factors shaping resource use and biodiversity loss.

Focusing not on the complexity they reveal but on the underlying pattern on which this complexity is built, reveals major similarities. Increased resource use due to changing domestic and global pressures, and policies and institutions guided by an inappropriate model for biodiversity protection, makes up the pattern common to each of the studies. The following sections review some of the main findings from the case studies, with a focus on the similar patterns of pressures on biodiversity at work in this very diverse set of cases. While our division of the important factors into domestic pressures, international pressures and responses necessarily conceals some of the complexity uncovered by the case studies, it also provides an interpretation and condensation of the findings that will help us begin to address the problem of biodiversity loss.

DOMESTIC PRESSURES

Domestic factors, whether local, regional or national, exert pressure on habitats and species that lead to biodiversity loss. The most common are population growth, migration, poverty, inequality and resource scarcity. In most of the studies these factors figured to a greater or lesser degree as critical drivers of biodiversity loss through their direct impacts on resource use. While these factors can be broken down into local and national components, as they are in most of the case studies, they are addressed together here since they tend to overlap considerably.

Demographic Pressures

Both natural population growth and migration appeared as important domestic pressures on biodiversity in many of the case studies. Population growth, whatever its source, generally leads to increased use of resources, particularly the expansion of agricultural land but also over-use of marine and forest resources, which directly affects habitat and species abundance. Poverty, limited education and poor access to reproductive health services cause increased natural population growth in a number of the sites studied. Migration, which often has more severe environmental consequences than natural population growth, occurs because of wars, civil unrest, lack of economic opportunity, population pressures on resources and deliberate government efforts to resettle people. For example, war played a particularly important role in driving migration in Vietnam, creating large-scale population pressures in the vicinity of several national parks. More commonly, land scarcity or poor economic opportunities drive migration, as is the case in Mexico. Landlessness has driven people to settle and practise shifting agriculture on the edges of a protected area, despite the very poor quality of the soil and low agricultural productivity, because they perceive few other options.

Population growth is directly linked to agricultural land expansion and other forms of resource use in most of the studies. Frequently, the more damaging patterns of resource use accompanying population growth are also linked with poverty and resource scarcity – more and more people are trying to eke a subsistence living from fewer and fewer resources. Over-use of agricultural land, with its consequent land degradation and incursion into forests, is clearly illustrated in the Chinese and Vietnamese cases, where most of the growing population is highly dependent on agriculture. In other cases, changes in resource-use patterns can be linked to new opportunities or techniques introduced by migrant populations, as has occurred in Cameroon, where loggers have played a catalytic role in the shift of indigenous populations from subsistence to commercial-scale hunting. Likewise in Pakistan, migrants to the coastal mangrove areas have introduced new, illegal fishing techniques that are driving rapid depletion of fishing resources.

Poverty and Inequality

The effects of poverty and inequality are manifested by a lack of alternatives to resource degradation and a lack of local control over resources. The populations in almost all of the study sites are poor and many support themselves with subsistence agriculture or subsistence extraction of natural resources. Given the scarcity of opportunities, people use the only resources that are freely available. In China, for example, the lack of affordable alternatives for food and fuel lead to clearing for agriculture and over-harvesting of fuelwood. In Mexico, too, shifting cultivation of staple crops provides the only option for survival, leading to forest clearing as the soil wears out. Population pressures, common to many of the sites, only exacerbate the resource shortage. In most of the cases, traditional community institutions, where they exist, are breaking down. Often central governments have deliberately removed decision-making about resource use from local hands, as in Cameroon, where all natural resources belong to the government. This lack of local control further reduces the opportunities for communities to either extract greater benefits from local resources or to manage those resources sustainably.

Persistent poverty often contrasts with the appropriation of valuable resources by the wealthy. Inequality of access to resources stands out most clearly in the Philippines, where a long history of land tenure inequalities, supported by the entrenched social and political systems, has consistently driven the poor onto marginal lands which support little production and are rapidly degraded. Meanwhile a small group of plantation owners have appropriated better lands for large-scale commercial agriculture. Similar inequality exists in Mexico where, despite a strong tradition of land reform, the lands allocated to the poor often do not even provide enough subsistence to support a family and are exhausted within a few years.

Isolation

Poverty is not only a matter of access to land or other natural resources. In a number of the cases poverty leads to resource degradation because of the site's isolation. Isolation or marginalization means that there is limited access to markets, education or other social or economic resources. For example, poverty largely drives degradation of the mangrove forests of Tanzania's river deltas. But a lack of infrastructure and social support services aggravates that poverty and its effects. The main economic activities – agriculture, fishing and harvesting of mangrove poles, bark and logs – all affect the mangrove ecosystem and consequently biodiversity. Of the products from these activities, only mangrove products can be reliably transported to markets, resulting, not surprisingly, in their over-harvesting.

Despite the isolation of many of these sites, the local people still depend on a cash economy. Even in the remote forests of Cameroon people need cash for basics such as salt, soap, medicines and school fees, so they must produce not only for their own subsistence but also for the market. Exploitation of the available natural resources for sale, such as mangrove wood in Tanzania, wildlife in Cameroon and Vietnam and timber in Mexico, becomes an important survival strategy as the need or desire for consumer goods grows. On the other hand, wage earners in Cameroon earn so little that they have to turn to subsistence agriculture and hunting to survive. Likewise in the Danube Basin, harvesting of floodplain resources provides an important supplement to agricultural incomes.

Well-intended efforts to bring development to people and lift them out of poverty often rely on heavy use of local natural resources. While these projects are often successful in creating jobs and raising local standards of living, they are rarely designed for sustainability and their long-term impacts on environmental resources are ignored. Development of commercial agriculture in Brazil, proposed shrimp-farming projects in India and Tanzania, the development of agricultural cooperatives in Vietnam and industrialization of the delta area in Pakistan are all examples of the way that efforts to reduce poverty destroy natural resources. Provision of infrastructure, such as the building of roads in south-eastern Cameroon, may only facilitate resource exploitation without bringing long-term benefits.

INTERNATIONAL PRESSURES

International pressures that directly and indirectly shape the use of resources and biodiversity have become stronger in recent years in many countries. Globalization is rapidly increasing the flow of goods, capital and ideas among countries. The economic crises of the 1980s and 1990s have acted as an important force behind the opening of many economies to the pressures entailed by globalization and have increased the role of international organizations in shaping national macroeconomic and sectoral policies. The effects of trade and macroeconomic pressures on domestic resource use are being magnified as a result. Countries of all political and economic shades – China and Vietnam, the new market economies of Eastern Europe, countries with a long history of protectionism and import-substitution such as India and those with a long history of export dependence such as the Philippines – are being affected by this trend.

Macroeconomic Change and Trading Relationships

International economic and political forces affect the way resources are used at the local level. Among these, trading relationships and macroeconomic factors were cited most frequently in the studies as drivers of biodiversity loss. Trade affects resource-use patterns at the sites in Brazil, Pakistan, India and the Philippines most directly, where expansion of production for sale on the international market causes habitat or species loss. Expansion of shrimp production for export from Chilika Lake in India has disrupted the food web of the lake, leading to decline of fish and bird species. At other sites trade factors have a less direct but still important impact. In Mexico, for example, changes in agricultural and land tenure policies intended to complement trade liberalization even affect regions such as the study site, where most production is for subsistence use. In Cameroon, the expansion of timber exports has also indirectly boosted domestic markets for bushmeat, leading to an increase in hunting.

Efforts to increase exports have been central to economic adjustment as countries have faced rising fuel prices, falling commodity prices and increased competition in international markets over the past two decades. The debt crisis and structural adjustment programmes carried out in a number of the countries increased the need for exports to provide badly needed foreign exchange. The shift toward market liberalization, occurring to varying degrees in both socialist and non-socialist countries, likewise promotes exports. The consequent growth in trade has facilitated both legal and illegal exports in many countries. The impacts of production for export are clearly visible in several cases. Export markets are largely responsible for industrial growth in Pakistan, which has seriously affected the mangroves of the Karachi delta. The new predominance of soybean products among Brazil's exports has entailed widespread conversion of habitat in the central plateau. The NAFTA agreement is reshaping markets for traditional agricultural products and export products in Mexico, changing the method and location of production. Illegal exports have also found new outlets. The opening of Vietnam, for example, has led to increased exports of wildlife and wildlife products, including endangered species, to China.

Trade growth makes even isolated areas more subject to the vagaries of international macroeconomic effects and markets. Changes in exchange rates, which may result from national policies or changes in international markets, directly affect production. Devaluation of the Central African franc (CFA) in Cameroon provided a sudden boost to timber exports by lowering the domestic cost of labour, entailing more widespread incursions into the forests in the south-east. The current Asian crisis has led to a sharp drop in the price of Matsutake mushrooms, which were one of the most important commercial products of remote Deqin County in China. Local people now need to exploit other natural resources to maintain their incomes. In Eastern Europe the shift toward capitalism has been accompanied by a period of economic chaos, which has reduced long-term investments and promoted unsustainable resource use. Changes in international demand also rapidly reshape resource use. Expanding global shrimp markets, for example, are opening up new opportunities for production in Tanzania and India, with consequences for mangrove and lake habitats.

At the same time that policy changes are boosting production for export, the shift toward liberalization and the budget cuts entailed by structural adjustment programmes have decreased governments' capacity to enforce environmental laws. Many countries have sharply reduced their budgets for enforcement. Liberalization has also meant reduced domestic control over resources. The Danube case points to a joint Slovak-Austrian gravel mining company that is destroying protected wetlands without any government intervention. The Tanzania case points to a proposed international investment in a large shrimp-farming operation that would substantially affect mangrove habitat.

International Political Relationships

Political relationships among countries also shape resource use. A clear case is found in US support for Philippine sugar production over many years, an effect not only of US colonial history in the Philippines but also of the large stakes US companies hold in sugar production in the archipelago. In turn, sugar plantations have driven deforestation both directly and indirectly. In Cameroon too, colonial history has had lasting impacts on the country's international relations, including its participation in the CFA union and relatively open borders with the other members of the union. This openness facilitates both legal and illegal trade.

International treaties designed to protect biodiversity, notably CITES and CBD, have not greatly benefited conservation. The Cameroon study finds that CITES provisions, such as quotas for exports of certain species, may have actually aggravated wildlife exploitation by raising prices and encouraging illegal trading in export quotas. The CBD remains a normative document with little on-the-ground application. The case studies give greater credit to aid agencies and international NGOs in promoting conservation. These organizations generally work at the local or regional level, however, and do not address the larger-scale issues raised by these studies.

POLICY RESPONSES

All of the factors discussed above – poverty, inequality, population growth, foreign exchange needs and international markets – create social, economic and political problems as well as environmental problems. Three basic mechanisms exist for resolving these problems: government policy, markets and community institutions. Government and market responses to these pressures often entail increased resource use, leading to habitat loss or alteration and species loss. At the same time these pressures are leading to the breakdown of communities and community institutions that provided viable mechanisms for managing resources sustainably, making the role of governments and markets increasingly central to conservation.

Government actions predominantly address the socioeconomic and political pressures discussed above, generally with little or no attention paid to the environmental pressures created by either the problem or the response. Policy failures, or so-called perverse policies, have received substantial blame in recent years for environmental degradation, and are noted in all of the case studies.[2] What must be recognized, however, is that these environmentally detrimental policies are addressing important social, economic and political goals. In many cases they are addressing such pressures as poverty, poor access to markets and foreign exchange needs. In others they address largely political or ideological goals deemed important by governments. Often these goals are met through private or government appropriation and exploitation of resources.

While such government policies are widely blamed for environmental degradation, including biodiversity loss, markets do not have a better record. Markets do not incorporate the value of either biodiversity or habitats, nor should they be expected to. Since much of the value of biodiversity is really unknowable, it has little meaning for people trying to earn a living today, for governments in need of financial resources or for companies trying to show an annual profit. Therefore decisions about natural-resource use are made within a context that does not place an economic value on environmental resources. Governments are the main institutions with the capacity to correct for market failures. This capacity is severely limited, however, by their need to meet other more pressing goals.

Policies Promoting Resource Use

All of the case studies implicate public policies in the loss of biodiversity. To varying degrees each case study reports expanding use of resources, entailing loss of habitat or species. Public policies and markets directly and indirectly promote expansion of resource use to meet a variety of goals or, in other words, to respond to a variety of domestic and external pressures. These goals may be those set by governments or those pressed on governments by economic- or political-interest groups.

Responses to domestic pressures, notably population and poverty, have perhaps had the greatest impact on habitats and species. The allocation of land or other resources for subsistence or commercial exploitation has been the most common response to these problems. Governments may legally allocate resources or may simply turn a blind eye to appropriation of resources by individuals or commercial interests. Given persistent inequalities of political and economic power, the resources allocated to relieve poverty are generally marginal, with little value to powerful interest groups. Such resources are often found in fragile environments and areas where biodiversity has been relatively undisturbed.

In Mexico, land reform has been the government's response to domestic pressures including social conflict, landlessness, population expansion and persistent poverty for most of the 20th century. The lands allocated to the poor, however, are often agriculturally poor lands with little access to water. Small agricultural subsidies, insufficient to improve living conditions, combined with the lack of other economic opportunities, keep people on this land. The need to continually shift plots and clear new forest means that impacts on habitat are substantial. Similar patterns of land allocation with insufficient credit or technical support to provide a real solution to the problems of low agricultural productivity or poverty are common. In the Philippines, expanding agriculture under government-sanctioned migration intended to relieve agrarian pressure on other islands threatens one of the last undeveloped islands. The case studies in China, Vietnam and Brazil describe the same pattern of settlement, clearing and land degradation.

Other natural resources are also allocated to individuals and companies in response to these domestic pressures, with similar results. In Cameroon the extension of roads into the south-east forests by logging companies entails not only increased logging but also increased hunting, which supports a large population of residents and migrants but is having serious impacts on some species. In Pakistan, the Danube and India, uncontrolled expansion of fishing for similar reasons is depleting marine, riverine and lake resources.

The macroeconomic problems of recent years, the trend toward economic liberalization and opening to foreign trade and investment, and the need for foreign exchange to finance development have increased the external pressures to which governments and producers have had to respond. Government response has largely been to support exports and, to a lesser extent in recent years, import substitutes through various combinations of subsidies, provision of infrastructure and access to resources for commercial interests. As subsidies have been reduced under recent liberalization programmes, private sector access to natural resources has often been opened up. Producers respond rapidly to new market signals and access to resources. This allocation of resources – land, water, forests – has direct impacts on habitats as use is intensified. There are also many indirect repercussions on biodiversity as commercial operations attract new populations in search of economic opportunities or displace populations to new areas.

Examples are numerous. Government policies in Brazil have addressed external pressures through expansion of agriculture. These policies have sought to meet foreign exchange needs through promotion of resource use by private farmers and agricultural companies. Expansion of commercial agriculture, supported by government research, subsidies for credit and inputs, and infrastructure, has affected large parts of the formerly isolated central plateau. This set of policies also responded to some domestic pressures, notably a land shortage in the south of the country, and to a perceived need to develop the less populated regions of the country. Since the expansion of mechanized commercial agriculture has created a large landless population in the region and driven many new settlers to the Amazon, the impacts on biodiversity are felt not only in the region but also in other areas critical for conservation. Other countries have responded similarly to external pressures. In Cameroon, the very limited range of available export products has led the government to promote logging by private companies to meet foreign exchange needs. The devaluation of the CFA and government willingness to grant logging concessions have attracted large commercial logging companies to the forests in the south-east. This expansion of production, as in Brazil, has also served to open up new areas of the country to government control and development. In Pakistan, natural resources have been exploited for export production, resulting in heavy contamination of the river deltas by export-oriented industries. At the same time, diversion of water for domestic agriculture has been increased to reduce import needs. Both are seriously affecting mangrove and other coastal resources. In none of these cases have the environmental costs entailed by the conversion of habitat and biodiversity loss been factors in decision-making about responses to external pressures. Immediate needs have taken precedence over long-term sustainability.

Domestic Political Economy

Policy-making and the effects of policies are closely linked with political economy factors. In other words, political and economic power as well as political ideologies have driven many inappropriate decisions concerning resource use and allocation. Underlying these strong links is the central role taken by the governments of all the countries studied in promoting development, which is understood as increasing consumption and transformation of natural resources. The ill effects of centralized decision-making about resource use are most obvious in the countries which have had socialist governments – notably China, Vietnam, Slovakia and Bulgaria – but the lack of local control over environmental resources is common to most of the cases. The political and economic goals of the government and of the social groups who have the greatest input into government decision-making are given precedence. In Vietnam, for example, collectivization of agricultural land in the 1950s for political reasons led to an agricultural crisis that drove many farmers to clear private plots, hunt and collect forest products. Under later food self-sufficiency policies, intended to meet economic goals, all were conscripted to clear forests for expansion of food crops.

Similar links are evident in every case. Landowners in the Philippines, particularly the sugar producers, have had a central voice in determining economic policies and in forestalling land reforms that might reduce migration to marginal areas. Large agricultural producers in Brazil also have been able to ensure that policies supporting capital-intensive production – including subsidies, construction of infrastructure, and price supports for export crops – remained in place. In Pakistan, agricultural land barons have forestalled any effort to raise the price or limit the quantity of water available for irrigation at the expense of the ecosystems and residents of the Indus delta, where the supply of fresh water has dropped dramatically. Government institutions and state-owned companies have direct interests in resource use as well. The case of logging in China provides a clear example of the way in which government entities may become dependent on resource exploitation.

These policies with their undesirable environmental impacts meet the needs of both private and government interests. The existence of an entrenched elite in a number of the countries studied explains the allocation of resources and a pattern of government policies that reinforces that allocation, most clearly evident in the case of the landholding elites in the Philippines, Brazil and Pakistan. Commercial interests, particularly those that have established a close political or economic relationship with the government and those that can promise substantial resources to help meet government objectives, also shape policies. Governments therefore have indirect interests in promoting resource use. Proposed private development of shrimp ponds in Tanzania and a rapidly growing shrimp industry in India are encouraged despite their environmental and social effects because of their export-earning potential. In Cameroon expansion of logging operations, carried out by private companies, has been a central component of government efforts to address economic pressures. Few if any restrictions have been imposed to control either the direct or the indirect impacts of timber extraction. Industries in the Philippines and Pakistan have been allowed to pollute vast areas. Government interventions in all of the countries, for the most part, promote or facilitate resource use rather than sustainable use.

International Political Economy

International institutions have been equally guilty of promoting resource use as a response to external pressures, without any environmental concerns. The International Monetary Fund (IMF) has supported liberalization and promotion of export production in many of the cases. In Pakistan, liberalization of the fiscal, tax, and trade structure occurred under IMF pressure. At the same time, however, the government continued its strategy of increasing production levels through expansion of industrial centres, regardless of associated environmental impacts. Furthermore, despite its emphasis on reduced government interventions in markets, the IMF has not been able to push Pakistan to reduce water subsidies or establish water markets, two changes which would improve freshwater flows to the mangroves of the Indus delta. Likewise, international trade agreements, notably the WTO, promote liberalization of trade and increased production without explicit recognition of the environmental consequences of these changes.

A clear ideological component to many policies also exists, including countries' drive for sovereignty and for freedom from external pressures. Food self-sufficiency policies, most damaging in Vietnam; the Cold War, which shaped resource use in the Danube Basin; the drive for national sovereignty that led to occupation of parts of Brazil, were all ideologically based policies that shaped relations with the international sphere. Today's push for market liberalization is likewise driven by current ideology as well as by pressing economic problems in the developing world. On the domestic side, government development projects take an important share of the blame for migration of people and increased exploitation of resources. These projects may enjoy political backing from particular groups but they also enjoy more widespread popularity as initiatives for economic advancement.

Poor Environmental Management

Coupled with a wide variety of policies and market structures that promote biodiversity loss is the overwhelming failure of government efforts designed to protect the environment. The lack of political will, managerial capacity and financial resources to ensure protection of biodiversity is repeatedly cited by the studies. This is manifested, for example, in the failure to protect parks from agricultural incursions or hunting, the failure to enforce restrictions on fishing or logging and the failure to enforce international treaties on trade in endangered species: it reflects the overwhelming lack of interest in protection of biodiversity on the part of governments, of many influential members of society and of international institutions.

In many cases, no serious, legally mandated management regimes to protect habitats or species have been established. In the case of Mexico, limits on resource use in the biosphere reserve, described by the case study, cannot be established until a management plan – which it still lacks even after ten years of existence – is approved. In the meantime, the resource-use rights of the local population remain unclear. The Danube River Basin, shared by a number of countries, cannot be managed adequately without an international agreement. However, only in 1998 did an international convention for river-basin management come into force among the interested countries. In the meantime, pollution and water diversion affecting downstream countries are common.

Even where environmental management regimes are legally mandated, weak enforcement of laws designed to protect the environment, either for lack of funds or lack of political will, is cited in virtually every study. The studies noted easy sentences for offenders as well as complete neglect of enforcement, reflecting the low priority given by governments to biodiversity protection. Economic development or similar goals generally take precedence over environmental concerns. When resources are cut, as under structural adjustment programmes, environmental protection is often the first thing to go. In Cameroon, for example, budget cuts under structural adjustment included the sale of all government vehicles, which clearly limited the government's capacity for enforcement in the field. Tanzania's national mangrove management programme has only one boat available for monitoring and enforcement and it is often without fuel.

Conflicts among the goals of various government agencies and policies, cited in most of the studies, clearly reflect this lack of commitment to environmental protection and the precedence of other goals. Positive incentives for land clearing and other resource use were common to many of the countries, despite laws on conservation, resource management and environmental impact assessments. Promotion of resettlement and agriculture, notably in Brazil and Mexico, hunting in the Danube Basin, logging in Cameroon and use of mangroves and wetlands for shrimp farms in India and Tanzania were among them. Conflicts among policies are illustrated in Mexico, where laws on land tenure and agricultural subsidies promote land clearing: since protected areas often include established agricultural communities with legal land rights, clearing is promoted even in protected areas. While many of the studies blame these problems on a lack of institutional coordination and communication, the problem runs deeper. The lack of attention or prestige accorded to environmental ministries and programmes reflects the very low priority given to environmental goals in the face of other critical domestic needs and external pressures.

Where serious efforts were made to protect the environment, conflicts with community objectives that have made environmental objectives difficult to achieve arose in several cases. Efforts to establish sedentary agriculture among ethnic groups in Vietnam, which would have reduced the amount of forest lost to shifting cultivation, have had limited success since they failed to account for local traditions or preferences, much less the local agricultural conditions. In Tanzania a new government-supported project to protect the mangroves requires rice farmers to plant their fields with mangroves, which would deprive them of their livelihood. The creation of a Biosphere Reserve in Mexico that overlaps with existing community and private lands has left local people concerned that their rights to what they see as their resources are being denied and has made them resentful of government intrusion. In other words environmental policies conflict not only with other government objectives but also with communities' own perceptions of their needs and rights.

Patterns of Development

The study sites present a mix of areas where modernization and development are well established, as in the Danube Basin, the island of Cebu in the

Philippines and the surroundings of Karachi in Pakistan, and areas that are only now abandoning traditional ways of life and resource management, such as the forests of Cameroon and Mexico. The governments in all of the countries studied clearly favour development, which is understood as control of resources and economic growth. In the Danube Basin, the drive for control of resources took the form of management of water resources. In Brazil, policies have controlled territory through occupation. The government-supported drive for increased production for economic growth has been seen in all of the countries – soybean production in Brazil, logs in Cameroon, shrimps in Tanzania and India, sugar in the Philippines, agricultural staples in China, Vietnam and the Danube Basin and industrial products in Pakistan and Cebu. Increased production in every case has affected habitats and biodiversity. The current ideological shift toward liberalization has brought a new belief in the power of markets and the importance of export production as part of the development package that is affecting all of the countries studied.

This resource-based approach to development has brought economic and social benefits to many countries. However, the environmental costs of addressing domestic and external pressures through increased exploitation of resources without adequate investment in environmental management must be acknowledged. Biodiversity loss, which is the end result of most forms of environmental degradation, is among the least recognized of these environmental costs. Even when high environmental costs become apparent, economic development programmes may not be abandoned. The expansion of soybean production in Brazil, for example, remained a policy priority even when international soybean prices fell. Government subsidies had to be increased to keep the sector solvent. Diversion of water for agriculture in Pakistan has severely affected the mangrove ecosystem, and therefore has reduced the productivity of fisheries and may make the area increasingly vulnerable to storms. Still, no effort has been made to reduce water use. In addition to these high costs, many such development programmes cause environmental damage while bringing few benefits, because they do not fit well with local conditions. Privatization of resources and an increased role for markets is being pushed, for example, in Mexico. However, in remote areas such as the forests of the Yucatan Peninsula, access to markets is very limited and new policies designed to increase the participation of farmers in markets may have more negative than positive effects.

Other common elements of this development package are a bias toward centralization, expansion, use of technology and urbanization. Socialist models of economic growth, with their heavy emphasis on centralized decision-making, have perhaps had the greatest impact on biodiversity because of the sheer scale of projects and policies undertaken. Prime examples are the food-security drives in China and Vietnam. These programmes vastly expanded the area affected by agriculture without substantially improving production or people's well-being. Many other developing countries have also favoured large-scale and centrally planned development, evident in Brazil's agricultural expansion and the industrialization of Pakistan, with similar environmental consequences. A frontier mentality – the belief in the need to extend development – is quite common, arising in the Mexico, Brazil, Vietnam and Cameroon studies. In some cases, as in Vietnam, frontier expansion is driven by the need to settle a displaced population; in others, as in Brazil, it is part of a policy to develop the country. Settlement is deliberately promoted in order to bring civilization or national control to remote areas and resources.

While the beneficial impacts of this pattern of development have been substantial in many cases, the direct impacts on habitat and species – land conversion, loss of mangrove habitat, over-fishing and hunting – have been negative. Often traditional community-based mechanisms for resource management are broken down under this pattern of development. The implementation of development policies has direct impacts on traditional ways of life, as well as indirect impacts, as migrants move into new areas, bringing with them social change. In India, Brazil, Mexico, and most clearly in Cameroon, the influx of migrants to previously isolated areas has brought changes in the use of resources with important consequences for habitats and biodiversity. New technologies, improved access to markets and ignorance of traditional systems of resource management lead to resource degradation and species loss. Development and migration also create social conflicts over resources, as in the case of the shrimp farm proposed in Tanzania, which has sharply divided the community between those who favour the farm and those who oppose it.

While many government development programmes and private investments that promote or facilitate resource degradation have enjoyed wide popularity, some local and national efforts to protect biodiversity are also enjoying some success. The island of Palawan in the Philippines, which is comparatively undisturbed, is benefiting from conservation and ecotourism investments and has created its own legally mandated environmental plan. In Brazil, the county of Alto Paraíso, which has been relatively unaffected by development programmes, is attracting a population with interest in the environment and is also beginning to see its future in ecotourism. Such cases, however, are limited.

OVER-DETERMINATION OF BIODIVERSITY LOSS

Most of the factors driving biodiversity loss – the 'root causes' revealed by these studies – can be brought together under a common umbrella of the prevalent approach to development. The economic, political, social and cultural structures that shape our world almost all promote resource consumption and transformation and recognize little value in biodiversity. The contribution of resource exploitation – logging, aquaculture, agricultural expansion, industrial growth – to development is widely accepted. The potential contribution of natural habitats and biodiversity is rarely recognized. Sustainability has not been part of development plans, the environment being treated as a virtually limitless source of resources and services. Socioeconomic institutions, including markets, laws, political bodies and social norms, favour and provide incentives for expansion of the consumption-driven patterns of development.

Root causes of biodiversity loss can be found in any or all of these socioeconomic institutions, affecting resource use at a particular site. They promote unsustainable resource consumption and degradation of ecosystems, frequently without resolving the fundamental problems of poverty or inequality that development efforts should address. In many cases all of these institutions or socioeconomic factors at once – either separately or in conjunction with one another – are driving biodiversity loss. Since any one of these factors alone would be enough to cause biodiversity loss, the loss is over-determined when many such factors are present. In other words, eliminating or reducing the pressure from one factor will not stop biodiversity loss since the remaining pressures will continue to drive this loss.

While biodiversity loss is occurring at all of the sites, heavily populated sites and easily accessible areas face a much greater number and variety of pressures than isolated areas. This suggests that intervention to prevent biodiversity loss will be easier in isolated areas.[3] For example, in Pakistan the proximate causes of pressure on the mangroves include industrial waste, overfishing, clearing of mangroves and water diversion for agriculture. Root causes of these pressures include water, industrial, environmental and international trade policies, agricultural interests, port development and inefficient institutions for allocation of water use. At the Danube study sites, which have a long history of occupation, proximate causes of environmental degradation include agriculture, fishing, industry and mining. Root causes of this degradation include economic turmoil, poor land tenure definition, a long tradition of biodiversity exploitation and lack of enforcement of environmental regulations. At both these sites a great number of factors are driving biodiversity loss. In Pakistan and in the Danube countries, the difficulty of slowing, much less reversing, biodiversity loss appears overwhelming since so many factors are contributing to biodiversity loss.

On the other hand, more isolated areas face fewer pressures. The mangrove ecosystems of Tanzania are under pressure primarily from over-harvesting, driven primarily by poverty and lack of economic options. In the Calakmul Biosphere Reserve of Mexico, direct pressure comes from still-limited conversion of forest to agriculture, largely driven by immigration, which is supported by government agricultural and land-tenure policies. In Tanzania and Mexico, points of intervention to address biodiversity loss emerge fairly clearly from the root causes analysis. Alternative economic opportunities in Tanzania could greatly reduce the pressure on mangroves, and in Mexico, a change in the agricultural and tenure policies that promote new settlement in unsuitable lands needs to be instituted.

As suggested in Chapter 2, a great variety of factors promote biodiversity loss while few act to mitigate this loss. At any given site one may find population trends, poverty, a variety of political and market factors and cultural understandings of biodiversity contributing to patterns of behaviour or resource use that cause biodiversity loss. Addressing one factor alone will not reverse biodiversity loss, clearly illustrating that biodiversity loss is over-determined at many of the sites. However, the number of factors that must be addressed at less accessible sites will often be fewer than at easily accessible sites. Only by understanding the complexity of the way in which many socioeconomic factors are working at a particular site can we begin to find new responses to biodiversity loss.

CONCLUSIONS

Several broad conclusions have emerged from this analysis. First, it is clear that understanding biodiversity loss requires looking well beyond what is happening at local sites if we are to understand and to address the underlying root causes of this loss. Second, the underlying socioeconomic causes revealed in all these case studies are two-fold: the heavy reliance on natural resources to address domestic and external pressures, and the common acceptance of a development model in which this use of resources is promoted. Third, environmental management systems are inadequately designed and inadequately supported to address the resulting pressures on habitats and biodiversity. Fourth, in many of the cases studied, biodiversity loss is over-determined, meaning that reducing biodiversity loss requires that we address various root socioeconomic causes. We cannot expect the current approach to environmental management – either the exclusively local approach to conservation that is at the heart of many international conservation programmes or the inadequate and poorly enforced management regimes of national governments – to address the overwhelming threats to biodiversity loss. In the face of the wide variety of factors that are working simultaneously and often in conjunction to drive biodiversity loss all around the world, a more comprehensive approach to conservation needs to be developed.

Each of the case studies tells the story of a variety of causal factors underlying local biodiversity loss that are often found beyond the local level. The local dynamics of resource use and biodiversity loss are often quite complex in themselves, but the story is not complete without looking at the ways in which regional, national and international policies and structures affect those local dynamics. The studies point to a very diverse set of causal factors – national and international corporations, migrants, government economic policies, international trade regimes, and market institutions, to name a few – which by design or by neglect promote the loss of biodiversity. In this context, environmental management efforts have been given little priority. The shortcomings of environmental management systems and difficulties encountered repeatedly by locally oriented conservation projects reflect not only a common failure to understand or address the larger socioeconomic causes of biodiversity loss but also the over-determined nature of biodiversity loss at many sites. The number of domestic and international pressures shaping the local behaviour that leads to biodiversity loss is sometimes overwhelming.

Governments and individuals have to respond to both these domestic and external pressures, not as environmental pressures, but as social, economic and political problems. Solutions to all of these problems, from population growth to balance-of-payments problems, are sought in natural resource use. For individuals and communities, resource use often provides at least short-term alleviation of these pressures. Similarly for governments, the permitting or promoting of resource use provides a temporary solution to economic, social and political pressures. Yet changing conditions that create new demand for resources and break down old regimes governing resource use – including globalization, technological innovation, population growth and increasing resource scarcity – mean that this approach is leading to ever more severe environmental degradation, habitat destruction and biodiversity loss. Even in cases where governments impose restrictions on appropriation of environmental resources, through the creation of protected areas or bans on hunting, for example, the lack of political 'will' and financial support behind these restrictions makes them ineffective. In all the cases studied, design of new environmental management systems is inadequate or they are poorly enforced.

The willingness of governments and the societies they represent to use natural resources unsustainably to meet current needs, despite the loss of biodiversity and long-term benefits, together with the very limited scope of real efforts to promote sustainable use, reflect the pervasive view of development. An understanding of development as economic growth and rising consumption is deeply entrenched in many economic and political systems. In addition, a social or cultural preference for this type of development has become widespread. Individual preferences, economic incentives and government policies favour transformation of natural resources at local, regional and national levels. The fundamental conflict between a development model that relies on increasing resource use to respond to domestic and external pressures on the one hand, and the conservation of habitats and biodiversity on the other hand, is ignored. Farmers clear land, loggers fell forests, fishermen deplete marine resources and governments build infrastructure to facilitate resource use to meet growing needs. In this process traditional ways of life that are less destructive of environmental resources are being lost. As the strength of external socioeconomic pressures on local communities increases, and as communities are increasingly integrated into a broader national and international context, the pressures on habitats and species are rising.

Specific recommendations for addressing specific problems are made in each of the case studies. However, a much more fundamental change in our approach to the environment is essential if we are going to confront the loss of biodiversity at a larger scale. A reorientation toward sustainable development and a real improvement in environmental management regimes are required so that environmental management will become a fundamental part of development. New thinking is needed to find ways to address the social, economic and political pressures facing developing countries without relying on ever-increasing resource exploitation. Governments and national and international organizations all have a role to play. Conservation of biodiversity will depend not only on addressing local, immediate pressures on habitats and species but also on addressing the wide range of regional, national and international pressures that may shape local resource use. We must look at this broader context in all its complexity to begin to address the underlying issues driving biodiversity loss.

Chapter 5

Recommendations on Addressing the Root Causes of Biodiversity Loss

Alexander Wood

In the previous chapter we faced the difficulty of drawing general conclusions about the causes of biodiversity loss when, in fact, biodiversity loss is expressed in unique local terms and processes. What we saw was that, despite the uniqueness of local conditions where biodiversity loss is occurring, there are systemic forces that act from many sides and converge to drive biodiversity loss. We characterized these forces as domestic and international pressures, and also highlighted the failure of current policies that reinforce, albeit unwittingly, the momentum to destroy habitats in which biodiversity can thrive.

The simple truth is that the race to save biodiversity is being lost, and it is being lost because the factors contributing to its degradation are more complex and powerful than those forces working to protect it. At the heart of this dynamic is a global failure to understand and implement sustainable development. Economic development continues to be defined as an increase in the efficiency of national economic performance and the expansion of a nation's productive capacity. Protection of the environment, and the benefits accrued to a country from the judicious and sustainable use of resources, continue to be marginalized in economic decision-making. Moreover, globalization of the world economy has proceeded at a pace that far outstrips the management and oversight capacities of environmental laws and institutions. The result is that any positive correction or mitigation effort put into place seems to have little enduring effect.

In the course of the project, we have come to recognize that the scale and scope of the challenge posed by root causes goes well beyond the single institutional mandate of the GEF. In fact, one of the important findings of the project is that root causes, no matter the particular issue they may reflect, operate at a number of scales. A critical outcome of this is the need for coordinated response that clearly defines the role of a number of actors, based on their particular competency and area of responsibility. This means that international institutions (including, but not limited to, the GEF), national governments, civil society (either large international NGOs such as WWF or community-based organizations) and the private sector all have a role to play, and all need to be part of the solutions to global biodiversity loss. This fact also explains why the recommendations in this chapter focus so much on the development of processes. Addressing root causes will mean the active participation of many actors, and will involve discussions and decision on the difficult trade-offs that countries will face. Putting processes in place and tools at the ready to examine and inform those trade-offs will be critical.

We have deliberately focused our work and recommendations on the institutional and policy context for biodiversity conservation. While this may seem to ignore the millions of individual decision-makers who make choices every day that affect biodiversity, it is our contention that their choices have a logic that is entirely attributable to the set of incentives these individuals receive from markets, institutions and traditions, amongst other sources. These incentives, and the political and economic context that creates them, are what we intend to influence.

With this in mind, the recommendations presented in this chapter are intended to suggest an operational approach to address the loss of biodiversity. To do so, however, the recommendations need to be firmly rooted in the notion that action on biodiversity loss needs to operate at the two distinct levels. For this reason the first set of recommendations focuses on the initiatives and innovation that have occurred at the local level. These positive steps, taken most often by civil society and parts of the private sector, are an integral part of any long-term strategy for biodiversity conservation, and they need, whenever possible, to be enhanced and supported.

In the second set of recommendations, we focus on the systemic level and so return to the underlying assumption of this Root Causes project. To reiterate, the activities that address biodiversity loss at the local level can only succeed in the long run if the proper set of policies and incentives exist at the national and international levels to support them. For example, and as a preview of some of the issues that will arise in the course of the conclusions, we can say that the emergence of certification and labelling schemes that promote 'green' products could be done away with by the stroke of a WTO pen, or a government's need for budgetary restraint can cause it to eliminate support for the management of protected areas, or in the most extreme example, the US$128 billion in private investment that flows into developing countries every year and the agenda for economic growth that it carries, outweighs by several orders of magnitude the amounts that are spent for conservation. This is why we believe a new approach to conservation is required, and so we end our recommendations by calling for the widespread adoption of a root causes framework to help guide future conservation strategies and activities.

SUMMARY OF RECOMMENDATIONS

At the local level

1. Activities that seek to ensure the immediate and effective conservation of biodiversity, and that focus on the local dynamic that is causing that loss, need to be identified and supported.
2. The role of civil society in promoting, implementing and monitoring the conservation of biodiversity needs to be recognized and supported by national governments and international institutions.
3. The private sector can, and should, take a more active role in the development of standards, management practices and business models that seek to integrate sustainability into their activities. The private sector should also use the increasing political power that it wields to promote the development and implementation of incentives for sustainable development and the conservation of biodiversity at the national and international levels.

At the systemic level

4. National governments, which bear the major responsibility for addressing the root causes of biodiversity loss, need to recognize that a deep-seated conflict exists between economic development, as it is currently pursued, and the preservation of biodiversity. They need to create national processes to define and resolve these conflicts.
5. The international community has to ensure that the context in which countries are being asked to make tough choices about their development is properly supportive of the objectives of sustainable development. International institutions and regimes need to create incentives and remove disincentives for sustainable development, and the conservation of biodiversity in particular.

6. Institutions and individuals concerned with the loss of biodiversity need to develop and integrate new approaches to understanding the root causes of biodiversity loss. This will ensure that new strategies and activities that aim to address the loss of biodiversity are built on as comprehensive and strategic an understanding of the factors involved as possible. These new approaches will be defined by a multi-disciplinary framework that will allow the complexity of root causes to be properly assessed.

RECOMMENDATION 1

Activities that seek to ensure the immediate and effective conservation of biodiversity, and that focus on the local dynamic that is causing that loss, need to be identified and supported.

Calling for a new way of thinking about the biodiversity loss does not mean that we believe that current approaches that focus on the local dynamic driving biodiversity loss should be set aside. To the contrary, we need to be clear in saying that the approach we are advocating in no way constitutes a replacement of existing approaches and strategies, many of which have been in place and effective for many years. Our policy critique of the GEF, which began this exercise, was not that the 'traditional' approaches it supported were ineffective, but rather that those approaches were insufficient to meet the objective of conserving the world's biodiversity. We believe it is important to recommend that activities resulting in the immediate and effective conservation of biodiversity need to be identified and supported. As we said in defining our assumptions, biodiversity loss is a significant and critical global problem, and all possible tools need to be deployed to address it.

In particular, the following types of activities need to be aggressively identified and supported by national governments, international institutions and civil society. This short list is derived from the findings of the case studies and is not exhaustive.

*   Conservation activities, such as the identification and establishment of protected areas, need continued support to ensure that important biological resources under severe threat are given some protection. To ensure their long-term viability, these activities should be based on an understanding of the human, social and biological background to the trends that affect those resources or habitats. The lessons from the Brazil and the Philippines case studies are instructive. In each case, the continuum of economic development in three distinct areas is shown to be inversely proportional to the degree of environmental degradation in these areas. Understanding these trends, and overlaying them with biological criteria, can help inform choices about where conservation activities can be undertaken in the most cost-efficient manner.

- Economic alternatives to unsustainable resource use, especially in areas of growing environmental scarcity, need to be identified and supported. The case of Calakmul in Mexico, as an example, shows us how the absence of economic alternatives (or access to markets) leads to the unsustainable exploitation of an area's natural resources and the loss of biodiversity.

- Markets for environmental products (such as water) should be developed in a way that promotes their efficient and equitable use. One of the recurring conclusions of the case studies is the fact that the lack of markets for common environmental products leads to their inefficient and unsustainable uses. In the case of Pakistan, for example, water flow from the Indus, which is supposed to be controlled to sustain downstream mangrove swamps, is affected by overuse by large and politically powerful upstream agricultural landowners. A responsive market for water-use rights could provide the government with revenue to mitigate the downstream effects, and could lead to more efficient use by landowners concerned with minimizing the costs of production.

RECOMMENDATION 2

The role of civil society in promoting, implementing and monitoring the protection of biodiversity needs to be actively supported by national governments and international institutions.

Civil society around the world has always played an important role in the conservation of biological diversity. We believe that this role, in the context of globalization and the reduction of governments' traditional role in regulating the use of natural resources, will now be all the more important. As such, it is critical that new financial resources from national governments, international lenders, and the private sector should support this role. This would allow civil society to carry out four distinct functions in addressing the root causes of biodiversity loss:

- Implementation. Organizations that have a direct interest and capacity in matters related to the conservation of biological diversity should focus their on-the-ground activities on measures that seek to understand and address the root causes of biodiversity loss. Many new approaches that increase the scope of conservation activities, such as WWF's Eco-Region Based Conservation, are currently being implemented. These should be increased and resources allocated to allow for their implementation. Similarly, civil society can play a role in setting international standards for the practice and conduct of sustainable development. Practical, market-based mechanisms, such as the certification of sustainable forestry operations by the Forest Stewardship Council, are beginning to be replicated for other environmental commodities.

- Research and innovation. Research must continue on how to address the root causes of biodiversity loss, especially with respect to implementing the recommendations of this project. Research organizations can, and should, play a role in researching and defining many of the pressing issues raised by the Root Causes project. They can also contribute directly to the development of inputs that will be required by national governments to inform the choices they face on sustainable development (discussed in Recommendation 4), and help international institutions understand the impacts of their activities and how to mitigate them (discussed in Recommendation 5).
- Advocacy. Civil society is well equipped to ensure that the difficult political choices that are at the heart of the recommendations of this project are given the full airing they require. An advocacy campaign can ensure that the national processes to examine the trade-offs between economic growth and biodiversity conservation (discussed in Recommendation 4) are carried out and their recommendations acted upon. Civil society can also act as an advocate for those whose voice, for whatever reason, is not present but whose input is critical to the success of those proceedings.
- Monitoring and Accountability. Much research in this area has pointed to the singular importance of ensuring adequate follow-up and monitoring to agreements reached and policies put in place. Again, civil society will have a critical role to play in making sure that all those involved remain accountable for the commitments they have made.

Biological diversity, and its conservation, is an excellent example of a 'voiceless constituency'. Civil society has always been at its most important and most relevant when it acts as a voice for those groups or issues that are pushed to the margins of political processes and decision-making. Civil society must be allowed to play this role openly and responsively if biological diversity is to be conserved.

RECOMMENDATION 3

The private sector can, and should, take a more active role in the development of standards, management practices and business models that seek to integrate sustainability into their activities. They should also use the political power that they increasingly wield to promote the development and implementation of incentives to sustainable development and the conservation of biodiversity at the national and international levels.

A growing number of organizations and individuals in the private sector are emerging as positive forces in the pursuit of sustainable development and the conservation of biodiversity. Many companies are recognizing that the long-term benefits of adopting policies and pursuing opportunities that focus on sustainability outweigh the short-term costs of doing so. A growing number of consumers who are concerned about the environment and are empowered by new information tools, such as labelling and certification, are beginning to reward these companies for their leadership role on these issues.

Companies need to capitalize on their position and create new models at the national and international levels that provide concrete examples of how the private sector can profit from making sustainability, and the conservation of biodiversity in particular, an integral part of their business. They can do so by:

- actively promoting the adoption of standards for environmental manage-ment. These would include reporting standards, the development of corporate responsibility strategies and the sharing of best practices in industry and sector groups to which they belong. It must also include the adoption of market-based schemes that allow for the labelling and certifi-cation of goods and services that are sustainable; and
- using their considerable political 'clout' to support the creation of incen-tives to sustainable development and the conservation of biodiversity. Industry groupings such as the World Business Council on Sustainable Development, their national counterparts, and the myriad other industry-based associations that have taken progressive positions on environmental issues, should work to promote the development and implementation of national policies that address the loss of biodiversity.

RECOMMENDATION 4

National governments, which bear the major responsibility for addressing the root causes of biodiversity loss, need to recognize that a deep-seated conflict exists between economic development, as it is currently pursued, and the preservation of biodiversity. They need to create national processes to define and resolve these conflicts.

Almost all the case studies carried out for this project point to a basic imbal-ance in the way governments at all levels make choices about how to deal with the preservation of biodiversity, with well-intentioned and designed environ-mental policies often being at odds with other policies being enacted. Similarly, policies that are put into place for the management of natural resources very often suffer from lack of supporting institutional, regulatory or enforcement frameworks.

Without making subjective judgments about the validity of those policy or resource allocation choices (which often seek to alleviate poverty, establish food security or reach some other important social goal), it is still possible to point to the deep-seated conflict that exists between the objectives of economic growth and environmental protection. The simple fact is that governments are called upon to make difficult decisions about where priorities should lie and that their choices often reflect an understandable bias towards meeting basic social needs. What we would like to argue, however, is that the choices that are made do not always reflect the needs and interests of society at large, either because they reflect the interests of a small segment of that society, and not the larger social interest, or because they are made on the basis of inadequate or non-existent information concerning the true long-term costs and benefits of the choices being considered. These factors persist because processes or institutions do not exist through which those ill-affected by such factors are given a voice.

If we look at examples of some of the contradictory policies that the case studies illustrate, we can point to some of the difficulties involved.

- Policies that regulate the use of natural resources often show how governments act in contradiction to their own stated objectives. In the case of Pakistan (closely mirrored by the cases of India and Tanzania), policies for water use are supposed to be governed by a number of laws and agreements guaranteeing access to all and ensuring the viability of downstream mangrove swamps upon which prawn fishermen depend. In reality, politically powerful agricultural landowners have managed to capture most of the flow of the Indus for irrigation purposes, which has led to severe deterioration of mangrove swamps in the Indus delta.
- Governments are often caught in a conflict of interest by assuming the dual roles of natural resource manager and natural resource user. This dual role illustrates the difficulty, and contradictions, inherent in choices governments make. In China, for example, local and provincial governments derive considerable revenue from exploiting the forests. This, together with the lack of controls exercised by the central government, contribute to environmental degradation and extensive flooding.
- Migration policies and settlement in unpopulated areas, such as in Vietnam and Brazil, are carried out to relieve pressures in other parts of the country, to achieve food security goals and to give poor populations immediate access to natural resources. But when these are undertaken, as is almost always the case, without due regard to a supportive economic and social framework (involving such things as agricultural extension programmes or rural credit schemes), their social benefits can be short-lived. The environmental costs, moreover, in the form of converted or degraded forests and other natural habitats, are immediate.
- Development policies that are made without adequate information, or without due consideration for their environmental impact, can have direct impacts on biodiversity. The case of bushmeat in Cameroon, where the establishment of an infrastructure for deforestation has facilitated and accelerated the extraction of bushmeat from areas that had been previously cut off from markets, illustrates this. The government's desire to promote the expansion of the forestry sector grew out of a need to address balance-of-payment difficulties. What was not taken into account was the impact this would have on the dynamics of the bushmeat trade, and the cost to biodiversity has been high.

To address these types of issues, and the conflict that underlies them, we recommend that governments and donors committed to stemming the loss of biodiversity create processes at the national level to try to reach a national consensus on the trade-offs inherent in economic growth and environmental protection. These processes would need to involve all affected parties, from local communities to civil society to large landowners or corporate interests. The process would have an obvious political dimension in that it would seek to mediate and resolve trade-offs and conflicting interests that are at the root of contradictory policies. Special attention would be given to the potential conflicts that exist between policies that encourage the productive use of natural resources and those that seek to preserve, conserve, or promote the sustainable use of those resources. An essential input into these processes would be analytical work to assess the relative costs and benefits of respective courses of action. Consensus will only come on the basis of informed choices and from the recognition that trade-offs will have to be made. A critical element in the implementation of this recommendation is the financial and technical support that must be given by the international community to the outcome of these processes.

RECOMMENDATION 5

The international community has to ensure that the context in which countries are being asked to make tough choices about their development is properly supportive of the objectives of sustainable development. International institutions and regimes need to create incentives and remove disincentives for sustainable development, and in particular the conservation of biological diversity. Impact assessments must be conducted for all significant legal and financial structures, as a way of understanding how they generate incentives, positive or negative.

We believe that government policies often reflect conflicting objectives and competing priorities and provide incentives that are contradictory to sustainable development and the conservation of biodiversity. Asking national governments to confront the tough choices that they face in conserving their biodiversity can only be done if the international community creates incentives for sustainable development and biodiversity conservation. A number of incentives to sustainable development currently account for a great deal of the progress that has been made. But an underlying system of disincentives to sustainable development and conservation also exists. The imbalance between the two, or more accurately the pervasive character of disincentives, needs to be addressed in a forceful way by the international community if sustainable development is to become a reality.

Of the two sections that follow, the first illustrates the imbalance in incentives that exists, and the second calls for an understanding of the impacts of these incentives. This recommendation is critical to the logic of the framework we are suggesting. But because the recommendation touches on elements that are not necessarily drawn from the case studies themselves, more background is provided to explain its rationale.

Incentives and Disincentives

Incentives

The international community has created positive incentives for the conservation of biodiversity and sustainable development generally. The first set of positive incentives are legal in nature and consist of international laws to govern the use of biological resources: they include the CBD, CITES and the Ramsar Convention on Wetlands. These conventions do a great deal to regulate the use of biological resources and, in the case of the CBD, set rules for how the benefits of that use are to be distributed. While concerns have been raised about their effectiveness and accountability, they ensure that issues of biological diversity are addressed in an international setting and that countries are called upon to make political commitments to the issue of biodiversity loss.

The second set of positive incentives are financial in nature. The GEF, which devotes almost 50 per cent of its budget to the conservation of biological diversity, provides the most prominent of these incentives. In addition the World Bank and regional development banks, the United Nations Development Programme (UNDP), UNEP and bilateral donors fund many programmes that support biodiversity conservation. A significant amount of financial support for the conservation of biological diversity also comes from private foundations, other philanthrophic organizations and from NGOs. More recently, international standards for how certain natural resources can be used in a sustainable manner are serving as positive financial incentives. These standards accept that some use of these resources is necessary and even desirable if the benefits of utilization are equitably distributed, and provided that labelling schemes allow consumers to readily identify them in the marketplace.

Disincentives

The preponderance of disincentives against the conservation of biological diversity and sustainable development creates an imbalance, which limits the gains attributable to positive incentives. These disincentives can be placed in the same two broad classifications used for incentives – legal and financial.

An imposing international legal framework is being erected that has the potential to limit the ability of governments to regulate the use of natural resources. Even if they are of a mind to regulate the use of those resources in a sustainable manner, governments arc slowly being asked to give up their traditional role as economic agents and regulators over those resources and economic sectors that are relevant to sustainable development. The general term globalization is given to that set of trends that is pushing the international economy to adopt global standards that are increasingly defined by the private corporation, not the nation-state. The legal framework for globalization is provided by the WTO and by the proposed but now abandoned Multilateral Agreement on Investments (MAI). What these agreements share is an objective to progressively reduce the barriers that exist between countries, either for the conduct of trade or the flow of investments. But those barriers can include policy instruments that governments use to limit or govern the use of a particular natural resource, or investment in a particular kind of development. Taking away that policy-making role reduces the options a government has to regulate the development of its economy and potentially acts as a disincentive to sustainable development.

As an example, the WTO has opposed national policies that seek to block the importation of goods that the country in question judges to be environmentally destructive. In cases like the GATT and WTO Tuna–Dolphin or Shrimp–Turtle disputes, panels have judged that the US restriction on importation of tuna and shrimp, based on concerns over how harvesting methods were harming dolphin and turtle populations, is in contravention of GATT and WTO rules. The trade-dispute panels have interpreted these restrictions as being discriminatory and thus illegal. This type of interpretation is growing increasingly narrow and moving away from allowing countries to define policies that promote the conservation of biological diversity and sustainable development (International Institute for Sustainable Development, 1996).

The financial manifestation of this globalization, and the financial expression of a disincentive to sustainable development, can be found in a rapid overview of the various financial flows to the developing world. The World Bank, as an example, lends over US$25 billion in an average year. In the past ten years, a growing percentage of that money has gone into sectoral or structural adjustment lending, to the point where almost 65 per cent of its annual lending now goes for those purposes. The environmental impact of this lending can be said to be mixed: it tends to increase the efficiency of a particular economic sector, or of an economy as a whole, and so can lead to a diminution in the use of natural resources. At the same time, however, adjustment lending almost always has the stated objective of reducing the role of the government as an economic agent. Again, the rationale for that may be justifiable; such lending is often made necessary by poor management of the economy by that government. By reducing the role of the government in management of that country's economy, however, these programmes have an impact on the regulatory function of government with regard to the use of natural resources. Reduction of the government's role is seldom accompanied by replacement with institutions or regulatory regimes that can play that role, leaving a vacuum. That vacuum, of course, means that the societal interest that is served through sustainable development is given no voice (Reed, 1996).

Another way to think about the financial disincentives to sustainable development is to compare figures that support conservation and sustainable development with those that support traditional forms of economic growth. The GEF allocates just US$2.75 billion over four years, distributed across a range of activities that include biodiversity and climate change. This compares with US$25 billion that the World Bank spends annually on development initiatives. Since 1988, the Bank has spent US$619 million on the conservation of biodiversity (in addition to activities it has carried out using GEF resources). Annually this works out to be just 0.03 per cent of the Bank's resources. When the GEF and World Bank figures are compared with the flow of private investment into developing countries – US$128 billion in 1997 according to the Organization for Economic Cooperation and Development (OECD) figures – it is clear that the financial incentives to conserve biodiversity are swamped by those that are flowing to economic growth. Moreover, these financial flows reflect the growing influence of private capital on decisions that affect national economic development.

As with many national situations, the recommendation to ensure that incentives to sustainable development increase and disincentives decrease is really a call for the international community to ensure that there is consistency in the priorities that it establishes. As pointed out in the first chapter, the concept of sustainable development was born out of an international dialogue on how economic development can occur in a manner that promotes equity and preserves the environment for future generations. Sustainable development, as an international standard, has already been established. The international community now needs to ensure that this standard is given the proper signals to succeed.

Understanding the Impact of International Incentive Structures

For an appropriate determination of the true impact of international legal and financial structures, and how such structures can support sustainable development and the conservation of biological diversity, much work needs to be done to analyse the full impact of current international incentives. The idea is to have legal regimes and financial support programmes that explicitly define sustainable development as an objective, and so make support of sustainable development a priority.

Practically, this will mean:

- Sustainability impact assessments will have to be conducted for those rules created by the WTO or agreements initiated by similar international regimes that are likely to have an impact on the ability of national governments to pursue policies in support of sustainable development. This will mean assessments not only for standards that pertain to natural resource sectors, but for any sector likely to be related to use of natural resources.[1]
- Strategic or sectoral environmental impact assessments should be conducted for policies and programmes carried out with support from the Bretton Woods Institutions (the IMF, World Bank, UN and GATT) and bilateral donor agencies. While these institutions do analyse the impact of individual projects that are deemed 'environmental', they do not analyse the impact of programmes that seek to reform or adjust the economies (or sectors of the economy that are not strictly environmental) of their client countries. Given

the large amounts of resources that are devoted to these activities, and the significant impact they have on the development of a country's economy, it is critical that information be gathered to ensure that these programmes support sustainable development as defined by national governments.

RECOMMENDATION 6

Institutions and individuals concerned with the loss of biodiversity need to develop and integrate new approaches to understand the root causes of biodiversity loss. This will ensure that new strategies and activities that aim to address the loss of biodiversity are built on a comprehensive and strategic understanding of the factors involved. These new approaches will be defined by a multi-disciplinary framework that will allow the complexity of root causes to be properly assessed.

The root causes of biodiversity loss operate at many different levels – both temporal and physical. The resulting loss is caused by many factors at many scales and with complex linkages all operating simultaneously: it is said to be 'over-determined'. Addressing or mitigating just one of those factors may lead to some limited success, but ultimately the objective of conserving biological diversity can only be achieved if the complex array of factors is considered simultaneously. As noted in Chapters 1 and 2, a lot of work has been done in the academic and policy communities on understanding the factors that contribute to biodiversity loss, and we owe a great debt to that work. What the development and implementation of this project has taught us, however, is that understanding these factors by themselves is not as important as understanding the complex way in which they operate with others. Even more important, perhaps, is the need to find an understanding of this complexity that is relevant to policy-makers and resource users.

Some specific institutional recommendations are:

- The GEF and CBD secretariats, as the leading international forums for matters of global biodiversity, should develop an international process to highlight new approaches to understanding the causes of biodiversity loss. This process should bring together leading practitioners and thinkers on the issue, as well as representatives from major donor organizations, national governments and civil society. It should focus on the need to develop new tools for understanding the complexity of factors that drive biodiversity loss and new operational responses that take such complexity into account.
- The GEF should work to better incorporate root causes issues into existing efforts to streamline and disseminate simplified operational guidelines to its implementing agencies (the World Bank, UNDP and UNEP). Efforts should also be made to incorporate root causes issues into the country dialogue workshop modules that are currently being developed for its partners.

- Governments and donors should incorporate specific operational policies into existing frameworks to ensure that root causes of biodiversity loss are more systematically addressed in projects.

This might include:

- requiring all biodiversity conservation and sustainable use projects to clearly address root causes of biodiversity loss in project documents, including conducting a root causes-type analysis;
- establishing specific criteria related to how effectively root causes of biodiversity loss are addressed in projects as part of the agency's internal decision-making frameworks; and
- requiring country and sectoral strategies to incorporate analyses of root causes.

Such policies should be shared widely with all agency staff and developing-country partner-institutions to ensure that projects are developed appropriately. Widespread distribution of such policies is especially important for agencies that operate in a highly decentralized manner.

- Donors working in the same country or region should compare analyses and coordinate efforts to more effectively assist developing-country partners in affecting necessary policy changes to address root causes of biodiversity loss. Mechanisms such as donor-convened consultative groups should focus more attention on these issues. To do so, donors must engage more directly in root causes dialogues among themselves. Numerous forums to begin these dialogues already exist, including the Development Assistance Committee of the OECD, the Conference of the Parties of the CBD, the Inter governmental Forum on Forests and the Biodiversity in Development project – supported by the European Community, IUCN and the Department for International Development in the UK.
- Conservation organizations (including WWF) should increase the use of new approaches to conservation that stress the integration of biological and socioeconomic analysis and the development of strategic responses in their programming.
- All organizations should develop programmes to increase the capacities of their partner organizations to address root causes of biodiversity loss.

FINAL THOUGHTS

These recommendations reflect elements of an emerging consensus on how to address biodiversity loss. We fully recognize that taking action along the lines recommended in this chapter will be a long and difficult process. The conflicts and contradictions that drive biodiversity loss represent some of the most intractable problems our societies face. They involve issues as complex as how to address poverty and inequity, and how to balance current consumption patterns and the needs of future generations. These are not easy problems, nor do they have easy solutions. It will mean the use of political will and active participation by all the major organizations and individuals we have identified. Only by engaging in such a global enterprise will we make headway in ensuring the adequate supply of natural resources and existence of biodiversity.

Chapter 6

Brazil: Cerrado

Research team: The technical team was composed of the coordinator
Denise Valéria de Lima Pufal (economist), *Robert Buschbacher*
(ecologist) and *Maria Angélica Garcia* (ecologist).
Periodic meetings were held with an advisory committee composed of
Celene Cunha Monteiro Antunes Barreira,
Maria Elizabeth de Oliveira, Jorge Madeira Nogueira,
Marco C Van der Ree and *Nurit Bensusan.*
Direct consultations on technical matters were held with
Renísia Cristina Garcia, Regina Helena Rosa Sambuich
and *George Eiten*

Summary: **Government policies in Brazil have driven the rapid expansion of large-scale commercial agriculture in the Cerrado region. Agricultural development has had a dramatic impact on the ecosystems where it has taken hold. However, government policies were more successful in introducing this agricultural model in some places than others, depending not only on physical conditions but also on socioeconomic conditions.**

The rapid loss of biodiversity in Brazil's Cerrado region is linked to the advance of the agricultural frontier, which has accelerated in recent decades. From the 1960s to the 1980s a set of government policies stimulated agricultural development in the Central Plateau. These policies were aimed at production of commodities for export, thus providing foreign exchange, while occupying the demographic vacuum in the Brazilian interior.

Among the reasons for choosing this region for settlement were the great availability of land and the favourable topography for mechanization, an essential prerequisite for modern grain agriculture. Provision of subsidized loans, development of infrastructure and other incentives had a dramatic impact on the form of development and the rate of opening of Cerrado areas (Klink et al, 1993). However, the social, economic and environmental costs have been high.

Recent studies indicate that just 35 per cent of the Cerrado biome is currently in a relatively natural state.[1] Within this area, the few large blocks of remaining intact native habitat must be considered priority for implementation of protected areas, since only 0.6 per cent of the Cerrado is officially protected.[2]

The principal threats to the biodiversity of the Cerrado are related to two distinct agricultural modalities: on the one hand, intensive, high-input grain monoculture (primarily soybeans) with associated infrastructure investments (waterways, roads and railroads); on the other hand, low-technology, extensive ranching that occupies more than 70 per cent of the area of agricultural establishments in the core area of Cerrado. Grain monoculture has a smaller direct, but a larger indirect, impact on the Cerrado, since it occupies approximately 15 per cent of the area farmed. Ranching has a direct impact, opening new areas and constantly threatening biodiversity through its use of fire.

Three counties (*municipalidades*) were selected as case studies on the root causes of biodiversity loss in the Cerrado: Rio Verde, Silvânia and Alto Paraíso de Goiás, all in the state of Goiás, which is entirely located in the core area of the Cerrado. These three counties presented different responses to the same basic set of public policies related to the insertion of the Cerrado within international markets via commodity production, especially grains. The comparison indicates a tendency for concentration of monocultures and industrial agriculture in regions with favourable infrastructure and socio-environmental conditions. On the other hand, areas without these characteristics demonstrated different development models, either oriented to small farmers who gained viability by forming associations and cooperatives or focused on tourism and extracting natural resources. But poor populations are primarily forced into other strategies for survival, such as charcoal extraction and extensive ranching, with uncontrolled use of fire and continuous expansion into natural areas.

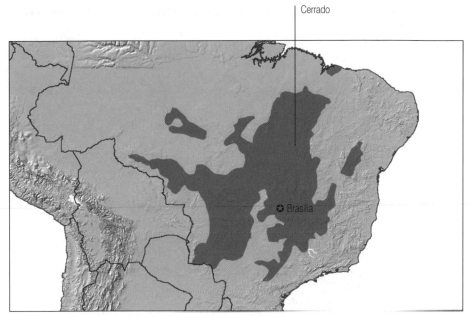

Figure 6.1 *Map of Brazil Showing Location of the Cerrado*

DESCRIPTION OF THE STUDY AREAS

General Characteristics of the Cerrado Biome

The Cerrado biome covers approximately 25 per cent of the Brazilian territory, or about two million km² (Figure 6.1). The core area of the Cerrado,
considered the most characteristic and continuous, covers 1.5 million km² on
the Central Brazilian Plateau – the states of Goiás, Tocantins, the Federal
District and parts of Minas Gerais, Bahia, Piauí, Maranhão, Rondônia, Mato
Grosso and Mato Grosso do Sul. The remaining 0.5 million km² consists of
fringe areas interspersed with each of Brazil's other major biomes: Atlantic
forest, Amazon forest and Caatinga (Cavassan, 1990). Due to the affinities of
its flora and fauna, Brazil's Pantanal wetland is often considered a special type
of (seasonally flooded) Cerrado, but land use and human occupation are
totally different. WWF considers the Cerrado biome as a single ecoregion,
which does not include the Pantanal.

The Cerrado is a complex of vegetative formations with varying physiog-
nomy[3] and floristic composition: grasslands (*campo limpo*), open savannas
(*campo sujo, campo cerrado*), woodlands (*cerrado sensu stricto*) and forests
(*cerradão*, dry forest on limestone and gallery forests) forming an ecological
mosaic.[4] The distribution of the different vegetative formations is a response
to differences in soil, climate and fire regime. For example, the forests occur

on more fertile soils and along watercourses, whereas the most open types often indicate the poorest soils.

The Cerrado has a tropical climate with a strong dry season. Two-thirds of the biome has total annual rainfall between 1200 and 1800 mm, and a five to six month dry season. The topography of the Cerrado region varies from flat to smoothly undulating, favouring the practice of mechanized agriculture and irrigation. The predominant soils are red or yellow latosols. These soils are acidic (pH 4 to 5.5), nutrient-poor (base saturation less than 50 per cent), especially low in available phosphorus (less than 2 ppm), and often present aluminium toxicity (saturation greater than 50 per cent). On the other hand, soil organic matter and physical structure are relatively favourable.

The vascular plant flora of the Cerrado contains over 6600 species in some 170 families and over 1100 genera (de Mendonça et al, 1998). Of these, 2150 species are herbs, 1291 shrubs and 1065 tree species, with the remainder in other forms or unclassified. The predominant plant families are legumes, composites, orchids and grasses. Of these the legumes are well represented throughout the tropics, while the grasses are typically found more in savanna habitat. The orchids are well represented in the Amazon and Atlantic as well, but in the Cerrado just over half of the almost 500 species are terrestrial. Cerrado species diversity varies with region. The grasslands contain 2055 species, the savannas 2880 and the forests 2540, the latter being remarkably rich given their relatively small area.

This heterogeneous biome also encompasses many different animal communities, varying in species diversity and abundance of individuals. In the Cerrado there are approximately 70 mammal genera, including 110 species, of which the large majority are rodents. This group presents the highest degree of endemism among the Cerrado mammalian fauna. The other mammals show, in general, a low rate of endemism. The Cerrado is home to about 25 per cent of the bird species of Brazil, with about 400 species. Bird endemism, 16 per cent of the species, is associated with the Cerrado forest systems. The invertebrate fauna and the diversity of microorganisms is not well known, but there are data showing that these fauna are rich and present a high degree of endemism.

Characteristics of the Three Case Study Counties

The county of Rio Verde, created in 1854, is situated in the south-west of Goiás, 220 km from Goiânia, the state capital, and 440 km from Brasília, the federal capital. It occupies an area of 8415 km^2 with an average elevation of 750 m. With a population of 100,000 inhabitants, 90 per cent of whom reside in urban areas, demographic density is 11.9 inhabitants per km^2.

Silvânia, the oldest county, is located in the Pires do Rio region, with occupation dating from 1770 (Borges, 1981). It occupies an area of 2860 km^2 at an average elevation of 900 m (SAGRIA, 1997). It is about 80 km from Goiânia and 220 km from Brasília. The population of 19,000 is distributed almost equally between the rural and urban zones. Demographic density is 6.5 inhabitants per km^2.

Previously a district of Cavalcante County, Alto Paraíso de Goiás was created in 1953. It is in the Chapada dos Veadeiros region in northern Goiás, 220 km from Brasília, and occupies an area of 2603 km^2 at an average elevation of 1200 m. The total population is 5500, with 64 per cent residing in the urban area. The demographic density is 2.0 per km^2, the lowest among the three counties studied.

In Rio Verde the savanna and woodland types of Cerrado vegetation predominate: *campo cerrado*, *campo sujo* and *cerrado sensu stricto*. Gallery forests are restricted to the valley bottoms and along watercourses. Due to the predominance of flatlands (*chapadões*), there is widespread use for monocultures.

In Silvânia the predominant vegetation is *cerrado sensu stricto*; however there are also extensive areas of *cerradão* (dense forest-like *cerrado*).

The region of Alto Paraíso is unique in containing a large proportion of high-altitude Cerrado, which covers only 3 per cent of the entire biome. This includes a great variety of Cerrado vegetation types, including *campo rupestre*, *campo úmido*, *campo limpo*, *campo sujo*, *cerrado sobre rochas*, *cerrado sensu stricto*, *veredas*, mesophytic forest, *cerradão* and gallery forest. The richness of the fauna and flora unquestionably makes the region a reference point for the biodiversity of the Cerrado. Surveys carried out in the region identified 186 tree species in 49 families with a mean density of 1035 individuals per hectare (Felfilli, et al, 1993). The species *Qualea parviflora* (Vochysiaceae) and *Psidium myrsinoides* (Myrtaceae) were the most important. The herbaceous and shrub flora is also rich, with 254 species identified and a mean density of 11,000 individuals per hectare (Mendonça and Filgueiras, 1995). The flora of this region, in spite of the numbers above, is still poorly known, with various rare species and some completely new to science and endemic to the Chapada dos Veadeiros being found. Among the most important are the grasses: *Trachypogon spicatus*, *Echinolaena inflexa*, *Lodetiopsis chrysothrix*, *Axonopus barbigerus* and *Ichnanthus camporum* (Filgueiras, 1995).

The main characteristics of the three case study counties are given in Table 6.1.

RESEARCH METHODOLOGY

The study was focused on the state of Goiás because it is totally within the Cerrado biome and can be considered representative of the entire region's history of occupation, land use and process of native habitat loss. A preliminary consultation of the bibliography and discussions with specialists on the region allowed identification of two predominant land-use models:

1. *Patronal:* a capital- and input-intensive production process, focused on generation of products for national and international markets; and
2. *Family:* more labour-intensive and normally oriented toward domestic markets.

Table 6.1 *Principal Characteristics of the Counties Studied (1996)*

	Rio Verde	Silvânia	Alto Paraiso
Area (km²)	8415	2860	2603
Population	100,000	90,000	10,000
Urban	19,000	9400	9600
Rural	5500	3500	2000
Mean elevation (m)	750	900	1200
Topography	Rolling (5% slope)	Irregular; 800–1100 m	Highly irregular; 400–1676 m
Predominant soils	Latosols	Latosols	Latosols, Lithosols, Cambisols
Predominant vegetation types	Disturbed areas; cerrado sensu stricto remnants	Cerrado sensu stricto	Cerrado sensu stricto; campo sujo
Area of agricultural establishments (ha)	720,242	263,283	100,419
Number of establishments	2231	2151	239
Area of agricultural establishments (% of county area)	86	92	39
in annual crops (%)	36	18	8
in pasture (%)	57	63	80
used for charcoal (%)	< 1	< 1	7
Cattle herd	422,000	127,000	18,000
Value of animal and plant production (US$000 per year)	129,000	26,000	92,700
plant production	93,000 (annual crops 91,000)	15,200 (annual crops 3500)	91,900 (charcoal 91,400)
animal production	37,000	10,700	800

Source: IBGE 1998 and other publications cited in the text

This preliminary analysis also led to the formulation of the following hypotheses:

- The expansion of the agricultural frontier in the Cerrado occurred as a result of government policies that promoted an intensive agricultural model aimed at producing commodities for export, especially soybeans.

- The degree to which this model was implemented depended on local conditions such as topography and infrastructure.
- The impacts on Cerrado biodiversity occur independently of the type of agricultural production system or model, but the rate of degradation promoted by patronal agriculture is greater than that caused by family agriculture.

To test these hypotheses we studied the history of occupation of the region, beginning with the 18th century. After this we analysed the relative increase of areas occupied by annual crops, permanent crops, ranching, mixed crops and ranching, horticulture, pisciculture and silviculture.

After reviewing census data from all of the micro-regions in Goiás, two counties were chosen as being representative of the two predominant forms of occupation and land use: Rio Verde for the patronal model and Silvânia for the family model. Due to the lack of scientific data about biodiversity in these two areas, another county was selected as a reference for the conservation relevance of the biome. This county, Alto Paraíso de Goiás, was subject to a similar set of public policy incentives for agricultural development but, due to unique local characteristics, these did not have the same effect on either agricultural practice or on the natural ecosystem. Alto Paraíso thus demonstrates a third development path.

The survey of the historical process of occupation of Goiás and of the three study areas provided the background for an integrated analysis of the economic, environmental, historical and cultural aspects of the three counties. We used the proportion of different types of land use as the key variable to characterize the three areas because of the strong relationship in the Cerrado between patronal agriculture and grain monoculture, while family agriculture is strongly related to ranching, permanent crops and some small-scale annual crops. Annual cropping has a much larger immediate impact on biodiversity and the environment generally, due to the ploughing of the soil, the intensive use of mechanization, chemical fertilizer and agrochemicals, and the creation of large areas of monoculture. Thus, the proliferation of annual crops such as soybeans results in a higher level of environmental impact than ranching or the other agricultural uses.

To collect data, surveys were carried out with institutions linked directly or indirectly to environmental and agricultural issues in Goiás, especially in Goiânia and in Brasília. Census data were obtained from the Brazilian Institute of Geography and Statistics (IBGE) and other information was gathered from the Brazilian Agricultural Research Agency (EMBRAPA), the Goiás Secretary of Agriculture, the Brazilian Agricultural Extension Agency (EMATER) in Goiás and the Federal District, the Goiás State Environmental Agency (FEMAGO), the Goiás state headquarters of the Brazilian Environmental Agency (IBAMA), the Institute for Society, Population and Nature (ISPN) and the University of Brasília (Cerrado database). Local offices of IBGE were also consulted.

Visits were made to Rio Verde, Silvânia and Alto Paraíso, where the principal public administration organs related to environment and agriculture were contacted, as well as teaching and research institutions, associations, unions and syndicates, agricultural and ranching cooperatives, agricultural credit banks and others.

The principal data limitation was in terms of local environmental conditions and their historical trends. Although the mapping of land use throughout the state of Goiás is now underway, it was not possible to obtain information on the target counties, with the exception of Silvânia, which had a historical study with images from 1978, 1981 and 1986.

In our demographic analysis, we made adjustments to control for historical changes in county boundaries that make direct documentation of population growth-rates impossible. In the case of Rio Verde, we used the area of the county in 1953 to analyse the region's population dynamics. In this way, we eliminated the effects of the adjustments to the county boundaries that occurred in 1953, 1987, 1991 and 1992. The population of Silvânia was also normalized this way. In the case of Alto Paraíso de Goiás, there were no problems with collecting or processing the data.

INTERNATIONAL CONTEXT

In general terms, the following international-level driving forces have been identified as playing a key role in land-use decisions and thus habitat and biodiversity loss (Klink et al, 1993):

- international trade policy, especially import agreements;
- exchange rate policy, which affects relative costs;
- subsidies to inputs and to production;
- policies of international aid; and
- other agreements that affect demand for products or tend to undervalue the real social worth of biodiversity and the quality of life.

In the case of the Cerrado, international trade linked to the need to generate foreign exchange was the key driving force for agricultural expansion and thus biodiversity loss, especially in the case of grain monocultures. These factors in turn were linked to the terms of trade (commodity prices and exchange rates) and global economic dynamics such as the petroleum crises of the 1970s, the global recession of the 1980s and the global financial crisis of the late 1990s.

The Brazilian economy has always been intimately linked to international trade, and Brazil has been characterized for many years as an agro-exporting nation. Since colonial times, agriculture has been a strategic sector for the Brazilian economy with successive cycles of products: Brazilwood at the time of discovery, followed by sugar cane and, later, cotton, tobacco, cocoa, rubber and coffee. These cycles were linked to international demand and subject to its oscillations, which resulted in moments of sudden increase and decline in production and trade. Only with industrial development has the Brazilian economy achieved a diversification of activities separate from the dynamics of its agricultural sector (Baer, 1995).

The decision to exploit Cerrado lands in a modern, commercial manner was made in the 1960s. The goal was to use agricultural modernization to meet the need to improve the balance of payments. This policy had the additional aims of diminishing demographic and land tenure pressure in the south and meeting the growing demand of urban centres. The rationale and approach were very similar to the programmes for colonization of the Amazon during the same period.

The increase in international soybean prices in the 1970s and 1980s inspired great interest in this product. At this time a highly interventionist military dictatorship ruled Brazil and took on a series of functions that would normally pertain to private enterprise and the market. In this context the government implemented selective credit policies to stimulate the commercial agriculture sector to produce crops, especially soybeans, for the international market. In this way Brazil evolved from being an importer to an exporter of soybeans in a very short time.

During the 1980s, the growing need for earnings to meet the balance-of-payments deficit stimulated soybean cultivation. At a global level, simultaneously, the rapid expansion of international trade in commodities increased competition among various countries producing the same crops, resulting in a drop in the price of soybeans beginning in the middle of the decade.

The maintenance of subsidized interest rates for the agricultural sector and an overvalued exchange rate drove macroeconomic policy during this period. On the one hand, the overvalued currency increased the price of exported products and, on the other, reduced the cost of imports, both key elements for the modernization of agriculture and industry. Fiscal policy involved large public investments in various sectors considered to be strategic for economic development, including agricultural expansion in the Cerrado and Amazon. These investments were funded through an increasing external debt, whose negative impacts on the country were not long in coming.

The petroleum crises of the 1970s, linked with a nationalist ideal of self-sufficiency and national security, created a need to reduce the country's dependence on oil imports. Thus PROALCOOL was created, a programme that promoted the production of alcohol from sugar cane as a substitute automotive fuel. This programme led to the establishment of various companies to plant sugar cane monocultures, especially in Goiás, the state with the fastest rate of growth in sugar cane cultivation in the country.

The worldwide recession of the 1980s, the fiscal crises in the US and Europe and the worsening debt of developing countries reduced global demand for imports, creating instability in the international trade in agricultural products, fostering protectionist policies and damaging agrarian structures in the developing world. This international scenario should have drastically reduced agricultural expansion to produce export commodities such as soybeans. Moreover, in the face of Brazil's debt crisis, the IMF imposed a sharp cut in government resources allocated to agricultural credit, which should have had a similar effect.

However, Brazilian national policies persistently counteracted these trends. In spite of fiscal restrictions and consequent cutbacks in credit, the Brazilian government instituted a policy of minimum price guarantees to the producer, committing to buy all excess production that could not be sold at prices above a predetermined floor. The Minimum Price Guarantee Policy (PGPM) neutralized the effect of the international market on the Brazilian producer, who would have his production absorbed, if not by the market, by the Brazilian government. In addition, a unitary price for fuels was established so that suppliers were forced to charge the same prices throughout the country, regardless of the high costs of delivering fuel to remote areas. These distortions spurred the continued growth of areas planted in monocultures for export in spite of the international crisis.

The incentive system for agriculture was not truly dismantled until the end of the 1980s, with the adoption of neo-liberal economic policies promoted by the Fernando Collor government; the PGPM, agricultural credit and, slightly later, the unitary fuel price were all eliminated, leading to a decline in the area cultivated in the country as a whole and in the Cerrado. With the dismantling of the PGPM (which was later reinstated but never received the financing to make it effective), producers began to base their investment decisions more on the behaviour of the market. They invested in quality and efficiency, seeking management models typical of other business sectors.

The international economic crisis of the late 1990s, in which Brazil has played a major role, has led the Brazilian government to look for solutions to the so-called 'custo Brasil' – the high cost of doing business in Brazil resulting from inefficiencies of transport, port and tax systems. The government is seeking to increase the profitability of companies beyond the São Paulo axis, particularly promoting exports. In this context, the vast areas of Cerrado have proven attractive to investments, especially for large-scale, capital-intensive enterprises

The government is creating three multi-modal export corridors, using roads, railroads and waterways. These measures should increase the profitability of Cerrado producers beyond the areas already known as pockets of profitability, of which Rio Verde is one. Given the large areas already deforested but underused by extensive agriculture, it is likely that new investments will concentrate on areas already deforested, where establishing cultivation will be less costly. Nevertheless, there is no guarantee that intact areas will not be affected (Pufal et al, in press).

Among other factors driving Brazilian land use is the expectation of Brazilian soybean producers that global demand for soybean will increase despite the current crisis in Asia. To increase production, genetically modified soybean may be introduced in Brazil, despite opposition from environmental and consumer protection groups, as well as entities linked to soybean producers who believe that greater competitiveness can be achieved in European and

Asian markets without genetic modifications.

Also pertinent is a significant reduction in the world coffee supply, due to recent natural disasters in Central America and Colombia. The Cerrado offers promising conditions for coffee production with irrigation: high elevations and abundant sun are factors that significantly increase coffee productivity (Pufal et al, in press).

Swine cultivation for export is also being promoted in the Cerrado. In Goiás, the Perdigão Company, a half-billion dollar enterprise, will supply swine to the regional common market, MERCOSUR. Additionally, according to one source, the Dutch government is studying the possibility of transferring 100–150 Dutch families to Mato Grosso to produce swine, an activity losing acceptance in Holland because of the large amount of manure produced. In Mato Grosso, the manure would be used as agricultural fertilizer. These two projects will consume a large part of the grain produced in their areas of influence, principally maize, which would provide an incentive to increase the area planted.

In summary, as an agro-exporting nation, Brazil's links to international trade have always been strong. Starting in the 1960s, the government saw a development model that combined capital-intensive agricultural modernization with expansion into frontier areas as a promising means to produce commodities for export and generate foreign exchange. Brazil borrowed internationally to modernize agricultural and industrial production in order to export commodities and industrial goods. National policies promoted a capital- and input-intensive model of agricultural expansion while international market demand for soybeans was high. Unfortunately, the petroleum crisis and global recession worsened the terms of trade, and Brazil found itself on a treadmill of ever-increasing indebtedness and need to export commodities. In the latest neo-liberal era, the government is investing more selectively in ever-larger agro-industrial projects to increase economic efficiency and international competitiveness.

This analysis also shows that even when the international terms of trade became unfavourable, Brazilian national policy continued to favour capital-intensive agricultural expansion in its frontier areas such as the Cerrado. We will now look at national factors which contributed to this scenario.

NATIONAL CONTEXT

While strongly linked to international markets and financial flows, the story of agricultural expansion in the Cerrado is very much the story of the national development strategy from the 1960s to the present. This brief overview explains how government development plans targeted agricultural expansion in the Cerrado and the instruments that were used in those plans. First, however, it is important to understand the cultural and political context that promoted a development model based on expansion and occupation, with the consequent devastation of natural habitat. We will also look at the demographic changes that occurred in Brazil's interior during this period, because they facilitated the process of agricultural expansion. Finally, we will look at the land-use policy instruments and institutions which, although currently marginalized by the powerful economic engine of development, could regulate and channel future development into more efficient and less destructive pathways.

Cultural Context

The patterns of a country's development, besides being intrinsically related to economic and geographic factors, are a response to cultural factors as well: the way in which the society sees and conceives development. Perhaps the exuberance of the Brazilian environment led Brazilians to treat the forests and jungles as something to be controlled or dominated. For a large part of the period we are focusing on, the ideology promoted by the highly nationalistic military government emphasized pride in Brazil's power and richness, promoting the image of a country whose environmental limits could not easily be surpassed.

In the case of the Cerrado particularly, its parched appearance during almost half the year, and the ecosystem's frequent natural fires, make it easy for the layman to perceive the biome as a wasteland rather than as a font of biodiversity and the birthplace of the nation's major river systems. Illustrative of this is the fact that the Cerrado, unlike the Amazon forest, Atlantic forest, coastal zone and Pantanal, was excluded from the regions considered 'National Patrimony' by the 1988 Federal Constitution. Low population densities and minimal economic activity made the region appear ripe for conquest. Furthermore, the fact that the Cerrado region, especially Goiás, had been isolated and poor made the mantra of development something desirable and glorified, even if it brought environmental destruction with it. Some politicians and many commentators have stated that with the introduction of new crops, especially grains, the ecosystem has reached its apogee.

Socio-political Context

Recent Brazilian agricultural development can be divided into two periods: the first, from 1945 to 1970, marked by the expansion of cultivated lands, and the second, from 1970 to the present, 'of conservative and selective modernization' (Mueller, 1992). The second period was considered conservative because it maintained the system of land-tenure concentration and exclusion of the small producers, and selective because it was aimed at a well-defined public – the capitalized farmer of the south and south-east – and focused on crops in demand by international markets, such as soybean, wheat and rice.

Two models predominate in Brazilian agriculture: family and patronal (FAO/INCRA, 1995). An estimated seven million agricultural establishments in Brazil occupy an area of 400 million ha. Of these only 7 per cent can be considered patronal, but they occupy 75 per cent of the area. The family sector includes 93 per cent of the establishments but occupies only 25 per cent of the area.[5]

The FAO/INCRA study came to the following conclusions about the two segments of Brazilian agriculture:

- The family sector supports greater diversification, including the mixture of agriculture and ranching.
- The patronal segment is technologically more intensive.
- Land use is more intensive in the family segment, due to the smaller property size.[6]
- The family segment is more sensitive to short-term changes, partly because of limited financial reserves to ride out market oscillations.
- The patronal sector lends itself to greater concentration of wealth because it uses less labour and because management is totally separated from labour.
- The family sector has greater environmental sustainability due to greater diversification and managerial flexibility.

In spite of the importance of both of these sectors to society and the development process, governmental policies have consistently given priority to the patronal sector. This can be interpreted as a consequence of the greater political power enjoyed by the patronal sector, which has the greater concentration of economic resources, including not only large agri-ranching landholders but also the industrial sectors of agricultural equipment and inputs. These groups are able to influence election of representatives to the National Congress. In turn, Brazil's federal system gives disproportional weight to the rural states, thus strengthening the power of the rural block in the Congress, whose members in turn occupy high posts in the executive branch.

The 'conservative and selective agricultural modernization process' expelled great numbers of producers from the south and south-east of the country toward the Cerrado and the Amazon (notably Goiás, Mato Grosso and Rondônia) where the landless poor could clear and temporarily occupy frontier areas. However, over time, even in these areas, the same model was reproduced over time, with concentration of landholding and capital-intensive production.

The FAO/INCRA diagnosis shows that the Centre-West region of Brazil, which contains the majority of the Cerrado, is the one that least favours the family segment. Only 43 per cent of the establishments in the region are family operations, while the average for Brazil is 75 per cent. In terms of area, family production occupies 5 per cent of the agricultural establishments in the Centre West, while in the country as a whole it occupies 22 per cent or over four times as much. This difference is due to the initial process of occupation of the region, which was strongly linked to extensive ranching and shifting agriculture,[7] and to the more recent government development programmes, which reinforced the unequal distribution of land and income.

Demographic Trends

Prior to the phase of agricultural modernization, other factors led to profound demographic changes in Central Brazil. The decision to relocate the capital from Rio de Janeiro to Brasília was in itself a reflection of the country's development strategy based on occupation of, and increased economic production from, the interior. As part of this process, the country made massive infrastructure investments: roads penetrated the Amazon (the Belém-Brasília highway) and crossed the interior of Goiás, while the federal capital was transferred to the middle of the Cerrado. On the one hand, this infrastructure reduced costs and increased returns from capital-intensive agriculture; on the other hand, the construction demanded a huge amount of unskilled labour. This meant both a decline in the agricultural population in certain counties at certain times and, at other times and places, an influx of colonists from very different regions. The specifics of these demographic changes are discussed for each of the three case study counties when we address the local context. For now, we can simply state that the cultural diversity (from the forested regions of São Paulo and Minas Gerais and from the arid north-east) and recent occupation led to a great openness toward the new development model that came from the south and south-east. The traditional local population showed some resistance, but it was not sufficient to block the entrance of the new, promoted by official propaganda, while the old model was viewed as backward and archaic.

National Development Strategies and Instruments

At the end of the 1960s, the transformation of the technical basis of agriculture began to figure among the goals of government development plans. In the First National Development Plan (PND I), covering the period from 1972 to 1974, a series of measures were delineated to:

> *'give Brazilian agriculture a system of fiscal and credit support, capable of producing a technological transformation and accelerated strengthening of market agriculture, sensitive to the stimulus of prices; achieve an expansion of area, principally through the occupation of empty spaces, in the Centre West (in the zone of the Cerrado), the North and in the humid valleys of the Northeast.'* (Presidency of the Republic of Brazil, 1970)

The plan targeted the Cerrado region for this development policy due to its extremely favourable socio-environmental characteristics: flat topography facilitating mechanization and great availability of land. In this period, EMBRAPA was created and became a key agent of the technological development that gave scientific support to the exploitation of the Cerrado. For most of its history EMBRAPA has focused on capital-intensive production techniques. In the case of the Cerrado, principal results included the development of soybean varieties suitable for low latitudes and techniques for correcting the soil's infertility and acidity.

PND II (1975–79) delineated effective measures to increase the share of agriculture and ranching in the country's GDP and its contribution to reduction of the public deficit and to increase the sector's net income enough to make it a potential buyer of consumer and capital goods. In this context, PND II presented the following strategies (Salim, 1986):

- expansion of the agricultural frontier toward pioneer regions and incorporation of new areas in the traditional producing regions;
- stimulation of specialization of production, aiming to increase the global efficiency of agriculture; and
- intensive use of scientific and technological development instruments, aiming to maximize productivity.

The principal policy instrument used by the federal government to implement these strategies was the Cerrado Development Programme (POLOCENTRO). This involved subsidized interest rates, incentives for scientific and technological development and for the use of equipment and other agricultural inputs, and development of infrastructure in frontier areas. Also important for expansion of the agricultural frontier were the minimum price guarantee and fuel subsidy policies. The former set a price at which the government committed to purchase agricultural produce that did not achieve the minimum price in the marketplace; this price was the same countrywide, without consideration of the distance to consumer markets or other specific characteristics of each region. The latter subsidized the price of fuel for regions far from refineries and distributors, reducing the cost of transport to urban markets.

PND III (1980–85) aimed to reduce social and regional inequalities, reduce urban over-expansion (especially in the Brasília geo-economic region) and create new opportunities for employment by promoting the development of agriculture and ranching and the expansion of infrastructure. Based on this national programme, the Alto Paraíso programme, which involved seven counties including Alto Paraíso de Goiás, was created with the intention of intervening in an area of 35,500 km² to promote diversification of production and inclusion of small and medium producers, with production still oriented for the export market. This programme resulted in the construction of storage and highway infrastructure, but it did not have the planned effect and the infrastructure was abandoned.

The Federal Constitution of 1988 established regional funds, such as the FCO (Centre-West Fund) as a mechanism to channel a portion of federal income tax revenues to development projects in the Amazon, Cerrado and north-east regions.

In the mid-1980s, when federal subsidies were drastically reduced, the Goiás state government adopted an aggressive policy of attracting industry to the state. The Sociedade de Fomento Mercantil (FOMENTAR) programme financed 70 per cent of the value-added tax for up to 20 years, with 2.4 per cent annual interest and no indexation to correct for inflation. This programme primarily attracted agro-industries in the food and textile sectors, as well as automotive assembly, including such companies as Parmalat, Nestlé, Ceval, Perdigão and Mitsubishi.[8]

Land-use Policy Instruments and Institutions

In Brazil, the sectoral division of policy-making and the separation of responsibilities for planning, agriculture and environment have led to contradictory and competing government policies. Most people still view conservation measures as anti-economic and have very little notion of the interrelated biological and socioeconomic impacts that can result when development initiatives do not adequately address environmental concerns. Less influential government departments generally make and implement environmental policy so that it does not permeate all sectors of public policy, limiting its application and efficacy.

Furthermore, the lack of long-term planning restricts understanding of the consequences and limits development of adequate mitigation measures for environmentally harmful projects. The lack of support for scientific research, especially for the Cerrado biome, which is underprivileged in the distribution of resources for research and conservation actions, also contributes to the lack of understanding.

Besides public policies instituted through specific programmes and projects proposed and carried out by the executive power, other normative and legal instruments regulated by legislative power are specifically directed at the agricultural and environmental sectors. For example, the Brazilian Forest Code (1965) requires each rural property to set aside 20 per cent of its land as a 'Legal Reserve'. With the advent of the Environmental Crime Law (1998), landowners are implementing the generally ignored law by documenting and registering the areas of reserve. In Silvânia, for example, landowners are taking urgent measures, after years of inactivity, to delimit the areas of legal reserve in each rural property. However, no legal way currently exists to ensure that these areas are good quality natural habitat. In the Rio Verde region, a movement of landowners is seeking to transform legal reserves into condominia of protected areas, combining the quotas of several large properties in one location of remnant vegetation, instead of small patches on each property. This alternative, which is not yet permitted by the relevant legislation, would reduce the 'edge effect' and could channel reserves into remnant natural areas, instead of occupying areas that are highly degraded. As long as it does not affect the requirement for permanent preservation areas on steep slopes and along rivers, this would be a positive measure.

Another policy instrument related to the appropriation of natural resources in Brazil is the Rural Land Tax (ITR). The new ITR law, promulgated in 1994, could have mixed results for the environment. The area subject to taxation no longer includes permanent preservation areas, the required area of legal reserve, or areas of ecological interest, if so recognized by a competent environmental agency. This encourages the creation of private nature reserves. On the other hand, the new law also institutes a land-use intensity factor to determine the tax rate – the more intensively the land is used, the lower the tax. This could promote more intensive land-use practices, including land leasing, that would have a greater negative impact on natural resources.

Since 1992, a bill to define the national system of conservation units, proposed by the executive branch, has been pending in the national Congress. Various meetings and revisions at several levels have been conducted to reach consensus on concepts, restrictions and criteria for different management categories of conservation unit but, as of early 1999, the bill was still awaiting final approval. There is an urgent need for a specific conservation policy that effectively establishes protected areas, especially in the Cerrado.

Various organizations and international agencies work in the Cerrado, among them WWF, UNDP and the GEF. Nevertheless, no integrated strategy has been created to ensure coordination and efficiency in the work of these agencies. Another problem is the difficulty of promoting a multi-disciplinary dialogue among those who work in the environmental arena. Professionals in the socioeconomic area have little knowledge of ecology, while biologists tend to attach little importance to socioeconomic factors that put pressure on biodiversity. The lack of integration of different sets of information on the Cerrado limits the efficiency of the few conservation measures that are taken. The few databases belonging to government and other agencies are little known and do not communicate with each other.

LOCAL CONTEXT

We have briefly explored contextual factors such as international markets, economic relations and cultural, political and demographic trends related to Brazil's Centre-West region. The principal result of all these has been a national development strategy, in place since the 1960s, that promotes a selective and concentrating agricultural development model, supported by massive investments in infrastructure, financial resources, subsidies and scientific support. This model favours capital-intensive production of commodities for export to the detriment of family farming.

Within this context, we now explore the results in terms of the actual dynamics of agricultural and economic development, social change and environmental degradation. This will be done on a comparative basis using the three case study counties: Rio Verde, which represents the patronal agricultural model; Silvânia, which represents the family agriculture model; and Alto Paraíso de Goiás, which followed an alternative pathway not representative of either of the predominant patterns. The international and national contexts are, of course, the same for each county and, with some variation of timing and intensity, the credit, subsidy and infrastructure policies used to promote the patronal agriculture model were also applied to each. However, the specific environmental, geographic and social characteristics of each county have acted as a filter, modifying the results generated by these driving forces.

Geographic Context

Rio Verde is located in the south-west Goiás micro-region, near the border with the states of Minas Gerais and Mato Grosso. Of the three counties, it is the most accessible to other economic centres. Thus, Rio Verde has been influenced by the economic dynamism of Minas Gerais since the beginning of the century and has served as a pathway to Mato Grosso, the most remote portion of Brazil's Centre-West. In addition to its favourable location, Rio Verde has significant deposits of lime, the key input in the new agricultural technology that allows high productivity of grains on the Cerrado's acidic soils. These two factors made Rio Verde ideally suited to take advantage of the public policies launched in the 1970s and 1980s; the result was the transformation of Rio Verde into the great granary of Goiás and an important regional economic centre.

Silvânia, having emerged as a mining village in the 18th century, passed through periods of growth and decline as a result of historical and political changes that altered the axis of economic dynamism of the county, leaving it in a marginal position. The construction of the new state capital, Goiânia, in 1935, reoriented economic activity to the south and south-west of Goiás. The construction of Brasília, inaugurated in 1960, attracted the economically active population from throughout Brazil, including nearby Silvânia, which saw a significant decline in agricultural production at the end of the 1950s.

The northern region of Goiás, where Alto Paraíso is located, is characterized by human poverty and environmental conditions inappropriate for agriculture or ranching. Geographically more isolated, its high elevation and rocky soils limit cultivation.

Demographic Trends

Population growth rates in Goiás have been well above the Brazilian average, due to the influx of migrants from other states. The analysis of population growth rates of the counties studied (Figure 6.2) leads to the identification of two distinct patterns. The first pattern is exemplified by Rio Verde which, during the period of most significant colonization of the state (prior to 1950), was more attractive to immigrants than other counties. After this period, municipal growth stabilized at around 3 per cent per year, maintaining net immigration. The county's population doubled between 1950 and 1960 and in the next twenty years jumped from over 40,000 to almost 75,000, a growth of about 85 per cent. The second pattern, observed in Silvânia and Alto Paraíso, shows a loss of population from 1960 to 1970 due to the proximity of Brasília, and a return to increasing rates of growth in the 1980s, especially in Alto Paraíso, which far surpassed the state average.

The reasons for the resumption of population growth in Silvânia are very different from Alto Paraíso. Silvânia resumed its economic growth with the rise of small family farms, promoted by the cooperative movement at the end of the 1980s. Alto Paraíso, on the other hand, attracts groups of mystics and

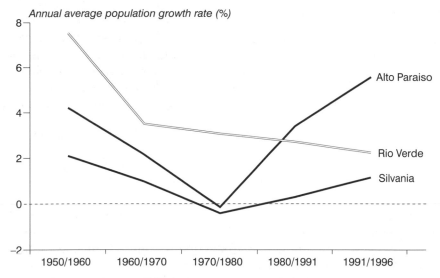

Source: Calculated from the IBGE Statistical Yearbook, 1996

Figure 6.2 *Mean Annual Population Growth Rates (1950/1960 to 1991/1996)*

environmentalists who see the region as a special place. Alto Paraíso had the highest mean population growth rate in the period 1980–96, with growth in the order of 3.8 to 5.6 per cent per year between 1991 and 1996, much higher than the other counties. For this latest period, immigration accounted for a large part of the growth rate – Alto Paraíso received 995 immigrants, corresponding to 18 per cent of the total population in 1996, more than half of whom came from other states (IBGE, 1996).

In Alto Paraíso the creation of the Chapada dos Veadeiros National Park introduced some legal obstacles to the development of certain economic activities in the park's buffer zone.[9] It also promoted a great influx of visitors, stimulating ecotourism, which seems to be the area's current economic vocation. With the implementation of plans to promote tourism in Brasília, Alto Paraíso will probably get even more visitors; thus the present rate of population growth may continue for some time, requiring caution in the planning of ecotourism and urban infrastructure. In 1980 the urban population was just 20 per cent of the county, but jumped to about 60 per cent in 1991.

Variation in the distribution between rural and urban populations was more accentuated in Rio Verde than in the other counties. The urban portion of the population changed rapidly, starting in the 1970s when the commercial character of modern agriculture developing in Rio Verde caused the displacement of the low-income rural population to the periphery of urban centres. Currently, although Rio Verde is heavily dependent on agriculture and ranching, the population is 90 per cent urban. Silvânia maintains an equilibrium between rural and urban populations.

Evolution of Land Use

In the 1970s the Rio Verde region was chosen as a priority area for POLOCEN-TRO, the set of public policies intended to transfer modern grain agriculture to the Cerrado. At that time Silvânia and Alto Paraíso were in areas of secondary priority. Cerrado development policy incentives targeted these two counties later than Rio Verde and with a view to controlling the population pressure on Brasília. Other political factors also contributed to an unequal distribution of public resources and infrastructure; these all contributed to Rio Verde achieving a more effective and rapid development process.

Figure 6.3 shows the increase of the areas of annual and permanent crops and of natural and planted pasture, relative to the size of the counties, from 1960 to present.[10] Being relative values, they show the rhythm of change and the temporal differences between the expansion of annual crops and planted pastures, identified with the advance of commercial, or patronal, agriculture that adopted new, capital-intensive production techniques (such as mechanization and the use of fertilizers and improved varieties). The figures also show the decline of natural pasture that is usually associated with family agriculture.

The advance of annual crops in Rio Verde began in the 1960s. Coinciding with the initiation of POLOCENTRO in 1975, the growth curve for annual crops and planted pastures became much steeper at the same time that the area of natural pastures declined, indicating a marked intensification in the use of land. The decline observed between 1985 and 1996 reflects the fiscal crisis of the Brazilian government, when resources for agriculture declined substantially; credit declined starting in 1980 and the minimum price policy was effectively abolished in 1989.

In Silvânia the advance of annual crops started in 1975, but the decline in native pastures was less rapid than in Rio Verde. The analysis of the other curves indicates that new areas were cleared for agriculture and natural pastures were replaced by planted pastures. The establishment of the FCO by the 1988 Federal Constitution enabled the establishment of associations of small producers, who were financed to obtain machinery and implements, expanding agriculture but within the family model.

In Alto Paraíso, the process came much later. Annual crops increased after 1980, but permanent crops also increased in this period – the result of the Alto Paraíso programme under PND III, which had as one of its principles the development of horticulture in the surroundings of Brasília. The area of natural pastures increased significantly between 1970 and 1975, declined in 1980, then stabilized. Soybean production is limited to a few plateau areas on large properties.

The intensity of occupation is indicated by the scale of each graph. In Rio Verde the area in annual crops reached 25 per cent of the county in 1996; in Silvânia it reached 12 per cent; and in Alto Paraíso 2.6 per cent. The different sizes of the counties and the areas dedicated to cultivation are shown above in Table 6.1.

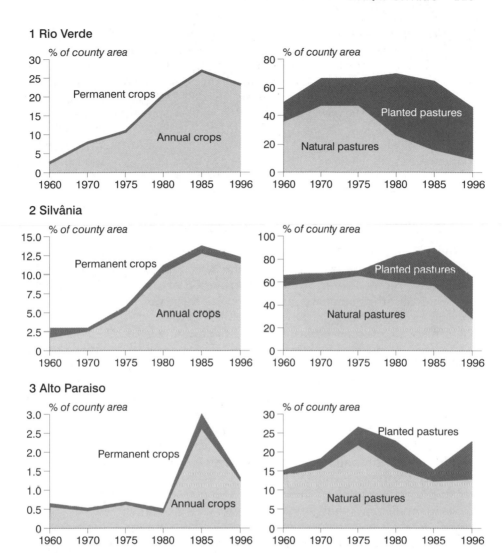

Source: Based on data from the IBGE Agricultural Censuses of 1950, 1960, 1970, 1975, 1980, 1985 and 1996

Figure 6.3 *Increase in the Area Occupied by Temporary and Permanent Crops, and Natural and Cultivated Pastures in Rio Verde, Silvânia and Alto Paraíso de Goiás (1960–96)*

The absolute values show more clearly the reality of each county: annual crops occupy 259,000 ha in Rio Verde, 5.6 times greater than Silvânia, where they occupy 46,000 ha, and 32 times greater than the area of annual crops in Alto Paraíso, which is just 8000 ha. Ranching occupies 411,000 ha in Rio Verde, 168,000 ha in Silvânia and 80,000 ha in Alto Paraíso. The size of the cattle herd in Rio Verde in 1996 was approximately 422,000, while Silvânia had 127,000, and Alto Paraíso 18,000. These data illustrate the economic inequality of the three counties; Rio Verde is far ahead in terms of concentration of capital.

These land-use dynamics are a direct result of the national development strategy as applied to the Cerrado. The changes that occurred in the 1970s and 1980s were a direct reflection of the three PNDs and the accompanying policy instruments such as POLOCENTRO, with its agricultural credit subsidies, the PGPM and the unitary fuel price. The specific conditions and processes in each county are a result of the differences in their geographic characteristics, which affected how the policy instruments were applied. In the following section we will also see the interaction between agricultural development and socio-cultural differences.

Social Changes Linked to Land-use Changes

In Silvânia as well as Rio Verde, the advance of the new agricultural model appropriated large areas of natural habitat for commercial activities. In Rio Verde this process also involved a redistribution of land tenure, with small properties absorbed into fewer, larger properties that were more economically efficient under the new production model. The number of agricultural establishments with less than 100 ha decreased significantly in the 1970s.

In spite of the rapid advance of annual crops and planted pastures in Silvânia, the drastic changes in the social relations of production that occurred in Rio Verde were not nearly as intensive in Silvânia. Occupation by modern agriculture, along the technological and commercial lines dictated by the agricultural credit policies, occurred in some parts of the county, while some small family farms, large traditional ranches and small commercial farms survived. This may be a reflection of the fact that Silvânia's population is more deeply rooted culturally because of the area's lengthy occupation and the existence of traditional communities.

In Rio Verde the social relations of production changed dramatically when the new production model demanded more qualified labour such as tractor drivers, machine operators and farm or ranch administrators at the expense of traditional labourers. These old ranch hands, sharecroppers and subsistence farmers became migratory workers who moved from town to country, based on the seasonal demand for unskilled labour. Furthermore, the appreciation of land values caused by the arrival of new entrepreneurs led to the exodus of subsistence producers, who moved to the periphery of urban areas.

The new model also introduced the figure of the capitalist tenant farmer who rents rather than owns farmland, and thus has a shorter-term relationship to the land and acts much more within the logic of capitalist exploitation – seeing the land as an inexhaustible resource that can be recuperated with fertilizer and other agricultural inputs. These tenant farmers are commonly people from other regions of Brazil who have difficulty understanding the Cerrado as a font of biodiversity and natural riches.

In Silvânia a movement developed to resist changes to the family production system. The county is currently experiencing an unmatched level of small farmer associations that is attracting the attention of national and international institutions and is supported by the federal government (EMBRAPA), the state government (EMATER and CAMPPO[11]), the UNDP New Frontiers Project and various NGOs. The principles for development of family agriculture in this associative movement are consistent with the National Programme for the Development of Family Agriculture, created by the federal government for this purpose.

Another relevant social change has been land tenure concentration, principally in Alto Paraíso and Rio Verde. Land tenure concentration in Goiás is related to the predominance of extensive ranching and to historical and political factors, in particular the advance of commercial agriculture, that have reinforced inequalities. Although the mean is not the best form of measurement, it does serve as a fitting illustration of inequalities. Silvânia's agricultural establishments have an average area of 122 ha, while in Rio Verde the average area is 323 ha and in Alto Paraíso it is 420 ha.

The data on establishments under 100 ha and those greater than 1000 ha reflect the land tenure concentration in the three counties (Table 6.2). While the establishments under 100 ha correspond to the greatest number of establishments, they occupy small areas. On the other hand, establishments with more than 1000 ha are fewer but occupy large areas.

Table 6.2 *Agricultural Establishments: Numbers versus Area*

| County | Establishments <100 ha | | Establishments >1000 ha | |
	% of establishments	% area	% of establishments	% area
Rio Verde	48	6.3	7.0	49
Silvânia	71	20.0	1.2	18
Alto Paraíso	55	2.8	9.6	69

The Special Case of Alto Paraíso

Two contradictory policies were initiated in Alto Paraíso in the 1980s: the first one, the Programme for Integrated Development of Alto Paraíso, was a pro-development programme that involved seven counties and sought to promote development of the region and reduce pressure on Brasília. Also in the 1980s, the Nipo-Brazilian Cooperation Programme for Development of the Cerrado (PRODECER) implemented the Buriti Alto colonization project, involving Alto Paraíso and another three counties.[12] The second policy was conservationist, including the regularization and effective establishment of Chapada dos Veadeiros National Park, which later, with the advance of Brazilian environmental policy, generated some legal obstacles to the establishment of certain economic activities in its buffer zone. This fact, combined with the very dynamic and environmentally-oriented migration to the region and the county's environmental conditions, may have contributed to the failure of the economic policies.

The development projects did not have the reach or effectiveness that was planned, although some large landholders did develop soybean cultivation, as well as semi-intensive and extensive ranching. The infrastructure developed in Alto Paraíso to support the production of fruits and grains was abandoned and the county remained economically stagnant. The reasons for the failure of the Alto Paraíso projects are not very clear. Possibly the remote location and the lack of an entrepreneurial class in the city are among the reasons, another being the resistance of various sectors of local society, including environmentalists, politicians and mystics.[13]

In Alto Paraíso the presence of the Chapada dos Veadeiros National Park and of various legends and beliefs about the region led to the immigration of mystics and environmentalists. Created in 1961 as Tocantins National Park, since it reached the river of the same name, the park had an area of 500,000 ha. Later it was renamed and the area was reduced, first to 172,000 ha and then to 60,000 ha. It is the only 'indirect use' conservation area in the region: the direct use of natural resources except for educational, recreational and scientific purposes is not permitted.

The failure of development projects in Alto Paraíso contributed enormously to the conservation of biodiversity in the county. More recently Alto Paraíso began to attract groups interested in its pristine nature and mystical location. Under a new development model based on ecotourism, with the Chapada dos Veadeiros National Park as the principal attraction, population growth has exceeded that of Rio Verde and Silvânia for the past 15 years. This development model involves restaurants, hotels, private nature reserves and a local association with over 100 guides, and primarily benefits recent migrants with interest and capacity to exploit such opportunities. However, several initiatives are seeking to expand the benefits, including vocational training efforts and small economic enterprises aimed at, for example, producing specialty products for the tourist trade. This process has contributed to the conservation of native habitat and, consequently, of the native fauna and flora.

In spite of this, Alto Paraíso is the principal producer of charcoal in the state of Goiás, an activity that generated US$91 million from the production of 912,000 tons of charcoal in the 1995–96 production season. Nevertheless, production comes from just five establishments; two of them have an area greater than 2000 ha and the other three have less than 200 ha.

Impacts of Agricultural Development on the Cerrado

The major impacts of agriculture and ranching on the Cerrado can be summed up as deforestation, destruction of habitat, alteration of the natural fire regime and introduction of exotic species, leading to the loss of biodiversity. Agrochemical pollution, erosion and the development of waterways extend these threats to aquatic ecosystems as well.

Capital-intensive agriculture – the patronal model – has the greatest environmental impact on a given area because of the high use of energy and agrochemicals, and mechanization which can lead to soil erosion. In addition, these agro-ecosystems virtually eliminate species diversity and bring a further threat with the introduction of genetically modified organisms that could escape and invade natural communities. Planted pastures have an intermediate impact, since the use of inputs is not as great. Natural pastures have a lower impact on a given area, since the cattle coexist with native vegetation, but many years of overgrazing and frequent use of fire will eventually lead to substantial degradation characterized by eroded soils and a low diversity of species.

At present the Centre-West produces 50 per cent of Brazil's soybeans, the product that was the driving force in the occupation of the Cerrado and is now Brazil's second leading export. Initially considered as the major direct cause of habitat destruction, we now understand that soybean monoculture has more indirect than direct effects on the Cerrado, since it occupies less than 15 per cent of the area of agricultural establishments of the Centre-West, while ranching occupies more than 70 per cent. Nevertheless, the economic development induced by soybean cultivation promoted the development of infrastructure, growth of cities and a series of impacts that resulted in environmental degradation.

The need to reduce costs and increase competitiveness of soybean cultivation recently led the federal government to define three export corridors within the Cerrado region. These corridors involve development of roads and waterways, projects that will cause major direct and indirect environmental impacts. Development of waterways requires modification of river channels and elimination of cataracts, while roads affect waterways and fauna that pass through or reside in the areas of influence. Indirect effects may be even greater, principally because access to remote areas promotes extensive land uses rather than intensive use of the most favourable areas, thus allowing for conservation of others.

The National Institute of Space Research (INPE) carried out a remote sensing study to estimate the integrity of native vegetation in the Cerrado, using primarily Landsat/TM images from 1992 and 1993 (Mantovani and Pereira, 1998). Only 35 per cent of native vegetation was detected without signs of human activity. The best preserved areas were where the states of Piauí, Maranhão and Tocantins come together, the region near the border of Tocantins and Mato Grosso and the Parecis Plateau (Chapada) between Mato Grosso and Rondônia. The areas of greatest degradation were found in the states of São Paulo, Goiás and Mato Grosso do Sul and on the border between São Paulo and Paraná.

The prospect of increasing profitability of soybean cultivation in remote areas of Cerrado, as a result of the expansion of transport infrastructure, threatens the few areas that are still relatively intact. Given the great species richness of the region as a whole and the endemisms that occur among different Cerrado areas, there is an urgent need to identify priority areas for conservation.

CONCLUSIONS

The national development strategies of the 1970s and 1980s were highly successful in promoting expansion of agriculture in the Cerrado. Soybeans are now Brazil's second largest export and both extensive and intensive cattle ranching occur throughout the region.

Our analysis shows that the ultimate root cause of this process was Brazil's pressing need to generate foreign exchange, first to cover the balance-of-payments deficit and later because of the debt crisis. This led national policy-makers to target agricultural modernization and intensification as solutions. The need for foreign exchange, combined with the political influence of large rural landholders, led policy-makers to favour the patronal (capital-intensive) agricultural model, which was seen as the most suitable to produce commodities for export.

The high international price for soybeans and the development of new agricultural technology, which allowed high productivity of grain monocultures in spite of the acidity and infertility of the Cerrado soils, were key enabling factors. In addition, the Brazilian cultural ideology of the period saw the Cerrado as a wasteland, nature as an obstacle to be overcome, and the Brazilian interior as a virgin territory ripe for exploitation – conservation and the possibility of wiping out an entire biome were not considered at the time. The drive to occupy the Cerrado was linked to the transfer of the national capital to Brasília and the development of associated transport infrastructure, which also facilitated agricultural expansion in the region.

The direct causes of agricultural expansion in the Cerrado were the national development strategies (three PNDs, POLOCENTRO) and the related policy instruments: subsidized agricultural credit, infrastructure investments, a minimum price guarantee policy and subsidized fuel prices for remote areas.

However, the results of these driving forces were not uniform throughout the region. For the three case study counties, we found that environmental, economic and cultural factors, such as topography, proximity to sources of lime and consumer centres, availability of infrastructure and presence of resistant social groups, determined the degree of agricultural expansion and the precise form which this expansion took.

Rio Verde was transformed into a regional agro-industrial centre. This county was both accessible to markets and had a local source of lime. In addition, the flat topography was highly favourable to mechanization and monoculture cultivation. These factors produced a positive feedback. The national policies to stimulate agricultural expansion in the Cerrado were magnified when Rio Verde was chosen as a priority area for POLOCENTRO and for infrastructure development. The result was intensive agricultural development, rampant habitat loss, extensive erosion and use of agrochemicals. Social disruption also occurred as the number of properties under 100 ha was dramatically reduced and farmers became labourers and urban dwellers. The future will see more of the same: Rio Verde is considered one of the most profitable areas for soybean cultivation and thus will be favoured by future infrastructure investments to create export corridors. Massive agro-industrial investments are already underway, with a US$500 million project integrating production of fertilizer, grains for animal feed and pork and poultry production.

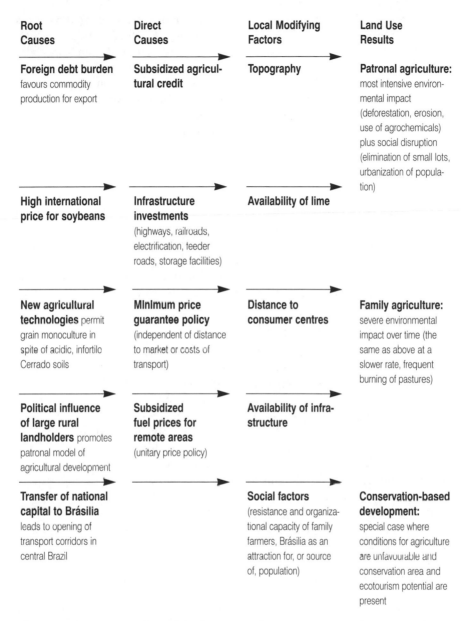

Root Causes	Direct Causes	Local Modifying Factors	Land Use Results
Foreign debt burden favours commodity production for export	**Subsidized agricultural credit**	**Topography**	**Patronal agriculture:** most intensive environmental impact (deforestation, erosion, use of agrochemicals) plus social disruption (elimination of small lots, urbanization of population)
High international price for soybeans	**Infrastructure investments** (highways, railroads, electrification, feeder roads, storage facilities)	**Availability of lime**	
New agricultural technologies permit grain monoculture in spite of acidic, infortilo Cerrado soils	**Minimum price guarantee policy** (independent of distance to market or costs of transport)	**Distance to consumer centres**	**Family agriculture:** severe environmental impact over time (the same as above at a slower rate, frequent burning of pastures)
Political influence of large rural landholders promotes patronal model of agricultural development	**Subsidized fuel prices for remote areas** (unitary price policy)	**Availability of infrastructure**	
Transfer of national capital to Brásilia leads to opening of transport corridors in central Brazil		**Social factors** (resistance and organizational capacity of family farmers, Brásilia as an attraction for, or source of, population)	**Conservation-based development:** special case where conditions for agriculture are unfavourable and conservation area and ecotourism potential are present

Figure 6.4 *Conceptual Model of Root and Direct Causes of Biodiversity Loss*

Silvânia also underwent agricultural expansion and widespread conversion of habitat. However, physical and geographic factors were not as favourable: the topography is not as flat, there is no local source of lime and consumer markets are further away. As a result, Silvânia was considered a secondary area for POLOCENTRO and agricultural development was more diversified – intensive agriculture in the most favourable areas, both natural and planted pastures and some tree crops. Social factors also strongly affected this process. Proximity to Brasília led to a loss of economically active population, especially in the 1970s. However, Silvânia also has a deep-rooted local culture, and advances in organization (cooperatives and associations) by small producers reinvigorated family agriculture. The county is seen today as a model for family agriculture and the cooperative movement.

In the same period that Rio Verde and Silvânia were undergoing dramatic transformation, Alto Paraíso remained economically stagnant. Its far more remote location and rugged topography made agricultural intensification economically unviable despite the fact that the incentive programmes were also applied to this region. In fact, several large-scale development projects were implemented, but they failed and were abandoned. In recent years an alternative development model has emerged, based on ecotourism and newcomers seeking quality of life and alternative lifestyles. The Chapada dos Veadeiros National Park is a key element in this process, which is bringing economic growth along with risks of degradation due to overuse and questions as to the breadth of the local population that it is benefiting.

Future Prospects for the Cerrado

The three case study counties show three development alternatives for the region: patronal agriculture, family agriculture and an approach tied to nature conservation. Public policies strongly promoted the first model, but it was only fully implemented in the favourable location and physical environment of Rio Verde. Silvânia generally evolved along similar lines, but the location and physical conditions were not as favourable (probably closer to the norm for the region) so the transformations occurred more slowly and incompletely. Environmental degradation is very high in Rio Verde. In the case of Silvânia, environmental degradation has been mitigated somewhat by less intensive occupation, but the trends are certainly in the same direction. However, with a concerted programme including effective implementation of the legal reserves required on each property, low-impact agriculture, and other conservation initiatives, the Silvânia model could be made much more compatible with biodiversity protection. This, in turn, would contribute to long-term sustainability of the development process and would bring significant economic benefits in terms of income distribution and social welfare.

The Alto Paraíso model is a special case. It would not be feasible to directly copy this model throughout the region. However, the experience should provide elements that would be relevant to a mixed development pathway along the lines we have suggested above: the family model of Silvânia could be modified to increase sustainability and social welfare by incorporating ecotourism, extractive activities, community participation, environmental education and protected areas as demonstrated in Alto Paraíso.

It is clear that the tendency of public policy is to invest massively in the patronal model. This means building infrastructure, principally to facilitate transport, and providing credit and developing technology that targets production of export commodities in input-intensive farming systems. From the environmental perspective, this means that the agricultural frontier is rapidly penetrating the last few relatively intact portions of the biome. The fact that only 0.6 per cent of the biome is in federal protected areas exacerbates this situation.

Our analysis indicates that the Rio Verde model is economically viable in the most favourable areas and will bring significant growth and income. While the sustainability and social welfare benefits of the patronal model may be questioned, there is little doubt that it will dominate the regions where its economics are overwhelmingly favourable. The question that remains open is whether there will also be space for the alternative models revealed by the Silvânia and Alto Paraíso cases. With careful planning and targeted investment, these models could coexist. Will public policy promote this coexistence or continue to favour only the patronal model? In the latter case, we expect intensive agriculture to be successful in some areas; in other areas it will be economically unsuccessful, but nevertheless act as an engine for environmental destruction and social disruption, reaching the remainder of the biome in a very few years.

RECOMMENDATIONS

The main recommendation is for the development of a more diversified development model for the Cerrado that includes intensive agriculture in the most favourable areas, a more diversified family agricultural model, and includes conservation as a third general approach to development for the region.

This proposal requires regional planning and zoning in order to channel the alternative forms of development to the most appropriate areas and incentives for the optimal implementation of each of the three different models.

Recommendations for Regional Planning

- Develop a register of research centres, databases, public authorities, NGOs and associations of rural producers and cooperatives that work in the Cerrado.

- Publicize the importance of the Cerrado biome in terms of biodiversity and the results of research on the environmental impacts of resource exploitation and infrastructure development in the Cerrado.

- Disseminate the case studies presented in this report, especially among environmental professionals and institutions, emphasizing the relevance and interrelationship between socioeconomic factors and threats to biodiversity.

- Promote better coordination among those setting priorities for management and conservation of the Cerrado.

- Hold meetings of stakeholders to develop an integrated strategic plan for the Cerrado, culminating in the preparation of an agreed zoning for land use and development in the region that orients credit policy, infrastructure development and pilot projects.

- Monitor the actions of government and the private sector in terms of infrastructure development, agricultural credit and major agricultural, ranching and tourism projects in the Cerrado.

- Ensure that environmental regulations are rigorously enforced for all major infrastructure projects, including preparation of environmental impact reports that fully consider indirect and cumulative impacts.

- Undertake a detailed study of the degree of implementation of legal reserves in the Cerrado, as well as proposals to change legal requirements to maximize the conservation impact of these areas; include analysis of the feasibility and benefits of establishing condominia of legal reserves.

- Map the distribution of legally required permanent preservation areas (steep slopes, watercourses and riparian vegetation and land at high altitudes) and carry out field verification to ensure that these areas are respected.

- Study the impact of recent changes in rural land tax on land use and habitat protection in the Cerrado, and propose measures to improve this policy instrument.

- Carry out biogeographic and land tenure analyses, and take urgent measures to increase the size and number of protected areas in the Cerrado, focusing on the regions with large blocks of remnant natural habitat.

- Promote expansion of the 'ecological value-added tax' that takes environmental considerations into account (especially the presence of protected areas) in the distribution of tax revenues among municipalities.

Recommendations for Specific Land-use Alternatives

- Develop standards and enforce regulations for the safe and limited use of pesticides.

- Monitor quality of ground and surface water, documenting impacts of siltation and pesticides, including possible health effects.

- Promote alternatives for sustainable development and the strengthening of family agriculture and communities extracting natural resources and test these in pilot projects.

- Promote ecotourism and rural tourism, as well as establishment of private nature reserves, and test these in pilot projects.

- Promote certification mechanisms for organic produce and sustainably produced charcoal. Set up special market channels near urban areas for family farmers who practise low-impact, diversified agriculture.

- Set guidelines for the form and substance of rural extension compatible with environmental sustainability in the Cerrado.

- Incorporate environmental concerns in the credit policy of official development banks to ensure that agricultural investments are consistent with the regional zoning for different development models, guarantee that pollution prevention measures are taken, and that legal reserves and permanent preservation areas are respected.

Chapter 7

Cameroon: Bushmeat and Wildlife Trade

Research team: This study was prepared by the team leader
Dr Fondo Sikod (University of Yaoundé II), *Estherine Lisinge,*
Dr John Mope-Simo and *Dr Steve Gartlan* (all with the
WWF-Cameroon Programme Office)

Summary: The bushmeat and wildlife trade in Cameroon is a growing threat to biodiversity. The development of a network of commercial hunters and markets is closely linked with Cameroon's dependence on primary product exports, including agricultural products and timber, which has led to land clearing and road construction without relieving local poverty.

The forests of Cameroon are extremely rich in flora and fauna. However, as in other tropical countries, Cameroon's biodiversity is under siege. The causes and the patterns that we describe are very typical, not only of Cameroon but also of the whole African continent and elsewhere. Two principal causes of biodiversity loss are examined in this study: the wildlife and bushmeat trades. The terms 'wildlife' and 'wildlife product' are used in this study to refer to any wild animal or bird that is caught and sold, alive or dead, and the skin, teeth, skull, horn, tusk or any part of the body sold. The term 'bushmeat' refers to any species of animal or bird that is shot, speared or trapped and sold for public consumption either fresh or preserved. In Yaoundé, Cameroon's capital city, an inventory of the four main bushmeat markets (Baillon, 1995) revealed a monthly arrival of 70 to 90 tons of bushmeat, with an average of 2.3 tons per day. The meat arrives in Yaoundé either by road (20 per cent) or by train (80 per cent).

Multiple root causes drive the wildlife and bushmeat trades. The principal driver is a complex of consequences of what might be loosely termed 'development' and the need to meet 'modern' consumption demands from a natural-resource based economy (logging, mining) or from primary agricultural production (coffee, cocoa, oil palm, banana). This takes place against a background of subsistence needs, high human population growth and significant economic decline.

The bushmeat and wildlife trades are examined at two different sites, Mount Cameroon and the south-east forests (Figure 7.1). Mount Cameroon's exploitation and development has been particularly intense over the last century. Mount Cameroon is close to the coast, easily accessible, located in an area of fertile volcanic soil, and adjacent to large population centres, notably Limbe and Douala, with good communications. In contrast, the south-east forests have been exploited for only the last two or three decades. They are remote from major population centres, have poor communications and, until very recently, have been inaccessible. Soils are infertile and human population densities have remained low. However, a course of development similar to that followed in Mount Cameroon is underway in these forests. Mount Cameroon may well present a picture of the forests of the south-east two or three decades from now.

DESCRIPTION OF THE STUDY AREAS

Mount Cameroon

Mount Cameroon is a biodiversity 'hotspot' located on Cameroon's western coast (Figure 7.2). The antiquity and isolation of the forests and a range of ecological formations from 200 to 2500 m above sea level are highly significant features. Mount Cameroon is thought to be the only place in West and Central Africa where the natural vegetation is effectively undisturbed from near sea level to the subalpine level (Environmental Resources Management, 1998). The area forms part of a Pleistocene refuge of the Lower Guinea Forest. The mountain shelters over 210 species of birds, eight of which are threatened

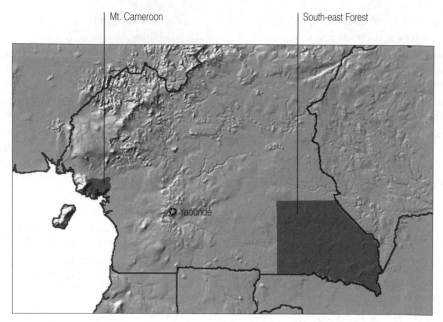

Figure 7.1 *Map of Cameroon Showing Location of Study Areas*

or near threatened. However, populations of large mammals have largely disappeared. The mean annual rainfall at Debundsha, on the west coast, is 10–12 m, making it the second wettest place on earth. The monthly temperature at sea level varies from 24 to 35°C, with the highest temperatures occurring in March and April.

The west-coast region is a cosmopolitan area inhabited by both Cameroonians and foreigners. The foreign community is significant, with Ghanaians, Beninois and Nigerians constituting the most important groups. The Cameroonian community includes the indigenous Bakweri, who have been settled there for generations. Though their main activity is fishing, many are involved in subsistence farming, the main crops being cocoyam, cassava and plantain.

A highly significant feature of the west coast in the context of this study is a parastatal institution, the Cameroon Development Corporation (CDC). CDC is an agro-industrial enterprise covering some 60,000 ha in the area, producing rubber, palm oil and bananas in the lowlands and low slopes between the Atlantic Ocean and the mountain. Significant external labour, including Nigerians, was brought in from the North-West Province to work in these plantations. This immigrant labour is involved in forest resource exploitation, including logging and hunting.

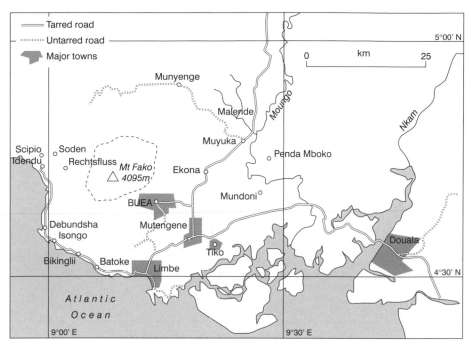

Figure 7.2 *The Mount Cameroon Study Area*

South-east Forests

The south-east study area lies in the Boumba and Ngoko Division of the Eastern Province (Figure 7.3) The vegetation is lowland forest of the Congo Basin with a high proportion of endemic flora and fauna. However, unlike Mount Cameroon, the south-east forests still contain significant populations of large mammals, including forest elephant, lowland gorilla, forest buffalo and bongo.

The region has an equatorial climate with an annual rainfall of 1.6 m. There are two wet and two dry seasons. The mean monthly temperature is 25–26°C and fluctuates little. The vegetation of the region is a mosaic of semi-deciduous, evergreen and swamp forest types. The topography is gently undulating, with valleys and ridges among flat basins, ranging in elevation from 300 to 700 m. Soils are red and red-brown clays with little organic material and are relatively infertile.

The local peoples of the south-east are the Bangando and Bakwele ethnic groups of Bantu origin and the semi-sedentary forager–farmer Baka pygmies, a small number of Muslim traders and other non-indigenous peoples who mainly work for the logging companies. Tribal groups and sometimes even families have members in more than one country. This facilitates movement and exchange between peoples of adjacent countries. Hunters pass from one country to the next without leaving what they consider as tribal land. Bushmeat has

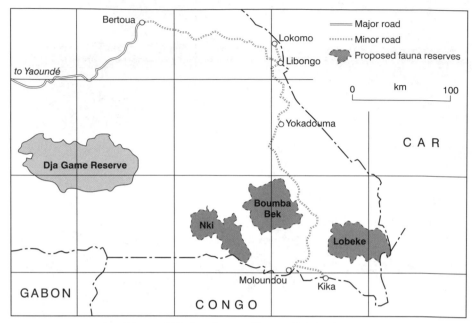

Figure 7.3 *South-east Forest Study Area*

always played an important role in human life in the Central African forest. Pygmy tribes such as the Baka still maintain elements of the hunter-gatherer way of life, which are increasingly being put to commercial use.

Intensive logging in the region started in the early 1970s. Because of the poor road network at the time, the logging companies constructed their bases along rivers for easy removal of timber. Over time and with the construction of roads, logs are now removed principally by road to the distant port of Douala. Five logging companies operate concessions and sawmills in the region and export unprocessed logs. The timber industry provides jobs for some 2000 people. Many of these workers are involved in bushmeat hunting and the timber trucks provide transport of bushmeat to distant urban centres.

RESEARCH METHODOLOGY

The major pressures on biodiversity of importance in this study are easily observed: high human population growth, economic decline and increasing levels of poverty and rapid escalation in exploitation of the country's natural resources. It is assumed that these factors are influencing the environment and promoting the loss of biodiversity. The problem is to determine the exact linkages and determine the relative importance of the various factors and of interactions among them. Because any individual behaviour can be the result of multiple causes, and because not all causes may be in the conscious mind of an individual, the process of working out these linkages is extremely complex. Initial hypotheses included the following:

- Development is the main root cause of biodiversity loss.
- The institutional setting of Cameroon facilitates wildlife harvesting, which leads to biodiversity loss.
- The economic environment of Cameroon has led to increased wildlife harvesting.
- Poverty is a root cause of the over-harvesting of wildlife.
- International demand for wildlife and wildlife products is a root cause of biodiversity loss.

Many different types of primary data were collected, using line-transect data on the distribution and intensity of hunting, participatory evaluations, questionnaires, interviews, checklists and discussions. Very little official data are available in these matters and official data that do exist, for example on the export of wildlife through the principal ports, are unreliable.

The principal secondary data source for the south-east was a two-year study on the spatial distribution and intensity of hunting in the western Dja Reserve (Muuchal and Ngandjui, 1997) and, for the Mount Cameroon region, a socio-economic survey (Ambrose et al, 1988). Data on the dynamics of the bushmeat trade and in particular the markets and trading links are unpublished WWF material (Baillon, 1995), supplemented by another unpublished report on the commercialization of hunting in the south-east (Zouya-Mimbang, 1998).

Analysis of information collected was carried out through a discussion and flow analysis of the linkages, both lateral and sequential, to bring out the causal relations that lead to biodiversity loss. At the local level, supply analysis and traditional linkages to nature were important. The introduction of markets brings in regional, national and international scales of analysis. The traditional situation breaks down and the driving forces change. Market and demand analysis, looking at such forces as income, poverty, tastes and preferences, and substitution, become important at this level of analysis. The importance and influence of socio-cultural variables diminish as the analysis moves from the proximate or local scale to the regional, national and global scales.

Almost all elements of this study would benefit from further research in order to better document the phenomena and to establish the causal linkages with more precision. The fact that both principal activities are essentially informal and illegal make accurate data collection particularly difficult and time-consuming.

LOCAL CONTEXT

Mount Cameroon

The Mount Cameroon area is dominated by the CDC, which has alienated much of the land from the indigenous Bakweri. There has also been significant immigration to satisfy the labour needs of the CDC. Population density is now about 48 people per km². Nearly 75 per cent of the Mount Cameroon study site is deforested.

Hunting in the Mount Cameroon area is carried out by means of wire snares and 'dane guns', which are locally manufactured single-barrel shotguns. Both types of hunting are nominally illegal but almost universally practised. Bushmeat is sold fresh or smoked. Fresh meat, which is the most common form for immediate consumption, is sold in local markets. Because smoking is the only means of conservation, hunters operating at distances of more than 15 km from their base smoke the meat on site in the bush. Smoking also facilitates transportation and reduces the weight. Smoking, especially of big game, takes at least two days. Many consumers prefer smoked meat.

Three different types of hunter as well as wildlife collectors operate in the Mount Cameroon area.

Indigenous Subsistence Hunters

Indigenous subsistence hunters live in the area and hunt on their subsistence farms and in the local bush surrounding the farms for animals to supplement the family diet. Snares and dane guns are commonly used. Most of the animals caught in this manner are essentially farm-pests that breed rapidly; there is little conservation significance.

Local Hunters

Local hunters are often resident immigrants who may not possess land and depend to a greater extent than the subsistence farmers on hunting and trapping. A significant part of the catch is sold in the local market to 'pepper-soup women', who cook and serve this local specialty of fiery hot broth with bushmeat in roadside cafes. The tools used by this type of hunter are the same as those used by the subsistence farmer. Because both the indigenous and the local hunter are part of the local community, they are susceptible, in principle, to community pressures.

Commercial Hunters

Commercial hunters are professional, full-time hunters who are rarely part of the local community and may arrive from distant areas where hunting is a strong local tradition but which are too far from suitable markets. They work in small, tribally homogeneous groups under a leader. Interviews with professional hunters indicated that they had moved to the Mount Cameroon area from their tribal lands not because wildlife abundance was higher in Mount Cameroon – the opposite was the case – but because the recently constructed west coast road provided quick and easy access to the major markets of Douala and Yaoundé. Market accessibility is all-important and overrides actual abundance of game in determining where commercial hunting is carried out.

These hunters avoid the indigenous villages. Sometimes they are based in the CDC 'stranger' (ie non-indigenous) labour camps. They stay for weeks in the forest, hunting by day and night. Wire snares are used, but in this case set in long fence traps which can extend for hundreds of metres. They also use dane guns, but more frequently use modern shotguns and even automatic military weapons. The meat is dried and smoked. After remaining in the bush for many weeks, they leave for distant towns such as Douala or Yaoundé to sell their meat; very little is sold on the local market.

Wildlife Collectors

Because Mount Cameroon is a biodiversity 'hotspot' and close to other mountains with high levels of endemism and protected wildlife areas such as Korup National Park, the area is popular with those involved in the wildlife trade. Unlike the bushmeat trade, the wildlife trade depends on sophisticated knowledge of species. The numbers of people involved in the wildlife trade are lower than those in the bushmeat trade. Teams of collectors may be led by either expatriates or Cameroonians. Species collected include songbirds, parrots, tortoises, snakes, lizards, amphibians, aquarium fish, butterflies, beetles and plants. The exclusive destination of the wildlife trade is the developed world, with a strong demand from the US.

The Cameroon Development Corporation

A major cause of biodiversity loss in the Mount Cameroon region has been the activities of the CDC. The development of plantations of rubber, oil palm, banana and tea in the Mount Cameroon region has been a direct cause of biodiversity loss. Plantations are essentially biodiversity deserts. Furthermore, when plantations are incompatible with wildlife, as when elephants destroy young oil palms, the tendency is to destroy the wildlife. In fact, a bounty used to be offered on elephants in Mount Cameroon.

The expropriation of Bakweri land by the German colonial regime in the late 19th century was later institutionalized by the government on a national scale and traditional land holding was abolished. Similarly, according to the forestry laws, all plants belong to the government. Neither the land nor the produce of the land belong to the people who live and work there: they belong to the government. The indigenous people, aware that they have no legitimate claim on either their traditional land or its products, still sell the right to hunt to commercial hunters and the rights to land to would-be immigrants. This is only rational. Formal laws regulating land tenure and natural-resource exploitation have therefore led to social instability and are not conducive to the responsible husbandry of either land or natural resources.

A further cause of biodiversity loss in the Mount Cameroon region is CDC policy and practice. The CDC pays very low salaries, daily rates ranging between US$1.45 and 2.25. Despite these low rates, food and other necessities of life are not provided by the CDC. Workers, in addition to completing their daily tasks, must farm or hunt in their spare time to obtain food. Therefore, many of the immigrant labourers have subsistence farms on Mount Cameroon. They not only degrade the forest through the creation of 'chop-farms', but also hunt and trap on the farms, so contributing both directly and indirectly to the reduction in biodiversity. Essentially, the natural resource base subsidizes the low salaries, thus depleting the natural capital of the region.

South-east Forests

The economy of the south-east forest area is dominated by the logging industry, which began intensive operations in the 1970s. Population density here is
only about four per km² and about 30 per cent of the area is deforested. The
logging companies have camps for their workers, who are primarily
immigrants from other regions of Cameroon. Since many of these workers are
hunters, they have become involved in the bushmeat trade, using the timber
trucks to transport bushmeat to distant urban areas. There are five main
bushmeat and wildlife commercial centres in the south-east, including
Yokadouma, the local government centre. Almost all bushmeat and wildlife
passes through Yokadouma. Demand for bushmeat for local consumption is
also high, as it is preferred to beef.

The traditional economic activity of the region is cocoa farming. Cocoa
farming is heavy work and requires both chemical inputs and access to transport. With recent disruptions in the marketing and support infrastructure for
cocoa, farmers shifted their focus to alternative activities that provide higher
incomes. The principal alternative activity is hunting and trapping. Unlike
cocoa, hunting requires few inputs, and middlemen take care of transport of
the product.

Hunting is carried out as elsewhere in Cameroon with dane guns and wire
snares, but in the south-east, military and automatic weapons are more
common. Many such weapons came in clandestinely from the Congo Republic
during the recent civil war. Baka pygmies of the region traditionally use nets
for capturing game, although this is becoming less common.

Four different types of hunter as well as wildlife collectors operate in the
south-east.

Indigenous Subsistence Hunters

The staple source of protein for the native population is bushmeat, so that all
households are involved in hunting, with trapping the principal method. Only
the excess is sold. Hunting in the region is both increasing in frequency and
becoming more varied. Baka pygmies, who once hunted exclusively with traditional methods, now often use modern weapons belonging to civil servants or
the elite of the village. The Bangandos and the Bakweles, who share the territory
with the Baka pygmies, were also traditionally mainly snare hunters. The use of
snares has increased dramatically, with villagers now setting hundreds of traps.

Subsistence hunting and trapping is carried out in the vicinity of the village,
but intensification of methods has meant that, around many villages, game has
become rare, obliging hunters to move further and further away from the
village. Indigenous populations are adding commercial hunting to traditional
subsistence hunting.

Local Hunters

Non-indigenous logging company workers and civil servants in the region also
hunt for subsistence. Most important among this group are the employees of

the logging companies. These companies have their bases in the heart of the forest, so far removed from urban areas where workers can procure supplies that they are obliged to use what is readily available. Like the situation of CDC workers in the Mount Cameroon region, the natural resource base subsidizes the logging companies' costs. Logging company workers and civil servants also supply snares and guns to the local population to hunt on their behalf; the hunters are rewarded with a portion of the kill.

Commercial Hunters

Many professional hunters and meat collectors are involved in supplying the bushmeat market. Organized similarly to the commercial hunters of the Mount Cameroon region, these hunters usually have special agreements with the vendors who sell their produce in the markets. The vendors supply the hunters with arms, cartridges and other supplies. Most commercial hunters are non-natives who use the natives as guides for token payments. These hunters are not susceptible to local community pressures.

The commercial hunters are able to penetrate these forests only because of the activities of the logging companies, which open up the forest and provide transport of meat to the urban markets. Without the infrastructure and communications provided by the logging industry, the commercial bushmeat industry would be unable to operate. Commercial hunting in the south-east is facilitated by the activities of Muslim traders and people with special status in society, such as senior administrators, politicians and members of the armed forces who provide financing, supplies and market connections for bushmeat and wildlife products.

Sport Hunters

This very small group of hunters hunt for trophies, usually elephant tusks or bongo horns. The hunting guides, mainly expatriates, set up luxurious camps in the forest for their mainly foreign clientele. Legal control and supervision of this hunting is not strong, and fraud and other illegal practices are common. The relationship of the hunting guides with local communities is very poor. Sport operators often attempt to drive out local communities. The damage done directly to biodiversity by sport hunters is less than that done by the other groups of hunters, but it is nonetheless significant.

Wildlife Collectors

Collecting wildlife is economically important in the region. The species collected are principally African grey parrots and some pigeon species. On occasions collectors have attempted to trade primates including gorilla. The wildlife collectors are organized in much the same way as commercial hunters. The birds are transported by road to Douala or Yaoundé and sent out by air; mortality rates often exceed 80 per cent. Much of the collection and export of these birds is characterized by fraud, and there is little doubt that quotas allowed under CITES are far exceeded.

The south-east forests have changed over the past three decades. Originally remote and inaccessible, with low human population densities, the area could meet its protein needs through subsistence hunting with little danger to the environment. The principal economic activity was cocoa farming. With the advent of the logging companies, immigrant labour was introduced and infrastructure and communications, especially roads, were improved. The infrastructure and practices of logging companies encouraged hunting and trapping not only for subsistence of the labourers, but also as a supplement to low incomes. Local communities, which had seen cocoa prices fall, also began to take advantage of this opportunity. Land-tenure issues, while not irrelevant, are not pivotal as they are in the Mount Cameroon region. The trend toward increased hunting and wildlife collection has been encouraged by the weakness of the central government in enforcing both wildlife regulations and the forestry law. Sanctions on illegal behaviour can easily be avoided by judicious bribing. Hunting, trapping and wildlife collecting are rational behaviours under the circumstances, where the resource is abundant and poorly controlled, where other economic activities do not provide sufficient economic returns and where ready markets are easily accessible.

The similarities between the two study areas are striking and far outweigh the differences. In both areas, essentially the same hunting structure exists and the same hunting methods and tools are used. Wildlife collectors operate in both areas, although they trade different species. In both areas immigrant labourers work for low pay and commercial concerns do not provide adequate supplies, with the result that people have to fend for themselves through farming or hunting. The main differences between the two areas arise from the fact that the south-east still has a complement of large mammals, whereas Mount Cameroon is basically reduced to rats, porcupines and squirrels. Subsistence hunting retains a more important role in the south-east because of the abundance of game. The processes that reduced the animal populations to virtual extinction on Mount Cameroon are already engaged in the south-east.

NATIONAL CONTEXT

National Policies

Development is the goal of both Cameroon and its citizens. Villagers often see the conditions in which they live as primitive and the features of their everyday environment as barriers to development.

Development is accepted as the national priority for the Cameroon government. Development in this context means provision of roads, ports, airports, modern buildings, telecommunications, an industrial sector and other infrastructure. Infrastructure development is also important to the government as a means of bringing all areas of the country under central control. The government sees the development of the logging industry as an important tool for bringing infrastructure to remote areas untouched by its authority. Those who think in this way consider clearing forest a useful goal. The government wants roads extended into the furthest forests, and the fact they are used by hunters and trappers to extract the wildlife is a matter of little concern. Short-term development and economic concerns prevail.

Government policies with regard to the forest sector are complex and often contradictory. While powerful sectoral ministries (such as finance and economy) have a strong say in policy, there is little collaboration among different ministries and considerable overlap of portfolios. Officially the government is committed both to the development of a permanent forest estate, sustainably managed over the long term, and to the development of community forests. However, it is also explicit government policy to use the forests to replace petroleum as the engine that drives the Cameroonian economy, which clearly leads to a short-term view and unsustainable exploitation. As a result of vastly increased commercial logging operations, Cameroon has become one of the tropical countries with the highest rates of forest loss. In the early 1990s, the IUCN estimated that the rate of deforestation in Cameroon's dense forests was 10 to 11 times higher than the rate of regeneration.

In this confused and contradictory situation, the government allocates small logging concessions to reward political allegiance. At higher levels there is a system of concession allocation under which large sums of money may be paid to secure large concessions. There is a very low rate of tax collection, and supervision of the forest industry in Cameroon is highly inefficient. There is little government control over the forest sector, forest guards lack equipment and their salaries are low. It is clear from the large sums of money available in this sector that it could be effectively policed and controlled. However, the situation suits the current institutional situation. Logging is not controlled because there is little political will to do so. Thus, while the government's explicit policy is long-term sustainable management of a permanent forestry sector, the implicit policy is almost the reverse of this. This implicit policy encourages uncontrolled exploitation of the forest sector and is a strong contributory factor to biodiversity loss. Short-term unsustainable use of the natural-resource base is encouraged under the laws, regulations and practices and is a potent contributor to biodiversity loss.

National Laws

The government of Cameroon has enacted three laws that have nationalized all land and all natural resources. The 1974 and 1976 land tenure laws effectively abolished traditional land tenure systems. The formal procedures for obtaining official title to national land set out in these laws are so tortuous, lengthy and expensive that few can afford it. In the 24 years that have elapsed since enactment of the laws, only 2.3 per cent of rural lands have been registered to private title, mostly by civil servants. Furthermore, in order to obtain title, land must be *mise en valeur*, meaning that there can be no title to an intact forest; the forest must be transformed into a cocoa farm or similar productive use before title is granted. Illegal, traditional systems of land tenure, however, still flourish. Similarly, the 1994 forest law nationalized all natural resources, including all plants and trees. Villagers have usufruct rights, including collection of specified forest products, trapping and some limited use of timber. The principal resources – timber and wildlife – belong to the state and can only be harvested with permission granted through the issue of concessions, licences or special permits. This alienation of land and resources is a source of considerable insecurity and is not conducive to sustainable management of resources. The relationship between tenure and sustainability is complex (Ruitenbeek and Cartier, 1998). Insecure tenure often leads to unsustainable use of resources. However, well-defined property rights do not guarantee sustainable management; they are probably necessary but not sufficient.

Cameroon is a party to CITES. Under this convention, the export of endangered species is either banned or controlled through the allocation of quotas. Exports under quotas – as in the case of African grey parrots, ivory and lizard skins – are controlled by the national Scientific Authority which issues a certificate of origin and certifies that a shipment is within the quota limit. These restrictions create high prices in export markets. African grey parrots sell for US$2000, for example. These CITES quotas are therefore routinely exceeded, and even when bans are in place, as was the case with ivory in 1997, exports still take place with fraudulent documents. When attempts are made to tighten international regulations, the trade immediately becomes more decentralized and harder to control. For example, when the CITES parrot quota for Cameroon was abolished and all exports were made illegal, birds were exported via the national airline from Douala to Libreville, from Libreville to Casablanca and from Casablanca to Spain on a chain of regional flights, thus avoiding international controls.

The fact that those who are responsible for monitoring the quota allocation also control the export of these valuable items from Cameroon leads almost inevitably to fraud and abuse. The possession of authority to issue CITES permits is virtually a licence to print money. The exploitation of the CITES mechanisms in countries of origin is a potent source of corruption and may encourage the loss of biodiversity.

Parrots and other natural resources such as medicinal plants are officially the property of the state and harvesting is regulated by the issue of special permits. The allocation of these, as in the case of CITES permits, is also open to abuse. There is virtually no supervision or control of harvesting, resulting from the proliferation of special permits.

The 1994 forestry law in theory espouses the principle of community forests. However, the law and its provisions are grossly flawed; communities do not possess title and management is still subject to supervision by the Ministry of Environment and Forests. As was the case with the 1974 land legislation, the law is also being subverted by civil servants who are registering community forests for their own use – generally for sale as logging concessions.

In sum, the primary land and resource laws of Cameroon are inconsistent with long-term sustainable use of natural resources. Well-intentioned legislation has been corrupted so that it aggravates, rather than prevents, the loss of biodiversity.

Against this background of legislative inadequacy is a history of economic decline, with several consequences. Structural adjustment policies imposed as a result of macroeconomic problems have sharply reduced civil servants' salaries, inducing corruption. At the same time that government capacity and budgets have been reduced, currency devaluation has led to a proliferation of logging because of sharply reduced relative labour costs. Declines in world prices for commodities such as coffee and cocoa, traditionally grown by peasant farmers, and the collapse of technical assistance schemes for these growers, have resulted in the abandonment of these crops and the search for more lucrative alternatives. Bushmeat hunting and wildlife trading are two such alternatives.

National Institutions

Government Institutions

The institutional framework in Cameroon is the product of a political structure that is centrist, hierarchical and geared to the collection and distribution of rents. It is essentially multifarious, fragmented, inefficient and functionally distorted. The government structure treats the natural resource base as a source of immediate and diverse revenue opportunities rather than as a resource to be managed over the long term. The resulting policies are revenue- and control-based, uncoordinated and inefficient. They do not provide the basis for rational management.

The enforcement of wildlife and forestry laws is the responsibility of provincial and divisional staff. These institutions have suffered a reduction in staff under the provisions of the structural adjustment programme. Operating budgets have also been reduced because of the inclement economic climate. One of the earliest government actions under structural adjustment was to sell off all official vehicles. Consequently the field offices of all branches of government suffered major losses in efficiency, effectively crippling their ability to function away from urban centres. Guards whose function is to control forest exploitation are forced, if they want to do their job, to beg lifts from the very people they are supposed to control. This is not conducive to efficient law enforcement.

There are many ministries whose mandates touch on the environment, but there is a lack of interministerial coordination even among different administrative branches within the same ministry. For example, the administration charged with allocation of logging concessions does not liaise with the administration in charge of protected areas and does not even have maps of protected areas. Frequently, therefore, logging concessions are allocated within protected areas.

Social Institutions

Changing social institutions and culture play a role in biodiversity loss. Traditional beliefs that the supply of animals in the forest is inexhaustible –

'beef never fit finish' – and the replacement of traditional taboos by Christianity that sees these taboos as evil and primitive both promote such loss. The taboos ensured that certain species and forests were protected, but the Bible, on the whole, is not a conservation-minded document.

Like much of sub-Saharan Africa over the last decade, Cameroon has been subject to large population movements. The most important of these has been a mass movement of rural people to the cities. Cameroon is soon likely to become a predominantly urban country rather than a predominantly rural one. Currently it is 45 per cent urban and 55 per cent rural. Strong regional migrations have resulted from overpopulation, for economic reasons or both. Immigration is a feature that tends to weaken and dilute traditional ways. Immigrants are usually economic migrants, workers in the logging or agro-industrial companies, traders or hunters, and their activities are often imitated and adopted by the local communities. Social instability caused by mass population movements is a driving force behind biodiversity loss.

The population of Cameroon has doubled over the last two decades. Today, 44 per cent of the population is under the age of 15 and only 5 per cent is over 60. Demographic pressures have important social consequences in the far north and western provinces in particular. Elsewhere, the consequences are mainly economic – too many people chasing too few productive occupations. Natural resource exploitation is a logical economic choice for this young population with few employment opportunities in the formal sector.

At the village level, anything beyond usufruct or subsistence harvesting is regulated in theory by the issue of special permits. Traditional hunting, which is usufruct, uses tools that are classified as illegal. Thus, virtually all hunting is illegal and, *ipso facto*, difficult to monitor and control. The combination of a centralized and somewhat impoverished administration, nationalized land and resources and controls by issue of permits present a situation that encourages evasion of the law and a short-term view. Secure rights over resources may not guarantee sustainable use, but are a necessary prerequisite.

Many local communities had just entered the cash economy and become dependent on it at the time that market prices for their agricultural commodities became uneconomic. In the areas penetrated by the loggers, a usable road network has been established and transport for bushmeat is available. Local people do have marketable hunting skills and, at least at the start, an abundant natural resource to exploit. Local communities and immigrant labour make use of the tools, skills, infrastructure and natural resources they possess to provide themselves with an income. This is rational economic behaviour given the circumstances.

National Economy

Up to 1985 Cameroon's economy had been growing steadily, supported by the agricultural sector. In 1986 the economy suffered a sharp reversal and GDP per capita declined by 6.3 per cent per year between 1985 and 1993. The country adopted an IMF-designed SAP in 1988, which was based on internal adjustments, emphasizing liberalization of economic activity, reliance on markets and increased competition and efficiency to reduce domestic costs and prices. As part of this internal adjustment, civil servants' salaries were cut by as much as 60 per cent and thousands were laid off. A World Bank study (1994a) showed that in the capital city of Yaoundé, which suffered the effects of the economic crisis least, the level of per capita consumption was 10 per cent lower than it had been 30 years previously. Rural areas, already quite poor, have suffered most. The number of rural households below the poverty line rose from 49 per cent to 71 per cent during the eight-year period. In January 1994 there was an external adjustment in the form of a 50 per cent devaluation of the CFA, aimed at increasing Cameroon's competitive position in international markets, which had been lost because of an overvalued currency. A principal beneficiary of currency devaluation was the logging industry, stimulated by an effective halving of labour and operating costs. The boom in the timber industry and the explosion in logging date from 1994.

A general decline in commodity prices in the 1980s sharply reduced the profitability of smallholder crops such as coffee and cocoa. Over the last five years, the price of robusta coffee has continued to decline. The price of cocoa has stabilized but cocoa producers were also negatively affected by the liquidation of SODECAO, the state cocoa development agency that provided fertilizers, fungicides and technical assistance to peasant cocoa farmers. These factors have mainly affected the cocoa-growing region of the south-east, where there were few agricultural or economic alternatives. As cocoa became unattractive as a cash crop, communities were forced to find other sources of income and abundant available natural resources were an obvious choice for exploitation. When the region opened up, following the logging companies' activities, the necessary infrastructure for the transport of these natural resource products to their market destinations became available.

Many tropical countries produce essentially the same range of agricultural products and this is the case with Cameroon, whose coffee, cocoa, bananas, oil palm and rubber compete with products from other countries, often with lower labour costs and much higher levels of inherent productivity. To a large extent the market prices for coffee, for example, depend on whether there has been a frost in Brazil, and for cocoa, on whether there have been forest fires in Ghana. In Malaysia the inherent productivity of oil palm is considerably higher than it is in Africa, and the African product is scarcely competitive on the world market. Overproduction and market speculation are additional factors that destabilize demand for products and prices for producers.

About 30 per cent of Cameroon's GDP is derived from the primary sector (logging, mining) and primary agricultural production (cocoa, coffee, bananas, rubber, cotton) which also accounts for virtually all of its exports. Cocoa, coffee and cotton are principally produced by peasant farmers rather than agro-industrial estates. The industrial sector of the economy, already weak, was also negatively affected by the economic crisis and many small factories have closed. The few job opportunities that were available in this sector declined. With primary agricultural products unprofitable, the economic choices have been harsh.

One phenomenon that is relevant here is the 'modernization' of society. Pure subsistence economies no longer exist, and people are, however marginally, part of the modern cash economy. Even in remote villages, certain commodities and services, for example salt, sugar, kerosene, soap, school fees and medicines, are seen as essential. Once a demand for these is established it is rarely reversed. Cash has to be produced to obtain these goods and services. Under current conditions, the only way to generate cash is to exploit the natural resource base. The skills that are necessary for a subsistence existence, that is, hunting and trapping, can be usefully transferred into economic activity with minimum modification. These are rational economic choices and in many ways the only available ones.

The growth in bushmeat markets is a relatively recent phenomenon. Franceville (1984) reported that bushmeat was 'rare' in Yaoundé. Today it is common, with an estimated 2.3 tons per day for sale in the four principal bushmeat markets of Yaoundé. The consumers of this meat are private persons and restaurants. The principal causes of this change, which appears to be supply-driven, are the development of road communications permitting transport of the meat, depressed economic conditions and low employment availability, which encourage diversification into alternate economic activities and rapid and uncontrolled urbanization. The cultural and symbolic association that the new urbanites have for bushmeat is another explanation for its consumption; it is associated with the village environment as well as rituals and festivals. The desire to partake of bushmeat despite its high cost, the dubious sanitation conditions under which it is sold and the use of hazardous chemical preservatives such as formaldehyde can be accounted for by taste, diet, curiosity, tradition, status and nostalgia. It transcends social divisions and ethnic origins.

INTERNATIONAL CONTEXT

The international context in which these processes of biodiversity loss are operating include both regional and global factors.

Regional Factors

Cameroon is a part of francophone Central Africa. It is a member of Communauté Economique de l'Afrique Centrale (CEDAC), the customs union which also binds together Gabon, the Congo (Brazzaville), the Central African Republic (CAR), Equatorial Guinea and Chad. Cameroon has common boundaries with these five countries and shares a currency and a similar linguistic, social and economic context. The CFA, which is convertible with the French franc, is legal tender throughout this region, facilitating trade, including informal trade such as smuggling. In the south-east, people move freely between Cameroon, the Congo and the CAR and the import of firearms and the smuggling of ivory and of parrots is facilitated by uncontrolled borders. There is also very little regional coordination in cross-border control of either people or goods.

Another significant international influence is regional conflict. Two of these have been important in recent times: the Congo (Brazzaville) civil war of 1997–98 and the border dispute between Cameroon and Nigeria in the Bakassi peninsula, which still continues. Regional wars may have important consequences such as regional destabilization, but more important for current concerns is the existence of firearms. These are used by the military for subsistence when fighting guerilla wars in the bush; subsistence easily turns to commerce and many armies in Africa have become involved in illegal wildlife trafficking. Military Kalashnikov or AK47 rifles are in use in south-east Cameroon, the Congo and the CAR to poach elephants and other game. In the Korup area of Western Cameroon, not far from the current Bakassi dispute, hunting still takes place with firearms remaining from the Biafra War of the late 1960s.

Regional networks and markets are important for the wildlife trade. Ivory is collected in south-east Cameroon and also from the Congo and the CAR. There is an important ivory market in West Africa, in Abidjan. Regional connections are used to minimize exposure to international controls. Ivory and skins are smuggled out through Ndjamena in Chad, which is accessible from Cameroon by road and has international flight connections to regional French cities, such as Toulouse, where international controls are far less stringent than they are in Paris. Regional routes are also important for the trans-shipment of wildlife.

Global Factors

The global context is more far-reaching and more complex than the regional context and can be examined under a number of different headings. These include historical factors, trade links, international treaties, macroeconomic factors and bilateral and multilateral aid.

Colonial History

The colonial era has had a profound effect on the present economic and ecological status of Cameroon. The 'Struggle for Africa' that characterized the final decades of the last century was essentially a struggle over resources and markets. Cameroon became part of the German Empire in 1884. Principal exports at the outset were ivory and rubber. The Germans acquired land by force from the Bakweri and established a network of plantations that were then planted with oil palm and later with rubber. Private individuals or German trading companies owned these plantations. At the end of the First World War, the plantations were confiscated but the original owners were then allowed to purchase their plantations back and did so. After the Second World War, instead of being returned to the Germans, the plantations were amalgamated into one enterprise, the CDC. The German colonial footprint on the Mount Cameroon area is very strong and the current situation there, ecologically and economically, is a direct result of the colonial era. The alienation of the land and the unrestrained exploitation of the natural resource base, destruction of the original vegetation and decimation of the fauna, and replacement with plantation agriculture, all major factors in biodiversity loss, were patterns established over a century ago.

In 1919, at the end of the German colonial period, Cameroon was divided into a large French-speaking area and a small English-speaking area – it was later reunited in 1960. French language and culture predominate, but even more important are the trade and financial links with France, including the use of the CFA as a common currency in Central Africa. The CFA is supported by the French treasury. France is a country where environmental issues are not of fundamental concern compared with much of the rest of the developed world. The logging companies operating in south-east Cameroon are principally French and, although the situation may be starting to change, there are few environmental concerns and little demand in France for sustainably produced timber. The trade links forged in the colonial period remain strong. Patterns of land and resource use, the legal and juridical context, financial mechanisms and control, development policy and markets are all strongly influenced by the colonial heritage.

Trade Links

Trade links between Central Africa and the rest of the world are ancient. By the 1850s, trade in edible oils, particularly palm oil, had replaced the outlawed trade in slaves. Trade links today are becoming increasingly fluid in the context of globalization. Ninety-three per cent of Cameroon's exports are either natural resources or the products of the primary agricultural sector whose production on smallholdings or in plantations actively reduces biodiversity. Table 7.1 illustrates the importance of petroleum, timber and plantation products to the economy.

Table 7.1 *Cameroon's Exports, 1996*

Product	Export value (US$millions)	Per cent of exports
Timber (logs, processed wood)	256	17
Petroleum	626	43
Coffee	127	9
Cocoa	182	13
Bananas	64	4
Rubber	78	5
Cotton	109	8

The wildlife trade includes live animals and wildlife products such as animal skins, ivory, rhinoceros horn, butterfly and beetle wings and hunting trophies.

These products comprise a highly lucrative trade, most of which does not appear in official statistics. Skins of snakes and lizards go to Europe for the fashion market. Ivory too is highly profitable and the destinations are many, including South Africa, West Africa, Europe, the US and Asia. Butterfly wings are used to make pictures and beetles are preserved in perspex for export. Ostrich eggs are sold to tourists. Hunting trophies, principally the horns of bongo and giant eland and elephant tusks, are exported to Germany, the US and Mexico. Live animals commonly exported include songbirds, parrots, tortoises, snakes, lizards, amphibians, aquarium fish, butterflies and beetles. Plants are also exported. There is no effective control over the collection of these species, and very little control over their export. It is a highly corrupt trade with very high waste. Major destinations include Europe and the US. The footprint of the developed world is very clear on the export of Cameroon's biodiversity.

Sport hunting represents another footprint of the western world on Cameroon's biodiversity. The principal species affected are elephant, bongo and giant eland. Sport hunting is socially disruptive in the south-east, where local communities are antagonized and marginalized. It is hard for local communities to understand why their own hunting, necessary for existence and economic survival, is illegal, while sport hunting, a pastime in which only the horns or tusks are taken, is legal.

While bushmeat serves a predominantly domestic market, the large numbers of Cameroonians and other Africans living in France and other countries, as a result of the colonial and cultural heritage, also like to consume bushmeat, constituting a small but highly selective market. Specialized restaurants supply these needs. Bushmeat orders are placed in Cameroon and meat is sent out in ice chests or plastic bags by air to Madrid, Paris, Brussels and Geneva, for example.

International Treaties

International treaties represent formal agreements prescribing and regulating interactions among nations. Their effectiveness is limited, however. First, international treaties are only as good as the precision with which they are written. It is also the case that countries ratify treaties for their own purposes, which may be only a subset of the major goals of the treaty. If a country perceives that this subset of goals is not being met, then there will be little political commitment to the implementation of the entire treaty. Countries also ratify treaties because they expect benefits, as was the case with the CBD, where ratification was expected to bring funds for biodiversity conservation. Under these conditions there may be no strong commitment to the responsibilities incurred under the treaty. Nevertheless, international treaties do provide the possibility of promoting biodiversity conservation and have the formal authority of international obligation.

CITES is the key text regulating trade in biodiversity. The treaty assumes efficient, honest and technically qualified administrations, but these are not a common feature in the developing world. In Cameroon illegal exports of ivory, parrots and lizard skins, all subject to CITES quotas, far exceed the legal exports. Far from reducing the illegal trade, CITES may make it more lucrative by adding scarcity value. CITES is not an effective treaty and may actually promote biodiversity loss rather than the reverse.

The CBD, a direct outcome of the Rio summit in 1992, entered into force at the end of 1993. The Convention is concerned with the conservation of biological diversity, sustainable use of its elements and equitable sharing of the benefits derived from the exploitation of genetic resources. Article 20 of the CBD outlines the financial mechanisms for providing the necessary resources to developing countries for the conservation of their biological diversity. Ratification of the CBD by member countries, including Cameroon, provides a very strong tool for national biodiversity conservation as it represents a formal, internationally recognized commitment. The CBD is a complex treaty, still developing its institutions and programmes, but does provide the possibility of bringing biodiversity conservation to the forefront of national political agendas.

Free Trade

The current trend in the international community, backed by the creation of the WTO, is toward free trade. This means the elimination of subsidies, premiums and taxes that distort trade and support for the unrestricted movement of goods throughout the world. Non-market provisions that increase the price of goods, such as sustainability conditions, are therefore discriminated against in some situations. Moreover, competition among producers is increased, which may drive them to exploit resources for short-term profits rather than for long-term sustainable use. For example, if it would cost more to establish a sustainable logging operation than it would to mine the forest, then opening of markets may push producers to mine the forest. Free markets too often favour short-term economic exploitation of forests to their sustainable use. As a result, trade liberalization may pose a major threat to the biodiversity of Cameroon. The development of demand for sustainably produced timber and reform of trade legislation so that it incorporates sustainability concerns are necessary actions for the preservation of biodiversity.

Macroeconomic Reform

The Bretton Woods institutions have had a significant impact on the environment of Cameroon. The government's decision to nationalize land in 1974 was essentially an initiative of the World Bank, aimed at doing away with the anarchic traditional situation, which was ethnically and tribally based, and replacing it with a system in which any citizen could legally acquire land anywhere in the country. These laudable goals have not been achieved. Similarly, structural adjustment in Cameroon has not been environmentally sensitive. Its implementation in an economy that is based on primary production requires increased primary production to be effective, which comes at the expense of the environment. Natural resource capital has been exchanged for immediate economic gain.

Cameroon has had a long history of state involvement in the economic sector. There are many parastatals in various stages of bankruptcy, with the vast majority characterized by inefficient management. The current economic remedy, promoted by the World Bank and IMF, is privatization. State owner-ship has become one of today's cardinal sins. In Cameroon, three state enterprises currently undergoing privatization are CDC, SNEC (the state water company) and SONEL (the state electricity company). Potential purchasers will have to invest heavily in these enterprises to improve the degraded infra-structure and will have to expand to recoup their investments. In the case of CDC, it is likely that the plantations which currently cover 40,000 ha will be sold with the potential for expansion by 20,000 ha, leading to further degra-dation in the Mount Cameroon region. Similarly, SNEC will have to create more reservoirs and SONEL will need to create more hydroelectric dams. All these plans for expansion will have highly negative effects on the environment.

Bilateral and Multilateral Aid

Most bilateral and multilateral aid programmes have similar goals: develop-ment, good government and poverty alleviation. However, many of the aid programmes are culturally, economically and ecologically inappropriate. For example, the EU road-rehabilitation programme, which is designed to upgrade cocoa transport roads and to end the isolation of rural communities, is ecolog-ically destructive in that it promotes extensive agriculture, provides access to the forest for hunters and fragments habitat. Many of these programmes are conceived in the West and present Western solutions to African problems. They represent what the developed world thinks the developing world needs or should be doing; they are not developed locally as a response to local needs. The implicit assumption is that present Western governmental and institu-tional structures are the best possible and should be adopted by the developing world. The root causes of biodiversity loss are not logging, mining and demographic trends; these are all proximate causes. The root cause is the need for social and economic development, both at the level of the individual and the level of the state. This need is met through depletion of the nation's natural resource capital, with clear ecological consequences.

CONCLUSIONS

Based on the analysis carried out for this study, all the initial hypotheses are retained. All are functional at different levels, directly or indirectly, in causing biodiversity loss. The principal cause is the complex of activities that constitute development, either at the individual level or at the level of the state. The economic root causes of biodiversity loss in Cameroon go back more than a century. The patterns of ecological degradation and biodiversity loss resulting from monoculture plantations, unsustainable exploitation of the natural resource base and establishment of trade links and development of markets for the natural resources of Cameroon were an early development. The growth and

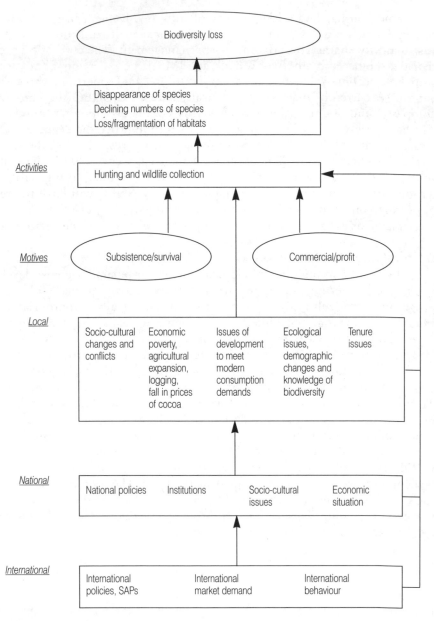

Figure 7.4 *Conceptual Model – Cameroon*

expansion of these trade links continues to the present-day. The cultural, legal and economic context inherited from the colonial past is also a powerful factor, defining patterns of activity both in terms of trade and in terms of development. Regional context is also important. The region is French-speaking, with a common currency, easy cross-border access and frequent outbreaks of war.

Cameroon and Cameroonians share a common goal of development. The shift from subsistence to a cash economy and the consequences for the environment at the local level are mirrored by the creation of a modern state with its development infrastructure. Development has involved depleting the natural resource capital in both cases, making it easy to see that development and biodiversity are inversely correlated. The depletion can be seen in terms of numbers of individuals of particular species (fewer elephants) or the loss of entire species (no rhinos), the degradation of ecosystems (lowland forest) or the loss of whole ecosystems (montane forest).

These powerful causes of biodiversity loss in Cameroon are to a large extent beyond the boundaries of the country. The causes of this loss can be both direct and indirect: biodiversity may be exported directly (timber, parrots, ivory, chameleons) or lost indirectly through expansion of commercial plantations (coffee, cocoa, rubber, banana). In an economy with natural resource and agricultural products accounting for 93 per cent of its exports, the causes of biodiversity loss are very clear. If there were no demand for bananas, pineapple, coffee, cocoa, tea, leather, rubber, logs, plywood, cotton, petroleum, songbirds, ivory, hunting trophies, aquarium fish, ornamental plants, medicinal plants, chameleons, frogs, parrots, butterflies, ostrich eggs, lizard skins, snakes or rhino horn, then the ecology of Cameroon would be in far better shape than it is today; the country would also be far less developed. It is, however, very clear that the process of development will continue but moderation of the demand in the developed world, including eco-labelling and more efficient import controls, would be a step towards reducing the loss of biodiversity.

The prescriptions of the World Bank and the IMF have major consequences for Cameroon institutions. Other bilateral and multilateral aid is also significant. Development aid should be a true partnership: it should be culturally and economically sensitive and not impose rigid and inappropriate models of development. The current focus on free trade is a potent threat to Cameroon's biodiversity. Privatization has also been prescribed for Cameroon, despite the fact that the transition to private ownership will surely involve negative impacts on the environment. Political fashion in developed nations is translated into policy for the developing world. The goal of many of these programmes is development and the consequences for the environment are rarely taken into account.

It is important to be realistic about what can be achieved within countries by mechanisms such as international treaties. Much depends on the precision of the language of the treaty and the effectiveness of the measures it prescribes. Some international treaties, such as CITES, are not particularly effective but could be made much stronger with more commitment to the detection and enforcement functions outside the producer countries. Others, such as the CBD, have a much greater possibility of effecting real change but require practical implementation instruments.

Countries are like people: Cameroon has entered the cash economy and needs finance to provide certain essential elements of life. Going back to a purely subsistence existence is no longer possible. But Cameroon gets her living from the natural resource base, which is increasingly being exploited in an unsustainable way. The only way to slow the process is to provide economic alternatives such as the development of a secondary sector of the economy. This would require substantial external investment, which would in turn require reform of the labour laws and establishment of a transparent and non-corrupt judiciary. The further up the causal chain one gets, the more complex the solutions to the problem become. Solutions at one level cannot be made without reference to higher levels. The local situation cannot be corrected without reference to the national context. The national context cannot be corrected without reference to the international context. The scale and costs involved at each level are much higher than would be the case if correction were possible at the lower level.

One cause of biodiversity loss is that there is no awareness of biodiversity and therefore no constituency for it within Cameroon. The environment is similarly perceived both by people in the village and by the government as an economic or nutritional resource, and not in terms of biological value. Such perceptions only come with education and with liberation from economic need. The potential for appreciating the beauty of nature is only possible when one has a full stomach. At this point, the loss of biodiversity is essentially a concern of the developed world.

RECOMMENDATIONS

It is not possible to undo colonial history, alter the linguistic and cultural context, or significantly reduce the need to trade. It is not possible, therefore, to stop biodiversity loss in Cameroon. However, with the implementation of some of the measures outlined below, it may be possible to slow the process. These are listed in two categories, national and global. Actions necessary at the local level have to be directed from the national level.

National Context

These goals will require political reform and not merely a cosmetic change in political parties but a radical streamlining of the government, reducing inefficiency and making it more transparent and effective, a strategy that requires strong political leadership.

- Develop a secondary sector of the economy to produce manufactured goods to add value and provide employment. This would reduce pressure on the primary sector. The reliance of Cameroon's economy on the primary sector is its Achilles heel.

- Reform land tenure and natural resource laws and the forestry sector to provide the basis for effective landownership with secure tenure which is essential to create conditions for sustainable use. This is not merely a question of reformulation of laws and decrees of application, but a true commitment to sustainability and an end to uncontrolled forest mining and unrestrained access to forests.

- Reduce the environmental damage caused by private companies and their workers. Legislation should be introduced to ensure that companies involved in agriculture or logging pay their workers at a rate that does not necessitate their living off the land. Companies should be held responsible for environmental damage caused by their employees. This legislation could be extended to control the transport of bushmeat. Logging companies should be required to destroy roads after logging has been completed. Industry should be discouraged from importing workers into ecologically sensitive areas, and should be required to repatriate workers at the end of their contracts.

- Explore the development of alternative, ecologically friendly crops for export in order to move away from reliance on the usual range of tropical products.

- Encourage the government to control the urbanization process and control migration from one area to another.

- Plan road and other infrastructure construction not only according to transport and demographic needs, but also taking biodiversity into account through adequate environmental safeguards. Similar standards should be applied to road rehabilitation and repair and to the construction of roads by logging companies.

- Manage harvesting of biodiversity and genetic resources (wildlife, medicinal plants) efficiently and sustainably. It is desirable to legalize traditional hunting and then manage it. Sport hunting must be controlled and efforts made to ensure that a significant portion of the proceeds is returned to local communities.

- Develop a national biodiversity strategy including a national plan for biodiversity protection that takes account of the distribution of biodiversity and the national protected area system.

- Promote education as a powerful tool for biodiversity conservation. Democratic and informed decisions on biodiversity need to be taken by an educated and informed population.

Global Context

- Develop information about the consequences of consumption of wildlife resources, especially in those countries that consume Cameroon's resources, either directly or indirectly. Steps would include making regulation of trade the responsibility of the consumer rather than the producer country; making aid more responsive to the needs of the country; and improving the quality of both bilateral and multilateral aid by moving toward more innovative projects directed toward quality of life rather than infrastructure development.

- Reform structural adjustment programmes to make them more sensitive to the environment, especially in economies that are principally primary producers. Emphasis should be placed on developing a secondary sector of the economy, so that value can be added to the primary products and opportunities for employment provided, and on diversifying the economy away from primary production.

- Reform CITES to increase the efficiency of detection and move the responsibility for monitoring away from the producer country. Efforts should strengthen control and reduce the import of wildlife into the developed world, including a redoubling of efforts to control and reduce the import of wildlife products such as ivory and rhinoceros horn into Asia.

- Promote effective international control of the arms trade. Cameroon should levy punitive duties on the import of guns, ammunition and hunting paraphernalia.

- Lobby for effective implementation of the CBD, especially with respect to provisions for access, benefit-sharing and development of protected areas.

- Lobby for reform of the free trade movement and reassess the environmental consequences of privatization. Work toward development of an international system to stabilize commodity prices for producers at a fair and acceptable level, perhaps through the introduction of direct marketing.

- Revitalize the cocoa industry. International cocoa prices have maintained an economically viable level. Cocoa is a crop that is consistent with biodiversity conservation since the forest cover is retained as shade. Revitalization of the cocoa industry could reduce the rate of biodiversity destruction in the south-east.

Chapter 8

China: South-Western Forests

Research team: The core members of the research team were *Prof Zhao Xiaomin* (Beijing Forestry University), *Dr Li Zhou* (Chinese Academy of Social Sciences Research Center of Ecological and Environmental Economics), *Mr Huang Zhengfu* (Chinese Academy of Social Science Institute of Rural Development) and *Prof Zhang Minxin* (Nanjing Forestry University Department of Forest Economics). *Dr Changjin Sun* (WWF China Programme) provided technical supervision and general guidance. Extensive use was made of field survey data prepared by the two project design teams for WWF field projects in Pingwu County and in Baimaxueshan of Deqin County. The core members of the Pingwu team were *Mr Lin Lin* (Sichuan Forestry Department), *Ms Xu Wei, Mr Wang Shizhi* and *Ms Gan Tingyu* (Sichuan Academy of Social Sciences), *Mr Han Wei* (Sichuan Poverty Alleviation Office), *Mr Wang Zhun* (Sichuan Academy of Forestry) and *Mr He Shengquan* (Pingwu Forestry Bureau). The core members of the Deqin team were *Mr Yang Weimin* (Yunnan Environmental Protection Bureau), *Mr Li Chun* and *Ms Liang Chuan* (Yunnan Forestry Department), *Mr Long Yongchen* (Yunnan Forestry Inventory and Planning Institute), *Ms Wu Yusong* (Oxfam Hongkong Kunming Office) and *Mr Dong Defu* and *Mr Xiao Lin* (Baimaxueshan Nature Reserve Administration)

Summary: **In two counties in China, agricultural expansion and commercial logging are destroying habitat of the giant panda and the Yunnan snub-nosed monkey. Deforestation is the result of limited economic opportunities and government policies that have led to unproductive agricultural expansion and created a heavy dependence on commercial logging.**

This case study of the root causes of biodiversity loss in China covers two sites, Deqin County of Northern Yunnan Province and Pingwu County of Northern Sichuan Province, both located in the same south-western China temperate forest ecoregion. The mountainous geography, together with diversified climate and soil patterns in these sites, harbour rich and diversified flora and fauna. In particular, two protected animals, the giant panda and the Yunnan snub-nosed monkey, live in these sites. The rich biodiversity formed in these mountainous landscapes is, however, very fragile in the face of disturbances. The local economies are heavily resource-dependent; the land is used for agriculture and grazing and the forest for harvesting timber, fuelwood and other forest products. These productive activities provide only a subsistence living for the people of the region; the local economy remains largely marginal to the regional and national markets.

Major threats to biodiversity in the two sites come from unsustainable resource extraction. In Deqin these include agricultural expansion, fuelwood collection, timber logging for subsistence and commercial sale, over-grazing and illegal hunting. In Pingwu agricultural expansion is a proximate cause of biodiversity loss in some communities, while historically, hunting and forest fires posed major threats to wildlife protection. The most important threat in recent decades, however, has been large-scale timber production, particularly commercial timber logging by state timber companies. All these activities damage wildlife habitats or directly reduce wildlife populations.

In order to conserve the rich biodiversity of this ecoregion, it is necessary to identify and understand the underlying socioeconomic forces that drive such destructive human activities and to take actions to address these forces. It is a gross simplification to say that subsistence needs or poverty are the root causes of biodiversity loss. This study explores how deep-rooted human institutions, including local customs, culture, religion, markets, laws and policies, determine human use of resources while poverty and lack of development further limit people's choices about resources. The two sites provide interesting confirmation of some of the causes of biodiversity loss common to the entire ecoregion. The two sites also allow for useful comparisons. While the Deqin case facilitates a more in-depth analysis of the root causes associated with a subsistence economy, the Pingwu case enables the identification of the root causes that drive commercially oriented logging.

In Deqin County population pressures and lack of development are contributing to unsustainable resource use in the local context. Viewed from the larger national context, government policies on population control, land reform, timber pricing, poverty alleviation and nature reserve management all

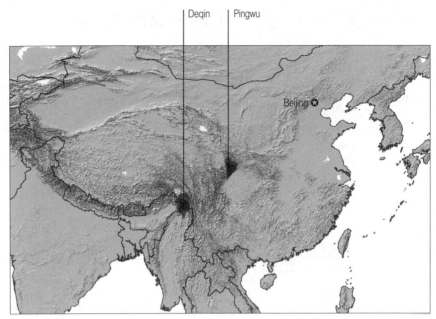

Figure 8.1 *Map of China Showing Location of Study Areas*

cause resource-use problems or aggravate the negative impacts of population pressure and lack of development on resources and biodiversity conservation in Deqin County. Political movements in modern China, which lacked economic rationales, have also caused much damage to biodiversity. Recently, the financial crisis in Asia has caused the collapse of the Matsutake mushroom business, leading to large disturbances in the local economy. Finally, logging and biodiversity conservation are found to generate externalities that are not incorporated into the valuation system of the market. This presents a major challenge for the future.

In Pingwu County, the major forces driving unsustainable logging are the dependence of the government and the local economy on timber revenues, logging firm survival, the presence of vested interests in the logging business, and the breakdown of the logging quota management system. These local root causes of biodiversity loss are found, in turn, to be sustained at the national level by a skewed investment incentive structure for timber production, an urban and state bias embedded in government policies, and destructive political movements. The government's new Natural Forest Conservation Action Programme, aimed at conserving old-growth forests and restructuring the state timber sector, provides a unique opportunity for addressing the threat of logging.

DESCRIPTION OF THE STUDY AREAS

Deqin County

Deqin County is situated in the southern stretches of the Qinghai–Tibetan plateau of Northern Yunnan Province. Deqin County is mountainous, with the highest peak reaching 6740 m and the lowest land at 1840 m. The Jinsha River, a major tributary of the Yangtze in its upper reaches, and the Lancang River, the Chinese part of the Mekong, flow across the county. Deqin has a cold temperate montane monsoon climate with a mean yearly temperature of 5.5°C and a mean yearly rainfall of 662 mm.

The county covers over 7500 km² and is sparsely populated with just 7.75 people/km². The total population is about 58,000 in 11,500 households. It has a total of 13 ethnic groups. Of these Tibetans alone account for over 80 per cent of the population. Other ethic minorities include Susu, Naxi, Bai, Yi, Dai, Nu, Pumi, Lahu, Hani, Miao and Zhuang nationalities (Editorial Office of Deqin Annals, 1998).

Agriculture is the mainstay of the county's economy, with 89 per cent of the population in farming and 75 per cent of the county's GDP of 78 million yuan from agricultural production. Farmland per capita is only 0.1 ha. The per capita grain output in 1997 was 305 kg, and per capita income was 607 yuan,[1] making Deqin a national-level 'poverty county' with 63 per cent of the population in poverty. Other economic activities include forestry, collection of forest products, and cottage industries. Fuelwood and Matsutake mushrooms, which provide a major source of income for rural households, are the main forest products collected. Transportation in the county is difficult and there are still 17 villages without access to highways.

Deqin County is one of the key counties in China with rich old-growth forests. Lands officially designated for forestry occupy 67 per cent of total land in Deqin, with actual forest cover of 37 per cent. State forests account for more than two-thirds of forest resources; the rest are in collective ownership. Timber production can be classified into three types: house construction materials, other subsistence use and commercial production. The production of house-building timber and other subsistence-use timber has been maintained at around 10,000 m³ per year, while commercial production varies from year to year, ranging from 64,000 m³ in 1994 to 19,000 m³ in 1996 (Editorial Office of Deqin Annals, 1998). Forestry and collection of forest products is an important economic activity with a total value in 1997 of 14 million yuan, or close to 18 per cent of the total county gross product. Of the total forestry value, non-timber forest products are dominant, with a total value of almost 11 million yuan.

Deqin County has a total of 200,000 ha of pasture, mostly distributed at an altitude of about 3500 m, which is being over-grazed. With a value of over 12 million yuan in 1997, animal husbandry plays an important role in the local economy, producing milk, meat, wool, and manure, and providing a means of transportation. The major grazing animals are yak and goat, followed by sheep and ox. In addition, most families have donkeys, mules and horses. There is a surprisingly low percentage of livestock used for meat production each year. With the exception of pigs, all other animals are slaughtered at a rate of less than 4 per cent of stock per year. For cattle, this rate is under 1 per cent. This reflects the value that local Tibetans traditionally place on livestock as a symbol of wealth.

Deqin County is rich in flora and fauna. The Baimaxueshan Nature Reserve was established in 1983. It has a total area of 190,440 ha, has 120 families, 397 genera, and 922 species of seed plants; 9 orders, 23 families, 68 genera, and 97 species of mammals; and 14 orders, 37 families, 4 sub-families, and 215 species of birds. While the total area of the nature reserve is only 0.76 per cent of the total land area of Yunnan Province, its mammal species account for 32 per cent of the provincial total and 16 per cent of the national total. There are 35 protected rare and endangered animal species in the county, of which 26 species are found inside the nature reserve (Editorial Office of Deqin Annals, 1998). The core habitats for the Yunnan snub-nosed monkey (*Rhinopithecus bieti*), which currently has an estimated population of 1000 to 1500 animals (Long et al, 1996), are found in Deqin.

Habitat reduction, fragmentation, and degradation, as well as illegal hunting, resulting in reduction of wildlife populations, threaten biodiversity in Dequin. For instance, a survey of one monkey colony indicated that it had decreased from about 300 animals in 1990 to about 200 animals in 1994. Other rare and endangered species such as the musk deer and red panda are also threatened in the region (Long et al, 1996). The most important proximate causes of biodiversity loss in the county include agricultural expansion for food self-sufficiency, fuelwood collection and timber production. Secondary proximate causes include over-grazing and illegal hunting.

Pingwu County

Pingwu County also has a mountainous topography of high ridges and deep valleys, with mountains over 1000 m occupying 93 per cent of its territory and with the highest mountain peak reaching 5400 m (Li, 1993). The county's complex topography creates a variable climate, primarily subtropical montane monsoon, and diversified soil types.

Pingwu County currently has 12 ethnic minority groups. However, Han Chinese are the predominant group, making up 97 per cent of the population, followed by Tibetans, accounting for 2.4 per cent. As of 1996, 184,900 people lived in the county, with a population density of 31 person/km^2 in a total territory of 5948 km^2. Pingwu is also a primarily agricultural economy, with a farming population of 163,890 people. Although the population density of Pingwu is four times that of Deqin, there is 0.15 ha of farmland per capita in Pingwu. Per capita annual income is currently 918 yuan, 1.5 times that of Deqin, and per capita annual grain production is 387 kg, compared with 305 in Deqin (Pingwu County Finance Bureau, 1997). In addition to agriculture, major economic activities in the county include animal husbandry, commercial forestry, construction, mining, power production, and food industries. While the subsistence living of native populations has been fairly stable for centuries, logging, mining and hydropower dam construction have brought in large numbers of migrant labourers.

Forests and forest-suitable lands, grasslands, and agricultural fields, respectively, occupy 63 per cent, 20 per cent and 5 per cent of total land in the county. There are over 27,000 ha of farmland. Pingwu is also endowed with mineral resources, particularly gold, and plentiful water. Pasture land in Pingwu is stocked at below carrying capacity. Nevertheless, animal husbandry plays an important role in the lives of local people. In comparison with Deqin, a high percentage of animals are slaughtered, an indication that farmers are raising domestic animals for consumption or commercial sale, not as a symbol of wealth.

The biological resources in Pingwu County are rich and diversified. The fauna includes 23 families, 37 genera and 87 species. Of these, three species, namely the giant panda (*Ailrupoda melanoleuca*), golden monkey (*Rhinopithecus roxellanae*) and takin (*Budorcas taxicolor*), are in category I of the national protected animals, eight species are in category II and seven in category III (Li, 1993). There are seven category I and 23 category II bird species. The giant panda has been found in 30 out of 39 townships in the county and the population is estimated at 183 animals, usually found in forests at 1600 to 3400 m. The Wanglang Nature Reserve, established in Pingwu in 1963, was among the first three giant panda nature reserves in China, and is one of the most important panda habitats (Ministry of Forestry and WWF, 1989). However, the 332 km^2 of this reserve plus two more planned panda nature reserves would only cover about 40 per cent of the total panda habitat in Pingwu County.

Forest cover in Pingu is about 48 per cent (Li, 1993). There are 78 common tree species belonging to 23 families and 37 genera. Forests located above 2000 m usually have a sub-storey of arrow bamboo, which is the staple food of the giant panda. About 37 per cent of the total stumpage volume, or 6.74 million m^3, is legally classified as viable for timber production. However, most of these forests are not really suitable for commercial timber production. They are often old-growth forests that support important wildlife habitats, they grow on steep slopes with shallow soils that are vulnerable to erosion, and they do not regenerate well after logging.

State timber production, mainly clear-cutting, is the primary proximate cause of deforestation and habitat loss in the county. Illegal hunting, fire, and clearing for agriculture are other threats to forests and wildlife habitat. The destruction of forests has caused widespread soil erosion and water siltation, which threatens wildlife. The population of the giant panda was 332 in 1975, 278 in 1983, and just 183 in 1985, a decrease of 114 animals in just 11 years.[2] The degradation of forest resources is another indicator of biodiversity loss. Logging and fuelwood collection have largely wiped out the subtropical evergreen broad-leaved forests historically distributed along river valleys and in low- to middle-altitude hills; they have also degraded many fir forests to bush and shrub forests, encouraging an overgrowth of the arrow bamboo, which in turn becomes too rough for the giant panda to feed upon. Yet another indicator of ecosystem degradation is the significant reduction in the volume of river flows in the county.

Comparison of the Two Study Sites

Major statistics of these two sites are shown in Table 8.1. The two case study sites share a number of characteristics. Both are considered critical sites for biodiversity conservation in China, and both are located in the same south-west China temperate forest ecoregion, which is a priority ecosystem at a global level (Carey, 1996). Located in the upper reaches of the Yangtze River watershed, they share a very mountainous topography and similar weather, soil and vegetation patterns. Nature reserves cover only a portion of the impor-tant habitats and biodiversity loss is a concern in both sites. Deqin and Pingwu both have primarily agricultural and resource-dependent subsistence economies. Timber production, particularly large-scale commercial logging of old-growth forests by state timber companies, is an important proximate cause of biodiversity loss in both sites. Economic activities and biodiversity conser-vation goals make conflicting demands on the local ecosystems.

There are also important differences between the sites which facilitate some interesting comparisons in this analysis. Deqin County is more remote and mountainous and is also poorer. Even though it is much less densely populated than Pingwu, per capita farmland and per capita income in Deqin are only about two-thirds that of Pingwu. In spite of the large number of livestock in Deqin, its animal husbandry is much less consumption-oriented than in Pingwu. Consequently, agricultural expansion, fuelwood collection, and over-grazing appear to be more serious threats to biodiversity in Deqin. Finally, illegal hunting is a more severe threat in Deqin as law enforcement in the Yunnan snub-nosed monkey habitats has never been as strong as in the giant panda habitats of Pingwu County. In Pingwu, commercial timber produc-tion appears to be more destructive and occurs on a much larger scale.

METHODOLOGY

Both the definition of biodiversity and the measurement of biodiversity loss are subjects of continued discussion. It has been suggested that species and their core habitats are good indicators of biodiversity. This study therefore uses species population size and habitat status as the indicators of biodiversity loss. 'Flagship' species, including the giant panda and the Yunnan snub-nosed monkey, serve as indicators for the health and integrity of the ecosystem of which they are a part. Analysis focuses on the proximate causes of biodiversity loss identified at each site in a field survey, namely logging activities in Pingwu and other development activities in Deqin.

Table 8.1 *Major Comparative Statistics: Deqin and Pingwu Counties*

Statistics	Deqin County	Pingwu County
Location	Northern Yunnan Province	Northern Sichuan Province
Altitude (m)	1840–6740	600–5400
Average annual temp (°C)	5.5	14.7
Annual rainfall (mm)	662	835
Total area (km^2)	7504	5948
Total population	58,000	185,000
Population density(/km^2)	8	31
Farming population (%)	89	89
Total farmland (ha)	5350	27,500
Per capita farmland (ha)	0.1	0.2
Ethnic minorities (% of total population)	98	3
Major religions	Tibetan Buddhism, Islam, Christianity	Buddhism, Christianity, Islam, Taoism, Catholicism
Total number of villages in the county	41 administrative villages, 470 production groups	250 administrative villages, 1,500 production groups
Total gross product (yuan)	78,320,000 in 1997	410,000,000 in 1996
Major economic activities	Farming, forestry, animal husbandry, collecting and logging	Farming, animal husbandry, forest industry, mining, food, construction, power
Agricultural output (yuan)	58,780,000	218,000,000
Per capita grain production (kg)	305	387
Agricultural output as % of gross product	75	53
Per capita income (yuan)	608	918
Population in poverty	33,000	–
Forest lands (ha)	496,000 (67%)	448,000 (75%)
Stocked forest lands (ha)	271,800	288,000
Forest coverage rate (%)	37	48
Size of nature reserves	190,000 ha	323 km^2 (+260 km^2 planned)
'Flagship' species	Yunnan snub-nosed monkey, red panda	Giant panda, red panda

The following categories of data were collected:

a. *Baseline socioeconomic and demographic data:* population size and sex division, land use, GDP, per capita income, government administrative structure, ethnic composition, fiscal revenue (size, division by sources), and major economic activities, including farming, forestry, grazing, logging, mining and hydropower generation.

b. *Biological data:* biophysical characteristics and changes; major flora and fauna resources and their change over time; the status of flagship species and keynote species (those listed as national-, provincial- or county-protected animal, bird, fish and plant species); change in the habitat of important wildlife (quantity and quality); change in forest resources (coverage rate, standing volume, species and age composition, structure of forest, extent of planted versus old-growth forests, stumpage growth rate); and change in environmental quality as indicated by the degree of soil erosion and water siltation.

c. *Data on government policy:* protected area development; land-use planning; control of hunting and poaching; nature reserves management (staffing, decision-making structure and funding arrangement); pricing of timber and other resources; taxation of timber and other resources; tenure arrangements for forest resources and land; population policy regarding ethnic minorities and the employment of migrant labour; and the development of rural extension networks.

d. *Data on timber production:* a company profile for each logging company, information on the organization of logging operations and on the enforcement of logging rules, and financial and economic data on timber production.

General data were sought from published secondary sources, from unpublished literature, and from various government departments, particularly the departments of statistics, finance and planning, taxes, forestry, agriculture, poverty alleviation, nature reserve management, and timber industry. Individual logging companies were approached for data on timber production and company finance. Finally, interviews and on-site surveys were carried out to collect data from rural communities using participatory rural appraisal methods.

On the basis of data collected, the linkage between habitat loss, including fragmentation, reduction, or degradation and hunting, on the one hand, and biodiversity loss, on the other, was established. Next, the proximate causes of habitat loss were identified by locating the major human activities that are associated with such destruction or damages. A stakeholder analysis was conducted to identify the major beneficiaries and victims of relevant human activities. To establish causal or interactive relationships among a set of social, economic, and political forces that govern human use of resources, ecosystem impacts, and biodiversity loss, the general lines of reasoning as outlined in Machlis and Forester (1996) were followed. Problem tree diagrams and numeric data presentation techniques were used to depict causal or interactive relationships visually and precisely and to depict trends or facilitate comparisons. Finally, the explanatory power of these constructed conceptual models was examined and recommendations that address the root causes, that is, the set of social, economic, and political forces driving biodiversity loss, were made.

The lack and unreliability of data presented a major problem for this study. This is particularly true for government statistics and records. The problem is most acute in Deqin since it has not had a forest inventory for the past decade, and many standard sets of statistics are either not available or are incomplete. Reluctance to share some data, particularly the financial data of logging companies, was also encountered.

LOCAL CONTEXT

Deqin County

The major indicators of biodiversity loss in Deqin include fragmentation, reduction and degradation of wildlife habitats and the reduction of wildlife populations. Threats to the Yunnan snub-nosed monkey provide an indication of biodiversity loss. While its typical home range is 100 km^2, one noted colony has lost 5 km^2 of its core zone over the last five years due to fuelwood collection. All four colonies in the Baimaxueshan region are isolated from each other by habitat fragmentation, which leads to in-breeding. Researcher Long Yongcheng recorded about 300 animals in the Wuyapuya colony in 1990 but found only about 200 four years later. In addition to habitat loss, hunting causes direct loss of wildlife. In 1980, over 30 monkeys were found shot in one village alone (Yunnan Provincial No 4 Forestry Survey Team, 1981). Other animals, such as musk deer and red panda, can be found now only in forests of higher altitude or on local sacred mountains.

Habitat loss is widespread, and is largely due to forest clearing for grain production. In 1949, farmland in Deqin covered 2000 ha. It increased four times in about 20 years, reaching 7500 ha in 1970 (Diqing Tibetan Autonomous Prefecture Statistics Bureau, 1998). Fuelwood collection is also contributing to habitat loss. A 1981 analysis indicates that about 210,000 m^3 of fuelwood are consumed annually in rural households, and 100,000 m^3 of fuelwood are consumed by industry, resulting in a loss of over 1800 ha of forest each year (Yunnan Provincial No 4 Forestry Survey Team, 1981). Commercial logging is the third important cause of habitat loss. Since 1985 over 9500 ha of forest have been logged in the county. The Deqin County Timber Company alone logged 3000 ha between 1972 and 1984 in the Adong forest at the northern edge of the Baimaxueshan Nature Reserve; it has since cut another 2000 ha in the Guomorong forest at the southern edge of the reserve. Other types of logging and over-grazing also contribute to forest loss, fragmentation and degradation. The relationship among these five proximate causes of habitat damage and wildlife loss – agricultural expansion, fuelwood collection, commercial logging, over-grazing, and illegal hunting – is discussed in detail below.

Agricultural Expansion

Deqin is not self-sufficient in food production, and increasing grain production has always been high on the local government's agenda. The government has been mobilizing available resources to expand farmland and to raise land productivity so as to address the problem of food shortages. There are two types of agricultural lands – paddy fields and dry lands, including irrigated and non-irrigated lands. Paddy fields are the most productive land, but account for only 2–3 per cent of total farmland. The major strategies employed by local people in addressing the problem of food shortages are to increase the area of farmland or to improve lower-quality land.

Historically, there has been a significant general trend of increase in total farm acreage, though with sharp fluctuations. Agricultural land covered 2000 ha in 1949 when the People's Republic of China was established, peaked in 1970 at 7500 ha, and started to increase again slightly in the 1990s. The single largest five-year increase occurred from 1955 to 1960 when the political movement known as the Great Leap Forward was in process. The area of paddy field has been relatively stable. With the exception of 1955 and 1960, it has been around 130 ha. The type of land with the largest fluctuations is shifting cultivation land, with the highest area of about 1300 ha in 1985 equal to 14 times that of 1949. It is interesting to note that shifting cultivation lands are generally created by deforestation, and that their peak in 1985 came much later than the peak of total farming area in 1970. This suggests that deforestation for agricultural land continues, despite a total reduction in farmland. Finally, it should be noted that over 90 per cent of farmlands in the county are dry lands, mostly located on very steep slopes, and are developed by clearing forests (Diqing Tibetan Autonomous Prefecture Editorial Office, 1984).

In spite of the steady expansion of agricultural land through encroachment on forests and wildlife habitats, food shortages have persisted. After 30 years of low per capita yields, grain production finally regained levels achieved in the mid-1960s in 1995. The highest production to date occurred in 1997, with per capita grain production reaching 395 kg, just above that achieved in 1965. Yet even in 1997, Deqin had to import 290 tons of grain.

Several factors have contributed to the persistence of food shortages. First, while total production has been increasing steadily since 1960, the increase in population has outpaced that of the grain production. Second, the small area of high productivity paddy fields and irrigated dry lands has seriously limited the growth of grain production. Third, the cold weather and lack of sunshine, together with the lack of irrigation water (rivers usually flow at the bottom of valleys whereas farmlands are high in the mountains), also limit the potential for raising land productivity. Per hectare yield in the bumper year of 1997 was still only 2568 kg, far below the national mean of 4500 kg.

The expansion of agricultural land has caused significant damage to forests and their associated ecosystems. The area of forests so lost has reached over 5500 ha per year. The soil erosion and water siltation accompanying deforestation and farming of newly cleared lands have been severe, leaving many areas close to villages barren.

Collection of Forest Products

Fuelwood is the most important rural energy source in Deqin County, accounting for 98 per cent of local energy use. Hydroelectricity is the only other locally produced source of energy. Many rural households cannot afford electricity except for lighting, which leaves a surplus of electricity in some locations. Even though fuelwood collection is costly in terms of time and labour, families prefer to use fuelwood since they have surplus labour but no cash. The predominance of fuelwood use is also associate with the local culture. Customarily an open fire is maintained in the hearth for 24 hours a day, year round. These fires are very inefficient in fuel use. The research team estimated that total land degraded each year by fuelwood collection may be as much as 1400 ha. The official annual quota for fuelwood cutting in Deqin is about 100,000 m³, far above the quota for commercial logging. The nibbling away of forests for fuelwood, like clearing for farmland, occurs in the vicinity of villages. Over time, the loss of forests near the villages has made fuelwood collection an increasingly demanding task.

The Matsutake mushroom business has made a significant contribution to the local economy over the past decade. Local farmers, working on collective land, are the primary harvesters of the mushrooms, which are found exclusively in the oak forests of the region. With fresh Matsutake selling to Japan at prices as high as 200 yuan/kg, the share of Matsutake in the total value of local commercial agricultural products has reached over 65 per cent in the late 1990s. This large share reflects in part the poor links between the local economy and outside markets. While Matsutake production has been relatively benign for the environment overall, unmanaged collection practices are resulting in the depletion of Matsutake resources. Fluctuation in the mushroom market also has a large indirect impact on the local ecosystem as it affects local income and the intensity of other resource-based activities such as fuelwood collection and grazing.

Timber Production

Compared with other forest-rich regions in China, commercial timber production in Deqin started relatively late, in 1972. The Dequin County Timber Company has monopolized production, distribution and sale of commercial timber from the state-owned natural forests. This company has a staff of 300, of which 90 per cent are long-term contracted workers. Seasonal labour, mostly local peasants, are hired to carry out the cutting and transportation. The Prefectural Planning Committee and Prefectural Forestry Bureau set logging quotas. A Logging Quota Management System (LQMS) has been implemented to control resource depletion but clear-cutting has been widely practised. Currently, the Jinshajiang Forest Products Corporation under the Provincial Forestry Department, or outside timber merchants, purchase the timber, most of which is sold domestically. Deqin County Timber is responsible for the regeneration of deforested sites.

The production of timber for subsistence started much earlier, in 1962. Production is organized by various township and village enterprises, and the timber produced is supposed to be consumed within the county. Some of this timber has been sold commercially to outside buyers in recent years. It is subject to roughly the same procedures of LQMS as commercial production. House-building timber is not subject to quotas. However, the government controls its volume by allowing one household out of 25 to cut house-building timber each year and by limiting the cut per household to 35 m^3 (Deqin County Forestry Bureau, 1992).

While commercial timber production volume varies greatly from year to year, the production volume for subsistence-use and house-building timber has been more stable. Commercial timber production has been carried out in the large patches of primary forests owned by the state, while the latter two usually are carried out in forests close to villages and in a more scattered fashion. Between 1985 and 1997, about 13,000 ha of forest were cleared for timber production, of which almost 8000 ha were cleared for commercial production, 2000 ha for subsistence-use, and 3000 ha for house-building.

The forces driving local timber production were examined by looking at the distribution of timber revenue and the contribution of timber income to local government revenue. Government taxes and fees account for over one-quarter of the total market price per cubic metre of timber, and the income retained by logging firms accounts for one-third to one-half of total market price. The logging companies, namely Deqin County Timber and the various town and village enterprises, are therefore the largest beneficiaries of commercial logging. A large portion of revenue earned by Deqin County Timber, plus a large share of timber taxes and fees, go to the local government.

The contribution of timber production to locally generated county revenue (revenue generated for the county government by all economic activities in the local economy) is very high, accounting for 44–89 per cent in the past decade, averaging 7 million yuan in recent years. The share of timber revenue in total local government revenue (the sum of county revenue plus fiscal subsidy from higher-level government departments) is comparatively low at around 20 per cent. This reflects the fact that Deqin County is heavily dependent on subsidies from higher levels of government. The rate of fiscal self-sufficiency in Deqin reached about 30 per cent at its highest in 1991, and 16 per cent at its lowest. However, local government expenditures have been increasing. Commercial logging is therefore largely motivated by the need to sustain a growing local government. Similarly, the production of subsistence-use timber by township and village enterprises is largely motivated by the needs of local township and village governments.

Also of importance are the externalities associated with forests. Forests are located in the upper reaches of the major river systems in Deqin. The soil and water conservation benefits generated by natural forests are not directly reflected in the local economy or enjoyed by local people in Deqin, whereas the harmful effects of logging on soil erosion are felt largely by downstream economies. This asymmetry of costs and benefits surrounding timber production contributes to local incentives for commercial logging.

Over-grazing

Animal husbandry is ranked after farming and forestry in the local economy with a value of about 12 million yuan per year. A large portion of the products of animal husbandry are consumed domestically, and family wealth is traditionally measured by the size of livestock herds. Butter, hides and meat are sometimes sold for cash income. Production costs are low, particularly since villages usually take charge of grazing, with households taking turns tending the animals.

During the past two decades, the number of domestic animals in Deqin has increased significantly, particularly the number of goats. Over-grazing has been a problem since the late 1970s. As of 1997, Deqin County was being over-grazed by 23,000 ox units, over 40 per cent above its estimated carrying capacity. The fact that tenure of grasslands is not clearly defined has further aggravated the problem of over-grazing – even state-owned grasslands with open access are grazed by household herds.

Over-grazing has caused degradation of grasslands, soil erosion, and water siltation, as well as under-feeding of animals, especially in the winter. Goats in particular are responsible for substantial damage since they tend to graze at lower altitudes close to villages, where ecosystems are vulnerable to a range of threats.

Illegal Hunting

Local inhabitants hunt to obtain meat or skins or to protect crops and domestic animals. Government employees and urban residents usually hunt for recreational purposes. Over the past 14 years, 280 incidents of illegal hunting have been reported and punished, over 50,000 iron snares and 60 skins confiscated, and over 600 people charged (Baimaxueshan Nature Reserve, 1997). In general, the problem of illegal hunting is becoming less severe as law enforcement grows stronger. Increased enforcement, however, is leading to increased damage to crops and livestock by wildlife. In 1997 alone, about 656 domestic animals were hurt or lost to wildlife attack (Baimaxueshan Nature Reserve, 1997).

Summary

The above analyses indicate that the most important proximate causes of biodiversity loss in Deqin County include agricultural expansion for food self-sufficiency, fuelwood collection, and timber production. Secondary proximate causes include over-grazing and illegal hunting. While agricultural expansion and fuelwood collection result in habitat reduction, timber production causes loss, degradation, or fragmentation of habitats. Over-grazing causes grassland and forest degradation, and illegal hunting constitutes a direct attack on wildlife.

Two underlying factors, namely population growth and lack of local economic development, or poverty, reinforce the impacts of the five proximate causes of biodiversity loss in the county. Demographic censuses reveal that, between 1953 and 1990, total population nearly doubled to about 56,000 people. Forty-three per cent of the local population was still illiterate in 1990, and only about 11 per cent had received education beyond primary school. The pressure of a rapidly increasing population on the production of food, fuelwood and house-construction timber, and for the expansion of animal husbandry, is enormous. Yet, despite the expansion of agricultural areas and the increase in land productivity, per capita grain production remained below its 1960 level for 30 years. At the same time, lack of education works against the adoption of new technologies that could improve productivity in local economic activities.

Lack of local economic development greatly limits the choice of viable economic alternatives. A poor county government means a lack of funds to subsidize hydro-power generation and a dependence on fuelwood, lack of irrigation facilities, and lack of inputs in farming and technological innovation. All these problems in turn sustain rural poverty and the natural resource exploitative local economy – particularly the exploitation of timber resources and over-grazing. Population pressure and lack of economic development are therefore the root causes of biodiversity loss at the local level.

Pingwu County

Habitat loss, fragmentation and degradation are serious threats to biodiversity in Pingwu County. Loss of wildlife is the first indicator of biodiversity loss. The Pingwu County Annal recorded a large wildlife population in Pingwu in the late 1950s and early 1960s (Editorial Office of Pingwu County Annals, 1995). Today, many wild animals, including the giant panda, clouded leopard, red panda and takin, are officially threatened animals.

Reduction of forest cover is the second indicator. Pingwu was historically endowed with rich old-growth forests. Currently, only one large patch of unlogged primary forest remains outside of the Wanglang Nature Reserve. A reduced diversity of vegetation types is the third indicator. Large-scale commercial logging and fuelwood collection have significantly reduced the diversity of forest types in the county. For instance, subtropical evergreen broad-leaved forests originally distributed in the lower hills and long river valleys have largely disappeared, and most Chinese-fir forests have degenerated into shrub forests. Finally, the increase in flooding incidents and the reduced flow in major rivers in Pingwu provides a fourth, though indirect, indicator of biodiversity loss.

The damages to biodiversity indicated by species reduction and habitat loss are mostly caused by human economic activities, the proximate causes of biodiversity loss – logging, farming and animal husbandry. Logging has been the most important. Large logging companies owned by the central government started to enter Pingwu in the 1950s and expanded their operations in the 1970s. The forest coverage rate in Pingwu was over 52 per cent in the 1950s, but was quickly reduced to less than 35 per cent by the 1970s. Regeneration was carried out on a small scale and in easily accessible sites, usually on natural grasslands, instead of on deforested sites. Beginning in the

1990s, clear-cutting of entire watersheds was carried out, wiping out even seedling trees. In 1995, the Pingwu Forestry Development Corporation initiated a concession-granting practice whereby private timber loggers were contracted to log an entire watershed with a lump-sum advance payment. This has further encouraged exploitative logging. Today the last stand of old-growth forests remaining outside nature reserves is being logged.

Agricultural expansion is not a major threat to biodiversity in Pingwu. The impact of farm expansion is largely historical and total farm area has been decreasing since 1980, falling from 31,558 ha then to 28,133 ha in 1995. The impact was concentrated in low-altitude areas of Pingwu which are densely populated and support large farmlands and intensive farming. Grazing also is not a major threat to conservation. Although the major impact of animal husbandry is on forested lands, either through clearing or direct grazing, the impact is limited since the number of animals raised is well below the estimated carrying capacity. Moreover, unlike the case of Deqin, Pingwu has relatively more oxen than goats (Editorial Office of Pingwu County Annals, 1995).

Forest fires, probably related to human activities, have historically caused severe damage to forests. Between 1950 and 1990, 45 forest fires occurred each year on average, causing damage to a total of 4000 ha of forests, equivalent to 100 ha per year. Forest fires were most severe from 1950 to the late 1970s. Due to increased forest fire prevention efforts, the threat of forest fires has been under control in recent years (Editorial Office of Pingwu County Annals, 1995).

The government encouraged and organized hunting for a long time, partially for the purpose of protecting crops and partially due to the lack of conservation awareness. In the 1980s, however, hunting was made illegal. In fact, some hunters of the giant panda were executed in 1987. However, scattered illegal hunting of non-protected animals continues, often entailing incidental damage to giant pandas and other protected wildlife, particularly when snares are used. Organized illegal hunting with advanced weapons by people from outside of Pingwu County also occurs occasionally (Lu et al, 1998).

The damage caused by farming, animal husbandry and hunting in Pingwu is limited. The following discussion focuses on the incentives that underlie logging, which is the main proximate cause of biodiversity loss in the county.

Logging

The problem of over-logging in Pingwu County is obvious. Between 1988 and 1995 the average annual volume of timber produced was 90,000 m³, of which 69,000 m³ were commercial timber. Given an average production coefficient of 0.6–0.7, this is equivalent to depleting between 130,000 and 150,000 m³ of standing forest stock each year. According to 1988 inventory data, the average annual growth in standing volume of forest stock in commercial timber forests in Pingwu is only 17,300 m³. The volume of actual depletion is therefore eight times the annual growth rate of these forests. Since most commercially viable forests in Pingwu are old-growth forests, this depletion inevitably causes major damage to biodiversity. Moreover, there has been a large gap between the area logged and the area replanted, although the law calls for reforestation. From 1988 to 1995, the average area cleared and not replanted was 5485 ha. By 1997, the forest resources in Muzuo and Baima townships were depleted and a logging operation was started in Huya township in the last remaining large patch of old-growth forest.

In Pingwu, collectives own about 250,000 ha or around 59 per cent of forest. The state owns the remaining 175,000 ha or 41 per cent of forest lands. Forest resources have three distinctive characteristics. First, production timber forests account for only a minor portion of total forests (under 9 per cent). Most forests (78 per cent) are protected for ecological reasons. Second, most timber forests (80 per cent) are mature or over-mature. And third, almost all mature or over-mature timber forests are distributed on very steep slopes (Pingwu County Forest Inventory Team, 1990). All these characteristics make logging damaging to biodiversity and ecological protection.

Timber production in Pingwu can be divided into two types: commercial timber production and subsistence-use timber production. While commercial timber production can be carried out in both state and collective forests, subsistence-use timber can only be produced from collective forests. Subsistence-use timber is used for building houses, fuelwood, and small-scale wood processing. The production of subsistence-use timber dates back to the early 19th century, but has remained modest in scale. Today, subsistence-use timber is mainly produced by township and village enterprises or by individual households. Between 1979 and 1990, the production of subsistence-use timber increased, averaging about 16,000 m^3 per year. A significant portion of this timber is used for fuelwood. There is also a fairly large commercial charcoal business using subsistence-use timber.

Commercial timber production by state companies is the major force behind deforestation in Pingwu County. While the area of state forests is only about 70 per cent that of collective forests, the volume of timber production by state companies in Pingwu from 1990 to 1995 was over three times that of subsistence-use from collective forests. Commercial timber is produced for sale to buyers outside of Pingwu County. Timber companies owned by the state or by town and village enterprises carry out production. The Northern Sichuan Forest Industry Corporation began large-scale commercial timber production in Muzuo and Baima townships in 1952. Even though replanting was done well, forests were deforested without any compensation to the local community or to the local government. In 1958, Northern Sichuan Forest Industry, owned by the provincial government, was dissolved and replaced by a company owned by the prefectural government, which was in turn replaced by a county government-owned company in 1994. In 1995, this last company was merged into the Pingwu Forestry Development Corporation. Currently there are also two smaller logging companies owned by the county government, namely Longmenshan Forestry Farm and Pingwu County Forestry Industry.

Socioeconomic Interests Driving State Commercial Timber Logging

Current logging practices are unsustainable both in terms of logging volume and methods. At the current rate of resource depletion, Longmenshan Forestry Farm can only sustain timber production for one more year, and Pingwu Forestry Development for eight more years. This destructive commercial logging by the state companies has continued because of deeply vested local socioeconomic interests. The first is the dependence of county and township government revenue on income from logging. In 1997, the Pingwu County government had revenue of 24 million yuan, of which about 47 per cent was from logging. The revenue of some villages and township administrations in forest-rich regions is also heavily dependent on timber exploitation (Lu et al, 1998). Since governments at various levels all depend heavily on timber revenue, there is a strong incentive for government to sustain commercial logging, even when each level of government recognizes that such logging practices are not sustainable.

Second is the dependence of state timber companies on logging. Pingwu Forestry Development has three major lines of business – logging, sawn timber, and calcium carbide. Yet it earned over 99 per cent of its profits in 1996–97 from logging alone. Moreover, a large portion of both the company profit and the taxes are retained by the county government. The government and the state companies have reason to support each other in sustaining commercial timber production.

Third is the existence of other vested interest groups which have developed around timber production over the years. In addition to the logging companies themselves and various governments, there are numerous other beneficiaries. The flow of revenue from prime fir timber provides a good example. Produced from collective forests by Pingwu Forestry Development and selling for 1000 yuan/m^3 in Chengdu City, the breakdown of the unit price is shown in Table 8.2.

This unit price composition illustrates both the large number of parties involved in the timber business, and the disproportionately large percentage of the total timber income taken by logging companies and middlemen. This is even more evident when the problem of truck over-loading is taken into account. It is reported that, while the nominal volume of a truckload of timber is 7.5 m^3, actual loads may reach 11 m^3. Thus the county government and other departments lose 500–600 yuan per truckload sold outside the county, significantly increasing the profitability for parties engaging in timber marketing and inducing bribery and corruption. Therefore, the forestry department, the various departments and individuals involved in organizing, administering and monitoring logging, and parties involved in timber transportation, all have a stake in maintaining the logging business.

The fourth is the breakdown of the LQMS in Pingwu. The LQMS was designed by the central government to ensure that annual resource depletion does not exceed mean annual growth in individual counties. Nationally the LQMS has run into major problems during the recent transition to a market economy. This is particularly true in Pingwu for two reasons. Firstly, the

Table 8.2 *Composition of the Unit Price of Fir Timber Produced by Pingwu Forestry Development*

	Revenue (yuan per m³)	Percentage of selling price
Village forest farm stumpage income	18	2
Fees collected by three timber check-points	50	5
County government revenue and other forestry department fees	124	12
Transportation costs	268	27
Revenue retained by the logging companies, private concession grantees and agents engaged in trading logging quotas	539	54

logging quotas have become a sort of security note in the market of Pingwu in recent years. Logging quotas are being granted for various reasons unrelated to logging capacity, including unemployment welfare, infrastructure development, repair of damages caused by natural disasters, staff salaries, fiscal deficits, or pure patronage. These quotas are then distributed and traded widely among different parties, without connection to the intended holder, the land owner. Since each and every transaction involves a profit, the price of logging quotas inflates significantly before reaching the ultimate producer. To break even, the producer is forced to produce timber in the least costly but often most environmentally damaging fashion.

Secondly, Pingwu Forestry Development pioneered a new practice in 1995 of granting logging concessions to private contractors instead of carrying out logging operations itself. When a private grantee obtains a concession, the price paid includes advance payment of all the stumpage to the owner plus all taxes and fees (including regeneration and tending fees) to the government. The concessionaire also needs to make a very significant investment in road construction and in high-priced logging quotas. The trading of logging quotas also induces a host of other problems, such as the purchase of logging quotas for use at sites other than that intended and over-loading of trucks. All this forces the concessionaire to take an exploitative approach in logging, clearing the entire accessible area. Local villagers often follow the concessionaire to gather whatever wood is left over. Finally, this arrangement does not assign responsibility for replanting to anyone.

NATIONAL CONTEXT

Deqin County

As throughout China, higher-level forces that are outside of the control of local resource users and decision-makers heavily influence resource-use patterns in Deqin County, primarily because the Chinese economy and society are centrally governed by various levels of government. In the three decades between 1950 and 1980, these forces took the form of government policies and political movements. Laws played only a minor role and the government tightly controlled the market. The major government policies in resource use cover population policy, land policy, natural resources use policy, pricing policy, poverty alleviation and general economic development as well as nature reserve management and wildlife protection. Beginning in the early 1980s, the local economy joined the national transition toward a market-based economy. Even though the local economy is still very isolated, market forces and fiscal devolution have begun to play roles in local resource-use patterns. In particular, the county government is now responsible for balancing its budget.

In demographic policy, the Chinese government had a policy of encouraging births until 1970, resulting in a large population boom. From 1949 to 1970 total population in China increased from 455 million to 800 million and the population in Deqin likewise nearly doubled. The family planning policy implemented after 1970 marked a major shift in population policy and gradually evolved into the well-known 'one couple–one child' policy, which has significantly reduced birth rates, particularly in the 1990s. However, total population nationwide has continued to grow as the population of reproductive age is disproportionately large. In the case of Deqin, population growth has been more significant since ethnic minorities enjoy preferential treatment in family planning. They are allowed to have two or three children instead of one. Migration and population movements within China had long been strictly controlled. The relaxing of control over population movements and tourism policies in recent years has had limited impact in Deqin. Tourism is bringing more outsiders to the area, but Deqin remains isolated.

Another important population policy concerns the separation of rural and urban populations, realized via the notorious 'Hukou' (resident permit) Administration System which prohibits people with 'Rural Hukou' from entering the urban sector to engage in non-agricultural activities. While peasants from the rural collective sector are responsible for earning their own living and do not enjoy much government assistance, the government generally employs people in the urban sector in administration, governmental institutions and state-owned enterprises. These government employees enjoy better living standards, with housing, medical care, schooling, utilities, insurance and pensions provided, and are guaranteed lifetime employment. One of the consequences of this policy is an over-sized urban sector that constitutes a fiscal burden for governments at various levels. In the case of Deqin County, the need to support more than 3000 workers and other county employees has been a major incentive for the government to encourage logging and other extractive businesses. The other consequence is an over-sized and impoverished rural sector that has not benefited from the process of industrialization.

In the field of commodity pricing, the government long had a very rigid pricing policy for timber. Timber was treated as a special material subject to state regulation instead of market forces. Before the market reform of the late

1970s, the price of timber was fixed artificially low by the government at 54 yuan/m^3. Today, timber prices are determined by the market and are much higher. However, a large portion of the timber price still goes to the government as taxes and fees and to monopolistic state companies as profit. For timber produced by collective forests, rural households receive collective compensation of 60 to 80 yuan/m^3 of timber for stumpage, only about 10 to 14 per cent of current timber prices. The other major problem with market pricing is the failure of the market to account for the social or environmental cost of logging in timber prices. Compensation is not provided for the loss of forests' ecological and biodiversity benefits, creating a problem of inter-regional equity. Local government administrators feel that the people of Deqin have sacrificed a great deal by putting aside 190,000 ha of good forests as a nature reserve; they have not been compensated for this contribution to ecological protection and biodiversity conservation.

China's land reform policies in the early 1950s established two forms of land ownership, namely collective and state lands. The larger patches of better forests went to the state while the smaller or lower quality forests were put under collective ownership. The exploitation of forests for commercial timber production had long been under strict control of the government. Since the price of timber was set artificially low and the share of the timber price left for the collectives was not distributed to individual households, farmers were not interested in managing the collective forests. Collective forests were not really owned and managed by individuals in the collective; rather, they were exploited by the government representing the collective. The opening up of the timber market in 1985 encouraged farmers to log in an unplanned fashion, which resulted in recent heavy deforestation in Deqin County.

Over the past twenty years of the reform era, the central government has given high priority and preferential investment treatment to the development of the eastern (mostly coastal) part of China. The lack of investment in inner regions such as Deqin and Pingwu has further aggravated the dependence of local economies in these regions of China on resource depletion. Further, these resources have mostly been sold in the form of raw materials with little value added. However, because Deqin is a national-level 'poverty county', governments from various levels have been providing subsidies to Deqin in an effort to combat poverty, bringing badly needed capital to Deqin. Unfortunately, most of such subsidies require matching financial support from the county government, which has turned to logging to generate such matching funds. In 1997, for example, the county government had to log 3000 m^3 of timber so that matching funds could be raised.

For close to three decades from 1950 onward, political movements or campaigns featured prominently in Chinese society and economy. The Food-First Movement and the Cultural Revolution had the largest impact on Deqin's environment. The Food-First Movement of 1960–70 prompted a large forest-clearing campaign, developing many unsuitable fields that were later deserted. From 1955 to 1960, a total of 2500 ha of farmland was added to local farming area, and a total of 7500 ha was added by 1970. The Cultural Revolution of

1966–76 rendered local governments largely dysfunctional and resource management institutions collapsed.

The progress of the reform era has been accompanied by a general growth of conservation awareness in China. The Baimaxueshan Nature Reserve was established in 1983 as a provincial-level reserve and upgraded to a national-level reserve in 1988. However, the funding for reserve management comes from the provincial budget, which is inadequate and very unstable. Also, the amount of funding for each nature reserve is set by the government in direct proportion to the size of the staff. This funding policy has led to over-staffing of reserves.

Government policies in population, land tenure, timber pricing, fiscal devolution, poverty alleviation, regional development and nature reserve management, as well as the strong urban and state bias, all have contributed to the loss of biodiversity. Political movements tend to reinforce the negative impacts of inappropriate policies, and the historical impacts of such political disturbances and inappropriate policies create difficulties for the corrective policies being implemented today. These political movements and inappropriate policies also tend to reinforce the impact of the two root causes in the local context, namely population growth and lack of economic development. Finally, the inability of markets to account for the externalities generated by nature reserves and logging tends to allow timber logging to continue at a scale that is not in the best interests of the country, but that is commonly seen as economically beneficial for society.

Pingwu County

Most of the government policies and political movements that influenced resource use and biodiversity conservation in Deqin have also had an impact in Pingwu. In Pingwu's case, however, the various government policies related to commercial timber production appear to be most relevant. These fall into three groups: a skewed incentive structure for timber production, a strong urban and state bias and destructive political movements.

Government policies have long supported an incentive structure that allows or even encourages timber production instead of forest protection. This incentive structure can be clearly detected in the valuation policy for natural forests and the pricing policy for timber. From 1950 to 1970, the central government, following the Marxist philosophy on natural forests, used timber as a 'gift' from Mother Nature to develop the war-torn economy in China. The Northern Sichuan Logging Company, for instance, produced over 700,000 m^3 of timber for the construction of the Chengdu-Baoji railroad. The better forests were put under state ownership. Every stage of timber production, including logging, distribution and marketing, was put under strict state control according to the philosophy of a planned economy. Timber prices were set artificially low, providing forest owners with little incentive to good stewardship. This period witnessed the first wave of major deforestation in modern China. A second wave followed with the Cultural Revolution.

The market reform begun in the 1980s freed timber prices. However, the opening of timber markets was not supported by corresponding policy changes in timber production management. Many government departments, businesses and institutions, such as schools and hospitals, jumped into the timber business. The breakdown of the LQMS as well as the practice of concession logging have added further incentives for unregulated logging. This has resulted in the third wave of deforestation.

The market pricing practised today does not address all the price distortions related to timber production, because market pricing does not represent the value of public goods that are produced by forests, such as wildlife sanctuary or water and soil conservation. This problem is becoming more acute as two new nature reserves are being set up in Pingwu County. Financing of these reserves is a burden for the local government, which receives no compensation for the services it provides.

Apart from the problems in forest- and timber-pricing policy and timber production management regimes, insecure forest tenure has also distorted the incentive structure. Collective ownership was not well respected under the planned economy. In the process of implementing the private contracting system in forestry in the 1980s, deforestation also occurred because of uncertainties felt by farmers regarding private use rights on contracted forest lands. From 1950 to 1990, state forests produced a total of 2.9 million m^3 of timber, depleting about four million m^3 of standing volume. Frequent changes (new company set-up, mergers and shut-downs) in state timber companies increased pressure on timber.

The problem of the strong urban and state bias in government policy is obvious in the entire rural sector in China. In timber production, this bias is represented by a benefit-sharing pattern under which the central government takes precedence in logging, followed by the prefectural government, the county government, and township and village administrations. Anything left over is for local communities. The bias is also reflected in the changes of state ownership of the logging companies in Pingwu and by the preferential treatment the government grants to state enterprises and their employees. On the expenditure side, the budget of Pingwu County in 1997 was 57 million yuan, of which 78 per cent was used for staff salaries and other expenditures in non-productive sectors. This expenditure pattern, while supporting the over-sized urban and state sectors, has very limited revenue-generating capacity. It clearly sustains the need for more timber exploitation.

The problems plaguing the state timber sector tend to reinforce the urban and state bias and contribute to unsustainable logging. State firms are notoriously inefficient in China. Financially the timber companies depend heavily on logging. Many attempts at diversifying their business, including expansion into timber processing or even non-timber activities, have met with a total failure. Workers are guaranteed life-long employment and are not willing to work hard. The firms often have to hire temporary peasant labour for the more physically demanding jobs, such as logging. Finally, these firms are often burdened with a large retired staff for whom they have to pay pensions,

housing and insurance, and take responsibility for the education and employment of their children. The government policy of life-long employment for
state workers, and the fiscal dependence of government on timber profits from
state companies, require the government to sustain the inefficient operations
of state timber companies.

Finally, the various violent political movements also played a destructive
role in forest management in Pingwu. During the Great Leap Forward, vast
amounts of timber were cut to fire the local steel furnace, which churned out
useless iron, destroying about 24,000 ha of natural forests. During the Cultural
Revolution, an additional 1500 ha of forests were cleared for grain production, and 180,000 m³ of timber were exported from Pingwu County at a price
barely covering the logging and transportation costs. Political disturbances,
the urban and state bias, and the skewed incentive structure for timber production, tend to reinforce each other, and together promote logging operations
and the destruction of wildlife habitats.

INTERNATIONAL CONTEXT

As discussed above, both Deqin and Pingwu still have largely subsistence
economies, which are marginal to the overall Chinese economy and even more
so to the global economy. The Matsutake mushroom business in Deqin is an
exception. The Matsutake mushroom is a highly commercial product that has
successfully entered the Japanese market. While high prices over the past
decade have encouraged exploitative collection and raised social tension in
some communities, the recent financial crisis in the Japanese economy has
caused a collapse of the Matsutake business. Prices came down from as high
as 200 yuan/kg in 1997 to a mere 15 yuan/kg in 1998 in the local market,
with no time for the economy to adjust to this price shock. The impact of the
collapse is felt most acutely by farmers, since the taxes collected on Matsutake
by the local government are relatively low. Farmers will have to increase their
production in animal husbandry, timber production or farming to maintain
their current level of income, adding to the stress on local ecosystems. The
impact of the Matsutake mushroom business on local biodiversity is strong
though indirect.

Deqin has had no major international aid project in the field. In Pingwu,
however, the WWF China Programme started to work with the Wanglang
Nature Reserve in 1995 on capacity-building in reserve management. Even
though no major field conservation activity has been initiated yet under this
project, in-depth understanding of biological and socioeconomic processes
underlying biodiversity loss in Pingwu County has been gained via a lengthy
and participatory project development process. Local partners' awareness of
the need to address the socioeconomic root causes of biodiversity loss has
been raised significantly. Implementation of this project may help develop new
ways to address many of the local threats to biodiversity.

CONCLUSIONS

The unique geographic and topographic features in Deqin have nurtured its richness of biodiversity. However, the fragility of local ecosystems make this biodiversity very vulnerable to outside disturbance. Over the past fifteen years, significant achievements have been made in biodiversity conservation in Deqin, notably the establishment and management of the Baimaxueshan Nature Reserve and the protection of the Yunnan snub-nosed monkey and other endangered species. The challenges facing biodiversity conservation in Deqin are still enormous. As revealed by this case study, these include the fragmentation, reduction, and degradation of wildlife habitats and the killing of wildlife. Agricultural expansion, fuelwood collection, logging, over-grazing and illegal hunting are the main proximate causes of these problems. Population pressure and lack of local economic development are the driving forces behind these problems, and are, therefore, among the root causes of biodiversity loss at the local level. Improper government policies or poor implementation of policies and highly destructive political movements are root causes at the national level. Such government policies cover population, land tenure, timber pricing, fiscal devolution, poverty alleviation, regional development and nature reserve management. These root causes are more significant not only because they have a very obvious and powerful impact on the proximate causes but also because they reinforce the effects of the two local-level root causes. Sudden changes in the international market associated with the recent Asian financial crisis are also found to be contributing to biodiversity loss.

These causal relationships are depicted in Figure 8.2. The dotted lines connecting illegal hunting and the killing of wildlife indicate a one-to-one direct relationship between the two that is not related to other changes in the ecosystem. The dotted line from Matsutake mushroom market indicates that conditions in the mushroom market have an indirect impact on local resource-use patterns.

The major proximate causes of biodiversity loss in Pingwu include timber production, agricultural expansion, forest fires and illegal hunting. Logging remains the most serious threat today. Over the past half century logging in Pingwu County has been carried out almost exclusively in old-growth forests and has caused three large-scale waves of deforestation. The first occurred during the Great Leap Forward, the second during the Cultural Revolution and the most recent one during the transition to a market-based economy. Logging has damaged wildlife habitats and caused degradation of ecosystems.

The root causes of logging in the local context include an economic structure heavily skewed toward logging, marked by dependence of local government revenue and state company profits on logging, and a group of vested interests promoting logging, including people involved in trading and approving quotas, concession grantees, administrators and timber merchants. The breakdown of the LQMS, including the trading of logging quotas and burgeoning of concession logging, further drives unsustainable logging. On a

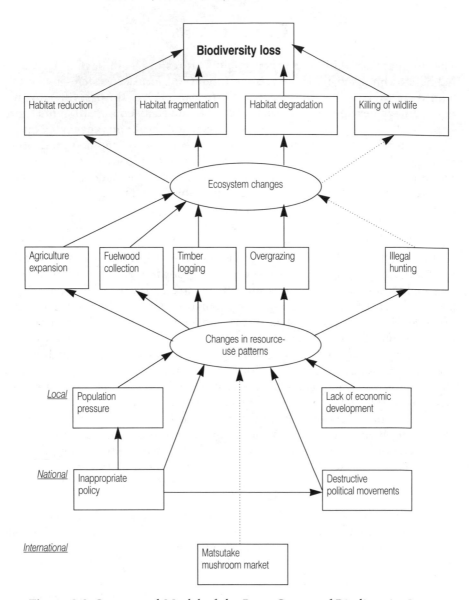

Figure 8.2 *Conceptual Model of the Root Causes of Biodiversity Loss in Deqin County*

national scale the root causes include a skewed incentive structure in logging created by inappropriate government policies or by poor enforcement of relevant policies, a strong urban and state bias and destructive political movements. All these factors contribute directly to the loss of biodiversity and tend to reinforce the effects of the local root causes of biodiversity loss. On an international scale, the local economy is still very marginal and there has been no international cooperation except the WWF China Programme's intended support.

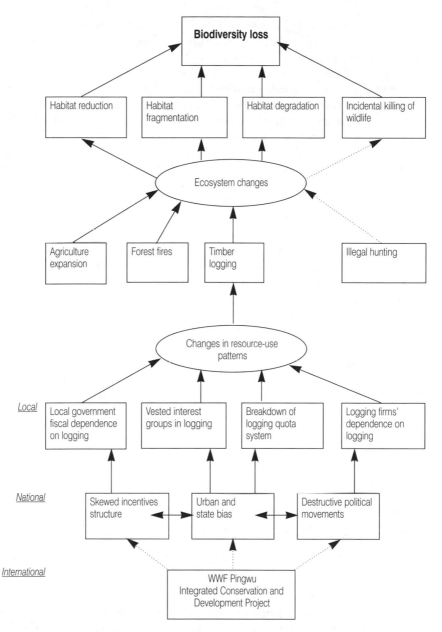

Figure 8.3 *Conceptual Model of the Root Causes of Biodiversity Loss in Pingwu County*

This complex set of causal relationships is depicted in Figure 8.3. Note that, as in Figure 8.2, the dotted lines connecting illegal hunting and the incidental killing of wildlife indicate a one-to-one direct relationship between the two that is not related to other changes in the ecosystem. Also, the dotted lines from the WWF Pingwu project indicate that such a project would have a positive impact in addressing the root causes of biodiversity loss and would directly change local resource-use patterns.

Although many of the causes of biodiversity loss are rooted in China's centralized planned economy, the move toward freer markets does not ensure the right incentives for conservation. In the market economy as practised in China today, new inefficiencies are emerging for at least three reasons. A fully functional market economy has not yet been established in these counties, which is evident from the lack of market institutions, such as secure tenure arrangements, and the government's various distortionary policy interventions. Due to the marginal and largely subsistence nature of local economies, many economic activities are not yet well integrated into the market. Even a fully functional market, however, does not provide appropriate signals for resource allocation that take into consideration positive and negative externalities, such as biodiversity and environmental damage.

New opportunities are emerging in these counties. In particular, the logging bans on natural forests that are being implemented under the China National Natural Forest Conservation Action Programme are removing the threat of commercial logging in the counties. This programme was prompted by the severe flooding in the central Yangtze region in the summer of 1998; both sites are located in the upper reaches of the Yangtze watershed. The difficulties in realizing the full potential of this opportunity include locating sound implementation mechanisms for the logging bans, land-use planning and management of forests to be saved by the logging bans, employment of workers from logging companies, reorientation of logging businesses and generation of long-term government revenue and local income from alternative economic activities. If well implemented, however, the programme would greatly promote biodiversity conservation in these sites.

RECOMMENDATIONS

Deqin County

The following recommendations are designed to improve the conservation of biodiversity. The expansion of farmland for self-sufficiency in food production has been a major proximate cause of biodiversity loss. Increasing food production is a real need in Deqin, as its physical isolation from the rest of the national economy precludes large-scale grain trade. The strategy of agricultural expansion has proven to be ineffective. However, strengthening agricultural technical extension could raise land productivity and promote biodiversity conservation. Through the adoption of new crops or new crop varieties, or the use of plastic groundcovers in farming, land productivity can be raised, reducing the need to expand farmland and perhaps supporting forest regeneration. A related intervention would involve training villagers and technical workers in veterinary medicine, manufacturing of ethnic crafts, and farming techniques to improve agriculture and animal husbandry and increase the value of local products. Also, actions should be taken to reduce the size of animal herds in Deqin and to raise the commercial value of products from domestic animals. All these interventions will need the support of the government and the active participation of local people.

To address the problem of fuelwood collection, mini-hydro-power stations could be developed in villages with access to adequate water resources. This could significantly reduce the pressure on forests from fuelwood collection and is almost risk-free. However, the relatively large one-time investment and high costs of electricity for households in the absence of government subsidies are potential limiting factors. Energy-saving stoves and fuelwood plantations could also be developed to address the problem of excessive fuelwood collection. Correspondingly, the Baimaxueshan Nature Reserve should be enlarged to ensure that key wildlife habitats are protected.

To reduce logging, demonstration brick houses that use little timber could promote the substitution of timber with other materials and reduce the domestic consumption of timber. Stopping all commercial logging would require fiscal subsidies from higher governments and transformation of the logging enterprises in the short term and alternative income-generating businesses in the longer term. Every effort should be undertaken to take advantage of the opportunity provided by the China National Natural Forest Conservation Action Programme. The development of tourism or ecotourism could be a sustainable alternative to resource-intensive industries in the long run.

All these measures will be much less effective if actions are not taken to control population growth and to promote local economic development. Preferential investment priority should be given to inner regions such as Deqin. The matching support requirement for investment in poverty alleviation should be abolished, and schemes such as household micro-credit programmes should be introduced to improve the efficiency of government poverty alleviation efforts. The government should strengthen family planning programmes among ethnic minorities in the region. It should be recognized that, despite Deqin's sparse population, its environmental carrying capacity has been reached, at least in the context of the existing economic structure and technologies. The county and village governments should be downsized and equal treatment of rural and urban residents should be gradually introduced.

Beyond local intervention measures, it is even more important to promote changes at the national level. First, an integrated land-use planning exercise should be carried out in Deqin County, allowing an optimal and ecologically sustainable division of land uses among farming, forestry, nature reserves and grazing lands. Second, it is necessary to carry out national-level research to devise a funding mechanism for nature reserves that can guarantee safe and adequate funding for their management. Third, since almost all forests in Deqin County are natural forests and should be given status either as protected areas or as soil-protection forests, higher governments, including the prefectural, provincial and central governments, need to work out a compensation package for local government revenue and for the relocation of logging company workers. Fourth, the central government should take active measures to downsize the overstaffed government sector and reduce the fiscal burden it creates on local government coffers, which would alleviate pressure for commercial logging. The recent government programme of restructuring and staff cutbacks in the central government is a good start and will probably be expanded to regional and local governments.

At the international level, it is necessary to look for alternative income sources to replace or supplement the Matsutake mushroom trade with Japan. One possible option would be to work with farmers to increase the commercial use of their domestic animals and to raise local processing capacity for animal products.

Pingwu County

Commercial timber production is the largest threat to biodiversity in Pingwu. Naturally, stopping all commercial logging activities and designating old-growth forests as nature reserves would be the first and foremost intervention for biodiversity conservation in Pingwu County. This would require a host of supporting arrangements, including the reorientation or restructuring of state logging companies toward non-logging activities, the development of alternative businesses and the diversification of the local economy to reduce local dependence on logging, and securing subsidies from higher level governments to replace lost revenue from logging. Also, hydro-power could be developed to generate government revenue and to reduce the need for charcoal.

In the case that logging cannot be completely stopped, it is necessary to change current logging practices and the management of logging operations. In particular, concession logging and the trading of logging quotas should be outlawed. Clear-cutting should be phased out and measures should be taken to ensure forest regeneration.

In the long run, downsizing local government and reducing government expenditure, reforming the management and ownership structure of state enterprises, unlinking social welfare from employment, strengthening reserve management and ensuring funding for nature reserve management are all interventions that could address the root causes of biodiversity at the national level. All these could be carried out under the general framework of the China National Natural Forest Conservation Action Programme. A policy study on funding of nature reserves management should be carried out for both counties and for the entire nature reserve system in China.

It is also important for the government to take advantage of the opportunity to collaborate with the WWF China Programme to introduce co-management and to develop alternative businesses in Pingwu County. Alternative income-generating activities to be carried out at the community level need detailed surveys and consultations with relevant communities.

Chapter 9

Danube River Basin: Wetlands and Floodplains

Research team: The methodology for this study was developed and piloted by AIDEnvironment of The Netherlands in cooperation with two WWF partners.
The research team consisted of *Mr Charlie Avis* and *Mr Jeroen Van Wetten* (AIDEnvironment, Amsterdam, The Netherlands), *Dr Jan Seffer* (Director, Daphne Centre for Applied Ecology, Bratislava) who coordinated the case study in Slovakia and *Mr Georgy Tinchev* (Head of the Protected Areas Division, Committee of Forests, Sofia) who coordinated the case study in Bulgaria. The research team had full responsibility for authorship of this report. Terms of reference and overall project direction were given by *Mr Philip Weller* (Director, WWF Danube Carpathian Programme, Vienna, Austria)

Summary: **Environmental degradation of the Danube River Basin began centuries ago. Some of the causes of habitat alteration and biodiversity loss are found to be historic and irreversible, such as the 40-year period of socialist government in Bulgaria and Slovakia. Other causes are still driving biodiversity loss in the current period of economic and political transition and offer a place for intervention to halt the unsustainable use of resources.**

Damage to natural resources in Central and Eastern Europe has been less widespread than in Western Europe and the region remains relatively rich in biological and landscape diversity. The two study areas selected for this project – the Danube floodplains and islands, and the wetlands of northern Bulgaria and the Morava River floodplain of western Slovakia (Figure 9.1) – exemplify this high biodiversity. The two case study sites, indeed, the two countries, share some common legacies in terms of the socialist experience, but differ greatly in their ecological character, intensity of development and location within the Danube basin.

The legacy of 40 years of socialist planning and maximum resource consumption, with little regard for sustainability and the conservation of scarce natural resources, has damaged the natural environment throughout this half of Europe. As the newly democratic countries of Central and Eastern Europe emerge from this painful period, new threats to the unique natural capital of the region have emerged. A new form of over-consumption can be observed, based not on the rhetoric of centrally planned, socialist ideology but on the adoption of free-market approaches, re-privatization of resources and seemingly uncontrolled and unregulated flows of international capital.

At the same time, the economic crisis that has accompanied these far-reaching political and social changes continues to bite hard into the daily lives and budgets of individuals and government. These new challenges to rational resource use in the region are a significant threat to biodiversity. The factors that influence this threat are complex and may be seen as an intricate network of interrelated, multi-level and temporally variable root causes.

Both Bulgaria and Slovakia have signed European Association Agreements that declare their intention to join an expanded EU, which means that their governments are committed to harmonizing their policy and legislative and management systems with those of the EU. Both governments have taken important first steps in this regard. The emerging environmental policy climate appears to offer significant opportunities for more sustainable management of natural resources – including wetlands – in these two countries. Further, the recent entry into force (October 1998) of the Danube River Protection Convention (DRPC) offers a framework for international cooperation and more integrated river basin management, which has been lacking.

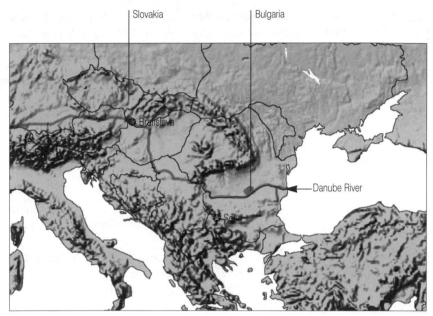

Figure 9.1 *Map of the Danube River Basin Showing Location of Study Areas*

DESCRIPTION OF THE STUDY AREAS

Wetlands in the Bulgarian Portion of the Danube River Basin

In Bulgaria the total area draining to the Danube basin is 46,896 km², or 48 per cent of the country's total territory. The Danube River forms the boundary between Bulgaria and Romania for 471 km, with the high southern banks of the Bulgarian side contrasting with the low marshy areas of the opposite bank. Permanently flooded marsh areas cover some 70–90 km², with seasonally inundated floodplains making up an additional area of 450–470 km². The numerous Danube islands, 61 of which belong to Bulgaria, total more than 10,000 ha in area and support significant biodiversity.

These wetlands constitute only a very small fraction of the former wetland, yet within the context of this case study represent a relatively large area. The study will concentrate on certain wetlands for which information is both readily available and relatively complete, such as the Belene complex of islands and marshes near Svishtov.

The marshes and islands of the Bulgarian portion of the Danube contain some of the richest wetland habitats in the Danube basin, with important plant, fish, animal and bird populations. Communities of white willow (*Salix alba*), almond willow (*Salix triandra*), purple willow (*Salix purpurea*), black poplar (*Populus nigra*), white poplar (*Populus alba*), Vardim oak (*Quercus longipes*) and elm (*Ulmus foliacea*) characterize the natural forests on the islands. These forests provide important habitats for a wide range of animals and birds and include at least one endemic tree, the Vardim oak population, that is adapted to extended periods of flooding.

Where intact primary and typical plant communities exist, for example on Kitka, Milka and part of Vardim Islands, a unique formation of specific flora and fauna has developed. Large numbers of fish and amphibian species are present, including pike (*Esox lucius*), carp (*Cyprinius carpio*), tench (*Tinca tinca*) and the rare amphibian spadefoot (*Triturus cristatus* and *Pelobates syriacus*), of which the latter two are included in the Bulgarian Red List of threatened species. The islands offer refuge and food for migratory and threatened bird species such as the dalmatian pelican (*Pelecanus crispus*), ferruginous duck (*Aytya nyroca*) and red-breasted goose (*Branta ruficolis*). Other rare and endangered species that can be found in locations within the study site include the white-tailed eagle (*Haliaeetus albicilla*), corncrake (*Crex crex*) and lesser grey shrike (*Lanius minor*).

The wetlands and forests house numerous and often very large heron colonies, including grey heron (*Ardea cinerea*), night heron (*Nycticorax nycticorax*), squacco heron (*Ardeola ralloides*) and spoonbill (*Platalea leucorodia*). Srebarna Nature Reserve, a Ramsar and UNESCO World Heritage Site, is home to 179 species of birds, 99 of which are known to nest here. Of these, 24 species are classified as rare or threatened. Highlights include a large colony of dalmatian pelicans and the only known Bulgarian nesting site of the white heron (*Ardea alba*).

Mammalian species of conservation value found in the Danubian marshes and islands include the wild boar (*Sus scrofa*), otter (*Lutra lutra*), red deer (*Cervus elaphus*) and jackal (*Canis aureus*). Wild boar, red deer and wolf populations are controlled by conservation authorities.

Current Levels of Protection

Wetlands, such as Srebarna and parts of the Belene complex, are designated nature reserves and are generally managed by the State Committee of Forests and/or Ministry of Environment. Further classifications include that of nature monument (eg on Belene Island) and protected site (eg on Vardim Island) while other wetlands in the Danube basin are found within national parks. Activities within such protected areas are theoretically strictly controlled and subject to management planning processes. However, due to a lack of financial resources and sometimes indifferent coordination between respective authorities, this is often difficult to enforce in practice.

The Belene complex includes nature reserves, protected sites and nature monuments and is managed by the State Committee of Forests. The state owns the land, including all the lands managed by the Committee and the main island of Persina, which is owned by the Ministry of Justice due to the presence of a prison. In total, the area with some form of protection is 1714 ha. Since all Danubian islands are border areas, they will remain property of the state, despite the re-privatization of land proceeding elsewhere. In such areas, the outlook for protected areas is relatively bright. However, as a result of the new law on nature conservation, protected areas management in Bulgaria is currently under debate, and it is unclear as yet which authorities will be responsible for management. Until this position is clarified, the situation is even more difficult than usual for conservation and resource managers.

Current Land-use Patterns

It is difficult to generalize concerning land use over this large area. Agriculture is the principal livelihood for many. Widespread drainage of Danubian wetlands has opened up large areas of land that have been used for agriculture and grazing. Some 25 per cent of the country's production (by monetary value) originates here, with the principal commodities including corn, sugar beet, orchard fruits and vegetables. This is also an important wine-producing area. The region also contains much industry, particularly around Russe, including machinery construction, chemicals, power generation, cellulose and paper plants and food production and processing.

There are almost 600 settlements in 49 municipalities, with a total population (in 1992) of more than 1.3 million, or 15 per cent of the country. Population density, at 73 inhabitants per km², is slightly below the national average. Unemployment is very high within the study area, in some municipalities as high as 50 per cent. Many unemployed or under-employed rely upon fishing as an economic fall-back and subsistence activity.

Forestry is an important and visible activity. It has been estimated that over 21,000 ha have been planted with intensive poplar stands, which have replaced the indigenous varieties of willow and poplar that now remain only as small remnants covering about 13 per cent of the floodplain. The Danube islands are generally uninhabited and commercial exploitation is often restricted to the managed poplar plantations of the Committee of Forests. The introduction of hybrid poplar trees on the islands and in the floodplains has been responsible for significant reductions in species diversity and large areas of such land are effectively under monocultural silviculture. Such activity is, however, being scaled down within protected areas while indigenous or rare assemblages are being protected and replanted.

Loss of Wetlands and Wetland Biodiversity

Intensive drainage programmes have drastically reduced the number and extent of the wetlands, marshes and floodplains of the Danube basin in Bulgaria. As yet, without extensive mapping, it is very difficult to determine the precise historical extent of these lost resources. At present, anecdotal evidence is all that exists, such as documentation of the drainage between 1925 and 1935 of 28,000 ha of Danube floodplains to accommodate refugees from the First World War.

The widespread drainage and dike construction programmes of this century have probably been the principal reason for wetland loss. Official documents and plans show this quite clearly. Systematic post-war pumping and diking followed the somewhat experimental and isolated works of the 1920s and 1930s. The years from 1947 until 1953 marked the height of such programmes, which were driven by the need to increase agricultural land. Earlier schemes had also been driven by the necessity to eradicate malaria, which was a significant threat to human health well into this century.

Other related factors causing wetland loss include agricultural encroachment and the conversion of seasonally flooded lands into forestry plantations. Less significant factors affecting biodiversity in the region include isolated but possibly intensive over-consumption of resources, such as fishery or reed and rush resources; the impacts of the many armed conflicts and wars; urbanization; and hunting of birds and game. Lastly, construction of the barrage scheme at Iron Gate significantly decreased the size of floods, according to reports, which negatively affects the forests, islands and remaining floodplains that rely upon annual replenishment for biodiversity support.

Probable Future Threats

Future threats to the wetlands are likely to include further agricultural and forestry expansion into natural floodplain areas, particularly the islands, if secure conservation management regimes are not put in place. The possible continuing invasion of alien or damaging species related to this expansion is also a danger.

Pollution from the Danube (industrial, municipal, river transport) is not a major problem for the region as a whole, but in localized and specific areas the hazard is significant. On the tributaries, pollution is more acute and 'inland' wetlands and those at river confluences could be threatened in this way. Immediate and localized threats to biodiversity include urbanization and small-scale drainage, over-consumption of wetland products, including over-fishing and hunting of rare or threatened species and the burning and over-grazing of meadows. Lastly, a recent joint Bulgarian–Romanian summit discussed the possibility of constructing another bridge over the Danube, with obvious environmental implications for the study site.

Morava River Floodplains in Slovakia

The Morava River floodplains are located in western Slovakia, forming the border with both the Czech Republic to the north and Austria to the west. The study area includes all wetlands and floodplains on Slovak territory between the confluence of the Morava and the Dyje in the north to the Danube in the south. The length of this section is 78 km, and the total area of active floodplain is 43.6 km^2.

Wetland landscapes include the river itself and its tributaries, oxbow lakes, sand and gravel banks, reed beds and swamps, temporary pools and floodplain meadows and forests. The latter two constitute more than 80 per cent of the study area. However, the floodplain is only 27 per cent of its original area due to extensive river regulation. Despite this, the area represents the largest complex of floodplain meadows in the whole of Central Europe.

As the river corridor actually formed the Iron Curtain between the West and the socialist countries, it remained out-of-bounds and relatively untouched for a long period. Since 1989 the land has been open once more for development and now constitutes both a popular recreation area and an important economic resource.

Floodplain meadows are the predominant habitat type and cover more than 2360 ha. More than 850 species of plant have been recorded, and Central Europe's largest complex of subcontinental cnidium meadows is found here. The number of higher plant species can reach as many as 60 to 70 per 100 m². The meadows are characterized by two dominant vegetation types: mesophylous *Cnidio–Violetum pumilae* (mesophylous subcontinental cnidium meadows) and *Gratiolo–Caricetum praecocis-suzae* (moist subcontinental cnidium meadows). The Slovak Red List of endangered plants includes 12 species of meadow plant and four species of water macrophyte.

As one of central Europe's major nesting and wintering sites, the meadows provide important sources of food and habitat for a wide range of birds, including many rare and endangered species. In fact, 176 species have been recorded, 118 of which nest here. As many as 50 pairs of corncrake have been recorded. White storks feed in the study site and nest on the Austrian side in the WWF Reserve at Marchegg, forming the biggest white stork colony in Europe. The study area is classed as an important bird area by Birdlife International.

The remaining floodplain forests total some 16 km², dominated by willow and poplar species. This wet softwood association, *Salici–Populetum*, is among the most threatened ecosystems in Slovakia. Hardwood associations such as *Fraxino pannonicae–Ulmetum* (elm, ash and oak) occupy the more elevated and drier sections of the floodplain.

The wetlands are also breeding and migration sites for fish, with 48 species recorded. Of these, 36 are endangered on a European scale and 10 are facing extinction. Some species, such as the Balon's ruffe and the larger and smaller Danubian perch, are endemic to the Danube basin.

Current Levels of Protection

Much of the floodplain area is included in the Zahorie Protected Landscape Area (PLA), which was designated in 1989. There are also two National Nature Reserves (NNR) which accord the highest level of protection. Horny les NNR (543 ha), which includes floodplain forests and meadows, and Dolny les NNR (186 ha), which includes valuable alluvial softwood forest and oxbow lakes, were both established in 1981. The study area has been a Ramsar Site since 1993. Despite these designations, protection and sustainable management of the floodplain meadows and forests remain problematic. The adoption and enforcement of a management plan in keeping with the area's Ramsar status are unlikely in the near future. The PLA Administration aims to promote environmentally sensitive management of the area. However, in terms of resources and legislation, it is severely handicapped. Problems over land ownership and the conflicting legislative framework and illegal activities effectively counteract the conservation measures that currently exist. The current levels of protection, both legislated for and enforced, are insufficient for proper

management and conservation of this highly valuable and scientifically significant wetland and the biodiversity it supports.

Current Land-use Patterns

Population pressure within the study area is relatively low, with a population of
46,000 and density of 85 inhabitants per km², compared to the national average
of 105 per km². Two large settlements, Senica and Malacky, together with other
urban districts, account for more than 50 per cent of the population.

Agriculture remains the dominant land use in the study site. Habitats
include meadows, arable land, forest and woodland and uncultivated tracts in
a natural or semi-natural state. Meadows are by far the most significant in
terms of biodiversity, although these have been reduced in area as a result of
post-war conversion to arable land, especially since 1971 when some 500 ha
of meadow were lost due to intensification of agriculture. Meadows outside
the inundation area have been converted to arable land. Within the active
floodplain, the meadows are mown either once or twice per year, depending
upon flood levels and financial resources. Hay is either used for domestic cattle
or exported to Austria. Mowing and traditional management of meadows
have created a unique habitat over centuries that is extremely valuable in terms
of biodiversity, despite being man-made.

The process of land re-privatization, begun in 1989, is far from complete.
Identifying the true owners of sometimes minute parcels of land is almost
impossible, and this constitutes a very significant obstacle to sustainable
management. Abandoned land has been invaded by weed and alien species,
while illegal operations are more easily carried out when ownership is unknown
or disputed. Ecological, or low-input, agriculture has been promoted in the
study area to good effect, making use of government subsidies and incentives.

Forestry management follows the updated 1996 Forest Management Plan,
in which the Zahorie PLA advocates environmentally sensitive practices.
However, the floodplain forests have suffered in the past from the invasion of
alien species and outbreaks of disease amongst elm and oak. Use of the area
for recreation is encouraged and is quite heavy as a result of the opening of the
river after almost half a century of restricted access. Fishing is especially
popular, with negative implications for the environment, and while motor
access into much of the floodplain is prohibited, the ban is ignored.

A large and particularly damaging gravel mining enterprise is located
within the study area, covering 420 ha. Operations began in 1972, and it is
estimated that since 1980 more than 40 ha of theoretically protected land
have been destroyed within the Ramsar site. Formerly a state company, this
joint Slovak-Austrian enterprise has continued and intensified its operations
despite their illegality, exploiting confusion over land ownership.

Loss of Wetlands and Biodiversity

The floodplain was formerly approximately four times its current size. The
total area of wetlands according to a reconstructed map of potential vegetation type was originally 160.8 km², compared to the present floodplain of

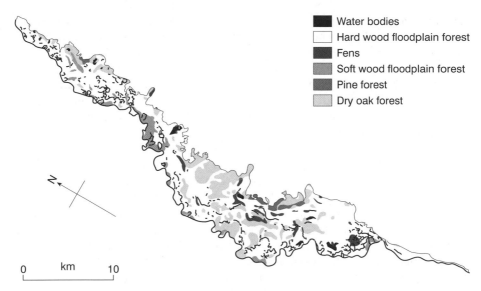

Figure 9.2 *Reconstructed Habitat Structure of the Morava River Floodplain*

43.6 km² (see Figure 9.2). River regulation has been the principal immediate cause of wetland loss. During this century, more than 90 per cent of the river's course has been regulated through dike construction, canalization and the cutting off of all major meanders. In the study site, the river's length has been shortened from 95 to 78 km.

Construction of river regulation infrastructure was carried out between 1969 and 1982 to specifications drawn up in 1935. The principal rationale was flood protection, and the net result has been a shrinking of the naturally inundating floodplain to only 20 per cent of its former area and a deepening of the channel bed. The river can now transport more than twice its former volume, accommodating 440 m³ instead of 210 m³. Losses to biodiversity include those associated with the reduction of the extensive floodplain meadows, shallow river and bank habitats and the desiccation of oxbows and floodplain forests.

Secondary causes of wetland loss include conversion of floodplain meadow to arable land and illegal gravel mining activities. Other factors that have affected the floodplains, or continue to do so, include environmental damage associated with fishing, problems with forestry management and water pollution. Water pollution is predominantly industrial and mostly derived from the Myjava tributary and from Austria. Urban areas contribute domestic municipal wastes since many do not have wastewater treatment plants.

Probable Future Threats

The gravel mining operation is the largest single threat to the floodplain ecosystems. The legislation dealing with protected areas post-dates that concerned with mining operations, and the private company responsible for activities in the study site has exploited this loophole and confusion to extend its operations well into the protected areas and Ramsar site. Uncertainty over land ownership has presented a similar opportunity in this respect.

Conversion of meadows to arable land is the second most important potential and current threat. Even if conversion is not widespread, ploughed fields present obstacles to biodiversity in the form of barriers to migration of plant and animal species. Furthermore, decreasing levels of traditional meadow management, for example, land abandonment or a reduction in mowing from twice to once per year, will also continue to affect species habitat.

Recreational use, principally fishing and water pollution, also threaten the study site. There is evidence of a decrease in the number of nesting birds since the re-opening of the area in 1989, and it is probable that bank-side damage and disturbance caused by quite large numbers of fishermen is responsible.

A number of engineering schemes have been proposed in the last two decades, including further dam construction, a Danube-Odra-Elbe canal and various bridge projects. Apart from bridge-building, these seem unlikely to take place in the present economic and political climate. Given that before the Second World War there were 11 bridges, and today just one, it seems quite possible that this will proceed. The engineering works, infrastructural development and increasing traffic are likely to have a significant negative impact upon the area.

RESEARCH METHODOLOGY

For this study, we followed the line of the actors responsible for, and influencing, the destruction of wetland biodiversity and ecological processes. The methodology for this project was designed with reference to the WWF/MPO approach paper (Stedman-Edwards, 1998) and the SEAn methodology (AIDEnvironment, 1997). The analysis concentrated on the underlying driving factors and policy or market failures that have led to the actions of the actors – those individuals, institutions and organizations responsible for the destruction of wetland biodiversity.

An actor is seen as having options to choose from and motivations that influence choices. Motivations are shaped by factors such as price and economic incentives or disincentives, and influenced by the actor's environment (socioeconomic, political, for example). Options are possibilities provided by, for example, the legal system or the soil conditions. Thus the motivations, options and decisions of the actor are a result of other surrounding actors – we call these the determinants (Figure 9.3).

The main guiding questions used in this study to uncover the root causes of biodiversity loss were:

- What are the root causes that have led to neglect of situations of policy and market failures, mis-pricing and unsustainable resource-use?

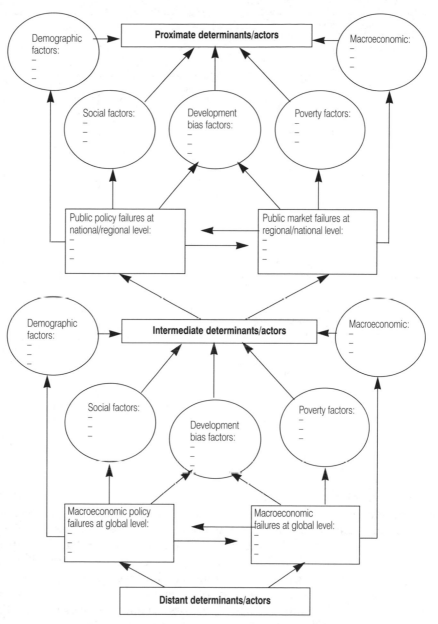

Figure 9.3 *Human Activities Leading to Alterations in the Ecosystem*

- Why does this situation not lead to adjustment of current policies?
- What are the other interests of actors involved so that feedback does not take place or is neglected or blocked?

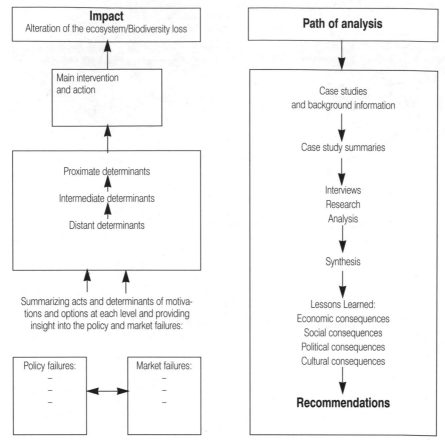

Figure 9.4 *Analysis Framework*

Primary attention was given to the dynamics in the human system and the influence of root causes (factors and determinants) that are responsible for maintaining situations characterized as policy and market failures associated with biodiversity loss. Policy and market failures are interrelated and often reinforce each other. In the framework used, root causes are identified at two levels, and are summarized as policy failures and market failures (Figure 9.3). To fill in the framework, use was made of a tentative list of guiding questions and a checklist of possible underlying factors driving biodiversity loss. The overall approach employed for this analysis is summarized in Figure 9.4.

OVERVIEW OF ROOT CAUSES

In both areas, historical loss of biodiversity was found to be widespread and due to similar underlying factors or root causes. Current threats were found to be less significant – in terms of area affected – but locally important in terms of existing, sometimes remnant, habitats and species. Root causes were identified by analysing and tracing cause-and-effect from impact through proximate cause to root cause. Emphasis was given to the chains of actors and causes that influence the motivations and choices of actors. The influencing factors were predicted to operate at three different levels: local, national and international.

Since for many impacts, causes and effects were operating at more than one of these levels, a series of root cause networks was constructed to help visualize the analysis and guide the reader towards the root cause. The root cause networks were developed, discussed and refined by the research team during the later stages of research. (One example is provided in Figure 9.5.)

Bulgaria

Historical records and documents show that the floodplains and marshes of the Danubian basin in Bulgaria were once much larger. The most important factors responsible for the loss of habitat and biodiversity in the Danubian floodplains were found to be river regulation and drainage; conversion of floodplain to forestry; killing of selected bird and mammal species; over-harvesting or otherwise inappropriate use of floodplain resources; and surface water pollution.

The following provides a more detailed analysis and description of the cause-and-effect chains for each impact and set of root causes, highlighting key policy decisions and legislative contradictions and responsible actors.

River Regulation and Drainage

The first systematic and significant drainage efforts were carried out in the Karaboaz floodplain between 1909 and 1912. Dikes were constructed near the villages of Boril and Gigen to protect the population from flooding and to drain 800 ha of previously flooded land for use in agriculture. In 1912, the government passed the 'law for the fund for cultural activities on waters and forests', which provided the financial means for the construction of irrigation systems, drainage of marshes, river regulation and forestry activities. The fund was generated through taxes on water users, sale of forestry products and a special loan from the Bulgarian Agricultural Bank. The first year's budget was used to drain two marsh areas – Batak and Straldja – outside the study area, and subsequent budgets were allocated to Danube marsh reclamation projects.

In 1920, the 'law for water syndicates' was passed to assist cooperatives and the private sector to engage in drainage and hydrological projects through the provision of credit facilities and other preferential conditions. In 1935 a syndicate in the study area built the first pumping station to drain the formerly extensive Vardim floodplain. In 1947 the 'law for water economy' of the new constitution of the socialist republic, which nationalized all waters and river courses, replaced the old law. Government grants were released to facilitate the drainage of Aidemir, Brushlian, Svishtov and Belene floodplains and wetlands from 1947 to 1953. Three principal motivations – flood control, agricultural expansion and the eradication of malaria – drove such programmes and policies.

The application of new technologies was central to these processes, funded by the state budget, and in keeping with the political climate of development and modernization. As is also seen in Slovakia, this climate of 'progress' did not take into account the full economic value of the floodplains and wetlands, since these were not known or understood. With hindsight, the drainage of these marshes was an operation that destroyed biodiversity and entailed greater costs than benefits. *No scientific or economic appreciation of biodiversity* is therefore taken to be a root cause of biodiversity loss. This root cause has operated from 1900 to the present day.

Malaria eradication was a major priority for the government since there were serious health problems and deaths well into this century. In 1919, the 'law for the struggle with malaria' was passed and the special Inspectorate on Malaria established. This law allowed individuals or firms a 15-year tax amnesty for operations located on previously drained wetlands and floodplain marshes. Capital projects were also funded at this time: the largest marsh in Bulgaria, at Straldja, was drained using finances from the budget of the Inspectorate on Malaria. The decision to encourage and fund such drainage programmes was made in response to the alarming public health problem. Accompanying measures included spraying wetlands with petrol and Vert de Paris in order to destroy mosquito larvae; filling in smaller water bodies and regulating the river through construction that damaged the embankments; and the introduction of the alien American fish species *Gambbusia affinis* in 1928. Such activities were presumably quite logical within the climate of the time and indeed possibly very necessary. *The presence of malaria* is therefore identified as a root cause of biodiversity loss. This root cause operated from 1900 to 1930.

The government instigated other flood control and agricultural expansion projects due to the need to resettle Thracian refugees from the First World War and land pressure elsewhere in the country. The demand for land and the need to resettle a large refugee population led the government to allocate funds for further marsh drainage works. Loan funds were provided to the Ministry of Agriculture and State Properties for wetland drainage, including the construction of the 38 km-long Karaboaz dike system and, between 1925 and 1935, some 29,000 ha of Danube floodplain was drained. *Population growth* and *war and civil unrest* are therefore identified as root causes leading to biodiversity loss. These root causes operated from 1918 to 1930.

Figure 9.5 illustrates the network of motivations and organizations that have led to river regulation and drainage in the Bulgarian section of the Danube, and so to biodiversity loss. Similar networks were created for each of the factors but could not be illustrated here.

Conversion of Floodplain to Forestry

Today, many parts of the floodplain and Danube islands are managed as intensive hybrid poplar plantations. This monoculture has reduced biodiversity significantly, although the plantations do provide habitat for some bird and animal species. The first attempts at commercial, intensive forestry in this area

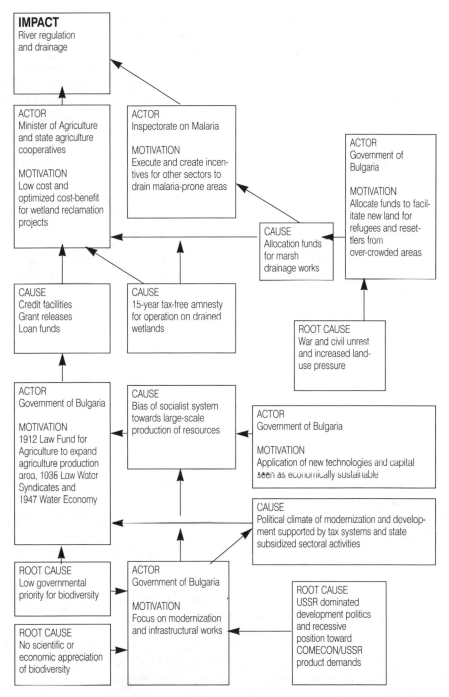

Figure 9.5 *Network 1: Bulgaria Danube Wetlands (1900–Present)*

were made during the 1930s, with the establishment of 3500 plantations. In 1956, the Council of Ministers adopted an order to promote the establishment of these plantations, charging the Ministry of Agriculture and Forestry with the planting of 21,000 ha of riverside areas by 1962. A national seminar in 1961 further guaranteed the legal, economic and scientific base for poplar development and, until 1991, between 2000 and 3000 ha were planted every year. Since 1992, with the economic crisis of the transition period affecting the budgets and operations of all state bodies, this planting rate has slowed to between 900 to 1600 ha per year.

The support for intensive poplar planting was very much in keeping with the socialist government's philosophy of large-scale, state-owned production and exploitation of natural resources. Such inappropriate planning and development activities were quite typical of such governments and very much a feature of the socialist development model imposed on the Warsaw Pact countries. Bulgaria fell into the Soviet sphere of influence following the end of the Second World War, and international geopolitics were perhaps of greater influence on such decision-making than the wishes of the Bulgarian people. *The Cold War and international geopolitics* is, therefore, taken to be a root cause of biodiversity loss. Such negative impacts have operated from 1950 to the present day.

Little or no consideration was given to the value of existing habitats lost to forestry plantations. There was an overwhelming lack of appreciation of biodiversity and the goods, services, functions and benefits of natural areas in general, and floodplains and wetlands in particular, which is easy to understand given the country's negative experiences with malaria earlier during the century. *No scientific or economic appreciation of biodiversity* is therefore taken to be a root cause of biodiversity loss, operating from 1900 to the present day.

Hunting of Selected Bird and Mammal Species

Government policies towards hunting also influenced biodiversity loss in the study area. In 1948 a law was adopted that classified as 'harmful game' many bird and animal species now afforded protected status as a result of their threatened numbers. No constraints were placed on the killing of these animals and birds in terms of seasons, numbers or methods. In fact, the government offered incentives in the form of rewards of money, timber or lower taxes. All representatives of the following genera were classified as harmful and were, therefore, subjected to massive hunting pressures:

- Genera: falcons (*Falco*), eagles (*Aquila*), sea eagles (*Haliaeetus*), short-toed eagles (*Circaetus*), ospreys (*Pandion*), kites (*Milvus*), harriers (*Circus*), accipiters (*Accipiter*), herons (*Ardea*), night herons (*Nycticorax*) and bittern (*Botaurus*)
- Families: gulls (*Laridae*), pelicans (*Pelicanidae*), cormorants (*Phlacro-coracidae*) and grebes (*Podicipidae*)

- Species: wolf (*Canis lupus*), otter (*Lutra lutra*), glossy ibis (*Plegadis falcinelus*), great white egret (*Egreta alba*) and little egret (*Egreta garzeta*).

In 1962, the 'order for game management' was passed, which further encouraged and rewarded such hunting through the development of quotas for hunters, obliging them to kill, poison, or capture a certain amount of harmful game. It is difficult to understand the government's motivations for such policies. Local hunters would have been attracted by the potentially lucrative economic rewards to be gained from the wildlife-rich marshes and wetlands in any case. Given the prevailing economic hardship in Bulgaria, and in particular in the relative isolation of wetland villages of this region, the poverty of the population is taken to be a root cause contributing to this hunting. *Poverty and inequality* are therefore identified as a root cause of biodiversity loss, operating from 1948 to the present day.

These policies and hunting freedoms also certainly encouraged other individuals, at least some of whom would not have been motivated by economic gain. The practice of 'shotgun ornithology', whereby biologists, other scientists, or interested amateurs pursue their interest in biology by shooting game, provides a perfect example. Local experts suggest this factor was not insignificant in reducing the numbers of some species to dangerously low figures. *No scientific or economic appreciation of biodiversity* is, therefore, traced as a root cause of biodiversity loss. This root cause operated from 1940 to 1980.

Over-harvesting or Otherwise Inappropriate Use of Floodplain Resources

Over-fishing, over-harvesting of reeds and other wetland products, burning and clearing of reed beds and wetland habitats, illegal poaching of wildlife and over-consumption of water have been cited as localized current and past threats to biodiversity. Some small-scale conversion of wetland habitats into private agricultural land is also occurring in some localities. The primary actors in these cases are largely the local communities, driven by the very real and widespread poverty that has accompanied the country's difficult and troublesome transition to a democratic, market economy. Real incomes have fallen alarmingly in recent years, from an average in the study region of US$934 per capita per annum in 1989 to just US$320 in 1996 (Bulgarian Institute of Statistics, 1998).

Unemployment in the region is high and families rely more and more on informal activities to survive. Among these informal activities, part-time fishing is common, but all opportunities for natural resource exploitation that might be financially rewarding are being pursued at a faster rate, and by a higher proportion of the population than in previous years. Some of these activities are illegal, although the risk of punishment is lowered by the limited capacity of the regulatory authorities to enforce existing legislation. Furthermore, yesterday's officially sanctioned and rewarded hunting is today's illegal and punishable poaching, while habits, attitudes and livelihoods are not changed overnight, particularly in rural areas.

The economic crisis of the current transition period can be traced to over 40 years of inappropriate and damaging socialist management of the country's economy and natural capital. The desperate economic situation of many individuals and families, while worse now than under socialism, can also be traced back to this same factor in terms of resource wastage, poor levels of infrastructure, inadequate health care, poor access to education and minimal provision of services. As argued above, the socialist system was largely imposed from outside the country and, therefore, one root cause of the current over-exploitation is the previous geopolitical climate. *The Cold War and international geopolitics* are therefore again taken to be a root cause of biodiversity loss.

Despite the overwhelming economic motivations and needs that drive this unsustainable resource use, other factors are also responsible. The apparently low level of environmental awareness among the local population could be ameliorated by a government committed to its obligations under various international conventions (eg CBD and Ramsar Convention) – so could the inadequate and insufficient levels of enforcement currently by the regulatory bodies charged with protecting the wetland and floodplain resources and natural areas (Ministry of Environment, Committee of Forests). These regulatory bodies are badly under-funded and lack the necessary equipment, training, numbers of staff, transport and resources to implement the existing legislation. There is also a seemingly unnecessary division of responsibilities for environmental protection between the two institutions mentioned above, and sometimes inadequate communication and coordination between them. These factors highlight a prevailing low government priority for biodiversity, which undermines the efforts of some authorities and underpins the chain of events described above. *Low government priority for biodiversity* is, therefore, taken to be a root cause of biodiversity loss, operating from 1990 to the present day.

Surface-water Pollution

Due to the enormous dilution capacity of the Danube, surface-water pollution is not seen as a problem, apart from localized and unusual accidental spills or other events. The condition and nature of the smaller tributaries that feed into the Danube is more problematic. The precise effects and nature of this pollution are not well-documented, partly as a result of the poor monitoring systems of this region during the post-war period and its sensitivity as a border region. However, a general and continuing decline in water quality was perceived up until the late 1980s. As in many other regions of Central and Eastern Europe, water quality improved during the initial stages of the economic and social transition period, due to downturns in industrial production and reductions in the levels of fertilizer and pesticide application (Klarer and Moldan, 1997).

This recent improvement notwithstanding, it is nevertheless felt that surface water pollution has significantly affected the health and integrity of remaining wetland ecosystems in the study area. The actors responsible for this pollution, in this case fairly diverse and well-distributed industrial operators, have been influenced by two factors when making decisions regarding the environmental performance of their plants or farm systems. These two factors have been the prevailing low level of environmental awareness and the insufficient enforcement of environmental legislation.

In many cases, the opportunity to pollute without government sanction arose because the Ministry of Environment did not have sufficient funds to enforce environmental legislation. Both these factors can, therefore, be traced to a single, deeper factor concerning the government's priority setting. *Low government priority for biodiversity* is once again identified as a root cause of biodiversity loss, operating from 1950 to the present day.

Regarding the insufficiency of the financial resources being made available to the responsible regulatory bodies, a further factor can be discerned. The current economic difficulties inherent in the economic and social period of transition make it very difficult – if not impossible – to finance the activities, structures, institutions and staff required for full enforcement. As we have argued above, the cause of these economic difficulties can be considered to be the legacy of 40 years of mismanagement and inappropriate decision-making during the socialist era. *The Cold War and international geopolitics* are again identified as a root cause of biodiversity loss.

However, the failure to set in place a more holistic approach for planning for these international waters cannot be ascribed purely and completely to these identified root causes. *The failure to employ catchment-level planning in the Danube river basin as a whole* is therefore identified as a third root cause of biodiversity loss, operating from 1950 to the present day.

Slovakia

The time-series maps (Figure 9.6) show the approximate historical habitat structure of the region from the early 18th century to the present day. These maps clearly show the impacts of human activity on the floodplain during this 250-year period. The most significant patterns to emerge are a decline in the area of bank-side forests (flooded forests); a drastic decline in the area of naturally flooding meadow grasslands (most of which were located along the smaller tributaries of the Morava); a large and relatively recent increase in the area under arable cultivation; and a significant and progressive straightening and regulation of the watercourses. The last map, for 1997, has an overlay of the recorded corncrake sightings to demonstrate the importance of the floodplain meadows for biodiversity

The floodplain forests and meadows rank among the richest habitats for biodiversity in Slovakia, but their widespread removal has severely reduced levels of biodiversity in the floodplain area. The most important factors affecting biodiversity in the Morava river floodplains are surface-water pollution, river regulation, conversion of floodplain meadows in diked areas to arable land, gravel mining, reduction or absence of mowing practices in floodplain meadows and damage to river banks, habitats and access areas.

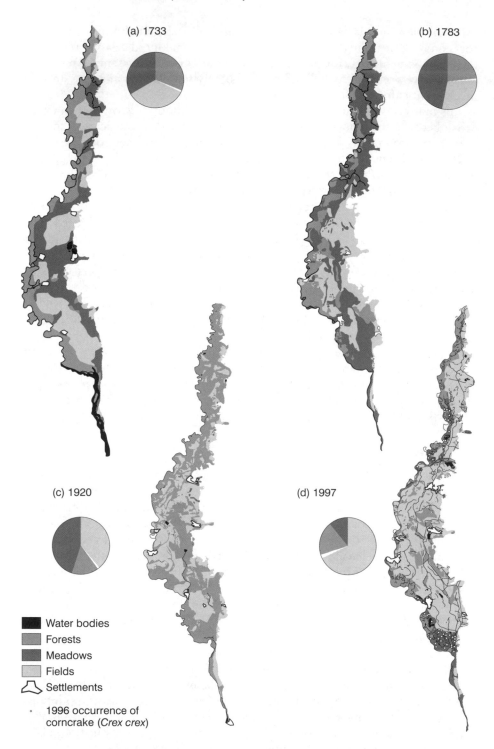

Figure 9.6 *Habitat Structure of Morava River Floodplain*

Surface-water Pollution

Surface-water pollution in this region comes from two major sources: industrial plants upstream (including those in Austria and the Czech Republic) and agricultural sources in the study site and upstream (again including those in Austria and the Czech Republic). As with Bulgaria, the precise nature and quantity of pollution is not documented, but an overall improvement has been discerned since the political and economic changes of the late 1980s. The rapid economic growth rates experienced in both the Czech and Slovak Republics during much of the 1990s, combined with an influx of foreign investment and eventual industrial recovery, however, mean that the reduction in pollution is likely to be temporary.

Surface-water pollution has significantly affected the health and integrity of wetland ecosystems in the study area. Two factors – the prevailing low level of environmental awareness and the insufficient enforcement of environmental legislation – influenced those responsible for this pollution, including industrial operators and the farming community in three countries, when making decisions regarding the environmental performance of their plants or farm systems.

In the case of the Slovak and Czech polluters, poor enforcement of environmental legislation was probably a consequence of the insufficient resources of the Ministry of Environment, a well-documented phenomenon throughout Central and Eastern Europe. In the case of Austrian polluters, who are arguably more important in terms of immediate effects on the Morava river, a general and pervasive low appreciation of the value of biodiversity, possibly coupled with a tendency to overlook exported pollution, is more likely to be the cause. Both the above factors can, therefore, be traced to a single, deeper factor – low government priority for biodiversity in all three countries. *Low government priority for biodiversity* is therefore taken to be a root cause of biodiversity loss, operating from 1950 to the present day

As in Bulgaria, the insufficiency of the financial resources being made available to the Ministries of Environment in the Czech and Slovak Republics due to the economic difficulties inherent in the current period of economic and social transition is a critical factor. The main cause of these economic difficulties is the legacy of 40 years of socialist mismanagement and inappropriate decision-making. *The Cold War and international geopolitics* are therefore taken to be a second root cause of biodiversity loss.

Again, the failure to set in place a more holistic planning approach for these international waters cannot be ascribed purely to these identified root causes. An international coordinating body, responsible for monitoring, information exchanges and for giving advance warning of pollution incidents, was lacking in the Danube basin until the establishment of the Danube Environment Programme and the very recent implementation of its constituent initiatives such as the Accident Emergency Warning System. *The failure to employ catchment-level planning in the Morava catchment*, and indeed the Danube river basin as a whole, is therefore identified as a third root cause of biodiversity loss, operating from 1950 to the present day.

River Regulation

The Imperial Austro-Hungarian Government carried out the first engineering works aimed at river regulation during the late 19th century. Efforts intensified between the two World Wars and continued well into the 1960s. Two factors were key to the regulation and drainage of the river and its floodplain.

First, the 18th and 19th centuries were marked by increased flooding events in the study region, which can be discerned in the time-series mapping from the abandonment of certain areas of arable land. Rapid erosion due to deforestation and agricultural development of the uplands in the upper Morava catchment caused increased flooding throughout the Morava catchment, and indeed the Danube. Such agricultural expansion and development was necessary to feed the growing (and increasingly urban) population of the upper Morava valley and parts of Bohemia (Czech Republic). *Population growth and increased land-use pressure* are, therefore, taken to be a root cause of biodiversity loss, operating from 1890 to 1965.

Second, the period was a time of rapid social, economic and cultural development within the Austro-Hungarian Empire, especially from 1740 to 1783 – the reign of Queen Maria Theresa. The urban development of the nearby cities of Brno, Vienna and Bratislava demanded increased agricultural production from these areas. Increased agricultural production demanded both greater protection from the already increased threat of flooding and an increase in the amount of land used for agriculture. Also, this region was used as a convenient and fertile testing-ground for the new agricultural, mechanical and, most importantly, hydrological techniques and technology being developed in these urban centres.

The combination of these factors meant that the political need and will, financial resources and technologies required for large-scale engineering works were all present in the same place and at the same time. *Geographic proximity to the markets and influence of Bratislava, Brno and Vienna* is therefore identified as a root cause of biodiversity loss, operating from 1890 to 1965.

Hence the river was regulated and the associated wetlands and floodplains, seen as unproductive in comparison to arable lands, were drained, using new methods and newly available investment capital. The whole political and social climate was one of development and so-called modernization, and significant advances were undoubtedly made. The application of new technologies – in many fields and affecting many sectors – resulted in economic growth the like of which had never been experienced before. Yet these advances were, with hindsight, at the expense of the biodiversity supported by the floodplains and wetlands. *No scientific or economic appreciation of biodiversity* is therefore taken to be a root cause of biodiversity loss, operating from 1890 to 1965.

Conversion of Floodplain Meadows to Arable Land

During the socialist period, particularly after the decision to develop collective and state farming production systems, some of the peculiar paradoxes of ideologically-driven decision-making became apparent.

The closure of the area had a positive impact upon biodiversity in some locations, as a result of reduced human influence for much of the post-1950 period. However, some locations were exploited, despite the illegality of activities within this border area. Local farmers illegally entered the area and converted the floodplain meadows into arable land. Insufficient environmental enforcement was a factor, itself caused by the lack of resources available to the regulatory agencies, driven by the pervasive low priority given to biodiversity and nature conservation within the government of the time. *Low government priority for biodiversity* is again identified as a root cause for biodiversity loss, operating from 1970 to 1990.

The illegal expansion of agriculture into the floodplain meadows was not a mere accident, but resulted from rational decisions. The motivation for this expansion, which would not have been a particularly lucrative economic activity given the unsuitability of the land for arable cultivation, can be traced through an analysis of the agricultural production of the time. Nearby collectivized and state-organized farm units were under pressure to meet certain production quotas and were rewarded for doing so or penalized for failing. All that was important was that the quotas be met. So an entrepreneurial collective might exploit nearby 'off-limits' land for cereal production and add those illegal yields to their legal yields, boosting their performance accordingly.

In this light, even extremely inefficient production from the floodplain meadow areas was of use, since it was a top-up to the legally obtained production and therefore had a marginal value – within this social-political-economic context – far higher than it would under other conditions. The true cost of such production was not relevant at the time. This is a powerful illustration of the concept of mis-pricing.

The perverse planning and production systems of the socialist regime, in this case agricultural production quotas and collectivization, were, therefore, the factors that influenced local farmers to exploit the floodplain. This system was itself a function of the overall inappropriate socialist development model. *The Cold War and international geopolitics* is, therefore, again identified as a root cause for biodiversity loss, operating from 1970 to 1990.

Gravel Mining

The large gravel mining enterprise in the north of the study area has a visible impact on the floodplain, has encroached significantly upon the Ramsar site and is a threat to the nearby nature reserve. It also affects surface water quality through the discharge of sediment-laden outflows.

The operator, a joint Austrian-Slovak private company, is engaged in an illegal activity made possible through loopholes and the inconsistency of the relevant legal provisions. The latter relates to the conflict between the Slovak mining and environment acts, which both theoretically apply to land used for such industrial activities. The incomplete and complicated re-privatization of formerly state-appropriated nationalized land further confuses the issue since the real owners of the many small parcels of land are either untraceable or unaware of their property rights.

Insufficient enforcement of legislation, including Slovakia's obligations under the Ramsar Convention, is clearly a contributing factor. Therefore, the previously described lack of resources available to the regulatory bodies, which is partly a result of the difficult transition period, can also be seen as a factor. These three factors – the legal contradictions, the unclear land ownership as a result of the nationalization and subsequent re-privatization, and the difficult economic transition period – can all be traced to a single deeper factor: inappropriate socialist planning and development. *The Cold War and international geopolitics* is, therefore, again identified as a root cause for biodiversity loss, operating from 1990 to the present day.

One reason that the gravel mining company is able to act illegally is that no one knows who owns some of the land which it is rapidly excavating. Progress towards full re-privatization has been difficult, drawn out, and not particularly transparent. It may be that the government or certain agencies or individuals have a vested interest in ensuring that this is so. *A lack of political will to equitably and rapidly re-privatize* is tentatively proposed as a root cause of biodiversity loss, operating from 1990 to the present day

Other factors also influence this activity. Because the funding for the enterprise is through an Austrian investor and the market served by the gravel enterprise is within Austria, the floodplain's geographic proximity to the building sites and roads of Vienna is presumably a significant factor in the viability of the company's activities. Anticipated trans-European transport routes, enhanced trade and market opportunities across the Slovak–Austrian border and anticipated infrastructure investments in Slovakia are additional factors that make this venture attractive despite its illegality. The absence of effective regulatory measures or mechanisms within the EU for controlling environmentally damaging investments in Central and Eastern Europe is therefore a root cause of biodiversity loss. *The exploitation of Central and Eastern Europe by EU private business, without an appropriate and effective EU control mechanism* is identified as a root cause of biodiversity loss, operating from 1990 to the present day.

Meadow-mowing Practices

Where floodplain meadows still exist, appropriate human activities maintain their unique ecological structure and value that has been created over centuries of management. Continuation of traditional mowing techniques is required to support the very high levels of biodiversity found within these rich, man-made habitats. Since 1990, mowing frequency has been reduced in many places from twice to once per year, while in other places mowing is no longer practised at all, because local farmers no longer need winter animal fodder. Some of the land-owners may have only recently re-acquired property rights to these meadows and may be absentee owners with little or no interest in engaging in such agricultural work. Others are untraceable. Unclear land ownership, resulting from the incomplete and difficult re-privatization of land, is again a factor. *The Cold War and international geopolitics* is, therefore, again identified as a root cause for biodiversity loss, operating from 1990 to the present day.

As with the gravel mining example, slow progress towards full re-privatization is a factor. *A lack of political will to equitably and rapidly re-privatize* is again tentatively proposed as a root cause of biodiversity loss.

However, this does not explain why local farmers still present and active in the area are reducing the frequency with which they mow. Clearly, the prevailing market forces within which they operate must make such a decision rational. The influencing factor is the government agricultural policy, including the drastic reduction in subsidies to agriculture since 1990. Cuts in the state budget have resulted in subsidies falling by 30 to 40 per cent, as government economic planning favours the urban over the rural sector. Again, these policies demonstrate an under-valuation of the meadows, their biodiversity and the true environmental benefits that they provide to the wider ecosystem.

While these factors may be partly explained by the difficult economic transition, and therefore are related to the Cold War history, they may also be attributed to the de facto priority given to the rural sector by the government. *Urban bias, to the detriment of rural interests, including conservation*, is therefore identified as a root cause of biodiversity loss, operating from 1990 to the present day.

Damage to River Banks, Habitats and Access Areas
The closure of the area for so long resulted, upon reopening, in strong interest in the recreational opportunities presented by the floodplain, the river and the open spaces. The nearby Slovak population has been understandably eager to visit and become reacquainted with this beautiful, tranquil, natural area to which access was denied for 40 years. Furthermore, the area's close proximity to Bratislava and other Slovak urban settlements as well as Vienna means that there are large numbers of urban residents with relatively few alternative options for recreation.

Widespread damage to river banks, habitats for birds and small animals and access areas is a significant problem in certain locations. Fishermen are particularly to blame for clearing bank-side vegetation, damaging trees, making fires, littering and generally acting with little respect for the environment. Two factors seem to influence such environmental damage by the general public: a lack of appreciation of biodiversity and insufficient enforcement of legislation.

The latter has already been traced several times to *the Cold War and international geopolitics*. This root cause is indicated by the fact that the very closure of the area as part of the Iron Curtain is one reason for its current popularity and the consequent pressures on biodiversity. As a result of this history, the influx of visitors has been far more rapid and intense than would otherwise have been the case. However, the lack of appreciation of biodiversity is a function of the poor environmental awareness and education levels prevalent in schools, the media and the general public. This poor environmental awareness can be traced back to poor implementation of current and recent government policy.

Pressure on the floodplains would not be so intense if there existed a range of natural areas to which the urban population could travel, within a short enough distance from the capital. Failure in the past to set aside sufficient protected or maintained natural areas for recreational uses is therefore identified as a root cause of biodiversity loss.

CONCLUSIONS

Many root causes operated in both study sites. While this is perhaps to be expected given the socioeconomic nature of the root causes and the somewhat shared social, political and economic recent history of the two countries, it is also a little surprising given the much deeper cultural, geographic, historical and ecological differences and that the most significant root causes were complete or no longer in operation. Two root causes in particular were especially frequent: the Cold War and international geopolitics, and low government priority or awareness of biodiversity.

It is a difficult task to rank the relative importance of the root causes. Weighing the relative importance of the perceived or observed impacts is less difficult. For both study areas, river regulation and drainage of floodplain areas have had the largest effect upon biodiversity and have probably caused the bulk of biodiversity loss. These impacts are both largely historical and completed. Firstly, population growth has contributed to these impacts by stimulating the drainage and reclamation of floodplains, either directly for additional agricultural expansion in Bulgaria, or indirectly through increased erosion upstream, necessitating further flood control measures in the study area in Slovakia. Secondly, and more significantly, the lack of a scientific or economic appreciation of biodiversity has continually been a root cause in both case study sites.

Most of the root causes discussed here should be considered as contextual, immutable factors that contribute to our understanding of the case studies' historical and political background. These historical root causes are important, but do not offer points of entry for policy interventions or remedies. In order to address biodiversity loss today, we must look at those root causes currently exerting an influence. These are active factors that offer points of entry for intervention activities.

What is particularly striking is that, of the identified root causes, none was assessed to be operating at the local level. Many, if not all, of the impacts on biodiversity are occurring at the local level yet, when traced backwards, it is found that the primary, socioeconomic root cause of impacts on biodiversity is either a national or international phenomenon. Since many of the root causes are still operating, it would appear that threats to biodiversity are still strong despite the largely historical nature of much of the biodiversity loss to date.

All root causes were operating at either the national or international levels, but local and national actors carry the true costs. Therefore, opportunities may exist to influence these actors through local- or national-level activities.

In particular, an appropriate approach is to advocate from the local/regional level towards the national and international the need to adjust policies, mechanisms and regulations connected with the root causes of biodiversity loss.

Full Valuation of Floodplain Ecosystems

In general terms, the reasons for biodiversity loss can be summarized as a widespread and persistent failure to properly understand, quantify, or value the goods, services, functions and capital value of natural resources. These resources have been and continue to be undervalued. The mis-pricing of natural capital continues to lead to the reduction of biodiversity.

This implies that if one or more of the actors responsible for the processes leading to biodiversity decline were to be made aware of the full economic value of a given resource and if the processes of mis-pricing in policy decision-making could be thus eliminated, more sustainable use would be the rational outcome. However, it is difficult to convince decision-makers, who, by their nature, often see a situation in purely economic terms or with a very strong sectoral bias, particularly when full knowledge of the true economic value of the floodplains does not exist. Wetland valuation is a relatively new and as yet still developing technique. Much progress is being made worldwide in the development of appropriate tools and methodologies (Barbier et al, 1997), but neither Slovakia nor Bulgaria are well-endowed with environmental economists, aware of such techniques and tools.

Only limited valuation work has been undertaken for Danubian floodplains in general (Andreasson-Gren and Groth, 1995). A major conclusion of this study is, therefore, that there is an urgent need to properly and systematically assess the true economic value of the remaining floodplains and wetlands in both the Bulgarian and Slovak study sites. Armed with fuller economic data on these ecosystems, it will be easier to convince decision-makers and the general public that these are resources worth conserving and using in a sustainable manner. Such economic valuation is dependent on a proper understanding of all the various functions an ecosystem performs, so that economic values may be assigned to previously under-valued functions such as groundwater recharge or flood absorption, which leads to the next major conclusion of the study.

Ecosystem Functioning

This study has largely concentrated on the ecosystem – or habitat – level rather than the species level for several reasons. Firstly, habitat loss in the two study areas is widespread, as has been shown by the historical reconstruction of previous habitats, stretching back in Slovakia for more than 250 years. Secondly, detailed data on species diversity, and especially genetic diversity, are generally not available for historical periods or are anecdotal at best. And thirdly, it is somewhat easier to assess ecosystem changes. This study concentrated upon these more visible trends. Finally, one can argue that, when implementing ecosystem or habitat-level actions, genetic and species diversity are implicitly included. Perhaps as important as species loss, if not more so, is the overall negative impact of such losses upon functional diversity. Functional diversity may be described as the range of environmental, ecological, cultural and economic functions that biodiversity, or an ecosystem, performs. This study has not considered the impact of the described changes upon the functioning of the wetland ecosystems.

Two examples among many are sufficient to demonstrate this point. Firstly, we do not know the impact on the downstream waters of the Danube of the loss of naturally flooding meadows along the tributaries of the Morava river in terms of nutrient removal, natural filtration and other water quality functions. Secondly, we do not know how the drainage of the Danubian marshes has affected the regional groundwater table balance and dynamics in northern Bulgaria, in terms of recharge functions and moderation of annual fluctuations of hydrological highs and lows. Further research is required to assess the impacts upon functional diversity – or ecosystem functioning – to properly understand the relative importance of the identified root causes. This is not to say that other proposed actions should not be undertaken before full knowledge is acquired. Rather, a thorough and applied programme of research should be developed that seeks to establish the functions of the various components of the wider system while also addressing the restoration and conservation of degraded or remnant habitats.

RECOMMENDATIONS

The following recommendations have been developed by the research team alone and represent simply a first step towards the drafting of an overall, integrated, long-term action plan. These recommendations are for actions requiring immediate implementation in order to lay the foundations for future activities agreed upon through stakeholder analysis and participatory planning processes.

Priority Actions

- Promote and stimulate an integrated approach to river-basin management in the two study sites, recognizing the importance of human quality of life and biodiversity conservation, through all appropriate means, including opportunities presented by the Danube River Protection Convention and EU approximation processes.

- Promote the establishment of more secure conservation status for the two areas: in Slovakia in the form of a Ramsar site involving Austria and the Czech Republic; in Bulgaria in the form of an international lower Danube green corridor involving Romania, Moldova and Ukraine.

- Set in motion a process of consultation with the identified stakeholders, using this report as a fundamental starting point for review and discussion, in order to agree upon the importance and urgency of action and the necessity of a participatory approach to any future decision-making.

- Develop and propose a series of sustainable resource-use scenarios, which guarantee a safer future for existing biodiversity, for presentation to the stakeholders at the outset in order to guide and lead the participatory planning process in a satisfactory direction towards the longer-term activities.

- Continue to assess and evaluate the functioning of the different ecosystems in the study area based upon fuller understanding of the dynamics and linkages of the floodplains, wetlands, groundwater, tributaries, main river channels and islands.

- Establish the economic rationale for sustainable use of floodplain and wetland resources, based on full economic valuation of floodplain and wetland goods, services, functions and capital. Detailed economic assessment of ecosystem functions and values is required in order to properly understand and value the true costs and benefits of different development and resource-use scenarios.

- Investigate the potential for establishing strategic rural partnerships in the two study sites, building upon the valuable foundation of community participation facilitated in part by the project partners in the field, in order to guide the participatory planning process in appropriate directions.

- Continue the valuable work on mapping and basic ecological applied research in the two study areas and expand the activities to include socio-economic components to ensure a more integrated synthesis of findings and implications, leading to holistic recommendations for possible land-use options and development scenarios.

- Continue investigation of the major impacts and the current causes of biodiversity loss in order to exploit opportunities to launch strategic interventions to stop, alter or diminish the influence of these root causes.

Stakeholder Analysis and Participation

Based upon the results, achievements and outputs of the above priority activities, WWF and its project partners must work to ensure the initiation of a truly participatory process. Such a process takes a long time, hence the need for the immediate implementation of the above recommendations and the following medium-term activities:

- Refine this root causes methodology, report and indicative recommendations, based on discussion and review with the relevant stakeholders, including the Ministries of Environment and other responsible state regulatory and planning authorities.

- Implement an awareness-raising campaign in the study areas, targeting the private sector, farming and fishing communities and municipal or local government, and within central and regional governmental bodies responsible for planning and decision-making.

- Develop a communications strategy for informing the wider international community, in particular funding agencies, about the importance of the study areas, the threats to biodiversity, the root causes of past and current biodiversity loss, and the opportunities for collaborative, participatory and effective action.

- Produce lobbying tools and design approaches and proposals for funding or implementation of specific packages of activities, in order to shape the evolving participatory debate and planning of activities.

Development of an Action Plan

The outputs of these medium-term activities should include an action plan and a portfolio of projects in order to seek funds for specific measures aimed at protecting biodiversity through the elimination of identified root causes.

Central to this process will be strengthening stakeholder commitment to biodiversity conservation through the demonstration of the economic and environmental benefits of rational resource use and wetland ecosystem restoration, and the provision and diversification of livelihood options for the populations in the two study areas. To these ends, we recommend that a consultation process start immediately with all domestic and international stakeholders, using the contacts and good name of the in-country project partners, and building upon existing activities.

A series of workshops and public awareness events should be designed in order to publicize the initiative and begin to identify appropriate individuals and organizations willing and able to push forward the development of an action plan.

It is estimated that this portfolio of projects could be developed in order to be presented to funding agencies within a period of approximately one year. At present, we make no recommendations as to the precise nature of these projects but the actions outlined above might form important components of any agreed plan.

Chapter 10

India: Chilika Lake

Research team: The research team included *Dr Gopal K Kadekodi*
(Research Professor in the Centre for Multi-Disciplinary Development
Research) and *Prof Subhash C Gulati, Dr Saroj Kumar Adhikari,*
Mr Ram Ranjan and *Mr Dharmendra Kar* (all in the Institute of
Economic Growth)

Summary: **The rapid expansion of commercial aquaculture, particularly
prawn culture, in Chilika Lake is contributing directly and indirectly to
the decline of the lake's fisheries and world-renowned bird population.
Changes both in India's economic policies and in global markets have
caused a rapid rise in the price of prawns and the abandonment of traditional fishing patterns in favour of aquaculture.**

Chilika Lake, the largest lagoon in Asia, covers about 100,000 ha on the east coast of peninsular India (Figure 10.1). It is one of six Indian wetlands listed in the Ramsar Convention of 1982. Chilika is a very rich preserve of ecological diversity, with over 400 vertebrates of both brackish and freshwater species, including several endangered, threatened and vulnerable species. Over one million migratory waterfowl and shore birds gather there during winter. A very large lake with a drainage basin of over 4300 km^2, Chilika provides a livelihood for over 100,000 fishermen and contributes to India's foreign exchange balance through tourism and exports of prawns and fish.

Though severe ecological degradation of the lake has been observed, it has received little attention at the local, national or international levels. Forest degradation, markets and international changes are usually portrayed as the main causes for such degradation. Finding the truth of the matter lies in understanding the various direct and indirect causes at the local, regional, national and global levels. Only such an approach can provide direction for policy formulation for better preservation of Chilika's biodiversity.

Like many wetlands around the world, Chilika Lake is subject to a multiplicity of pressures, ranging from local to global in geographic scales, with impacts over short to very long periods, and with long-term effects on the socioeconomic development of India. All these are driven in part by market forces and in part by socio-political situations. In the case of each type of pressure, different sets of root causes of biodiversity change are identifiable. With this backdrop of highly diversified possible root causes, it is important to study this wetland more closely, with a view to its conservation.

This study found that the major root causes of biodiversity loss, in order of importance, are population dynamics, globalization, aquaculture technology and, lastly, if at all, forest degradation and other ecological changes. This important finding leads to the conclusion that the root causes for biodiversity loss in the lake lie in regional socioeconomic factors.

DESCRIPTION OF THE STUDY AREA

Because it is connected with the Bay of Bengal, the Chilika wetland is actually an estuarine lake or lagoon. Hemmed between green hills in the south and the Bay of Bengal in the north-east, the lake is dotted with numerous small rocky islands. Its pristine beauty has fascinated the people of the region for centuries. Over the last 100 years, Chilika has attracted the attention of biologists, fishery scientists, geologists, oceanographers, planners and administrators and, in recent years, ecologists, naturalists and conservationists.

The lake is about 64.5 km long, varying in width from 18.5 km in the north to 5 km in the south. At its southern end, the lake has a major link with the Bay of Bengal through an irregular 29 km-long channel (with several small, sandy and usually ephemeral islands). About 1.5 km wide, the channel runs parallel to the bay and is separated from it by a very narrow spit, 180 to 275 m wide. The lake also has another link at its southern end (through Palur

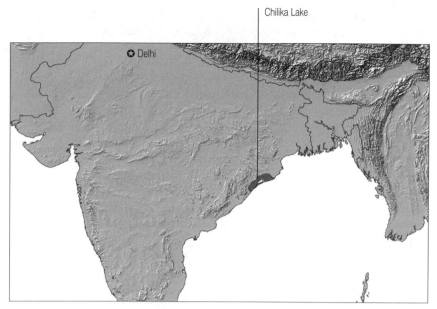

Chilika Lake

Delhi

Figure 10.1 *Map of India Showing Location of Study Area*

Canal from Rambha Bay to the mouth of the Rishikulya River, a distance of about 18 km) which is separated from the lake by lowlands, some of which are used as salt pans.

Largest among the lake's islands, Nalabana is a low-lying marshy island of about 35 km², covered with low vegetation. Designated as a bird sanctuary in 1973, it is the only protected part of the lake. Generally, it is completely submerged after the monsoon. Several rocky islands in the southern sector, including Kalijai, Somolo, Dumkudi, Honeymoon, Breakfast and Bird Islands, represent the inundated remnants of the Eastern Ghats. On the coastal side, many islands, made up of sand dunes, cover about 728 km².

The drainage basin of the lake lies between the rivers flowing into Mahanadi and Chilika in the north, while in the north-east, areas draining into the Bhargavi River make up the watershed. To the west and south-west, the watershed boundary lies between streams flowing into the Rishikulya River and those flowing into Chilika. Many other smaller rivers, rivulets and tributaries also flow through the area.

In addition to the 1100 km² area of the lake itself, the drainage basin of Chilika includes 2325 km² of agricultural land (mostly dry land), 525 km² of forests, 190 km² of permanent vegetation predominantly used for plantations, 70 km² of swamps and wetlands and 90 km² of grassy mud flats in the north-east of the drainage basin. Only 50 km² of the basin are occupied by human settlements, roads, railways and other infrastructure.

Chilika Lake is home to several ecologically important species of flora and fauna. Some of the most common varieties of crab species found in the lake are *Scylla serrata, Neptunus pelagicus, Varuna litterata, Ocypoda sp* and *Paratelphusa sp*. Commonly known as Chilika's famous 'tiger crab', *S serrata* is the most important species and occurs in greater numbers than all other species combined. However, it is now on the list of vulnerable species due to over-exploitation. Five species of prawn form the basis of the commercial prawn fishery in the lake. These are *Penaesus monodon, P indicus, Metapenaesus monoceros, M affins* and *M dodsoni*. The famous 'tiger prawn' (*P monodon*) is also over-exploited by the fast-growing prawn industry.

There have been very large biodiversity losses in Chilika Lake. The number of fish species is estimated to have fallen from 126 in the 1920s to around 69 in 1988. Prawns used to be abundant in the lake and provided prey for a variety of fish. Now prawns are scarce, a fact reflected by a decline in both fish and prawn landings. Chilika also used to be home to a variety of marine animals including crocodile, green sea turtle and gharial, all of which have become locally extinct.

Some of the ecological changes that are taking place are worth noting. The rate of annual siltation in the lake has reached alarming proportions. The progressive increase in silt, predominantly due to deforestation in the Chilika drainage basin, has reached a rate of almost 13 million tons annually, brought into the lake by an estimated annual freshwater flow of 375,000 million cusec. The influx of silt is the chief cause of lake shrinkage. The current annual rate of lake and wetland shrinkage is about 14.7 km². Shrinkage of the lake area alone has been approximately 1.5 km² per year. Compared to the fast fresh-water inflow, particularly during the monsoon months, outflow is slow due to the constricted channel. This channel runs through a sandy trough, frequently changing course because of the shifting of the sea mouth. The mouth of the lake has been shifting northwards at a rate of 3 km every 10 years, thus making the channel longer every year. The sea inlet has also been narrowing over time. At present, the width is about 180 m, down from 195 m in 1992.

Progressive decline in average salinity from around 22.3 ppt in 1957–58 to present levels of 3.6 ppt is another serious ecological change. Declining salinity is mainly due to the increasing flow of fresh water from the north and clogging and shifting of the lake mouth in the south. This affects the entire spectrum of fishing practices for both brackish and freshwater species, since it contributes to the shift from traditional fishing methods known as *uthapani, jano, diano* and *bahani* to pen and cage aquaculture.

The growth of chemical-based industries in the catchment areas, agricultural intensification in the Chilika basin and, most importantly, the spread of prawn-culture ponds since the mid-1980s, have increased pollution and eutrophication of the lake. The presence of toxic heavy metals including mercury, lead, copper, chromium and nickel in the lake has been reported. The net effect of eutrophication is excessive weed growth, because of the high influx of rich organic silt and sedimentation over the years and progressive decline in salinity. Weed invasion has been claiming 14.3 km² per year since 1973. *Potemogeton pectinatus*, locally known as charidal, is the most common weed. It grows luxuriantly from the silty northern area of the lake to the sandy southern end, and can tolerate wide salinity variations (0.2–15 ppt).

The lake boasts 150 species of birds including the dowitcher, one of the least known Asian shorebirds, and the spoonbill sandpiper, one of the rarest. In addition to its impact on fishing, weed growth has contributed to drastic reductions in these bird populations, particularly noted near the Nalabana bird sanctuary. Also noted is a decline in the quantity and variety of fish on which these birds prey. Deforestation in the Chilika basin and hunting of 15,000 to 20,000 birds every year are also contributing to this decline. This decline, in turn, has resulted in a substantial decrease in international tourists and ecotourism, which used to contribute greatly to the local economy.

FISHING AND AQUACULTURE PRACTICES

Because of their strong links with the habitat and human livelihoods around the lake, it is very important to note the changing fishing and aquaculture practices in this region. The lake provides an excellent brackish-water environment with more than 6000 ha for prawn and fish culture, about 19 per cent of the total available brackish-water resources in the State of Orissa. For centuries the people of this region followed traditional methods of fishing. Prawn culture is a relatively new activity.

During the early 1980s, brackish-water commercial prawn farming grew rapidly in and around the lake. Large-scale conversion of various traditional fisheries to aquaculture has taken place. While *diano* and *uthapani* fisheries were converted to aquaculture by newcomers and the government, other fisheries such as *bahani* and *jano* areas have been converted both by the government and by some fishermen's cooperative societies, either themselves or through sublets to third parties.

Under a programme for landless and rural poor, developed under the Brackishwater Fisheries Development Agency and strongly supported by the Orissa State Fisheries Department, 1550 shrimp ponds covering an area of 487 ha were established in the periphery of the lake. Several financial institutions provided more than Rs1.1 million for these projects. About 600 very poor families in the Chilika area have improved their incomes through prawn culture under the 'Economic Rehabilitation of Rural Poor' scheme sponsored by the state government. In addition, 165 private agencies have developed prawn-farming projects in the lake area using bank credit, and 20 farmers were engaged in prawn farming under a central government-sponsored scheme. Most of the projects were developed in the north-east and south-east parts of the lagoon. Recently there has been an attempt to opt for small-scale brackish-water shrimp culture, which has fewer ecological impacts. Development of low-cost technology for prawn culture has facilitated rapid expansion of aquaculture in confined brackish-water ponds as well as in seasonally dry areas in the lake periphery and in the adjacent areas of saline soil.

RESEARCH METHODOLOGY

Possible socioeconomic root causes of biodiversity loss were analysed together with key ecological factors using statistical techniques to arrive at priorities for policy prescriptions. Some of the likely socioeconomic root causes of biodiversity loss in Chilika Lake identified in initial hypotheses were population growth; urbanization and industrialization; conversion of lake area to agriculture; pressure on land; intensification of land use and changing cropping patterns; deforestation in the catchment; increased demand for fish and prawns; pricing and growth of the market system; changing caste configuration of fishermen and caste conflicts; changing aquaculture practices; intervention by money lenders; and the legal, political and institutional role of the state.

Variables for Analysis

The hypothetical ecological and socioeconomic root causes or variables can be grouped into four basic blocks, namely geographic, ecological, socioeconomic and temporal. Three broad geographic levels are considered here: global, national (including regional) and local. In Chilika, the influence of the global on the national and of the national on local processes and institutions is visible. Natural phenomena such as floods, rainfall, deforestation and climate change, as well as human resource use such as aquaculture and agriculture, are considered as ecological factors. Under socioeconomic factors, caste systems and their conflicts, population dynamics, poverty, industrialization, urbanization, ecotourism and markets are considered. The geographic scale and socioeconomic factors provide the most useful basis for organizing this study.

For the purposes of geographic analysis, the entire lake area was divided into four ecological sectors: northern, central, southern and the outer channel. This division is based on salinity and depth. It is assumed that the salinity would normally increase from the north to the outer channel, and that with the increasing freshwater inflows from the northern sector and clogging of the lake mouth in the outer channel, the central and southern sectors would lose their distinct characteristics over time. If that happens, biodiversity losses will be very high. On similar lines, the 128 villages around the lake have been grouped into five zones. The zoning was based on demographic structure and change, fishing and agricultural practices and geographic contiguity.

To analyse the socioeconomic aspects, the first step was to take a close look at the different socioeconomic groups and their differing perceptions about the state of lake biodiversity. They were grouped in four categories for the analysis. Geographically, they are grouped as local – people of the villages around the lake, totalling about 100,000 in about 128 villages; regional – people of the districts around the lake (Khurda, Puri and Ganjam); state and national – the governments of Orissa and of the Indian Union; and global – middlemen, organizations, market operators, exporters and importers. Temporally they are grouped as present generation and future generation. Economically they are grouped as fishermen, profit-makers in aquaculture, export-earners and ecotourists. Socially, they are grouped as class and caste groups, money lenders and politicians.

Data

A large statistical and scientific database already exists on the ecological aspects of the lake. These secondary sources provide significant insight into the ecological changes over the last 100 years. The major ecological factors included are salinity, siltation, weed growth, lake shrinkage and depth changes, pollution, eutrophication, avifauna, fish catch and aquaculture. In addition to compiling these data, interviews were held with scientists, bureaucrats, social workers and citizens with knowledge of the lake. These interviews elicited additional information about historical and current lake characteristics, inhabitants and fishermen in the surrounding areas and their perceptions and suggestions for improving biodiversity conservation.

The existing literature contains little information on socioeconomic and anthropological factors. Available information from secondary sources covered fishing licences; fish landings, exports and prices; fish processing; employment, cooperatives and financing; census data on population dynamics; and legal issues. To provide more information on the socioeconomic variables for this study, a survey was carried out of cultural practices, livelihood status, demographic structure of the family, social dimensions of fishing communities, perceptions regarding causes of biodiversity changes, income and consumption patterns and willingness to pay for biodiversity conservation.

Eight villages with distinctive characteristics were selected in order to capture the important socioeconomic and cultural root causes affecting biodiversity in the lake. Two villages in the south-central sector of the lake, Krishnaprasad Garh and Berhampur, were selected because new fishermen, along with traditional fishing communities, are practising intensive prawn culture along the shore of the lake in this area. Two villages located at the entrance of the outer channel to the lake, Satapara and Arakhuda, were selected because both prawn culture and fishing are intensive in this region. Juvenile prawns are being caught and sold to fishermen in areas where pen culture is common. One village on the northern side of the lake, Soran, was selected because siltation and weed growth are major problems in this part of the lake. Bhasandpur and Chandraput, also in the northern part of the lake, were selected because of the settlement of immigrants from Bangladesh in this region, which has generated caste conflicts. The eighth village, Sabuli, in the southern sector of the lake, was selected because the village is located in the mountainous region of Chilika basin, an area covered with thin forest. A split among the fishing cooperatives has led to many conflicts affecting fishing rights in this village.

Through interviews and group discussions, about 40 households in each of the eight villages answered a pre-tested structured questionnaire. To generate interest in the survey among the villagers, group discussions of Chilika's deterioration and the problems faced were held before the interviews were conducted. Additional information was gathered through discussions with community leaders and older villagers.

Analysis and the Conceptual Model

The linkages among economic, social, demographic and ecological variables were estimated using statistical techniques. The socioeconomic aspects and factors were linked with the ecological dimensions and characteristics using a conceptual model, which was developed around the ecological framework of the lake. Socioeconomic pressures are understood to affect the ecological conditions and, in turn, those conditions are understood to cause socioeconomic changes.

This conceptual model was then simulated for various scenarios including the following:

1. Impact of globalization: price changes, exports, tax and subsidy policy changes.
2. Impact of demographic changes: literacy, mortality, fertility, migration.
3. Impact of legal changes: licensing, lease policy.
4. Natural ecological changes: deforestation, floods, changing lake mouth.
5. Technological interventions: aquaculture practices, dredging in the lake.

The conceptual model developed here suggests both the direction and extent of the impact of root cause factors responsible for the change in the Chilika Lake region. The analysis suggests that biodiversity changes themselves do not set off any chain reaction of changes in the ecology of the region. Rather, it is the population and socioeconomic dimensions, fuelled by global factors, that have been bringing significant biodiversity changes to the region. The rate of change in the ecological situation of the region is, in turn, a threat to the socioeconomic life of the region.

LOCAL AND NATIONAL CONTEXTS

Local Issues

The local region refers to the lake periphery and the lake basin, which falls in three districts of Orissa (Puri, Ganjam and Khurda). Several demographic, social, economic, ecological, institutional and legal characteristics are relevant in this context.

The most important local issue is the sustainability of fishing in the lake. The local population depends on fishing. Until the 1970s the human population and fish production grew consistently at almost the same rate of about 2 per cent per year. Prawn fishing did not play a special role until the 1980s, when there was a shift to prawn farming as a new technology which overtook traditional methods. Then came a phase of high population growth rates, which reached 4 per cent per year in the 1990s. Prawn and crab became the main catches, accounting for 45 per cent and 17 per cent respectively, and pen and cage culture gradually replaced traditional *jano* and *bahani* techniques. Prawn culture also attracted those other than fishermen to the trade, since it does not require any traditional knowledge of fishing. The number of active fishermen swelled from about 8000 in 1957 to over 27,000 by 1996. The consequence was that local fishermen were forced to opt for intensive prawn farming. In the early 1990s, the effects of globalization could be seen in the fast-rising prices of prawns compared to those of fish, which made exporting commercially attractive, and attracted middlemen, politicians and money lenders into the business. In addition to conventionally or legally assigned fishing sites, people started prawn farming in open areas and the lake periphery. Not surprisingly, per-family catch fell drastically.

These changes in aquaculture practices have important environmental effects. Expansion of fishing grounds is one of the main causes of over-fishing in the lake and its outer channel, which, in turn, seriously affected the movement of adult prawns into the sea for breeding purposes as well as the return of young prawns through the lake mouth. Moving prawn larvae and catching juvenile prawns for sale to prawn culture ponds have adversely affected the mature prawn population in Chilika, leading to the decline of several fish species that prey upon prawns. Thus, over-harvesting of prawns since the mid-1980s has gravely affected the ecosystem of Chilika, and yield rates have fallen drastically since 1986. Interestingly, while the landing rates of prawns have been falling in Chilika, landings in the state as a whole are increasing. In 1985–86, the share in total production from Chilika was 22 per cent, which fell to only 2 per cent by 1995–96. Therefore, the primary root cause for biodiversity loss is identified as local population dynamics, driven by the expansion of prawn farming.

The second most important local issue is the link between the unsustainable aquaculture practices and the neglect of lake biodiversity. This study found that it is through local socioeconomic conditions that the ultimate effect of these practices is felt on lake biodiversity. The starting point is the poverty of the people, which leaves them little choice but to over-exploit Chilika's fisheries. Catching juvenile prawn and crabs, social conflicts, over-exploitation of lake marine products, growth of weeds, declining salinity and lake shrinkage have all adversely affected the biodiversity of the lake. The people of the region seem to understand these problems but are helpless to act because of their poverty. Local fishermen are in perpetual debt because of loans taken from money lenders. As many as 67 per cent of fishermen stated that they are unable to repay the loans on time, largely because of the declining fish catch. These fishermen have few other resources. Even among those fishermen with some education and exposure to the external world, almost 88 per cent of the households reported that they have no participation in the onward fish trade. Ideally, vertical linkages with processing, marketing and sale and distribution activities would be developed while maintaining fishing as the primary activity in the region. Such an expansion of economic activities would facilitate sustainable management of the lake.

A breakdown of the caste-based division of work in the fishing profession is a third major local root cause. Traditionally the fishermen caste was stratified in terms of professional skills in the fishing industry trades, divided as boat and fishing gear-making, net-making, fishing and trade, for example. The restrictions entailed by this social system have been lost in the process of globalization, as technology and markets have changed and as new fishermen have entered the business.

How is the state of the fishery affecting the livelihood of the local people? Notably, very few 'desirable' fish are consumed by the fishermen and their families or other local people. The bulk of the fish catch from the lake is consumed elsewhere, mainly in Calcutta and abroad. For instance, in 1996–97, out of a total production of about 1600 tonnes of fish from the lake, only about 20 per cent was consumed locally, whereas 80 per cent was exported to other states and foreign countries. Similarly, out of total shrimp production, only 22 per cent was consumed in the Chilika area whereas 78 per cent was sent to other markets. Though no direct estimate of income from fishing was possible, income from agriculture among fishermen and other families was found to be about Rs 4300 and Rs 8500 per year respectively (US$1 = Rs 42). The field survey indicates that income from fishing is little better.

Analysis of the primary data indicates that dependency on fishing and the share of the population engaged in fishing are inversely correlated with literacy and educational levels. Literacy is also correlated with high rates of migration from the region for jobs elsewhere. At approximately 43 per cent, the literacy rate is quite low, a factor that should be considered in designing balanced regional development plans.

State and National Issues

What is the role of the government in these local issues? The people of Chilika believe the root causes of environmental problems are class conflicts, illegal encroachments and the role of mafia, government and politicians. They believe that the government should give priority to restricting the entry of new fishermen to the fishery, removing weeds and protecting the lake mouth from clogging and shifting. The state government, however, treats the problems of social conflicts and biodiversity loss as law-and-order issues. The Revenue Department is considering armed policing of the lake. The usual approach to restricting exploitation of the lake and reducing related conflicts is to limit new fishing licences. Order after order has been passed restricting illegal and unauthorized farming, banning intensive prawn farming and conversion of *diano* and *uthapani* leases to pen or net fishing, banning unregistered societies and imposing strict licensing policies for both fishing and motorized boats. At the same rate, however, communities and individuals have been going to courts over social conflicts about these issues. The district authorities are unable to reduce either the conflicts or the increasing number of court cases.

The major push for exploiting marine and wetland resources began when a national process of structural adjustment and liberalization was started in India in 1991. These policies created a price gap between traditional species and those in demand for export, such as prawn and crabs. As a result, aquaculture farms, cold storage and export houses specializing in marine products have been mushrooming throughout the country's coastal regions. Several multinational companies have started ventures.

Another important national link is through ecotourism. The national and state governments have both recognized this wetland ecosystem under the Ramsar Convention. Several sites in the lake area have been recognized as important tourist areas. Nalabana Island has been declared a natural bird sanctuary with all human interference barred. Though the lake offers tourism based on religious, aesthetic and marine and avifauna attractions, very little has been done to facilitate ecotourism. Tourist visits increased from 83,000 in 1983 to 148,000 in 1994, registering an average growth rate of 3–4 per cent. There is still much more scope for this sector to grow. Expansion of ecotourism, however, could bring indirect pressure to preserve the lake's biodiversity.

National concern about the loss of biodiversity in this lake was registered only when the Supreme Court passed a historic judgement in 1996. This judgement strongly advocated the establishment of an authority to implement protection of coastal zones based on the principles of 'precaution' and 'polluter pays'. This order set guidelines for elimination of aquaculture and industries in the coastal zones, creation of an environment protection fund, and a ban on converting agricultural, mangrove and forest lands to shrimp ponds. It is to be hoped that this national policy will become a reality.

INTERNATIONAL CONTEXT: GLOBALIZATION

Like many other sectors of the economy, the Chilika fisheries have undergone a process of liberalization, globalization and a shift to greater market orientation. This aspect of the development of Chilika's fisheries has been analysed closely for this study. Both spatial and economic dimensions are involved in the transformation. For Chilika's fisheries, the process of market orientation began in the 1980s, spurred further by the government's new economic policy in 1991. These two phases of globalization are considered separately.

Sufficient evidence exists to say that, until the 1970s, the fishermen of this region, known for their community organization, had confined their fishing mainly to local and domestic use. From 1929 to 1970, production exceeded 5000 tonnes in only four years. In most years, production averaged around 3000 tonnes. The average annual growth rate of fish farming was about 2 per cent, very close to the population growth rate of the region. No external market forces caused growth in fish farming or created pressure to export fish products from this region.

From 1970 onward, fish production jumped in Chilika. The highest production was registered in 1972–73, with almost 9000 tonnes. In the 1970s and 1980s, fish landings ranged between 5000 and 6000 tonnes, although with a negative annual growth rate of about 1.7 per cent. Growing national demand and, to a lesser extent, growing foreign demand have led to rising prices that have more than compensated for the decline in production.

Price effects rooted in growing global demand changed the scenario in the 1980s. Exports of fish increased in the 1980s, with an average of about 85 per cent of the landings exported to foreign markets, as against 60 to 75 per cent of landings exported in the 1970s. Until the 1980s, though the prices of prawns and crabs were rising, exports did not respond. In the 1980s, exports of fish and prawns rose as high as 97 per cent of the landings in some years while production rates remained around 6000 to 7000 tonnes per year. Production started to fall in the mid-1980s, hitting a low of about 1200 tonnes in 1995–96 as the lake was over-fished.

As mentioned earlier, construction of prawn-culture ponds, which began in the early 1980s, intensified over the subsequent period with associated changes in fishing technology. New capital-intensive fishing techniques using fine-meshed nylon nets, motorized boats and larger prawn culture ponds have become common. Twenty-four ice plants and three fish-processing plants with a daily total capacity of 166 tonnes were established. In terms of the change in fishing techniques, it should be noted that, by 1993, prawn and *diano* fishing grounds had swelled to 69 and 88 respectively, and most of the *jano* fishing grounds had been converted to prawn culture. Today, there are as many as 5000 licensed boats, many of which are motorized. Fishermen have opted for more and more boats, even though the average cost of each boat is about Rs 40,000. The field survey reveals that almost 50 per cent of financing for the boats came from money lenders. Thus, more investments, new technology and introduction of new people into the industry have all gone hand-in-hand since the 1980s.

What is the end result of globalization and the ecological degradation of the lake? Total fish landings from Chilika started falling sharply after 1986–87. Annual fish landings reached a low of about 1200 tonnes in 1995–96, just 14 per cent of the all-time high production of almost 9000 tonnes in 1986–87. Fish landings increased slightly in 1996–97 to over 1600 tonnes, still only 18 per cent of landings in 1986–87. The sharp decline in fish catch poses a threat to the traditional fishermen's livelihood. If this trend continues, fishing in the lake will soon be a thing of the past. Over-fishing in the lake periphery partly explains the drastic reduction in fish and shrimp landings. In addition, very intensive fishing at the shallower and choked lake mouth makes it increasingly difficult both for mature prawns and gravid fishes to reach the sea and for juveniles to enter the lake. The fall in fish, shrimp and crab landings over the years clearly indicates loss of fauna in the lake, and the equivalent loss of other aquatic species is highly probable. In response to a question on species loss in the field survey, 85 per cent of people expressed their awareness of species extinction.

How does prawn culture persist when the lake is ecologically degraded to the point that this degradation is threatening the livelihood of the people? The answer lies in the pricing of prawns. The market price of prawns varies with the size and type, from Rs 45 to Rs 500 per kg (prices as of July 1998). The price of export quality tiger prawn increased rapidly from Rs 280/kg in 1992 to Rs 420/kg in 1996–97. Fishermen received a price of Rs 180/kg in 1988, which increased to Rs 300 by 1996–97. This sharp increase in export prices more than offsets the declining rates of prawn (and also crab) landings. It is this price effect that has kept the prawn culture going, despite the ecological degradation.

An important comment on the rate of exploitation of local resources can be made at this stage. A comparison of the local value of exported shrimps with the free on board (fob) unit values indicates that the degree of exploitation of local resources in the name of export earnings has been increasing over time. While local prices of export products have only doubled over the last decade, the fob unit values more than tripled.

In summary, the effects of globalization and market orientation include:

• Adverse income distributional effects, benefiting middlemen primarily and leaving a large sector of the population outside of the beneficiary group.
• High domestic prices, even for traditional varieties of fish.
• Social tension between fishermen and other castes, and social conflicts induced by court cases, money lenders and the mafia.
• Loss of cultural identity, for example the disappearance of cooperative fishing.
• Drain of local resources and income from the region.
• Ecological degradation of the lake due to over-fishing, encroachment and unsound fishing techniques.

CONCLUSIONS

The major conclusions of this study were drawn from the conceptual model (Figure 10.2) and statistical analysis of the main variables. The first major conclusion is that the root causes of biodiversity changes in Chilika are not ecological, and that ecological changes in the surrounding area, such as deforestation, have not brought as much degradation as previous studies have suggested. Ecological factors can be viewed in terms of lake biodiversity or landscape biodiversity. One of the issues is whether changes in the lake periphery are affecting the ecology of the lake. The second is whether land-related ecological changes have any major effects on the lake. Land-related changes include deforestation in the catchment area, conversion of the lake periphery to agricultural land and changes in the rainfall pattern. Important lake-related ecological indicators are salinity, weed growth, lake depth, siltation and lake shrinkage. Contrary to expectation, the land-related biodiversity factors do not seem to affect the lake ecology as much as the latter affects the land ecology. The lake-related ecological changes bring about changes in the landscape around the lake, though only indirectly, by increasing human demands on the environment.

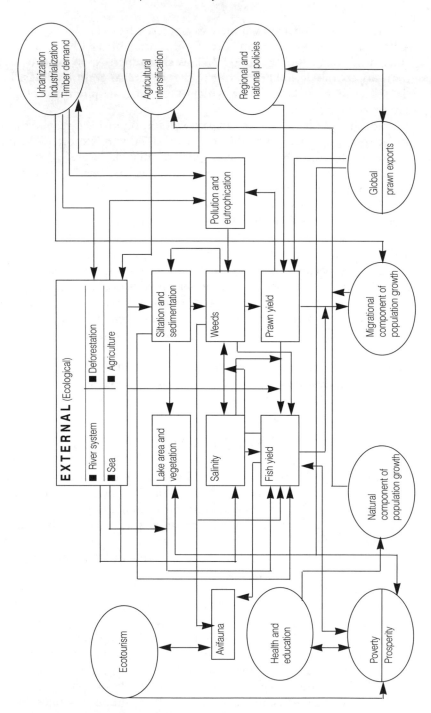

Figure 10.2 *Conceptual Model for Chilika Ecosystem*

The second major conclusion of the study is that the root causes of biodiversity change in the lake are found among socioeconomic factors, such as population dynamics, globalization and aquaculture technology. Until the 1970s the human population and fish production grew at almost the same rate. Then came the shift to prawn fishing exclusively, and hence the growing use of commercial prawn-farming technologies. The pen and cage culture gradually replaced the *jano* and *bahani* techniques. Population growth, together with the shift of others into fishing, forced traditional fishermen to adopt intensive prawn farming, a change magnified by the effects of globalization. The fast-rising price of prawns, as against that of traditional fish, made export production commercially attractive. The significance of population pressure on the lake and land ecology must be seen from the perspective of sustainable regional and human development. Population concentration in areas of prawn culture over the years has put pressure on the lake in terms of over-fishing and expanded agriculture on the lake margins. Together with the recent development of markets and globalization, national and global benefits have attained overriding importance at the cost of local benefits, thereby affecting the lake ecology significantly.

RECOMMENDATIONS

Socioeconomic Measures

Population Dynamics
Chilika is central to the traditional life and culture of the people of this region. Fishing provides food, social status and employment. The importance of the lake must be understood in these terms, rather than just as a means of economic support. Compared to many coastal regions of India, the annual population growth rate in Chilika is low at only 2 per cent, but the exploitation of the lake's resources is unsustainable at this rate.

A three-pronged policy is required.

- First, the views of the people must be given due weight in determining fishing sites, aquaculture practices, financing, marketing avenues and secondary employment opportunities. To ensure socially sustainable development, local fishing traditions should be respected.

- Second, the scope of Chilika fishing should be expanded to include marine fishing. The Chilika Development Authority (CDA) can play an important role here by training the fishermen in modern marine fishing, providing financial assistance, organizing marketing and monitoring aquaculture.

- Third, a network of small-scale businesses should be promoted by the CDA and the Orissa government in fishing, cold storage, marketing and processing. Fishing communities can be encouraged to take up these activities in addition to routine fishing. With an educated population of around

20 to 30 per cent and a literacy rate of 40 to 50 per cent, such a move towards more balanced regional development should be feasible.

Globalization and Technology

Globalization affects the ecology of the region directly and indirectly. The price differences between prawns and other fish have all been prompted by technical solutions, such as dredging the lake, developing cold storage, introducing mechanized boats and financing for fish exports.

- Measures such as dredging should be carried out only after thorough biological investigations of the lake ecology, species settlements and juvenile growth rates, for example.

- Introduction of mechanized boats for both fishing and tourism should be stopped completely if possible, with a heavy user tax applied to users.

- The globalization process has led to selective fishing, which was not permitted in traditional fishing. Cooperatives for traditional fishing should be encouraged and provided with support, and financing and boat licensing should be strictly monitored by an independent agency such as the CDA to reduce over-fishing.

- Export targets should have some links with local needs. An environmental tax could be introduced on all exportable marine products on the lines of the 'polluter pays' principle. Such a tax should not become part of the general fund of the government treasury but be retained exclusively for lake development.

Leasing Policies and Social Harmony

Changes in regional fishery leasing policies, especially since the early 1990s, have resulted in encroachment on the centuries-old fishing rights of traditional fishermen. The changing composition of the labour force and the people involved reflect the influx of newcomers into the lake area, leading to social tension and disharmony.

- Leasing policies now cater mainly for the interests of businessmen, middlemen and outsiders. This situation should be reversed by levying heavy fees on new fishermen entering the trade.

- Prawn and fish exports should come under heavy export duties.

- Outsiders should be encouraged to develop ecotourism activities or to find jobs in industry.

Ecological Measures

A progressive decline in average salinity from around 22 ppt in 1957–58 to present levels of 3.6 ppt is a serious matter. Hypotheses regarding seasonal and sectoral variations in salinity in the lake proved true. As expected, salinity reaches a maximum during the summer and is lowest in the monsoon season. Salinity is highest in the southern margins because of the link with the sea through the outer channel. The decline in salinity, due to siltation and sedimentation, is contributing to excessive weed growth in the lake.

- Recommendations by experts to raise the average salinity levels to 15 ppt should be implemented with a view to sustaining several fish species. Biologists must examine proposed measures for increasing salinity, such as dredging operations for the outer lake and other recommended sites near the Satpada and Palur Canals.

The increasing influx of rich organic silt and sedimentation over the years, combined with the decline in salinity has resulted in rapid weed growth which now infests around 52 per cent of the lake area. Pollution and eutrophication in the lake caused by chemical-based industries in the catchment areas, agricultural intensification in Chilika basin and the spread of prawn-culture ponds have also become issues, especially since the mid-1980s. Growth of prawn-culture ponds all around Chilika has contributed to the influx of nutrients facilitating weed growth. If the trend of progressive weed growth goes unchecked, the whole lake could be overgrown in another 50 years.

- The environmental tax proposed on prawn culture should be used to pay for removal of organic matter.

These ecological changes have drastically affected avifauna of the lake. More than a million migratory birds used to winter here, but the number is falling fast because of weed growth near the Nalabana bird sanctuary and because of the decline in quantity and variety of fish on which these birds prey. Deforestation and hunting in the Chilika basin are also contributing factors. The decline in avifauna has led to a substantial decline in ecotourism and international tourists, resulting in a local economic loss.

- Afforestation in the Chilika basin as well as bans on hunting of birds and on exports of fish and prawns from the area would improve conditions for avifauna and hence for ecotourism, not only improving economic and social conditions of poor inhabitants in the surrounding villages but also sustaining biodiversity.

Government and Legal Measures

At present, political efforts to reverse biodiversity loss in the lake area are limited to a few issues.

- The approach should be holistic. The starting point should be bridging the gaps between the fishermen and others, with attention to human dignity, rights and entitlements.

- Alternative activities, including ecotourism, should be integrated with aquaculture. Such an integrated approach is possible only if an authority such as the CDA takes responsibility for all these tasks.

- Logically, the CDA should have a broad representation of the people of the region on its board, not just serve as an official organ of the government.

- The government should not treat preservation of the lake as a policing exercise.

- The village communities should be involved in all major tasks such as monitoring, weeding, technological choices and generation of secondary employment.

Many of the findings of this study are based on a limited set of data and information about the habitat, culture, aquaculture, ecology and socioeconomic conditions of the region.

- In order to conserve the lake properly as a Ramsar site, a unit should be created within the CDA or in an organization such as WWF-India to generate and regularly collect scientific data.

- The information and data should be made available to scientific and socioeconomic agencies to support evaluation of policies.

Chapter 11

Mexico: Calakmul Biosphere Reserve

Research team: This study was prepared by *Dr Pamela Stedman-Edwards* (consultant to the WWF-México Program Office). Background reports were prepared by *Gloria Tavera, Eckart Boege* and the *Bufete Jurídico Tierra y Liberdad AC.* Substantial comments and contributions were also provided by *Jenny Ericson, Julia Murphy* and members of the WWF-México Program Office, including *Dr Guillermo Castilleja* and *Dr Eduardo Iñigo*

Summary: In the isolated region of Mexico under study, rapid population growth and persistent poverty are driving forest clearing that threatens a biosphere reserve. Failure to address the problems of poverty and social conflict underlies this threat to conservation. Government policies intended to improve the use of resources, including recent changes in tenure laws, do not have their intended impact in such a marginalized region that has only limited links with markets.

The Calakmul Biosphere Reserve and its surrounding forests remains one of the most isolated and least populated regions of Mexico. Nevertheless, important changes are taking place in the region that threaten the conservation of the tropical forest ecosystem and the biodiversity it supports. Poor ecological conditions for agriculture drive some of the degradation, but many of the changes are driven by socioeconomic forces. Rapid immigration to the area ranks among the most important, driving an expanding agricultural frontier. The lack of real economic alternatives to shifting cultivation is equally important in shaping resource use. The political and economic marginalization of the area has made it difficult to improve local socioeconomic conditions or support sound resource use. Recent extensive changes in laws and policies shaping markets and land tenure may have important effects in the region in the long term, but for the moment remain distant from local resource-use patterns. The creation of the reserve, however, has brought attention to the region. Together with valuable local efforts to exert control over resources, international conservation interventions in the area offer some hope of slowing the loss of biodiversity.

Mexico is an important case in the study of biodiversity loss; the country ranks fourth in the world for biodiversity. Calakmul is representative of the conflicts and problems surrounding many of the protected areas in Mexico, given unsustainable resource exploitation, inappropriate policies, poverty, population growth and marginalization of the local population. The national policy context in Mexico, notably the liberalization of a state-managed economy, parallels that of many other developing countries over the last decade. Mexico's tradition of communal land tenure makes this case of interest in other countries that are pursuing decentralization of resource management as a means to both development and conservation. The programmes aimed at promoting conservation in the region are typical of conservation programmes in under-developed regions in Mexico and around the world; they focus on settled agriculture and improved management of natural resources by local communities. However, conflicting pressures for development of rural areas and for protection of biodiversity have created a mesh of incompatible policies that promote land clearing and forest degradation.

DESCRIPTION OF THE STUDY AREA

The Calakmul Biosphere Reserve covers 723,185 ha and is located in the south-east of the state of Campeche. The reserve forms part of a larger system of lowland tropical forests, known as El Gran Petén, which spans about three million ha (Figure 11.1). Created in 1989, it was accepted as a UN Biosphere Reserve in 1993. There are two core zones which comprise 32 per cent of the reserve. The forest in this region is transitional between the dryer scrub forest of Yucatan and the humid tropical forest of the Petén.[1] Precipitation can vary greatly from year to year, and flooding is not uncommon during the hurricane season. There are no permanent sources of running water in the area and few

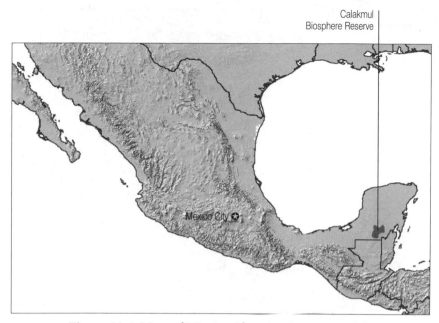

Figure 11.1 *Map of Mexico Showing Location of the Calakmul Biosphere Reserve*

sources of standing water during the dry season. Soils are shallow and calcareous and overlie a limestone platform. Biological inventories (INE and CONABIO, 1995) show that the reserve is home to at least 147 vertebrate and 18 plant species endemic to the Petén ecosystem. Twenty-five species of threatened vertebrates, including the spider monkey, tapir, jaguar, ocelot, margay and king vulture, and 17 endangered plants, are found in the region. The area is of particular importance for migratory song birds; over 20 per cent of species recorded in the reserve are migratory winter residents (Berlanga and Wood, 1991). Many species that are becoming increasingly rare in other parts of Mexico still have large populations in Calakmul (Galindo-Leal, nd). The reserve is also noted for several Mayan archaeological sites within its boundaries, which are contributing to the development of a local tourism industry.

The physical design of the Calakmul Biosphere Reserve is inappropriate for the purpose of a biosphere reserve and the requirements of biodiversity conservation (Galindo-Leal, nd). The boundaries were set with insufficient ground-truthing and little biological study of the area (Figure 11.2). The angular boundaries in no way relate to the shape of ecosystems or habitats, nor are the core areas clearly the most important for biodiversity. The southern core area in particular is problematic because it has no buffer zone on its eastern side, precisely where there are a number of settlements (Figure 11.3). The most obvious problem with the reserve is that it is virtually broken into two pieces. The narrow middle section is cut by a highway. Perhaps most importantly, both the core areas and the buffer zone include lands already

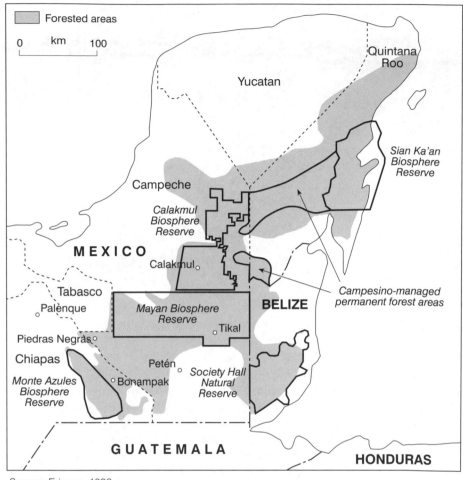

Source: Ericson, 1996

Figure 11.2 *The Calakmul Biosphere Reserve Region*

allocated by the government for agricultural and extractive purposes. Given these problems with the design of the reserve, it is essential to consider the fate of biodiversity in the surrounding areas, since the reserve itself may prove inadequate for conservation.

Biodiversity loss in the region is resulting from at least two proximate causes – loss of habitat and extraction of flora and fauna. Growth in the local population over the last 50 years has clearly affected the extent of forest cover and the availability of water around the reserve. In the reserve itself, the process of forest fragmentation is observable, especially in the central corridor where it is cut by a highway and along the eastern boundary, which is paralleled by a highway.[2] In addition to outright clearing and water diversion, biodiversity loss is probably resulting from extractive activities and hunting,

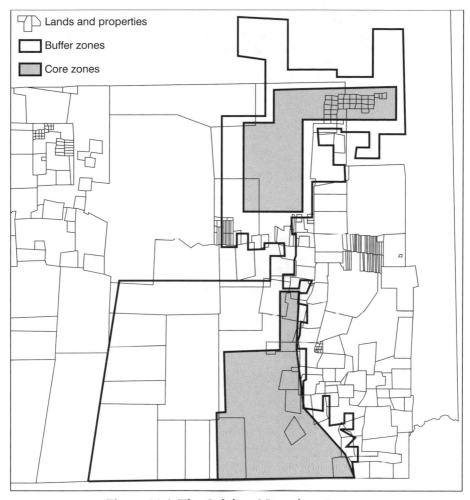

Figure 11.3 *The Calakmul Biosphere Reserve*

which may have a critical impact on some species including the wild cats, tapirs, ocellated turkey, mahogany and cedar.

RESEARCH METHODOLOGY

This study explores factors affecting biodiversity loss in and around the biosphere reserve.[3] It aims to understand the root socioeconomic forces and circumstances driving biodiversity loss, and the linkages among these root causes, across various scales from the local to the international. It begins with a description of local population and resource-use patterns, which are the direct or proximate causes of biodiversity loss. From there it moves outward to describe the various levels of socioeconomic factors that are shaping local resource-use patterns. These include regional development forces; national policies and institutions shaping settlement, tenure, agriculture and forestry practices; national policies defining Mexico's relationship with the international sphere; and international markets. The final section examines local responses to these forces and local understanding of conservation efforts.

The conclusions of this study were reached by asking a series of questions to examine the layers of factors affecting biodiversity in the Calakmul region to create a chain of explanation (Blaikie and Brookfield, 1987). The basic questions were:

- What are the direct causes of biodiversity loss and deforestation in the region?
- What explains the expansion of agriculture and other unsustainable resource use in the region?
- What are the connections with national markets?
- What local patterns of resource use can be traced to incentives and limitations from national policies?
- What connections are there between local resource use and international markets?
- How are local communities trying to affect their circumstances?

The existing literature on Calakmul and on Mexico, as well as a broader literature on the socioeconomic causes of environmental change, offered a ready-made selection of hypotheses that might explain patterns of resource use in Calakmul. These hypotheses were explored in turn to determine their relevance and importance in explaining biodiversity loss in Calakmul. Existing evidence pointed to some of these hypotheses as more probable than others, and further questions were asked in the field to better evaluate their applicability.

The information in this study is drawn from a variety of sources. These include extensive local field studies conducted on demographic change and patterns of resource use, using local surveys and interviews; and in-depth case studies of local views on the relationship between population and environment, carried out in two communities using participatory rural appraisal methodologies (Ericson, 1996; Pronatura, 1997a and 1997b). It also draws on several descriptive documents written by people with long-term experience working on conservation projects and on academic studies in the region,[4] as well as on documents produced by the conservation programmes in the region.[5] Information on the national and international context is drawn from documents from the governments of Campeche and Mexico, international organizations, academic papers and periodicals. Finally, information was collected specifically for this study from state and municipal government sources, WWF-México Program staff and local interviews about markets, patterns of production, land tenure disputes and investment of government funds, in order to define the relationship between local patterns of resource use and national and international factors.

Serious gaps in data on the region could only be partially filled by this study. Physical and biological data on deforestation and species loss were seriously lacking; yet deforestation was the only available proxy measure for biodiversity loss. The isolation of the region, its frontier character and the rapid changes that are occurring there, in terms of population growth, legal status of lands and political boundaries, make socioeconomic data scarce and unreliable. The clandestine nature of many activities in the area and the uncertain legality of others make it difficult to get honest responses from local people or government officials about local activities.

The other major methodological problem faced was in linking local activities to national and international factors. The links, for instance, between national policies and local responses, are indirect. Policies pass through layers of political manoeuvring and corruption, local understanding or misunderstanding, and contradictions with other policies. Then, the limited range of possible responses in Calakmul means that the response elicited at the local level may be minimal or may be unrelated to the original objectives of the policy. This limited range of possible responses may well mean that biodiversity loss is over-determined in Calakmul. Perhaps the most interesting conclusion of this study is that the effects of direct and indirect interventions by the government and of major marketplace changes on local resource-use patterns are significantly limited by the isolation and poverty of options in the region.

The results of this study are not offered as proof of what is happening in Calakmul, but rather as a set of hypotheses that seem to explain the dynamics of the region and for which there is some good evidence. There are, of course, many ways of understanding and describing biodiversity loss in Calakmul. This study has sought to find a way of understanding the problem that gives a point of entry to policy-makers and conservation organizations to begin to slow biodiversity loss.

LOCAL CONTEXT

Population and Settlements

Current patterns of settlement and resource use in and around the Calakmul Biosphere Reserve are shaped by patterns of land tenure that were established over the last 60 years and by patterns of resource exploitation that have an even longer history. As a result of the revolution of 1910, Mexico established a distinctive system of communal lands, known as '*ejidos*'. There are about 114 communities, primarily *ejidos*, home to about 25,000 people, in and around the reserve.[6] The lands of at least 27 *ejidos* and several small private properties overlap with the reserve area; almost 52 per cent of the reserve is also established *ejido* land and private property. An estimated 4000 people live within the boundaries of the reserve, and another 6500 hold lands within it but live outside. *Ejidos* in the reserve retain their tenure, but have lost the right to exploit many of the land's resources. Three types of *ejidal* lands are found in the region.[7] The oldest are large forest *ejidal* extensions, established primarily for extraction of chicle (*Manilkara zapote*).[8] They have been, until recently, among the least disturbed areas. In the 1960s, forest *ejidos* were created for timber extraction. In the 1970s and 1980s, many small, densely populated agricultural *ejidos* were created to accommodate a large landless population from other regions of Mexico.

Isolated by distance and the poor quality of the roads, the Calakmul region has the ambiance of a frontier. The region's history of interaction with national and international markets has always been one in which one or two resources were extracted, without creation of local economic development and without concern for the degradation of resources essential to the local economy. The Calakmul region was one of the primary sources, worldwide, of natural chicle in the first half of this century. Chicle markets collapsed in the 1950s, following the invention of a synthetic substitute, and valuable timber in the area has been seriously depleted. From the 1940s until the late 1980s, much of the Calakmul area was under the control of a large logging company, which devastated the populations of cedar (*Cedrela odorata*) and mahogany (*Swietenia macrophylla*). Left behind is a network of logging roads that facilitates access to the forest *ejidos* and reserve areas.

Two features characterize the local population dynamics in the Calakmul area: rapid population growth, due to high fertility rates and immigration, and rapid turnover of the population (Ericson, 1996, 1997; Ericson et al, 1998). The 1970s marked the beginning of extensive spontaneous and planned immigration to the region. Offices of the agrarian reform agency actively promoted migration to Calakmul.[9] Seventy per cent of the local *ejidos* were only recognized officially in the 1980s. Population growth for the new Calakmul municipality was about 400 per cent from 1980 to 1995, and many communities are expected to double in size within ten years (Ericson and Maas, 1998). The average age of the local population is about 19; rapid population growth can be expected to continue for a number of years (Ericson, 1997).

The heterogeneous population of the region includes migrants from 23 different states. The majority of migrants are Yucatec Maya, Chol and Tzeltal peoples from the surrounding states of Chiapas and Yucatan or other parts of Campeche, who have come in search of land or to escape conflict (Pronatura, 1997c). Yucatec Mayans, the traditional inhabitants, now constitute a small minority. Emigration occurs frequently. Colonists come in search of land but are often driven away within a few years by the poor agricultural conditions, particularly the lack of water, the prevalence of tropical diseases and the lack of economic opportunity. Many migrants to Calakmul have already moved several times (Haenn, 1996). Although the local population is comprised of indigenous and non-indigenous campesino populations, most have arrived in the last 30 years, and few of them have long-term roots in the region.

Local Resource Use and Management

Local conditions significantly shape resource use.[10] In the 1980s and 1990s, agriculture has taken on increased importance in the region as the population has grown and timber resources have declined. Cleared land has necessarily expanded. The direct or proximate cause of most deforestation and forest fragmentation in the Calakmul area is clearing for agriculture. Forest habitat degradation is resulting from extraction of wood and other resources. Decline in fauna may be resulting from both habitat degradation and over-hunting. The creation of the biosphere reserve has, on paper, placed important limits on the use of local resources, as do national laws on forestry and hunting. However, given the overlap between the reserve and numerous *ejidos* and private lands, and the lack of clarity and lack of enforcement of resource-use restrictions, the constraints imposed by the reserve have had little effect on resource-use patterns. The isolation and poverty of the region drive expanding subsistence production and exploitation of forest resources.

Poverty is ubiquitous in the Calakmul region.[11] Cash is earned from sales of agricultural and forest products and from day labour, but subsistence agriculture provides the main source of support for most of the local population. Agriculture remains small-scale as a result of ecological and economic limitations. Serious ecological challenges to agriculture include a chronic shortage of water during much of the year, poor quality of soils, high frequency of pests and unpredictable weather patterns. *Ejidatarios*, inhabitants of the *ejidos*, make varying use of the forests (Ericson, 1996; Murphy, 1992). The forest *ejidos* pursue more diversified production strategies, extracting timber, chicle, xate palm (*Chamaedorea sp*) and allspice (*Pimenta dioca*) and producing honey, among other forest products. The small *ejidos* concentrate on agriculture. Cultural traditions are very important in determining the range of activities pursued by *ejidatarios*.[12] While Yucatec Maya have a good knowledge of forest resources, recent immigrants have introduced commercial production of chilli peppers and cattle and see little value in the forest.

Traditional shifting cultivation methods are used for both subsistence and commercial crops. *Ejidatarios* farm an average of 4.5 ha.[13] At least 10,000 ha are planted in the immediate area each year; the total area affected by agricultural production is much higher because plots are shifted every few years.[14] These practices degrade lands as fallow periods are shortened in response to population pressures and as new migrants, with little knowledge of local conditions, expand the area under agriculture. Subsistence agriculture accounts for most of the planted land, and almost every family has a plot of staple crops, including corn and, to a lesser extent, beans and squash. The primary commercial crop in the region is chilli. The heavy investments required for chilli production, and the frequency of crop failures, have prevented large-scale production from becoming widespread. Although many *ejidatarios* are interested in cattle production, the shortage of water has prevented much development of cattle ranching. Corn and other subsistence crops are sold only locally and are often repurchased later in the season as the need arises; more often, they are used for barter purposes. Chillis and squash seeds, used for oil, are sold to *coyotes*, itinerant buyers of wood, chicle and other local products. *Coyotes* are able to control prices as long as their numbers are limited and producers are not organized.

A variety of products are extracted from the forest, both for subsistence use and for sale. The extent of timber extraction[15] in the region is unclear, since possibly as much as 80 per cent of felling is illegal. Recent efforts to place legal controls on timber extraction and implement management plans have been ineffective. While some *ejidos* have obtained permits for legal extraction, cutting often exceeds legal rates. The core areas of the reserve, along with the contiguous Guatemalan Maya Biosphere Reserve, may be furnishing much of the illegal production of high-value timber. Because harvesting is very selective, and because it depends on old logging roads rather than creation of new ones, the direct impact on biodiversity may be low. However, over-harvesting of valuable timber species is reducing the standing value of the forest. Like agricultural products, timber is sold to *coyotes*. Local efforts to develop a processing industry have failed because of mismanagement, corruption and lack of access to markets.

Calakmul remains one of the most important areas for the extraction of chicle, which is largely exported. The collapse of chicle markets, as well as forest clearing and extensive damage to chicle trees from over-extraction, however, have reduced local production. Even with careful practices, few trees survive more than five or six tappings (Snook and Jorgenson, 1994; Jorgenson, 1993). The development of a new cooperative system in the region seems to be boosting both production and profits for chicle harvesters (Tavera, 1997). Honey is another sustainable forest product,[16] primarily produced by Yucatec Maya, who have many years' experience with beekeeping,[17] and who have received extensive support from the state and from environmental organizations. A local cooperative has provided important assistance to producers but still suffers from management and marketing problems. Hunting,[18] for both commercial and subsistence purposes, may be having a substantial impact on local biodiversity, particularly jaguar, puma, peccary, ocellated turkey and great curassow. Many people rely on game as an important source of protein. Since most hunting is illegal, figures on numbers of animals taken for subsistence use or by sport hunters are unreliable.

Despite the variety of activities available, subsistence agriculture remains the backbone of the local economy. Since timber and chicle, the two primary resources of the area, no longer offer serious possibilities for development of the region, the local population is left dependent on unproductive agricultural lands. Most other activities, such as chicle extraction and beekeeping, can be integrated with subsistence agriculture. While it would appear to be more financially profitable to plant commercial crops or work as day labour than to plant corn, *ejidatarios* routinely choose the security of subsistence production.[19] Conservation activities in the area have aimed to curb the expansion of agricultural land by improving agricultural productivity and increasing incomes from forest-based activities. Yet it is uncertain that improved forest-based incomes would reduce the expansion of agricultural land in the absence of substantial land-use planning.[20] Extraction of forest products is not a substitute for, but rather a complement to, subsistence agriculture. *Campesinos* adjust their production patterns within the limited range of production possibilities, given limited natural resources and limited capital, to meet subsistence and cash needs.

Market failures in both agriculture and forestry shape resource use and economic development in the region. Yet, participation in the market economy is essential for *ejidatarios* in order to meet food, transport, education and health expenses. Almost all products are sold to the *coyotes* at low prices. Even when the government guarantees prices, the government office often refuses to buy local agricultural products. Local producers have neither the resources nor the knowledge to seek out better markets. New national policies, however, assume the efficacy of markets in fostering development.

National Context

Mexico's neo-liberal economic reform package has included major reforms in agricultural policy, land tenure and forest laws, all of which are intended to change land use and production patterns at the local level. Mexico has also been undergoing profound political changes, and democratic competition is becoming a reality. The isolation and poverty of the Calakmul region and the small range of production possibilities clearly limit the range of responses to these changes. Until the shift toward market-based policies in the 1980s and 1990s, Mexican policy sought to raise agricultural production and relieve rural poverty largely through the redistribution of land.[21] Agricultural and land tenure policies have both promoted clearing for extensive agricultural production. Development policies, focused on land distribution and increases in agricultural production, have outweighed conservation-oriented policies. Forestry laws, which offer some protection to biodiversity, have been notoriously complex, contributing to general evasion of the laws and the development of bureaucratic impasses in their implementation. Recent dramatic changes in agricultural policy and *ejidal* law may lead to changes in production patterns, but they may not provide better incentives to conservation. Some common hypotheses about their role at the local level are considered here in an effort to understand their impacts on land and forest use, and thence biodiversity, in Calakmul.

Government interventions are often contradictory, in part because a variety of government agencies have responsibilities in the Calakmul region. As a prime example, the creation of the Calakmul Biosphere Reserve occurred at the same time that the agrarian reform agency was allotting land in the area. The federal government has intervened directly in the region, not only through the creation of the reserve, with all of its attendant land tenure issues, but also through sponsored colonization and development programmes. Development-oriented agencies provide funds for infrastructure and other projects without consideration of the requirements of conservation. Resource use and development within the reserve should legally be governed by a management plan, but none has yet been approved. Current development plans focus on road construction and tourism (Box 11.1). Construction of an airstrip on the edge

---

Box 11.1 Ecotourism Prospects in Calakmul

The growth of tourism in the region offers prospects for both economic improvement and a stimulus to conservation, if development is carefully planned. The large number of Mayan ruins in the area, in addition to the presence of the Calakmul Biosphere Reserve, offer considerable attraction to tourists. Numbers of visitors to the region have increased notably in recent years, and there are many plans for investment in tourist facilities. An airstrip is being constructed in Xpujil and a first-class hotel has been opened nearby. Other land has been bought up in Xpujil for construction. Local highways are being improved, and a new highway from Calakmul to Tikal in Guatemala, intended to promote tourism, is being discussed.

Current plans for tourism development do not take into account the requirements of conservation in the Biosphere Reserve or the need of local communities for improved economic opportunities. Construction of the tourism corridor is planned along the highway that cuts across the narrow part of the reserve. Further construction in this area will completely separate the southern and northern halves of the reserve. In addition, plans have not properly considered the shortage of water in the area which will be aggravated by an increased number of visitors. Equally important, plans do not foresee benefits for the local population in terms of creation of jobs or sharing of revenues. Although a number of local community members have been trained as guides to the reserve, they have received no further support and their services are rarely used.

---

of the reserve, intended to boost tourism, is underway. There is also a large-scale water project underway that will service 22 *ejidos* (Ericson, 1997). Improvements in infrastructure are encouraging migrants to remain in the region (Ericson et al, 1998).

The failure to resolve social conflict and poverty issues elsewhere in the country, particularly in Chiapas, drives continued migration to the region. Very limited efforts to resolve local land tenure questions or to enforce protection of the biosphere reserve make it clear that government priorities lie elsewhere. *Ejidos* are demanding compensation for what they see as effective expropriation of their land rights, while illegal loggers and poachers are benefiting from lax enforcement of conservation laws (Tavera, 1997). Many local residents see the reserve as a mechanism by which the government or other outsiders, including conservation organizations, are appropriating resources that are rightfully theirs (Haenn, 1996; Ericson et al, 1998). Moreover, given the local abundance of forests and wildlife, no sufficient rationale has been presented to them for permanently setting land aside. The government has softened the blow of this appropriation of resources directly through funding from agricultural subsidies and development funds. Indirectly, the government has avoided opposition to the reserve and environmental restrictions by poorly enforcing these laws.

Agricultural Policies

Through the 1970s, government policy in Mexico aimed for self-sufficiency in agricultural production.[22] Under the recent liberalization programme, many of the supports to domestic agriculture have been reformed. The aim of current policy is to promote the competitiveness and productivity of the sector. Until recently, guaranteed prices supported staple crops, a system that has been replaced with the Procampo programme, which was intended to cushion the impact of the removal of trade barriers and price subsidies. The stated purpose of the Procampo programme is to induce more market-based decision-making among small farmers, who are expected to move from traditional crops to more profitable forms of land use. The programme provides direct subsidies to farmers, based on hectarage planted.

Ejidal agriculture has rarely provided more than the minimum needed for subsistence,[23] either because of the small amount of land granted or, as in the case of Calakmul, because of its poor quality and distance from markets. Government support to subsistence production has long served to mitigate rural poverty and to compensate in small part for the marginality of the lands disbursed to most *ejidos* and for the lack of capital and credit available to *ejidatarios*. Protection of subsistence producers, primarily corn producers, continues *de facto* under the Procampo programme. Procampo contributes significantly to the income of *ejidatarios* in the Calakmul area but has not altered production patterns, given their limited access to markets and reliance on subsistence crops. The government has also provided assistance to Calakmul in the form of food, water supplies and job creation in years when hurricanes and droughts have destroyed crops. In effect, support to subsistence producers may have maintained the rural population on the land even when harvests are poor.[24]

As part of the Solidaridad programme, a larger rural development programme established under President Salinas, of which Procampo is a part, the government provides cash for local development projects if the local community provides labour and some materials. Since this requires some coordination and cooperation on the part of communities, the programme has increased the importance of community and grassroots organizations throughout the country. In Calakmul it gave the impetus and the funds for development of a local union of *ejidos*, known as the *Consejo Regional de Xpujil* (CRAX). Solidaridad has since been renamed *Alianza para el Campo* and expanded under President Zedillo. Funding in Calakmul has been primarily for road construction, water infrastructure and reforestation. Investments under these programmes have been uneven and highly politicized, answering the immediate demands of communities in hopes of garnering support for the ruling party (*The Economist*, 1993).

New Laws and *Ejidal* Rights

The failure of the *ejidal* system to produce an agricultural surplus or resolve the problem of rural poverty has led, finally, to some significant reforms in the

Mexican agrarian law.[25] The debt crisis and the turn toward liberalization created the context in which it became both politically possible and necessary to change some fundamental features of the system. The impact on conservation of the new *ejidal* laws, in combination with changes in the forest law, is debated widely; as yet, the reforms have only just begun to effect changes in land-use patterns and the long-term consequences remain unclear. The land tenure system, at least prior to the recent reform, has encouraged deforestation and forest degradation.[26] The system has favoured allocation of cleared parcels to *ejidos*, who are granted usufruct rights only, so their tenure is insecure and access to credit is limited. *Ejidal* law has required that *ejidatarios* keep working their land. Moreover, the boundaries between public lands and *ejidos* and between *ejidos* have been ill-defined. Clearing provides a way of claiming disputed lands, as logging provides a way of claiming disputed forests. All of these factors add up to a preference for clearing and immediate appropriation of natural resources. The new agrarian law addresses the failure of the *ejidal* system to provide tenure security and demarcation for cleared lands but does not address the tenure issues on forested lands. Incentives for deforestation remain strong.

Under the new agrarian reform law, approved in 1992, *ejidatarios* now have the right to parcel *ejido* lands and to sell them or use them as collateral. Commercial operations, which were previously prohibited from owning agricultural land, now have the right to purchase *ejidal* lands. *Ejido* property will now be treated much more like private property. Some predictions suggest that the reforms will lead to little immediate change in the sector (DeWalt and Rees, 1994), given the marginality of much *ejido* land. Titling and registration will not solve the fundamental problems, which are lack of capital and, as in Calakmul, poor ecological conditions for agriculture. It is unlikely that the private sector will provide services, such as credit, technical assistance and agricultural research, that have been provided, however scantily, by the government for such marginal lands.

Ejidal forest lands are treated differently from agricultural lands under the new law, with serious implications for conservation. Forest *ejidos* can enter into joint ventures or offer long-term concessions for the exploitation of their forests with private companies. However, lands considered forested by the law cannot be parcelled or sold. If an *ejido* privatizes its agricultural lands and disbands, its forest lands revert to the state. Yet forest lands are often considered by *ejidatarios* to be agricultural lands held in reserve. *Ejidos* in the Calakmul region have unofficially parcelled their land, in lots of 20–100 ha, much of which is forested land (Ericson et al, 1998). There is a clear moral hazard inherent in the law: *ejidatarios* have every incentive to clear forest lands if they are planning on privatizing their land. The law is faulty too in that it applies a single definition of agricultural and forested land to the whole of Mexico. Not only does the law need to encompass vastly different ecosystems, but also vastly different systems of agriculture and forest use. In areas such as Calakmul where shifting cultivation is commonly practised and

BOX 11.2 LAND TENURE RIGHTS AND THE CALAKMUL BIOSPHERE RESERVE

Protected areas in Mexico are threatened by long-established resource-use rights, which have not been altered by recent reforms. The federal decree creating the Calakmul Biosphere Reserve, the environmental law, the forestry law, and the agrarian reform law all have some bearing on land tenure in the reserve. Legally, however, the extensive property rights granted by the Constitution take precedence over the resource-use restrictions imposed by these other laws. According to the Constitution, the government cannot impose limits on property rights without a judicial hearing. Article 14 states that, 'No one can be deprived of... his property, possessions, or rights without judicial proceeding'. Article 27 adds that *ejidal* property is protected 'equally for human settlement and productive activities'. Other articles support these strong property rights. As a result, *ejidos* and private property owners have great leeway to carry out various activities on their land. Two *ejidos* located in the reserve that were threatened with expropriation have taken the case to court and won. The government now makes no effort to control their use of land even within the core of the reserve.

The restrictions on resource use imposed by the Biosphere Reserve, therefore, are legally tenuous. The government does not have the legal right to confiscate property or restrict property use without due compensation. Many *ejidos* with land in the reserve in fact want to have that land expropriated, given the restrictions imposed on its use. The decree which created the reserve, however, does not foresee compensation for expropriation of the land. In fact, it states that residents 'will be required to conserve the area'. At least four communities that have been denied access to their land since the imposition of the reserve in 1989 are planning to go to court. They are demanding not only payment for *de facto* expropriation of their land but also compensation for the income lost over the last eight years. They appear to have the law on their side.

Even if the environmental laws had full legal force, they allow for extensive human use of the biosphere reserve. Virtually any activity is legally permissible within the reserve, according to the decree creating the reserve, once the appropriate authorization is obtained. The law is unclear whether this includes the core as well as the buffer zones. The environmental law states that only those communities that were living in the reserve before its establishment have rights to its resources. However, this limitation appears to be superceded by the agrarian reform law. While the decree creating the reserve expressly prohibits the creation of new *ejidal* lands within the reserve, several *ejidos* were established on reserve lands after 1989. These *ejidos* have the same legal rights as those established before 1989. Long-time squatters in the *ejidal* and national lands of the reserve have the right to demand title to the lands they have occupied, with complete rights to use of that land. Estimates of the number of squatters in the reserve vary, but the population appears to be substantial.

Source: Tierra y Liberdad, 1997

agriculture depends on the existence of large areas of secondary forest, separating agricultural from forest lands in this way is not possible. There is an ongoing debate among various government agencies about how to handle this situation. In the Calakmul region, little official parcelling and titling have been carried out. *Ejidatarios* do not see that they will gain anything by giving up their claims to forest lands (Tierra y Liberdad, 1997) (Box 11.2).

Forest Policies

Over the last century, Mexican forest policies have attempted to counter the effects of land tenure and agricultural policies that have promoted deforestation. However, land rights and agricultural objectives have generally taken precedence over forestry or conservation concerns. Government control and intervention in forestry have been heavy, handicapping forest *ejidos* and the timber industries; the forestry sector has been plagued with inefficiency. Forest management plans are at the heart of Mexican forest policy. While the requirements for extensive management plans and other documents may be admirable on paper, in fact, they create insurmountable obstacles for local *ejidos* (World Bank, 1995a; Boege and Murguia, 1989). Poor *ejidatarios* retain the rights to the forests but rarely have the resources to manage them effectively. The difficulty and expense of complying with government regulations promote corruption and deforestation. A 1986 law increased the onus on forest *ejidos* by adding environmental regulations to existing requirements. The forestry law was revised in 1992 to shift the focus of government forest agencies from direct intervention to a more normative role. Legislation for forests and wildlands remains very ambitious, however, given the government's limited resources. Enforcement, at least in the Calakmul region, is minimal, and those willing to participate in illegal logging are able to extract private income from a community resource.

Policies in other sectors favouring not only conversion of land to agricultural use but also commercial exploitation of timber have also undermined conservation-oriented forestry laws. In addition to subsidies for agriculture and livestock, import barriers in the timber sector have favoured exploitation, and timber industries have been allowed easy access to resources. Direct protective measures have often failed, illegal logging is common and many large reserves are virtually unprotected. The 1992 agrarian reform has not clarified ownership or responsibility for forest lands, and the land titling programme leaves many forests as virtually open-access resources and still encourages people to clear land to claim ownership.

Markets and Politics

The obstacles to local resource management and successful participation in markets are the result not only of legal arrangements but also of institutional arrangements that foster poor access to markets, enforcement failures, corruption and political manoeuvring. Intervention and involvement by business and government in Calakmul has been limited by the fact that the surplus available for extraction is small; however, the influx of funds for conservation and sustainable development is attracting interest to the area. The government has routinely provided assistance when problems were particularly severe in the region. *Campesinos* expect the government to step in during times of crisis, and they operate accordingly (Haenn, 1996; Ericson et al, 1998). Not surprisingly, current environmental regulations and conservation-oriented programmes appear to *campesinos* as just more in a series of government efforts to control their resources (Haenn, 1996). On the one hand, *campesinos* seek to evade government demands and restrictions that limit use of natural resources at the same time that they rely heavily on the government to provide land, income and services. On the other hand, the government has granted *campesinos* little more than what is needed for their survival. Calakmul has served as a last resort for *campesinos* without access to land. Although government subsidies form an important part of local income, the government has not solved basic problems in the area such as the lack of water and health services. The imposition of the Biosphere Reserve is seen locally as a restriction on basic rights to agricultural land and forest resources. The government is seen to be giving with one hand and taking away with the other (Haenn, 1996).

Neither the agrarian reform law nor the various changes in the forestry law address the situation in Calakmul. There is a complete disjunction between the goal of the agricultural policy changes, which is to create greater efficiency and commercial productivity, and the evident marginalization of Calakmul and subsistence needs of the population. Likewise, the conservation goals of the forestry law, which emphasizes long-term planning but is jeopardizing community management of forests, are at a disjunction with the needs of the expanding local population for an immediate cash income, which timber and forest products can provide, and for land for subsistence agricultural production.

INTERNATIONAL CONTEXT

The international pattern of developing-world debt default, structural adjustment and liberalization has been played out in full in Mexico. Trade and the exchange rate have been liberalized, debt renegotiated, extensive privatizations carried out, foreign investment substantially increased and import-substitution policies abandoned since the 1981 crisis. Mexico has dramatically liberalized trade with accession to the GATT and NAFTA. The crisis of the early 1980s forced these changes in Mexico's relations to international markets, and open participation in international markets is now accepted as the key to Mexico's economic development. Like the changes in national sectoral policies, trade liberalization is intended to increase productivity and efficiency of domestic production. The effects on markets based on natural resources, particularly timber and agriculture, have the most relevance for the Calakmul region.

In agriculture, exposure to international prices and opening of new market opportunities is expected to decrease small-scale subsistence production, which is uncompetitive, and boost efficient commercial and export production. A shift from staple foods, destined for domestic use, to production of fruits and vegetables for the US and Canadian markets is predicted. Optimistic projections, from the standpoint of forest clearing, suggest that agriculture and livestock production will be concentrated in the most suitable lands. Such projections, however, make strong assumptions about the absorption of rural labour by commercial agriculture and urban economies (DeWalt and Rees, 1994; Levy and van Wijnbergen, 1992). Continuing rapid population growth in rural areas is likely to mean continuing deforestation for subsistence production. *Ejidatarios* on poor agricultural land are unlikely to have the option of purchasing better land in areas more suitable to agriculture. Population growth in Calakmul continues to outpace emigration, and the ready availability of land in the area combined with a shortage of capital continues to make subsistence agriculture attractive.

In Calakmul limited physical, economic, political and knowledge resources shape agricultural production patterns more than international market prices. Subsistence agricultural production falls outside of the market. The isolation of the Calakmul region and its marginality to national and international markets has precluded large-scale production. Falling prices of staple goods induced by liberalization cannot be expected to affect production by *ejidatarios* such as those in Calakmul who remain in agriculture because land is their only asset, and who produce corn for their own food security. Changes in external agricultural markets may have little impact on deforestation or production of staple crops locally.

Nationally, timber markets may change substantially under liberalization as the price of imported timber falls. Because of high costs of transport and processing, Mexico currently cannot compete internationally in most wood products.[27] While market liberalization may eventually spark investments to increase competitiveness, in the medium term when Mexican wood is still uncompetitive, liberalization may result in more conversion of land to agriculture as the commercial value of the forest falls. Under NAFTA, Mexico has a comparative advantage in tropical timbers since they are produced only in Mexico. There is also a limited but growing demand for certified sustainably-harvested tropical timber. However, of the tropical woods, only mahogany and cedar have apparently unlimited market potential. In much of the Calakmul area these are scarce, and competition with cheap, largely contraband mahogany from Guatemala reduces incentives for sustainable management of these species. Moreover, the access of *ejidos* to timber markets is seriously limited by the cost of transport, lack of capital and lack of technical and business knowledge. Recent attempts to establish a local processing industry in Calakmul have been halted by lack of expertise, limited markets and corruption.

Regardless of the behaviour of international timber markets, many localized Mexican timber markets will continue to function. Moreover, much timber use lies outside the market, including extensive use of fuelwood.[28] The fear has been expressed that, by lowering the price of timber, liberalization will reduce the apparent value of forest conservation and thus provoke more clearing. However, given the current small contribution of timber to local income, and given the dependence on agriculture and preference for cattle, it seems unlikely that falling timber prices will spark more clearing than is currently occurring in Calakmul.

LOCAL RESPONSES TO DEGRADATION AND CONSERVATION

Both local *campesinos* and international conservation interests recognize the problems created by the lack of local control over the socioeconomic and ecological situation. International funding to promote conservation in the Calakmul region has had important effects not only through its direct contribution to the local economy and improvement in resource management but also, indirectly, by attracting political attention to the region. Creation of the new Calakmul municipality in 1997 should further this process. Local *campesinos* and conservation groups, however, have different goals and understandings of development and conservation. These divergent views spark resentment of conservationists on the part of the *campesinos* and reduce the effectiveness of conservation initiatives.

The development of CRAX in 1990 differed from the formation of earlier grassroots organizations in that it was established, with government assistance, to attract government and other funding.[29] CRAX represents more than half of the *ejidos* in the buffer zone. It has functioned almost as a government institution in the area, given the lack of other local representation (Haenn, 1996). CRAX now bills itself as the key local organization promoting sustainable development. Many of its programmes are conservation-related, but it also has substantial interests in other development projects. CRAX is responsible for most federally-funded conservation-oriented programmes in the region, primarily agroforestry, reforestation and apiculture. Almost all NGOs work with CRAX in some way. Projects supported by CRAX include several committees which function essentially as cooperatives, including committees for honey, chicle and allspice producers, which provide marketing services, credit and technical assistance. They suffer, however, from their lack of preparation for participation in markets, and internal corruption. A recent turnover in the governing committee may resolve these problems, but CRAX appears to be losing its local strength. Outside organizations relying on the local participation offered by CRAX cannot avoid entanglement in local politics and risk overlooking many *ejidos* and *ejidatarios* not linked to CRAX.

The two largest internationally funded conservation programmes working to protect the biosphere reserve are those of the Model Forest Network (Bosque Modelo) and Pronatura Península de Yucatán. The Model Forest Network programme, jointly funded by the Canadian government and the Mexican government, aims to foster sustainable management of forests and sustainable development of rural communities on the eastern side of the reserve (Model Forest Network and SAHR, 1994). The programme is predicated on the idea that, by improving agricultural production and increasing incomes from diversified use of well-managed forests, land clearing will be controlled and local people will come to see the value of standing forests. Model Forest Network works through CRAX, which designs and implements the projects. Specific projects include forest assessment and management, water conservation, wildlife management, beekeeping and environmental education. Matching government funds have supported reforestation, agroforestry, integrated forestry management studies and plant nurseries. The programme has been successful in promoting apiculture and sustainable agriculture and in fostering the establishment of several wildlife reserves on *ejido* lands. Projects have been introduced in 40 *ejidos*, and management plans developed for 16 *ejidos*. The greatest obstacle to the forestry component of the programme has been the lack of marketing capacity and markets for local wood products; very little timber has been legally harvested and marketed under the programme.

Pronatura Península de Yucatán, a Mexican NGO, also bases its work on the assumption that settled agriculture and the generation of economic value from sustainable forestry will decrease deforestation in the area (Pronatura, 1997a). Pronatura has supported strengthening of the management of the biosphere reserve, sustainable development and environmental education programmes for the local communities, ecotourism and basic research. Pronatura's work in Calakmul was one of the pilot Integrated Conservation and Development Programmes (ICDP) supported by The Nature Conservancy, WWF, WRI and the US Agency for International Development (AID) funds. Sustainable development programmes are promoted primarily through support to the organizational development of CRAX and to CRAX projects in organic agriculture, beekeeping, environmental education and water conservation. In order to reduce deforestation resulting from shifting cultivation, Pronatura has promoted low-input sustainable agriculture, using green fertilizers, reduction of agrochemical inputs and elimination of burning among local *ejidos*. The agricultural project has reached at least 720 *campesinos* and been implemented on 1000 ha with apparent success; at least 120 *ejidatarios* have adopted beekeeping. However, neither of these programmes can keep pace with the rapid expansion of the local population.

The sustainable development programmes in the area have spread the word about conservation. How successful they have been in instilling their message is unclear. Some *ejidos* have deliberately decided to accept no more *ejidatarios*.[30] Others recognize that they may have reached a saturation point but have not yet made the decision to accept no more immigrants. The decision of *ejidos* to restrict the number of newcomers may play an important role in slowing population growth in the area. A number of women in the area have expressed interest in family planning, but access to these services remains limited and family size is large.[31] There remains an optimistic expectation that the government will provide more lands when they are needed, including lands in the biosphere reserve (Pronatura, 1997a and 1997b).

The various legal restrictions on land and resource use that have been imposed, if not enforced, within the biosphere reserve, are widely viewed as restrictions placed on *campesinos'* ability to make a living. Conservation programmes are viewed as little different from other development programmes with further policies to be taken advantage of or avoided. Some *ejidatarios*, and most notably CRAX, have adopted the language of conservation and are receiving substantial benefits in terms of cash, food aid and training. However, their focus on getting more resources from the conservation programmes has led to significant factionalism within *ejidos* and exclusion of many community members from the benefits of these programmes. These programmes have not addressed expanding resource needs nor addressed the problems of marginalization or the disjunction between the demands of conservation and local subsistence needs.

CONCLUSIONS AND RECOMMENDATIONS

Biodiversity loss in and around the Biosphere Reserve is driven by local population growth and the heavy local reliance on natural resources, particularly cleared forest land. Underlying these immediate factors is the failure to resolve the problems of poverty, population expansion and social conflict in Mexico. Population growth in Calakmul cannot be attributed to the attractions of the region. But for a *campesino* with no other options, a plot on an *ejido* in Calakmul can afford at least a meagre living. Frontier expansion is driven not by the profits that can be extracted from timber, other forest products or agriculture, but rather by the large population that is excluded from other economic opportunities. The continued dependence of local *ejidatarios* on few agricultural products and government aid reflects their limited access to other resources in the economy. They remain at the margins in terms of knowledge and both financial and political resources.

In the Calakmul region, some forest *ejidos* have maintained their forests largely intact, but where population is denser, clearing has been extensive. The maintenance of forest reserves reflects a lack of resources for agricultural expansion as often as an understanding of the value of the standing forest. Various factors underlie the unsustainable use of the forest. *Ejidatarios* trying to produce timber products on their own face competition in the market from private companies for which they are unprepared. Complicated government controls and unclear resource-use rights discourage long-term planning for forest use. Clearing and illegal extraction are facilitated by poor enforcement of laws and the lack of clarity about land and forest tenure in the region. Nevertheless, the need to expand agricultural production must take a greater share of the blame for deforestation than the failure of forestry, land tenure or protected area policies. Agriculture is essential to the support system of the local population.

The array of laws, government interventions and changes in government policies designed to shape agricultural practices, forestry and most notably the conservation of the Calakmul reserve, have had a limited impact on the region. Despite the ubiquitousness of commercial activities, subsistence remains the backbone of the local economy. Trade and price liberalization are unlikely to affect patterns of land use and deforestation in marginal, tropical areas such as Calakmul in the foreseeable future. In the short-term, subsistence farmers will not change their choice of crops, which is based on tradition, food security needs and local markets. Government policies are taken advantage of when they increase local incomes, as is the case with Procampo funds, and evaded when they may reduce local control over resources, as is the case with the current titling programme. This is possible in part because of contradictions among various government efforts, such as the creation of a reserve on *ejido* lands. It is also possible in part because of the disjunction between government goals and policies and the situation in Calakmul, epitomized by a land titling programme that does not account for shifting agriculture or forest lands. Perhaps the greatest gap is found between the overall direction of current Mexican policies, which emphasize the role of the market in economic development and the marginalization of Calakmul from the market economy.

The *campesinos* of Calakmul face the classic problems of a marginal economy. Although they are dependent on the cash economy, they are not able to participate in that economy on an equal footing. All of the government and other programmes have failed to address the problem of securing access to markets. Nevertheless, better access to markets would not compensate for the poor agricultural conditions. The exhaustion of valuable timbers and the small scale of today's chicle markets have left the Calakmul region without competitive products. The production of honey and certified timber and, most promisingly, tourism do offer new prospects. If the problems experienced with timber and chicle are to be avoided, careful planning of the development of these resources is essential. Protection of biodiversity will require not only real protection of the reserve but also economic alternatives for the local population that wean them from forest clearing and over-harvesting of natural resources. Sustainable development programmes have not yet accomplished these goals.

Sustainable development programmes in the Calakmul region have for the most part addressed deforestation and biodiversity loss at the local level. While there is clearly further work to be done at the local level, the connections between local resource use and outside factors must not be ignored. Work in the region must recognize the broader context in which the reserve is situated. We must ask what are the appropriate and feasible roles of international organizations, the national government, the state government and local organizations. Most importantly, these various groups need to work together in planning for land and resource use in the region that will not only promote conservation but also provide long-term economic alternatives for the local population. Serious consideration must be given to whether there are any real options for development in the region – options that would take local *campesinos* beyond a precarious subsistence living but that would not threaten biodiversity.

On a broad scale, the following issues and problems, which are common to many protected areas in Mexico, need to be recognized, understood and addressed:

- A variety of forces are driving migration to the area. Migration to the area may continue at high levels for a number of years. Problems in other regions, including social conflict, lack of land and, perhaps, under the new law, sales of *ejidal* lands, drive migration to the region. Calakmul is not attracting people but rather accepting people who have nowhere else to go. These problems must be addressed if population growth in the reserve and the surrounding forest areas is to be controlled.

- Local communities have been divorced from the national economy and policy decisions. Political decisions and policy frameworks such as the current liberalization policies that do not recognize the socioeconomic reality of areas such as Calakmul may only serve to aggravate existing poverty and unsustainable resource use. Production in these areas is driven not by profitability but by the lack of alternatives. Adjustments in prices may have little effect on production levels or practices.

- Lack of clarity in land tenure and resource-use law promotes land clearing and over-harvesting of resources. Despite significant changes in the law to increase security of tenure and impose controls on resource use, in protected or forested areas such as Calakmul, the failure to clarify land ownership and use rights leaves broad leeway and incentives for land use incompatible with conservation. Before serious land-use planning can be carried out, the discrepancies in the agrarian law and in the laws on protected areas and in their implementation need to be resolved.

- There is an absence of land-use or development planning. Development in the region has been haphazard and without planning for sustainable economic activities or consideration of impacts on conservation. Government investment in the region has focused on meeting the immediate demands of settlers for land, roads and water. The results of this failure can be clearly seen in the development corridors along the eastern side and across the middle of the biosphere reserve.

  In addition to these general considerations, many particular issues need to be recognized and addressed by conservation efforts.

- This land, as agricultural land, will not provide more than subsistence living. The continued use of this land for subsistence agriculture cannot be seen as a long-term option for the region. Currently people remain in the area even when the land will not adequately support them. Continued expansion of agriculture in this area comes at the cost of loss of forest land that has a value for conservation and possibly for forestry higher than the agricultural value of the land.

- Extraction of wood, other forest products and hunting may be having an impact on the reserve. The role of these activities in the local economy needs to be addressed more realistically, with the understanding that increasing incomes from other sources, such as honey production, sustainable agriculture or tourism, may do little to control this outflow of resources. Management plans will be ineffective unless illegal trading is ended and communities accept the limitations imposed by the plans. Moreover, sustainable uses, such as extraction of forest products and tourism, may not adequately support a population of the current size.

- *Ejidos* need to participate in limiting population growth in the buffer zone and preventing settlement in the core zones of the Biosphere Reserve. Given the current overlap between many *ejidos* and the Biosphere Reserve lands, control of the population in the buffer and core zones of the reserve must rest with the *ejidos*. Only if *ejidatarios* are convinced of the necessity of controlling land clearing and resource use will they be motivated to limit immigration and their own population expansion. Provision of readily available reproductive health services would make an important contribution.

- Local development projects need to be carefully considered with regard to the impact on conservation. Various projects underway in the area, including the large water diversion project, the paving of roads and the development of a tourism corridor, have been undertaken without consideration of the effects on the reserve, local population growth or resource use. Land-use planning not only at the *ejidal* level but at a regional level is essential to prevent serious compromise of the reserve's potential contribution to biodiversity conservation.

- Market access for sustainably produced products must be improved if they are to provide a real option to shifting cultivation. Conservation programmes have promoted production of managed timber, honey and other sustainable products without addressing administrative and marketing problems. If these efforts are unsuccessful, local interest in pursuing sustainable options will diminish rapidly.

Chapter 12

Pakistan: Mangroves

Research team: The team was composed of coordinators *Sarah Ahmad* and *Osman Mian*, team leader *Akhtar A Hai* (economist), *Najam Khurshid* (environmental expert), *Abdul Rafiq Qadir* (hydrologist) and *Noor-un-Nisa* (sociologist). The team would like to acknowledge the contributions of *Dr Arshad Ali Baig*, *Qaisar Anjum, Shaukat Ali* and the WWF-Pakistan staff – *Salman Ashraf, Fayyaz Rasool, Rahat Jabeen* and *Akram Farooqi*. The team would also like to express its gratitude to local community members, fishermen, officials, researchers and scientists for the valuable information and guidance extended during the course of the study

Summary: **Coastal mangrove ecosystems in Pakistan have been seriously degraded over the last 50 years as a result of freshwater diversion for agriculture, industrial and urban water pollution and overfishing. These proximate causes are largely driven by national policies that have favoured agriculture and industry over the coastal regions and that have given high priority to exports.**

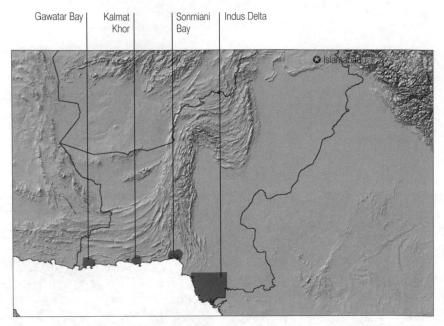

Figure 12.1 *Map Showing Location of Study Sites on the Pakistan Coast*

Pakistan is largely arid and semi-arid, receiving less than 250 mm annual rainfall, with the driest regions receiving less than 125 mm. It has a diverse landscape, with high mountain systems, fragile watershed areas, alluvial plains, coastal mangroves and dune deserts. Forests cover approximately 4.58 million ha in Pakistan, less than 6 per cent of the total area (Government of Pakistan, 1996). Of these, 0.132 million ha are coastal mangrove forests, which occur mainly in the Indus Delta and in a few patches westward along the Baluchistan Coast.

The Indus Delta covers approximately 600,000 ha with a coastline of 250 km, bordering the city of Karachi in the north-west. The delta is comprised of 17 major creeks, numerous minor creeks and extensive areas of mudflats. Mangroves cover approximately 129,000 ha (97 per cent of the total) in the Indus Delta and about 3000 ha on the Baluchistan coast in the Miani Hor, Kalmat Khor and Gawatar Bay areas (Figure 12.1)

There has been considerable loss of mangrove forest in Pakistan over the last 50 years. A significant reduction in the river water supply and increased marine water pollution in the Indus Delta as well as over-harvesting of mangroves by the local communities, sedimentation and coastal erosion are generally considered to be the proximate causes of this loss. Another threat is emerging in the form of over-harvesting of fish resources, largely provoked by increased pressure for exports with little or no consideration for the existing environmental laws and regulations. Policies and decisions made at the national and international levels have determined these proximate causes.

Note: The structure of this chapter has been rearranged to follow that of the other nine case studies. It therefore no longer reflects the sectoral organization chosen by the research team.

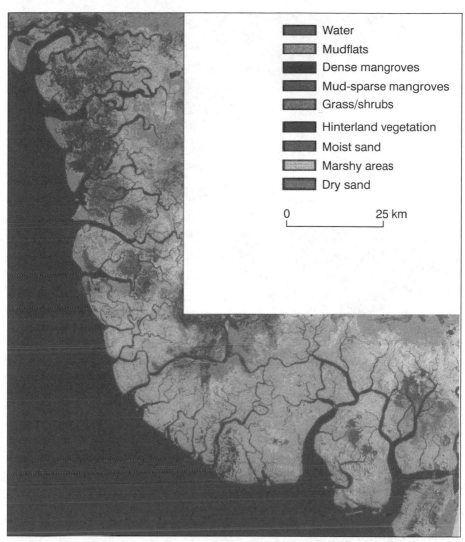

Figure 12.2 *Indus Delta Landforms and Habitats (Landsat, 1998)*

This study investigates the root causes of biodiversity loss in the mangrove ecosystem using the mangrove forests as the primary indicator of ecosystem health and the fish resources as a secondary indicator. Through the analysis, links have been established among factors at the local, national and international levels to reveal the pattern in which various causes affect the ecosystem. The conceptual models prepared for this purpose were developed with the help of a detailed household survey of coastal communities and Landsat satellite images of the forests (Figures 12.2 and 12.3).

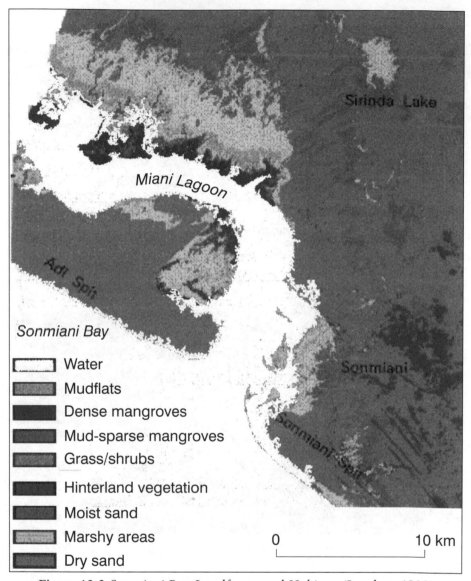

Figure 12.3 *Sonmiani Bay Landforms and Habitats (Landsat, 1998)*

DESCRIPTION OF THE STUDY AREA

Nearly 95 per cent of the mangroves located in the Indus Delta are of the species *Avicennia marina*. Very small patches of *Ceriops roxburghiana* (Rhizophora family) and *Aegicerias corniculata* (Myrinaceal family) are found near the mouth of the Indus at Keti Bunder. Small areas of *R mucronata* and *Ceriops taga* (Rhizophora family) have been planted in disturbed areas. The

Indus delta is believed to have had as many as eight species, but some of these no longer occur.

The 800-km long Baluchistan coastline, running along the North Arabian Sea, includes lagoons, bays, alluvial plains, mudflats, cliffs, beaches and marine terraces. The continental shelf here is only 40 km wide and the exposed coast is subject to strong waves. Mangroves occur in relatively protected lagoons and bays at Miani Hor, Kalmat Khor and Gawatar Bay.

Miani Hor, 95 km from Karachi, is a swampy lagoon covering an area of 7500 ha on the coast in the Lasbela district, where the climate is very arid, with less than 200 mm of rain a year. The sources of fresh water for Miani Hor are the seasonal rivers of Porali and Windor. The nearest river to the other lagoon, Kalmat Khor, is the Basol River which runs 15 km east of Khor, 315 km from Karachi. The lagoon covers an area of over 10,000 ha. Gawatar Bay is 515 km from Karachi. It covers over 26,000 ha, and is open to the sea with a mouth almost as wide as its length. Its freshwater source is the Dasht River, the largest seasonal river of Baluchistan.

Miani Hor mangrove species are *R mucronata, Ceriops tagal* and *A marina*. It is the only area in Pakistan where the first two species grow naturally. Kalmat Khor and Gawatar Bay support only *A marina*.

The study sites together have 12 varieties of halophytes and three varieties of algae. Common and important marine organisms include shrimps (three species), oysters (four species), gastropods (eight species) and crabs (three species). Mud skipper, thread fin, pomfret, mullet, palla and dolphin are also present. Endangered green and olive Ridley turtles are found in the vicinity of the mangroves in the Sandspit area (Sindh). About 90 per cent of the commercially important marine species spend at least a part of their life cycle among the mangroves.

The human population in and around mangrove forests on the coast of Pakistan is estimated to be about 1.2 million. Nearly 900,000 (140,000 households) reside in the Indus Delta and 300,000 (30,000 households) on the Baluchistan coast. Over 90 per cent of the population is directly or indirectly engaged in fishing. On average, the population in the coastal areas has been growing at a rate of 6–8 per cent annually over the last ten years. Migrants from other areas of the country and from Bangladesh and Burma have contributed to this growth, particularly in the Indus Delta where they are attracted by the high returns from fishing.

During the last decade concern has grown over the ways in which human activities have altered the mangrove ecosystems of Pakistan. Freshwater scarcity due to upstream diversions of river flows for agriculture, water pollution, overgrazing, cutting for fuelwood and timber and unsustainable fishing levels are seen as the main factors associated with biodiversity loss. The rate of degradation of mangrove forests in the delta has been estimated at 6 per cent between 1980 and 1995 and only 15 per cent are considered to be 'healthy' (Thompson and Tirmizi, 1995)

RESEARCH METHODOLOGY

This study focuses on four issues that contribute to biodiversity loss in the mangrove ecosystem. The analysis was divided into four modules which were studied in local, national and international contexts. The research objectives were:

1. To investigate the causes of scarcity of fresh water in the coastal areas and its impact on mangrove ecosystems. This required an assessment of demand for water, water rights and policies, the legal framework and its implementation and associated political constraints.
2. To assess the impact of pollution resulting from industrialization, port activities and land clearance on mangrove forests. National and international policies, institutional effectiveness in maintaining and improving environmental conditions, and political factors were examined.
3. To ascertain the extent of human pressure on mangrove forests and fish resources; to determine the relative importance of over-harvesting of mangroves and fish resources; and to identify economic, social and institutional factors causing such changes.
4. To identify the geophysical factors affecting the mangrove ecosystem.

In order to determine the extent of biodiversity loss, the study selected quantitative and qualitative change in mangrove cover as the primary indicator and the quantitative and varietal change in fish resources as the secondary indicator. The study presents an estimation of biodiversity loss by comparing the mangrove cover over a period of eight years using Landsat images for two of the project sites – the Indus Delta and Sonmiani in Baluchistan. There is little scientifically comparable information on changes in mangrove area with time, but Landsat digital images provide comparable data for the period from 1990 to 1998.

The main proximate causes of biodiversity loss were identified, and an initial conceptual model as well as individual models for the four main issues were developed. The actual impact on the biodiversity of the mangrove ecosystem was then investigated to assess the importance of each module at each site, followed by a comparative analysis from the local to the national and international levels. Based on the analysis and the comparative framework, future projections were made for biodiversity in these sites. The conceptual model was then revised accordingly.

After visiting the sites, reviewing the literature and holding initial discussions with the major stakeholders, household-level information was collected from different sites in both the regions. Using the information gathered from initial visits, two questionnaires, one for the household and one for the village, were designed. Questions were asked about demography, occupation, accessibility of services, mobility, fishing and other economic activities, perceptions about and use of mangroves, use of camels and, finally, assets and income flows. A total of 198 households were interviewed in 14 locations. Of these, 125 were interviewed in the Indus Delta and 73 in Baluchistan. Questionnaires were completed in 24 villages.

Lack of scientific and other information meant that for most of the issues covered, a first-hand data sample had to be generated and then extrapolated to the whole area. To provide an explanation of biodiversity loss, the local, national and international levels had to be linked, but because the impact of the various factors could not be tested scientifically, a large part of the analysis was based on qualitative assessments.

LOCAL CONTEXT

Scarcity Of Fresh Water

Biological Aspects

Reduction in the flow of fresh water to the Indus Delta from 140 to 40 million acre feet over the last 50 years has created two problems. First, the salinity of the sea water has increased to 50 ppt, which is detrimental to mangrove growth. Second, the flow of alluvium has declined from 160 million to 60 million tons per year. Figure 12.4 highlights the proximate and root causes of scarcity of fresh water in the coastal areas.

The effect of freshwater diversion is aggravated by reductions in silt flow resulting from damming upstream. Three large storage dams and 20 barrages which divert river water for agricultural use have been built during the past 50 years. Dams and diversionary barrages affect bed load and transport of suspended sediments during the flood season by capturing the material and preventing its uniform dispersal over mangrove areas. As a result, the surviving Indus Delta mangroves are sparse and stunted.

Eight different species of mangrove were reported in the Indus Delta during the 1950s but at present only three are extant, with *Avicennia marina* accounting for about 95 per cent of the total area. The other two species, *Ceriops tagal* and *Aegiceros corniculatum*, are restricted to localized patches, indicating ecological stress. Along the Baluchistan coast, Sonmiani is the only area where the three mangrove species occur naturally; at Kalmat (Pasni) and Jiwani (Gawatar Bay), only *A marina* is present. In addition to the loss of species, there has been a consistent decline in mangrove cover in the delta and Sonmiani. Though the estimates show little change in the total area under mangroves between 1990 and 1998, the qualitative decline from dense to normal or sparse cover is very evident.

Mangrove development is best in areas that have significant freshwater run-off. Although the freshwater requirement of mangroves has not been established scientifically, one estimate prepared by Sindh Forest Department suggests that an average flow of 1 cusec (28 litres/second) of fresh water for each 40 ha is required for healthy growth. However, it is unclear whether this is a constant need throughout the year or whether occasional supplies, as

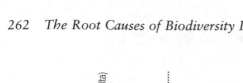

Figure 12.4 *Scarcity of Fresh Water*

might be expected during large natural riverine floods, are sufficient (IUCN, 1993).

Based on the estimated water requirement per unit of land and the Landsat estimates on area under mangrove cover together with area under mudflats (land that is potentially suitable for mangroves), the annual requirement for fresh water is about 6.8 million acre feet. Since water releases for the delta are made at Kotri (Hyderabad), which is about 100 miles from the mouth of the delta, the conveyance losses (about 40 per cent of the total) were also added to the net requirement. In gross terms, the requirement for healthy mangrove cover is about 9.5 million acre feet, which is close to the current Water Accord allocation of 10.0 million acre feet.

The above discussion clearly shows that, as a result of freshwater scarcity, mangrove cover has been reduced both qualitatively and quantitatively. In addition, the survival of *A marina* in the delta, which has a higher tolerance for salinity, and the gradual extinction of other species that are less resistant to higher salinity levels, indicate the increased levels of salinity in the delta.

Socioeconomic Aspects

The coastal areas of the country lack basic amenities such as drinking water, fuel sources and road infrastructure, but the coastal population has grown as a result of increased returns from fishing, despite the poor physical infrastructure. Consequently, the demand for fresh water for household consumption has increased, but because the local authorities have not assessed the requirements, the meagre water supplies from seasonal rivers on the Baluchistan coast, in particular, are insufficient.

The status of local governments has not been clearly defined in Pakistan. These governments are dominated by local feudal structures, and the role of local communities in assessing their water needs has remained extremely weak. Local political representation has not been effective in resolving the issue. These tendencies are not unexpected, given that the feudal structure prevailing at the regional and national levels restricts participation by the end-users in local development activities.

The loss of five mangrove species from the Indus Delta during the last 40 years, stunted growth of mangroves and the analysis of plant pathology under these conditions provide sufficient evidence to show that reductions in freshwater supplies in future may further reduce the genetic diversity of mangroves in the area and affect the biodiversity of the whole mangrove ecosystem. Fish resources may be depleted in the process.

Pollution and Land Clearance

Pollution of the marine environment is another proximate cause of biodiversity loss in the coastal areas of Pakistan. Three areas in the coastal region of the Indus Delta are significantly polluted: Keti Bunder (to the south near Sir Creek), the metropolitan centre (Karachi, Port Qasim and Rehri) and the coastline in the west (extending from Sonmiani to Jiwani). The loss of mangrove

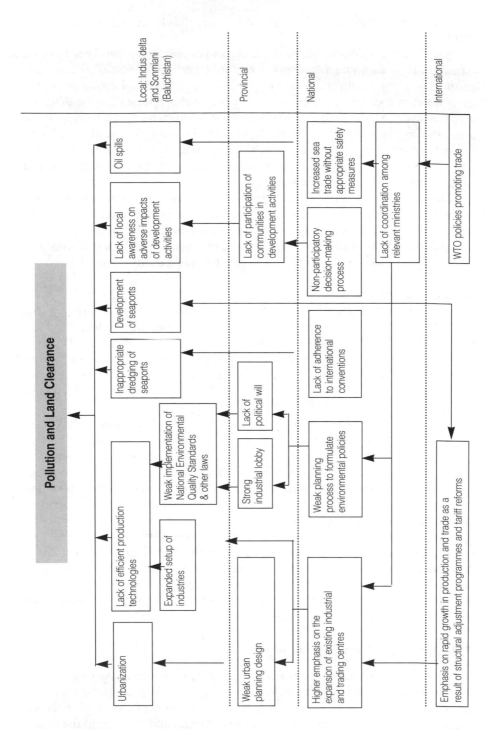

Figure 12.5 *Pollution and Land Clearance*

species during the last 50 years, besides being consistent with the reduced supply of fresh water to the delta, is also consistent with the increased volume of untreated waste-water discharges from industries and the city of Karachi and its vicinity. In addition, land clearance for the construction of new seaports, extension of existing seaports and establishment of industrial units near the coast has also contributed to the depletion of mangrove cover, particularly in the northern part of the delta. These factors have not yet affected the mangrove cover on the Baluchistan coast.

One of the direct and major causes of pollution in the Indus Delta is the industrialization and urbanization in and around Karachi (Figure 12.5), where more than half of the industrial units and over 70 per cent of the country's international trade are based. Being the biggest and only natural seaport, Karachi has attracted investments from all over the country. The situation thus created is largely an outcome of the national industrial policies that have emphasized centralized growth for industrialization. With improved infrastructure, Karachi has been rapidly transformed into one of the largest cities in the world. Rapid migration to the city raised its annual population growth rate to over 6 per cent. Rapid urbanization was accompanied by weak urban planning. The centralized industrialization approach was not accompanied by requisite urban development strategies. As a result, the generation of domestic and industrial effluents could not be assessed nor was the rapid population growth rate in Karachi taken into account. Correspondingly, there was no emphasis on safe or environmentally friendly approaches to the disposal of municipal and industrial wastes. Over time, pollution has affected the coastal areas of the Indus delta, causing stunted growth of mangroves and biodiversity loss in the marine ecosystem.

Industrialization, in addition to indirectly increasing pollution by promoting urbanization and therefore increasing domestic waste, also directly increases pollution. Due to the lack of efficient production processes in the industrial sector, resulting in an increased supply of untreated industrial effluent, marine pollution has worsened and poses a constant threat to biodiversity. Effluents from tanneries, including lead and mercury, are among the most harmful to marine life.

Due to the poor standard of living, local communities eagerly anticipate all types of development activities, without understanding the long-term adverse effects on themselves or their environment. For example, the development of a new seaport or establishment of an industrial complex is normally welcomed by the local communities since these developments offer employment opportunities. More often than not, the communities are unaware of the detrimental impacts of such development activities on the marine ecosystem and, consequently, on their fishing and other natural resource-based income and use. Unless the ineffective and non-participatory approach followed so far is changed, the social cost of land clearance and polluting industries will continue to rise and the environment will continue to suffer.

Based on past trends, one can easily ascertain the long-term environmental consequences of existing industrial pressures in and around Karachi and of the ineffectiveness of the environmental policy framework. A continuation of the present trend will cause more stunted growth of mangroves, and the biodiversity of mangrove areas will be reduced. Given the lack of land in Karachi, future economic growth will require reclamation of land from the sea at the cost of removal of mangroves. Although this analysis is most relevant to the Indus Delta, this trend will eventually affect the Baluchistan coast, and in particular the Sonmiani region, because it is close to the industrial complex planned at Hub.

Over-harvesting of Mangroves and Over-fishing

Over-harvesting of mangroves and fish by coastal communities is a third cause of mangrove degradation. It is, however, difficult to determine the extent of damage due to use by local communities.

Mangroves
Earlier studies covering specific locations in the delta and on the Baluchistan coast have reported logging of mangroves for fuel and timber at an increasing scale. Some studies have also highlighted the effect of camel browsing. However, empirical work has been confined to specific locations. The economic rationale behind the over-harvesting of mangroves rests with the scarcity of fuel alternatives at a comparable or lower price. Figure 12.6 shows the causal links among factors at different levels for the over-harvesting of mangroves. As a consequence of increased population and poor physical infrastructure, demand for mangrove wood for fuel increased at the local level. Lack of alternate fuelwood aggravated the problem. Alternatives, such as kerosene oil or natural gas, are either not available or too expensive for the local communities.

In order to understand the links among the factors mentioned above and to establish the trends with regard to over-harvesting of mangroves and fish resources by the local communities, a household survey was carried out. The data show that 46 per cent of the 125 households interviewed in the delta use mangrove wood as fuel. In Baluchistan 22 per cent of the 73 households reported use of mangroves. Overall, 37 per cent of the 198 households reported use of mangrove wood. The proportion of households using mangrove wood for fuel declines with the increase in distance to mangrove forests.

Mangrove forests have remained a source of fuel, timber and fodder for coastal communities in almost all estuaries. Because of their remoteness, resident communities have always had a stake in maintaining the forest. Logging and cutting have, therefore, remained within safe limits. However, these communities remain unaware of the greater role mangroves play in their own lives by maintaining diversity of biological resources in the marine environment and protecting coasts from erosion. This can be linked to a failure to increase the awareness of such communities about the greater role of mangroves.

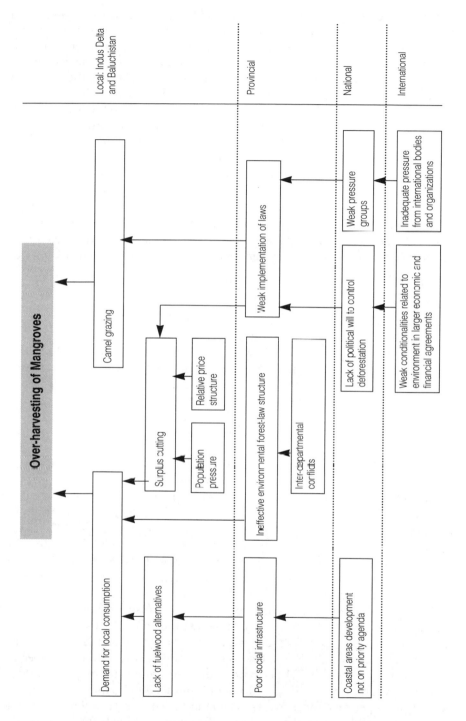

Figure 12.6 *Over-harvesting of Mangroves*

Camel browsing in the mangrove forest is harmful to the growth and regeneration of mangroves, but ineffective control by relevant departments allows this degradation to continue. The impact of camels, however, is limited to certain pockets in the dense forest of the delta, and has lessened with the decline in the camel population in coastal areas. This has been caused by both a reduction in camel exports to the Middle East and an increase in the relative profitability of cattle and buffalo over camels. Only 31 households out of 198 keep camels and on average there is only one camel per household.

Despite the fact that, in certain areas, cutting is prohibited and the Forest Department has taken over control, easy access to mangrove forests has led to cutting for commercial purposes, as for example at Keti Bunder, since mangrove wood is cheaper than other wood (Rs 60 per 40 kg as against Rs 80–100 per 40 kg). Although commercial cutting is limited to certain areas, the weak implementation of laws prohibiting this activity has long-term implications for the management of mangroves. On the whole, however, the current dependence of local communities on mangroves for fuel and fodder does not pose a serious threat.

Fishing

The over-harvesting of fish resources was investigated and a set of causal factors and relationships determined (Figure 12.7).

The household survey data show 168 households, out of a total of 198, involved in fishing. For nearly 85 per cent, fishing is their main source of income. On the whole, average earnings per household per annum were nearly three times the average income in rural Pakistan. Hence, in a relative context, these areas do not suffer from financial poverty but suffer from great social poverty, notably the lack of social amenities, and therefore have a poorer standard of living than other rural areas.

The Indus Delta is suffering population pressure from three sources – local population growth, migrants from within the country and migrants from without – but so far in Baluchistan there has been no immigration from abroad.

The survey data indicate reductions in the catch of different fish species in the Indus Delta and Baluchistan coast over the last five years. Of the 92 households surveyed in the delta, only six reported no change in fish catch; in Baluchistan only one household reported no change. These assessments, based on the experience of local fishermen, are consistent with the general impression gathered during initial site visits.

Published data on fish catch were not used because a significant part of catch is not reported by the fishermen. However, the official statistics published by the government tend to confirm the over-harvesting of fish resources (Government of Pakistan, 1996). Between 1985 and 1995, the total number of marine boats increased by 74 per cent in the delta to a total of over 13,000. On the Baluchistan coast the 1995 total of almost 5000 boats represented an increase of 84 per cent. Since marine fishing in Pakistan is carried out within a 50-mile range of the coast, the increase in the number of boats indicates significant pressure on inshore fishing resources.

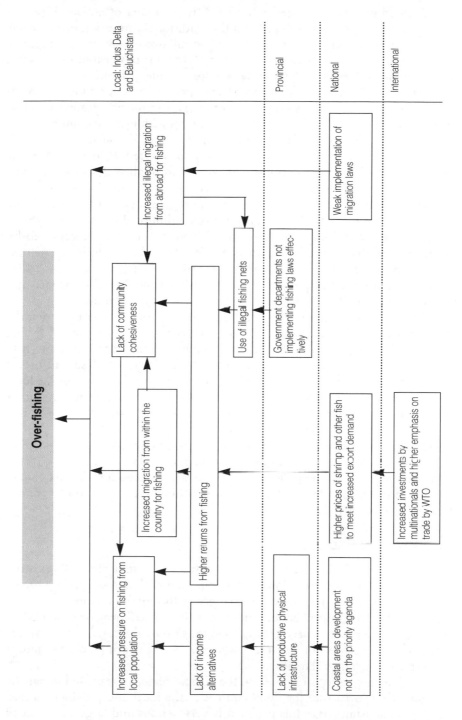

Figure 12.7 *Over-fishing*

Increased pressure on fisheries is caused by a number of factors. First, the coastal area is largely undeveloped and the traditional profession of the locals is fishing. With the rapid increase in coastal population – 6–8 per cent annually over the last ten years – together with extremely poor physical infrastructure, the coastal area does not offer alternatives for income generation.

Second, higher returns from fishing emerged at the same time as coastal population growth, resulting primarily from the government's strategy to boost exports. Increased investments from abroad along with increased international emphasis on trade were instrumental in shaping national policies.

Third, the higher returns from fishing promoted further significant immigration from within the country as well as from abroad, further increasing pressure on fish resources. In the process, local communities became more and more heterogeneous in their ethnic and tribal characteristics. Their cohesiveness started to decline and this exerted additional pressure on fishing, as respect for traditional rules and sustainable practices were replaced by profit. New settlers in the coastal areas increased damage to the local environment by propagating the use of illegal small-mesh fishing nets to further enhance the financial returns from fishing. After some initial resistance and hesitance in using illegal nets, the local fishermen also joined in.

The Indus Delta reports loss of a larger number of fish species during the last five years (1993–98) than the Baluchistan coast. The use of illegal fishing nets is widespread in the delta but in Baluchistan they have only recently arrived in Sonmiani, which is close to the Indus Delta. Widespread use of illegal nets demonstrates ineffective implementation of fishing laws at the local and provincial levels. The Fisheries Department is not implementing other fishing laws, such as the ban on inshore fishing of certain species, and this further promotes over-harvesting.

Over-fishing is increasing in both the regions. The higher income possibilities from fishing and the total disregard of fishing laws are leading to the extinction of certain fish species. There is an urgent need for effective implementation of existing laws related to both fishing and migration to coastal areas for the effective control of fishing

Geophysical Factors

Geophysical factors affecting the mangrove ecosystems include existing problems and the threat of global warming. Figure 12.8 describes the proximate and root causes of geophysical changes in the coastal region.

The Indus Delta exists because the deposition of sediments transported by the Indus in the past has been greater than erosion by the sea. Sediment transport is basically a function of river discharge. As a result of reduced sediment flows, the delta is now retreating.

The damaging effects of floods in the coastal regions are caused in part by the lack of infrastructure for flood control at the local and provincial levels. On the Baluchistan coast, this problem is very serious and largely a result of strong wave action and coastal current patterns (Mirza et al, 1988). The coastline is open and hence subject to strong wave action.

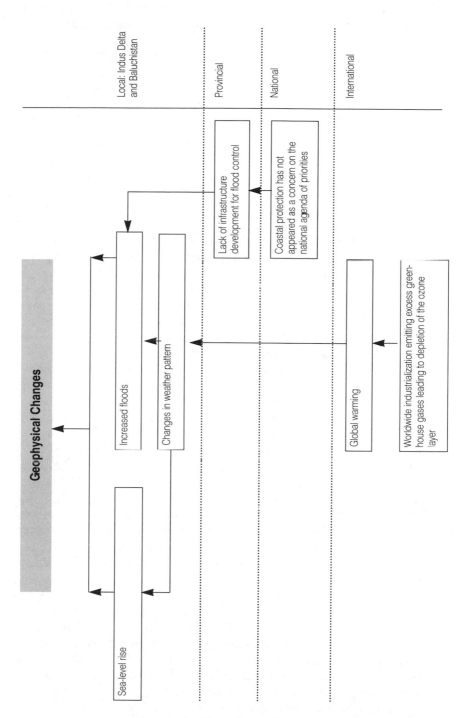

Figure 12.8 *Geophysical Changes*

Global warming will cause changes in weather patterns. Sea-level rise may cause coastal erosion and depletion of mangroves, aggravating current patterns of physical damage.

NATIONAL CONTEXT

Scarcity of Fresh Water

Agriculture is the leading sector of Pakistan's economy. Over two-thirds of the population live in rural areas and depend mostly on agriculture for their livelihood. Being arid, the country continually faces scarce surface water supplies, and irrigation water is considered the life blood of the economy.

Efforts to increase agricultural exports to support the growing industrial sector and to ensure adequate food supplies for the rapidly growing population focus on irrigation water supplies. Therefore, three large storage dams and over 20 barrages were constructed to hold the Indus water for irrigation, greatly reducing the flow to the delta, both in terms of the total amount and annual distribution. In addition, feudal-style landowners, backed by economic and political power, have managed to procure and maintain huge public subsidies on irrigation water. In addition to capital subsidies on irrigation projects, there is a massive recurring subsidy on irrigation water covering nearly 60 per cent of the operation and maintenance costs of the country's irrigation systems. Consequently, water-use efficiency in the Indus basin has remained low. According to the National Conservation Strategy (NCS) report, only 30 per cent of the total of 200 million acre feet of water – available in an average year through all sources – is applied to farmers' fields. As a result of these huge subsidies, neither the farmers nor the irrigation authorities have any incentive to use irrigation water more efficiently.

In the water management process at the national level, coastal areas are neglected. Allocations for the coastal areas are determined after accounting for all other needs. While the Water Accord of 1990 does guarantee 10 million acre feet for the delta, this allocation is not based on any scientific or need-based assessment and could be subject to further reduction in the wake of greater shortfalls in the system. Over the past 50 years, all additional requirements for irrigation water have been met through increased diversion of water upstream, thereby reducing the flows to the delta.

At the irrigation-system level, because of the failure to improve water-use efficiency, any additional cultivation of land reduces the flow downstream. Since the government has not succeeded in establishing a water market, due to the pressure from the agricultural lobby, inefficiencies in the use of water are likely to continue. International agencies such as the World Bank and IMF have stressed the need to reduce the water subsidy and establish a water market. However, since the agricultural lobby dominates the assemblies in the country, these suggestions have been ignored.

It is quite evident that, unless appropriate policy measures are taken to increase water-use efficiency, population growth and increased demand for irrigation water will continue creating shortages in the Indus Delta. Adequate supplies of fresh water and silt to the delta are critical for the health of mangroves and the region's biodiversity. Any reduction will restrict the mangroves in performing their vital role as primary producers in the ecosystem.

The problem of reduced flow of fresh water to coastal areas is most pertinent to the Indus Delta because of the larger variations in the total availability in the river system and increased diversions upstream for agricultural uses. Here, the root cause appears to be at the national level, where water use and allocation policies are made with political biases and remain largely devoid of the economic measures required to conserve water resources.

Pollution and Land Clearance

Local public institutions in Pakistan have not been accorded autonomy to design and implement policies or mobilize resources on their own. Rather, these institutions have historically remained dependent on meagre grants from provincial or federal governments. At the national level, ministries of commerce and trade, finance and urban and environmental affairs do not have coherent decision-making procedures for urban planning. The lack of coordination among local institutions or departments and among related ministries and departments aggravates the problems of urbanization.

Since domestic industries were protected from foreign competition under import-substitution policies until 1988, they are uncompetitive and inefficient. A study of 48 manufacturing units from Pakistan found that the value added of nearly half of the units was negative when measured at world prices. Industrialization in Pakistan has depended on a steady inflow of foreign aid and paid little or no attention to environmental costs. To support the expansion of trade, a new port was established at Bin Qasim. The dredging of port channels was carried out with a complete lack of adherence to international dredging laws. Not only was land cleared for the port facilities, but the dredged material was dumped on mangrove forest. Although in recent years donors have recognized environmental needs, the considerable damage to environment and ecosystems caused by earlier national and international policies will take decades to remedy.

The federal government approved a National Conservation Strategy in 1991. This strategy formed the basis for the Pakistan Environmental Protection Act of 1995 (revised in 1996), which covers issues related to marine pollution and conservation of biodiversity in addition to air, water and soil pollution and handling of hazardous wastes. In order to exercise the powers and functions established by the Act, the government established the Pakistan Environmental Protection Agency (PEPA) and created the Pakistan Environmental Protection Council (PEPC), with the Prime Minister as its chairperson, to approve national environmental policies. Similarly, each provincial government established an Environmental Protection Agency (EPA) to exercise the powers and functions delegated to them by the PEPA.

With a top-heavy institutional structure, the PEPC requires a minimum of 15 non-government officials as members out of a total of 41. These officials, however, are appointed by the federal government. Although such officials may represent different sectors of society, given their low proportion in the PEPC and their nomination by the government, it is not likely that they will exert significant pressure to ensure that environmental issues are better understood and political biases are minimized. This lack of representation reflects a major deficiency in the country's current institutional structure for environmental protection.

National Environmental Quality Standards (NEQS), also established under the 1995 Act to cover all sectors of the economy, have remained largely unenforced as anticipated. Government agencies responsible for enforcing the NEQS are understaffed, underequipped and unprepared. They are, therefore, unable to fulfil their roles of carrying out environmental impact assessments, monitoring or enforcement. The industrialists, on the other hand, do not share responsibility for improving or protecting the environment and have made virtually no attempt at recovery of by-products or minimization of wastes. The NEQS have, therefore, had minimal success in reducing pollution.

Since the largest seaports of Karachi and Bin Qasim and industrial units are located in the Indus Delta, the issues of pollution and land clearance are currently relevant to the delta only. The untreated industrial effluent thrown into the delta will continue to be a major threat for mangroves and fish.

Over-harvesting of Mangroves and Over-fishing

Over-harvesting of mangroves is a result of negligence in the development of Pakistan's coastal areas. Lack of basic amenities has, in certain locations, left no alternative to the use of mangrove wood for fuel.

Responsibility for protecting mangrove forests has lain with the Forest Department since the late 1950s, but only very recently has this department shown any interest in their conservation. A mere expansion of responsibilities, without the requisite resources, will not help the department implement the existing laws. For example, one forest guard alone is given an area of 8000 to 10,000 ha of mangroves to monitor. At the national level, weak environmental groups coupled with a general lack of political will to control deforestation allow weak implementation of laws to continue. These environmental groups receive inadequate support from international bodies and organizations, while the absence of strong conditions related to environmental protection in larger economic and financial agreements does not promote political will on the part of the government to control deforestation.

Inter-departmental conflicts have created barriers to improving forest laws, particularly those related to the marine environment. The Indus Delta has been divided among three authorities, namely the Sindh Forest Department, the Bin Qasim Port Authority and the Land Revenue Department. As a result, mangrove forests within the jurisdiction of each department are being protected in different ways. For example, the Bin Qasim Port Authority has declared mangrove forest within its control as protected area. But improper dredging of port areas by the authority itself has included clearing of mangroves. The Land Revenue Department has not prepared any plan for the conservation of its forests.

Given the high returns associated with fishing and a general lack of implementation of fishing laws as well as migration laws, the issue of over-fishing is likely to escalate in future and may affect the entire coastal belt. The increased pressure on fisheries from the local population indicates a lack of other income alternatives, which is itself a reflection of poor infrastructure. Coastal area development is not a priority for the government, due to the absence of strong political representation of the local area at the national level. Poor infrastructure has made the area unattractive to investors who could help in the diversification of local economic activities.

Emphasis on the expansion of exports, given increasing trade imbalances, has been supported by rapid devaluation of the rupee in relation to major currencies. Devaluation has led to rapid increases in the local price of shrimp and other fish. Since fisheries are treated as a sub-sector of agriculture, which enjoys total exemption from direct taxes in Pakistan, it remains extremely attractive financially for fishing communities to expand fish catch at all cost and to ignore the environmental consequences.

INTERNATIONAL CONTEXT

Pollution and Land Clearance

Increased pressures from the World Bank and the IMF for structural reforms do not explicitly emphasize the need for reform of centralized growth strategies. Rather, they stress liberalization of the fiscal, tax and trade structure, reduction in public expenditure, and incentives for private investments in order to move toward a market-based economy. However, the government has responded by a hastening toward increasing production levels with emphasis on the expansion of existing industrial and trading centres, largely ignoring associated environmental issues.

With increased sea trade, the probability of oil spills increases. These accidental spills pose a great threat to marine life and mangrove estuaries. Available safety measures are insufficient to check and control such oil spills. A lack of coordination among the relevant ministries and departments at the national and provincial levels prevents them from taking safety measures to protect the environment from such hazards.

Such circumstances are in part a reflection of the inefficiency of the bureaucracy and also an outcome of the strong emphasis on international trade by international agencies. GATT, to which Pakistan has been a party since 1964, and now the WTO, restrict government use of trade policies to protect the environment. The effects of incentives (or disincentives) from international agreements and policies on national and local decisions are often far reaching. However, there is no simple and straightforward link between the WTO's policies and the government's poor environmental performance. A detailed institutional analysis is required to unfold the layers of factors between these levels. Nevertheless, the prescriptions for increased trade will continue posing threats to the marine environment through increased pollution and land clearance until environmental issues are correctly understood and effective remedial measures are enforced.

On the whole, it appears that, whereas the WTO is facilitating significant expansion in world trade, coverage of the associated environmental concerns is in a stage of transition if not infancy. At present, short-term gains may be achieved by WTO-member countries by ignoring long-term environmental losses. Since environmental effects cannot be confined within national boundaries, it is likely that incompatibility between the WTO and multilateral environmental agreements will create environmental as well as political conflicts.

Over-harvesting of Mangroves and Over-fishing

International trade agreements, including tariff reforms, and greater emphasis by international organizations on the expansion of world trade have jointly created opportunities for exports. These agreements do not address the long-term sustainability of the coastal environment. As a result, increased export of fish is likely to cause depletion of fish species and biodiversity.

Since the major argument presented by the government for the devaluation of the rupee is to boost exports as well as to reduce exchange rate controls (which fulfills the requirements of the structural adjustment programme and is consistent with the emphasis on increased trade), it is not surprising that international agreements do not address over-fishing and degradation of the marine environment.

It is interesting to note that most WTO-member countries are also signatories to multilateral environmental agreements, and the number and scope of these agreements grew significantly during the 1980s and the first half of the 1990s. The failure to achieve compatibility between the WTO and environmental agreements appears to be a binding constraint in linking trade and environment. The trade sanctions envisaged under environmental agreements would be difficult for the WTO to adopt.

Geophysical Factors

Pakistan has been included in the list of ten countries most vulnerable to the impacts of rising sea levels. Qureshi (1989) has estimated a land loss of about 1700 km^2 in the Indus Delta due to sea encroachment over the last half century. Along the Baluchistan coast, historical records show that sea encroachment has destroyed several towns and villages. The lack of focus on coastal area development at the national level has given rise to issues related to coastal protection. National flood control and coastal protection measures are virtually non-existent. At the international level, global warming poses a regional threat. The advances made since the Rio Summit in 1992 to address this problem are encouraging, but stricter implementation of the agreements is required.

CONCLUSIONS

The loss of mangrove species over the last 50 years is highly consistent with the reduction of freshwater and silt supplies to the Indus Delta. The survival of salt-tolerant *Avicennia marina* in the delta provides evidence of higher levels of salinity in and around the mangrove forests. The comparative Landsat images of mangrove cover in the delta also suggest decline of mangroves over the last two decades. Although the Water Accord of 1990 guarantees a minimum of 10 million acre feet of water annually for the delta, the high public subsidies to irrigation water for agriculture upstream provide negative incentives for the conservation of water resources. In the event of any significant water shortage, the delta is likely to receive a smaller quantity. If the mangroves are to be conserved effectively, a larger water supply has to be assured. This would require improved water-use efficiency in the upstream areas.

The root cause of the reduced supply of fresh water to the Indus Delta is found at the national level. The decision to apportion and divert water supplies for upstream uses only takes agricultural needs into account. The strong agricultural lobby has managed to procure various government subsidies since most of the elected officials are feudal landowners who benefit directly from them. An efficient water market has not been allowed to develop. National policies have aimed at increasing agricultural growth by increasing crop area and water supply instead of focusing on higher productivity and efficient water usage, despite the fact that 40 per cent of irrigation water is wasted.

The loss of mangrove species is also consistent with the increases in volume of untreated industrial and domestic waste-water discharges from Karachi and its vicinity. Since domestic industries were consistently protected from foreign competition, they are non-competitive and production processes are inefficient and highly polluting. Moreover, the dredging of port channels is carried out with a total disregard for international dredging laws. The increased level of marine pollution in the delta, which is likely to be repeated in Sonmiani in Baluchistan, has stunted mangrove growth, and marine pollution poses a constant threat to biodiversity.

The government agencies responsible for enforcing NEQS are understaffed and underequipped. The general public and the industrialists, on the other hand, show no desire to share the responsibility for improving or protecting the environment. The ineffectiveness of the EPAs in controlling marine pollution will continue to contribute to environmental degradation. Instead of changing the environmental laws, efforts are needed to increase local participation in the PEPC if the effectiveness of the EPA is to be improved.

The household data show that most households are directly or indirectly linked with fishing. Because of relatively high incomes – by national standards – from fishing, the area does not suffer from financial poverty relative to other rural areas in the country. However, there is widespread social poverty as a result of the lack of social amenities.

Household fuel consumption patterns show that nearly two-thirds of the resident communities do not use mangroves at all. This indicates that pressure on mangroves for fuel is low and, given the high returns from fishing, it is likely that people will shift to other fuel sources as they become more afford-able. Though the over-harvesting of mangroves is a serious problem in selected areas, it is not a major threat in terms of impact on the entire mangrove area. This refutes the commonly held notion that over-harvesting by the local communities is the biggest threat to the mangroves.

Over-fishing emerged as a very important factor for biodiversity loss in the mangrove ecosystems. Over-fishing results in the extinction of certain fish species, causing changes in the biodiversity of mangrove forests where local fish species spend at least a part of their life cycle. In the rural household survey, over 95 per cent of households reported a loss of fish species over the last five years. Over-fishing is primarily caused by improved financial returns resulting from increased export demand and opportunities. Factors contribut-ing to this phenomenon include use of fishing nets of illegal specifications and poor control by the relevant authorities, including the Fisheries Department, as well as changes in economic policies.

The root causes of degradation of mangrove forests seem to stem – at the national level – from industrial, trade and conservation policies (Figure 12.9). Industrial policies favour centralized growth, with subsidies promoting ineffi-cient production technologies and leading to increased marine pollution. Trade policies, marked by tariff reductions and influenced by international prescrip-tions, emphasize export expansion to reduce trade deficits and revenue gaps. On the conservation side, over-fishing in shallow waters indicates a complete disregard for the existing environmental protection laws. Tax and water pricing policies have promoted inefficient water use. Due to the lack of environmental assessment of these policies, biodiversity loss in the mangrove ecosystem has neither been understood nor given due attention.

Understanding the economic rationale for the conservation of mangrove forests requires that the entire problem be viewed from a broader perspective. The costs of degradation must be weighed simultaneously with the benefits of resource use. Mangrove protection will require a comprehensive planning effort, with integration of the relevant ministries or departments and the local communities. Further research efforts would be extremely helpful in designing a comprehensive plan to conserve biodiversity in mangrove forests.

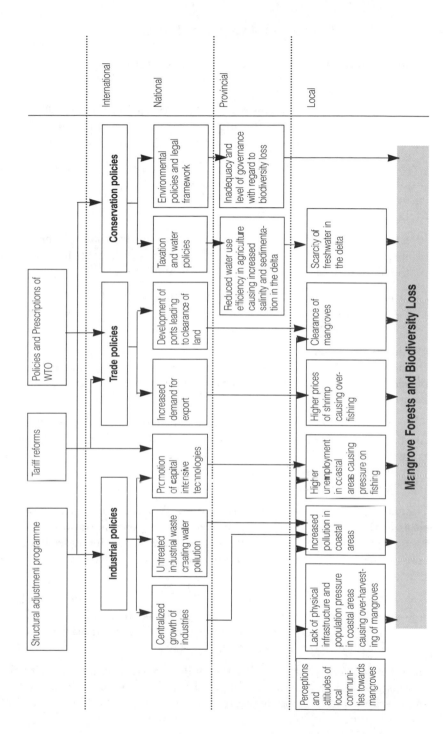

Figure 12.9 *Revised Conceptual Model*

RECOMMENDATIONS

The following recommendations are made, based on the analysis carried out for this study:

- Environmental impact assessments should be carried out by the EPAs on a regular basis and published officially to strengthen the mandated efforts to increase public awareness about environment and promotion of research.

- Given the extent of over-harvesting of fish resources, close coordination should be maintained between fishermen and fisheries departments to ensure implementation of existing fishing laws, particularly those related to illegal fishing nets.

- Effective policy actions at the national level are needed to check the influx of migrants promoting the use of illegal fishing nets and exerting pressures on the marine environment through over-fishing.

- Reforms need to be formulated to promote cooperation between the Forestry Department and coastal communities in order to ensure effective protection and conservation of mangroves.

- Qualitative assessment of the status of the fishing communities indicates the need for a vocational training programme for fishermen to help them develop their resources in a manner conducive to the protection of marine environment.

- The levels of income from fishing are promising for the development of financial markets in coastal areas. Credit to develop offshore fishing capacity would reduce pressure from inshore fishing. In the initial period, provision of subsidized credit may be instrumental in reducing over-fishing, particularly shrimp.

- Despite the guarantee of water flows in the Water Accord, further reductions in flow to the delta are probable. The only viable option left is to increase the efficiency of water use in order to minimize increases in diversions upstream and to ensure an adequate supply of fresh water to the delta.

- Changes in the legal structure of the PEPC are needed in order to include non-appointed members in the Council and to ensure an adequate balance between officials and others for better understanding of environmental issues and for effective implementation of laws.

- In order to avoid conflict of interest and for strict compliance with the International Dredging Convention to which Pakistan is a signatory, dredging operations need to be monitored by agencies like the EPAs instead of port authorities.

- Appraisal of foreign investments, particularly those affecting the mangrove ecosystem, should account for the full costs of environmental degradation they may cause.

- For a pragmatic solution to the increased water pollution in the marine environment, a restructuring of NEQS is needed so that the polluters' ability to pay the associated costs and the technological constraints are taken into account.

- Dialogue needs to be initiated to address the causes of biodiversity loss and discuss the role and constraints of those involved. Such dialogue would lead to viable and agreed steps for improving the environmental situation.

- Scientific studies should be conducted on the following issues:
  1. The adaptive behaviour of mangroves in the face of technical, socio-economic and environmental changes in the coastal areas.
  2. The freshwater requirements of mangroves in terms of quantity and distribution.
  3. The willingness of coastal communities to pay for alternate sources of fuel for household consumption.
  4. The institutional factors at all levels that affect mangrove ecosystem biodiversity.

Chapter 13

Philippines: Cebu, Negros and Palawan

Research team: Members of the project team were team leader
*Dr Celso R Roque, Dr Prescillano M Zamora, Dr Rufino Alonzo,
Dr Sabino G Padilla, Mirriam C Ferrer* and *Maria Dulce M Cacha.*
Editing, research and administrative assistance were provided by
*Maria Isabel Garcia, Edgar G Imperio, Amelia T Tapia,
Mary Rose Bungayon* and *Perlita M Padilla*

Summary: Three islands in the Philippines illustrate the strong correlation between population density and biodiversity loss. The study explores the root causes of population trends on the three islands to show how different historical patterns of political and economic power and access to land continue to shape resource use and biodiversity loss today.

The Philippines is experiencing a very high rate of biodiversity loss, indicated by a decline in quality and number of habitats such as forests, coral reefs and mangroves. This loss has deleterious impacts on the long-term sustainability of communities, political cohesion and governance and overall national welfare. It is becoming evident that biodiversity loss has root causes in the social, institutional, economic and political spheres. A host of socio-economic factors, including economic and political history and rapid population growth, contribute to the loss of environmental quality and biodiversity. Conservation efforts have failed to reverse the trend in large part because of inattention to these root causes. Despite investments by government agencies, other organizations and international development banks, forest cover and other important habitats continue to decline.

The direct causes of biodiversity loss in the Philippines are overharvesting and habitat alteration. The major proximate causes of primary forest loss are commercial logging, community logging, *kaingin* (shifting cultivation) and conversion of forest lands to other uses. In mangrove ecosystems, extraction of fuel and construction materials and development of fish ponds have caused rapid destruction. In the case of coral reefs, fishing techniques using dynamite and cyanide are probably the most important cause of biodiversity loss.[1] Access is an important variable in determining the impact of these activities, for example the distance of forests from waterways and roads and the ruggedness of the terrain.[2] Commercial logging provides access. Thus, besides being in itself a destructive force, it also induces migration to the uplands, timber poaching and shifting cultivation through the construction of logging roads.

In this study, we examine the root causes that are, in turn, driving these proximate causes, and look at the problem from two perspectives, the national and ecosystem levels. We analysed the situation at the national level by looking at relevant sectors such as the political economy. We also investigated the historical and current social, economic and political causes specific to the ecosystems of three islands: Cebu, Negros and Palawan. These islands are situated in different biogeographic zones of the Philippines and have very different histories and political economies.

DESCRIPTION OF THE STUDY AREAS

Over 40,000 species of wildlife exist in the Philippines. Because of the isolation of some of the islands since the Pleistocene era, Philippine forests are home to numerous endemic life forms. Rapid deforestation, transformation of mangrove swamps and destruction of coral reefs all point to significant loss of biodiversity. When the Spaniards first came to the country in 1521, forests covered about 90 per cent of the total land area.[3] Forest cover decreased to about 70 per cent by 1900, 49 per cent by 1950 and 18 per cent by 1994 (Environment Management Bureau, 1996). The present rate of forest cover loss is 180,000 ha per year. Conditions in other Philippine ecosystems are similar. Only 27 per cent of mangrove forest remains, and 95 per cent of coral

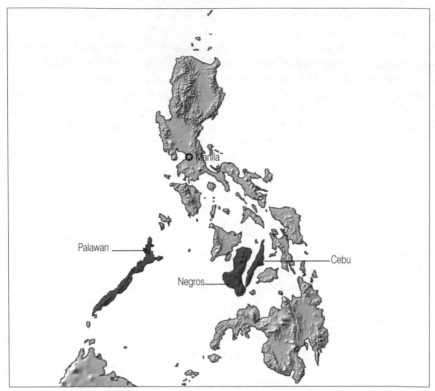

Figure 13.1 *Map of the Philippines Showing Location of Cebu,*
Negros and Palawan

reefs are in bad condition. As a result, at least 192 species are threatened or
endangered, including 86 bird species, 33 mammals and three reptiles. About
60 per cent of endemic Philippine flora are now extinct (Department of
Environment and Natural Resources, 1990). The tamaraw (*Bubalus mindoren-
sis*) and the Philippine eagle (*Pithecophaga jefferyi*) are on the verge of
extinction. Human encroachment has degraded all the national parks of the
Philippines to the point that about half are no longer biologically important.

Cebu is a long narrow island with a mainland area of 4400 km², and lies
geographically at the centre of the Philippines. Of the three islands in this
study, it has undergone the most development and urbanization. Much of the
island receives limited rainfall. A saw-toothed mountain range runs its whole
length. Limestones and marls are evident and karst topography is present
(Barrera, 1956). About 73 per cent of the island has slopes of more than 18
per cent. Although Cebu was still forested at the beginning of Spanish
colonization, its forests were almost totally gone by the end of the 19th
century. Many factors including colonial history, the continuing shift of land
use from agriculture to industrial and urban development purposes and
increasing population pressures have played a major role in biodiversity loss.

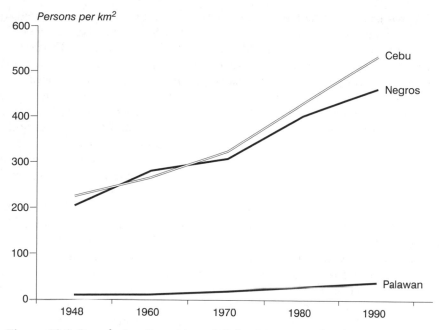

Figure 13.2 *Population Densities of Cebu, Negros and Palawan (1948–90)*

Cebu also illustrates the 'contagion effect' – how its own degradation affects nearby islands.

The total population of Cebu is over 2.6 million. Population density is 518 persons per km^2 (Figure 13.2), with 52 per cent in the urban areas. Settlements are situated mainly in the narrow coastal plains of the island (Fleiger, 1994). Only about 30 per cent of Cebu is suited for agriculture. Soil erosion is a serious problem in the interior because of the steep slopes and loss of forest cover.[4] The richest agricultural districts of the island are within a 30 km radius of Cebu City (Gwekoh, 1937), but these fertile lowlands are limited and Cebuano peasants occupy marginal areas where soils are now exhausted.

Negros, which lies to the west of Cebu, has a land area of 12,700 km^2, making it the fourth largest island in the Philippines. Negros has pronounced wet and dry seasons. Rolling hills, plains and mountain peaks characterize the island's topography. A group of volcanic mountains traverses the length of the island. Mount Canlaon is the highest peak on the island at 2450 metres. Negros offers the case of an island-ecosystem that has been largely transformed into a plantation economy.[5] Seventy per cent of the country's sugar plantations are concentrated in Negros, primarily in Negros Occidental, the larger part of the island. Other economic activities, including mining, forestry, fisheries and industry, have been of secondary but important consequence to the island's biodiversity. Since sugar traditionally formed the bedrock of the Philippine economy, Negros made a significant contribution to the country's economy and, correspondingly, Negros elites exercised considerable political influence.

Negros has very little remaining forest cover, old growth being limited to the steep slopes and tops of the high mountains. Mount Canlaon is the only protected area in Negros and is highly degraded – it has an area of 32,300 ha.[6] Large mangrove trees in south-western Negros and in small coastal islands have all practically disappeared because of the creation of fish ponds and saltbeds. Although they were abundant in the 19th century, only about 1000 ha of mangrove remain. Less than 5 per cent of living coral reefs in Negros are in excellent condition while almost 75 per cent are in poor to fair conditions. The wastes from industrial activities, notably sugar mills, ultimately end up in coastal and marine waters (Davies et al, 1990). In recent years, pollution of coastal waters has also been traced to excessive amounts of fertilizers and pesticides originating from nearby fish ponds.

Palawan is the fifth largest island in the Philippines and lies in the west, about 240 km south-west of Manila. Palawan province consists of 1768 islands with almost 2000 km of coastline. The climate is tropical and monsoonal. Palawan soils are largely alluvial or formed from underlying bedrock (Eder and Fernandez, 1996) and are of low to moderate fertility. The island is bisected by a chain of mountains, and 75 per cent of the total area has slopes over 18 per cent. The steep inclines are prone to erosion and have discouraged logging until recently. The province's natural vegetation differs from most Philippine islands, and there are many endemic species of fauna. Flora and fauna are predominantly Bornean in character. The island is a refuge for several species, such as the blue-naped parrot and Philippine cockatoo, which are threatened elsewhere in the archipelago, and for the last Philippine crocodile population (Eder and Fernandez, 1996).

Palawan has been referred to as the last ecological frontier of the country because of its relatively intact ecosystems. Development started late in Palawan and forests still cover 54 per cent of its total land area.[7] It also has the second largest remaining mangrove forest, with some 28,000 ha, which has been declared a Mangrove Swamp Forest Reserve. About 38 per cent of Philippine coral reefs are located in Palawan (Fernandez, 1997). In 1990 UNESCO designated the province as part of the international network of Biosphere Reserves.

Over the last four decades, Palawan has attracted immigrants from all other regions of the country. With a population density of 35 persons per km^2, compared to a national average of 202, Palawan is perceived to have the capacity to accommodate more people. However, concerns are already being expressed about the rapid loss of biodiversity and environmental degradation. Development began to accelerate at the same time that environmental activism and concern with conservation began to gain ground. This has given the local government the opportunity to take an alternative path to development – its Strategic Environmental Plan (SEP) now provides a comprehensive framework for sustainable development of Palawan.

RESEARCH METHODOLOGY

This study consisted of national sectoral studies of Philippine biodiversity, demography, economy and politics complemented by multi-sectoral studies of the three island ecosystems. An interdisciplinary team used systems dynamics for the analysis of root causes of biodiversity loss. For the time frame of the study, we chose the century between 1890 and 1990, which includes the last decade of Spanish colonial rule, the entire period of American occupation and Philippine independence.

The objective of this approach is to construct a computerized model of complex systems, usually involving linkages of economic, demographic, political and environmental components. In such a model, concepts are necessarily defined quantitatively. Quantification has the advantage of fixing the meaning of concepts, since variables must be expressed as objective measures. For example, we may claim that political influence of a certain social group is a strong driving force in deforestation, but political influence is not an acceptable variable in systems dynamics. Instead, in this particular case, the number and size of forest concessions owned by the social group are better variables because they are objectively measurable.

This study did not attempt to develop a computerized simulation model. We simply used systems dynamics to achieve clarity and identify causal loops and linkages among the many independent variables. Concentrating on feedback loops greatly diminishes the number of variables and focuses attention on those variables that are crucial in generating and controlling social and economic problems. Our interest goes beyond the identification of root causes. Ultimately, we want to discover policies that could moderate or control the loss of biodiversity. For policy purposes, the most important factors are those enclosed within feedback loops.

Data on biodiversity, as rigorously defined, do not exist in any form for the islands. The pragmatic alternative is to infer biodiversity loss from proxy measures, for which we used loss of forest cover, corals and mangroves and decreased populations of indicator species. Similarly, we limited the spectrum of direct causes by considering only a few important categories: over-harvesting, habitat alteration, species introduction and chemical pollution.[8] Given the limits of available quantitative data, the project undertook a largely qualitative analysis of the models to deduce conclusions about root causes of biodiversity loss for the three islands.

LOCAL CONTEXT: CEBU

The high population density of Cebu and the easy natural access to its forests provided by its long coastline are the most important root causes of the loss of its biodiversity. Cebu serves as an important example of how deforestation has been carried to its ultimate end. By the end of the 19th century, Cebu's forests were almost totally gone. In 1903 the forest cover of Cebu was about 17,000 ha out of a total land area of about 508,000 ha. By 1974 the forest area had declined to a negligible 400 ha. The destruction of the original forest cover is said to have contributed immensely to the extinction of at least nine species and sub-species of birds from the island (Magsalay, 1993). Cebu illustrates the history of the forest and biodiversity under conditions of persistent poverty and increasing population density. The case of Cebu also shows that forest cover is a good proxy indicator for other biodiversity indicators, such as mangroves and coral cover.

A large part of Cebu's rugged terrain is unsuitable for agricultural production. The island has relied heavily on trading and industrial manufacturing. Since early colonization, pressures on Cebu's environment, particularly the forest, have been immense. Export of forest products, shipbuilding, domestic consumption for fuel and industrial use for mines were among the major reasons, and reclamation projects also destroyed large areas of mangroves. The concentration of the best agricultural areas in the hands of the religious orders and later of a few *mestizo* families have also pushed people to occupy steep areas, where uncontrolled shifting cultivation has eliminated the original vegetation.

The central, strategic location of Cebu played a significant part in the development of the island as a major entrepôt or intermediary point of trade. Foreign trade influenced Cebu's settlement pattern in three ways. First, it induced the growth of concentrated settlements along the coast and near the mouths of rivers. The reclamation of wetlands by people who wanted to establish their residence within the city facilitated Cebu's urban expansion. Second, since exports consisted mainly of forest products gathered by inland villages and even from neighbouring islands, a web of trading relationships evolved within the island. Local goods flowed toward the coast as imported wares found their way inland. Lastly, long-distance trade induced a change in the social structure and led to the development of a social hierarchy.

The Legacy of Spanish and American Rule

In 1903 Cebu was already the most densely populated island in the Philippines. Throughout the 19th century, the number of persons per hectare of arable land was about six times the national average. The implications of the critical shortage of arable land vis-à-vis the constantly growing population in a dominantly agrarian economy are obvious. First, landless farmers seek subsistence in the most easily accessible and commonly owned forests and convert them to areas of shifting cultivation. The narrow shape of Cebu meant easy access by sea to most parts of the island except the middle portion, which is steep and rugged. In addition to increasing agricultural land and consumption of firewood, people cut trees to supply the boat-building industry and export markets. The beach forest and the mangroves were converted to residential areas and cropland. Limited fertile coastal plains pushed the Cebuano peasants to occupy marginal areas that should not have been used for agriculture.

The Spanish colonial policy of concentrating good agricultural land in the huge haciendas of the Spanish clergy and the elite, which further limited the land available to the masses, aggravated problems created by population density. The American regime did not alter land tenure patterns, although it abolished the Spanish system of tributes. The result was the continuous conversion of forest land to agriculture. The other reaction to the shortage of land in Cebu was emigration, but there was little until the 20th century. Under Spanish rule, mobility was severely restricted by the colonial government, because the tribute system, as well as the budget of the parish, depended on the population under its wings. Getting a passport required numerous clearances in order for a native to travel to other islands. Moreover, the passports were valid for only three months. The Americans encouraged resettlement, particularly in Mindanao, but this had little effect on the demographic crisis in Cebu.

In the 19th century the church owned the best agricultural lands on the island, expanding them through donations and purchases. The religious orders encouraged agricultural production on their haciendas. In the 1850s, increased production of export crops, notably sugar and tobacco, resulted in the recruitment of migrant peasants as plantation workers for religious estates and haciendas. Tenants and wage labourers were hired to plant tobacco, cacao, corn and sugar. In this period, Spanish and Chinese *mestizos* engaged in land speculation and acquisition inside the port area and nearby towns, triggered by new business opportunities in agriculture and trading. These *mestizo* families continued to play a key role in the island's commercial life, drastically changing the land tenure and crop production systems. In the 1860s, foreign vessels began to load cargoes of sugar and hemp and customs houses were built. American and British business houses also opened in the island. Streams of migrants flowed toward the trading centres. Business opportunities became available in the urban areas owing to increased foreign participation in the economy. During this period, people from Cebu started settling in northern Negros.

On the eve of the demise of the Spanish colonial government, wealthy *mestizo* families not only ruled Cebu's commercial life but also its political life. A few of them participated in the short-lived Philippine revolutionary government. When the revolutionary army began suffering major setbacks, they shifted allegiance and served in the new American colonial regime. They also expanded their business networks into the nearby islands, ultimately dominating business.

The American colonial era saw a series of policies designed to ease the population pressure in some highly populated areas and bring more people to the provinces with fewer inhabitants. In 1903, US colonial authorities promulgated the Public Land Act to influence population redistribution, encouraging pioneer settlements, particularly in Mindanao. Between 1910 and 1939, migrant workers and settlers were transported to other islands to fill labour needs. Over 40 per cent of the total transported labourers and home seekers originated from Cebu. In 1938, the National Land Settlement Administration launched a project to settle people in the Koronadal plain of Cotabato (Pelzer,

1948). Resettled families came from areas of agrarian conflict, particularly those with high tenancy rates. Agrarian unrest remained a major snag in the American colonial regime. Armed uprising during this period showed the seriousness of the agrarian problem. Efforts to redistribute the church estates failed. Tenancy and usurious practices ruled the lives of Cebuano peasants in part because of the high resale value of land, which was beyond their reach.

Independence and Current Conditions

In the post-colonial period, with the forests almost totally gone, industrialization emerged as the only alternative. Mining, manufacturing and tourism grew. Now the second largest urban economic centre in the Philippines, Cebu is a major destination of direct foreign investment. In the 1980s, massive construction of economic and tourism infrastructure began in Cebu, including special economic zones that were primarily situated in the coastal areas. The regional development council has prescribed the establishment of industrial estates that are government-owned but privately managed.[9]

Industrial growth, however, has not benefited the majority of Cebu's population. The island's migration flows reveal the limited economic opportunities available to the Cebuanos. Between 1948 and 1960, the island's population density increased by almost 19 per cent, and between 1960 and 1970 by over 22 per cent. A number of post-war migrant families came from provinces plagued with agrarian problems. In 1990 there were 520 persons per km^2 in Cebu compared to 221 persons per km^2 in 1948. Poverty is still rampant. Most households still use firewood, giving the forest very little chance for recovery.[10] In any case, most of Cebu's forest lands have already been converted to other uses. Today, land availability remains a big problem.

Despite the government's various land reform programmes, there is still a high incidence of tenancy in the rural areas of the province. The biggest landowners in Cebu are either top government officials or powerful politicians.[11] Just 595 families in Cebu, or about 1 per cent of the total household population, control over 38 per cent of all cropland and as much as 94 per cent of the total private agricultural lands included in the recent Comprehensive Agrarian Reform Programme. The Department of Agrarian Reform (DAR) has allotted 25,688 ha for redistribution but, since 1988, only 36 per cent have been awarded to beneficiaries. The delays were due mainly to the many protests and petitions, which have gone all the way to the Supreme Court and to the office of the President, for exemptions from coverage filed by landlords.

Confronted by a degraded environment, hordes of Cebuanos are migrating to other parts of the archipelago and even out of the country, a familiar recourse for Filipinos in the face of diminishing lands coupled with low yields. However, at the same time, the economic growth of the cities has prompted the arrival of streams of rural migrants to urban areas of Cebu. This influx facilitated the rapid transformation of the island's landscape from predominantly rural to predominantly urban, a trend that is common in the rest of the country, but the relationship between demographic factors and environmental degradation is highlighted in Cebu.

Much of the environmental pressure has now shifted from extraction of resources to pollution: water treatment facilities are non-existent; waste disposal facilities are insufficient; industrial firms lack anti-pollution devices; and there is an acute shortage of water.[12] Thus, in addition to deforestation, pollution from industries, owned and managed by Cebu's elite, has added to the environmental woes.

The Cebu case study contributed the following to the national model for biodiversity loss (Figure 13.3):

- The significance of a large initial population and the failure of demographic policies to prevent migration to the uplands.
- The ease of access to forest lands demonstrated the role of the access factor.
- Although Cebu has been industrializing with some success, the generation of non-agricultural jobs has been inadequate to absorb excess farm labour. Industrialization has attracted immigrants.
- Deforestation led to the loss of other habitats, such as mangrove and coral covers, supporting the assumption that forest cover is a good proxy for biodiversity.

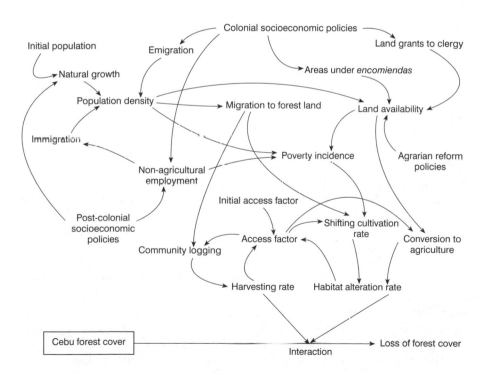

Figure 13.3 *Causal Loop Diagram for Forest Cover in Cebu*

LOCAL CONTEXT: NEGROS

In Negros, two significant factors have affected biodiversity loss: the conversion of large tracts of land to sugar plantations in the second half of the 19th century and, consequently, phenomenal population growth. Beach forests gave way to dense human communities while low-lying dipterocarp forests were converted to agricultural lands. Colonial systems created the sugar elite and established trade policies that fed the growth of the plantation economy. Two types of settler were attracted by the opportunities offered by the sugar economy: the traders and capitalists who acquired large tracts of land, and the farm hands and their families, who were contracted as workers. In due time, while the sugar lords amassed wealth, the impoverishment and underemployment of many farm workers and settlers in Negros contributed to upland migration and clearing of upland forests.

The Legacy of Spanish and American Rule

In the early years of Spanish rule, Negros was sparsely populated, especially in contrast to neighbouring islands such as Cebu. Through the 1770s, Negros towns were isolated from each other. Only in the early 19th century, when effective defences were put up against Muslim invasions, was it possible to establish towns near the sea. The intensive cultivation of the island began in the second half of the 19th century when the Spaniards introduced agricultural monopolies for export production. Sugar cane soon became the island's primary export commodity. After the first sugar hacienda was established in 1849, more and more tracts of land and forest were cleared. Chinese *mestizos*, edged out of the money-lending and trading arena by Western financial and trading houses, immediately moved into agricultural production. They secured titles to fairly large tracts of forests in Negros, which they cleared for agriculture. In addition to clearing for fields, the needs of a plantation economy contributed to forest cover loss in other ways. Demand for firewood for the mills and household needs was met by the mangrove forests, lumber requirements for construction led to felling of more trees, and other areas were cleared for access roads and railways as the economy grew. The expansion of haciendas and the increase in the volume of trade were almost uninterrupted up to 1898, when Spanish rule was ended.

Various factors hastened the conversion of the island into the leading sugar-producing area in the Philippines. British and American investment firms provided capital for local traders and planters as well as efficient milling equipment. Improved technology, in turn, made for more favourable economies of scale, and improved profits led to bigger land acquisitions. A sharp increase in sugar prices in the mid-1850s, an effect of the Crimean War, boosted the industry. The opening of the Suez Canal in 1869 facilitated exports to Europe and, for the next 15 years, Britain remained a major purchaser. The Spanish colonial government's restrictions prevented other European participation in plantation development. However, since the *mestizo* class was dependent on

European merchant capital, especially in the purchase of machinery, commercial ties between the two were strong.

The population of Negros increased rapidly during the next 50 years, creating more towns and parishes. The prospects of large returns from agricultural land and the promise of jobs lured many speculators and farm workers to settle in Negros. In 1855, the opening of the port in Iloilo, Panay, facilitated the flow of people and produce. By the 1860s most migrants came from nearby Panay, which was one of the most densely settled islands in the archipelago. Immigration reached its peak in 1885. At this time business-minded Negros planters chose to hire day labourers, rather than work with a tenancy system. Thus, the sugar plantation economy was instrumental in introducing modifications to the Philippine socioeconomic structure. By the 1890s, most coastal forests of Negros had been cleared, prime land had been mostly acquired by the new *haciendado* class, and a monoculture economy was put in place.

Before the sugar boom, natives who refused to be incorporated into the colonial society made up most of the upland migration. Although these small bands of fugitives from the colonial law cleared patches of upland forest, they also served as a deterrent to extraction of forest resources by lowlanders. These 'guardians' of the forest, however, did not survive the advance of the sugar haciendas. After exhausting the more accessible areas, speculators targeted the uplands, starting the second wave of migration and settlements in the uplands, mostly richer migrants who brought with them their families and workers. The creation of more towns and establishment of more plantations in the lowlands and foothills created a reverse movement of people from the hills lured by jobs, especially during the harvest season.

By the 1890s, most Philippine sugar exports were going to the US, while the European market was taken over by sugar beet. Under American rule, beginning in 1901, tariff reductions were instituted to support the sugar industry, and free trade ties were established, making the US the most important trading partner of the Philippines until the 1970s. US colonial policy on crops exported from the Philippines up to the 1930s – notably the removal of tariffs and mutual trade preferences – supported the expansion and modernization of sugar production. As a result, more areas were cleared for sugar cultivation. A succession of US and Philippine laws modified the trading agreement but, on the whole, sustained the dependence of the island's economy on its preferential market relations with the US. The Laurel-Langley Agreement extended the preferential trade status given to Philippine sugar until 1974.[13] After 1974, production dropped by 50 per cent. In 1982, the US reinstated a Philippine sugar quota at a lower rate. US sugar quotas further declined, beginning in 1991 when the Philippine Senate rejected the extension of the US lease for military bases in the country.

These preferential trade agreements enjoyed by the Philippines from the beginning of American rule up to the 1970s sustained the island's sugar economy. Profit margins fluctuated, but government loans and subsidies to the industry and the guaranteed US quota nurtured the industry. Duty-free access and generous US quotas are attributable to the interests of American corporations, which own half of the Philippine sugar industry's milling business. Conversion of land to sugar production continued up to the mid-1900s. The sugar oligarchy, which had a powerful lobby in government and whose industry leaders occupied top government positions, was able to secure government assistance and influence policies subsidizing the production and trading of sugar. For its part, the Philippines had a stake in sustaining the sugar industry, since sugar remained the country's major export until the 1970s.

Independence

While the phenomenal population growth of the 19th century was not replicated in the 20th century, population in Negros continued to increase at about the national average rate. By the 1960s the western region of the island had become an area of large-scale emigration of landless families, partly owing to harsh tenancy conditions in the sugar haciendas. Poor Negrenses went to Metro-Manila and other cities to work as household help and factory workers. Landless farmers also sought escape from hacienda bondage by becoming *kaingineros* (shifting cultivators) or workers in the logging industry, adding to the upland migration.

Sugar cane production has remained largely inefficient and suffers from low productivity. Production increases from 1850 through the 1970s can be largely attributed to increased areas planted, rather than improvements in productivity. Production decreases manifested in later decades can be attributed, on the other hand, to non-planting due to low world market prices and market disruptions.[14] In the 1970s, one quarter of the total land area of Negros Occidental was still planted to sugar. Today 76 per cent of the agricultural land in Negros Occidental is planted in sugar. In northern Negros, some 55 per cent of cultivated lands are devoted to sugar. On the plains of western Negros, about 41 per cent of cultivated area is devoted to sugar, producing 40 per cent of total Philippine export sugar.

In Negros Oriental, the level areas between coastal and mountainous areas are densely populated and intensely cultivated for corn, rice, coconut, cotton, banana and sugar cane production. On the whole, however, there is less arable land on this part of the island. Interior areas are rugged and mountainous. Careless logging and shifting cultivation have given way to secondary forests with associated soil erosion. Steep slopes have been cleared for planting upland rice and especially corn, not so much because the land is suitable for the latter, but because it is one of the few crops that can grow under the conditions. In 1994, 65 per cent of the total employed labour force of Negros Oriental was in agriculture.

By the 1940s, the island derived a significant portion of its income from its primary forests. Rainforests thrived throughout the central mountainous region of Negros. Concessions were issued to various lumber firms. Due to weak law enforcement, illegal logging took place alongside legal cutting. By the 1960s, sparse stands of secondary, non-commercial forests characterized the northern Negrense highlands. Nonetheless, dense stands of virgin tropical forests still clothed the Negros *cordillera*, and forested areas could still be found in the more inaccessible parts of the Tablas Plateau. In Negros Oriental, much of the clearing of primary forests occurred in the early 1950s.

In post-colonial Philippines, sugar oligarchies, which constituted a powerful lobby known as the sugar bloc, dominated the national political system. Negrense sugar planters and millers continued successfully fighting for quotas, cornering credit facilities and ensuring legislation and trade agreements protecting their interests. Provincial political leadership has been limited to the circles of large plantation owners. They have successfully twisted economic and foreign policy to serve their short-term ends. To meet the US quotas, the government created the Sugar Production Council in the 1960s and provided financing for the construction of more sugar mills. The devaluation of the Philippine peso and the adoption of export-oriented policies in the 1960s proved to be profitable for agricultural exports. Coinciding with the US trade embargo on Cuba, sugar producers doubly benefited from this shift in government policy. The World Bank and Japanese interests in Philippine economic development showered the sugar industry with loans for modernization. Between 1964 and 1979, the World Bank provided US$76 million for a range of rural development programmes. The sugar industry succeeded in securing over half of this credit facility. During martial law, marketing was taken over by the government and placed under centralized trading agencies, with the rationale that the economic and social stability of the country rested on the sugar industry.

The sugar bloc has also successfully thwarted attempts at land redistribution. Their strong lobby limited the land reform programmes of the 1950s, 1960s and 1970s to rice and corn. A strong sugar-bloc lobby in Congress compromised President Aquino's Comprehensive Agrarian Reform Law. The Department of Agrarian Reform has placed 27,000 ha of sugar cane lands in Negros Oriental and 127,000 ha in Negros Occidental under land reform. In the former, 40 per cent of agrarian reform lands have been distributed, but in the latter the figure is only 26 per cent. Land ownership remains highly skewed. The 9 per cent of planters whose lands are above 50 ha own about 52 per cent of total sugar lands according to the Sugar Regulatory Agency (SRA) data for 1988–89. An estimated 140 sugar barons in north Negros and 125 in south Negros own 100 ha or more. Of the labour force, 65 per cent is in agriculture and only 10 per cent in manufacturing and construction. Manufacturing activity largely revolves around sugar milling (SRA Report).

Although the government enacted laws to enhance the welfare of sugar workers, it failed to ensure the full implementation of these laws. The government not only turned a blind eye to injustices, it also used its military might to harass sugar union leaders and members. Negros Occidental emerged as one of the most impoverished and insurgency-prone areas in the country by the 1980s. To survive, displaced sugar workers took the initiative to work on idle lands. Planters, fearful of social consequences, lent land for subsistence production to their workers during those bleak years. To a certain extent, the food crisis in the 1980s and the uncertainties in the world market prepared the ground for diversification efforts and some voluntary land transfer.

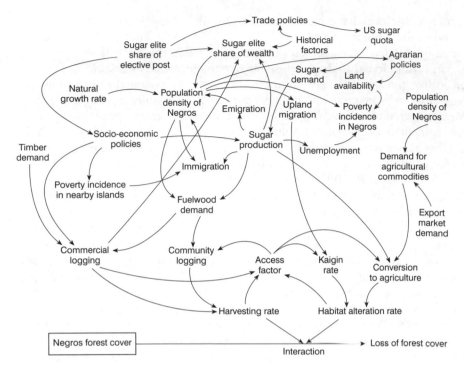

Figure 13.4 *Causal Loop Diagram for Forest Cover in Negros*

In the mid-1980s, difficulty in getting crop loans and the economic collapse faced by the whole nation, in view of the upsurge in the anti-Marcos protests, prompted many sugar planters to convert their lands to other uses, notably prawn farming. Japanese financiers lent money and expertise to Negrense entrepreneurs, making the venture possible. Coastal sugar lands were converted to capital-intensive prawn ponds and hatcheries. Between 1984 and 1994, agricultural lands declined by almost 12 per cent while fish pond areas grew by almost 120 per cent. However, the profitability of prawn production has declined as prawn farming expanded elsewhere in South-East Asia. Only the most efficient producers have survived.

The major causes of environmental degradation are clearly rooted in the historical factors that converted the island, particularly the province of Negros Occidental, into a monocrop sugar economy. This monocrop character makes the Negros case distinct from the rest of the Philippine archipelago's island ecosystems. Exponential increases in cultivated land and population beginning in the late 19th century led to deforestation and the consequent biodiversity loss. In the 20th century, the encouragement of commercial logging boosted destruction of forest cover. Extensive agricultural exploitation of the island has, in addition, brought about serious sedimentation problems in the mangrove forests and coral reefs. The brackish-water fish ponds created for prawn farming have been criticized for their adverse impact on the quality of the water supply and ground water.

The Negros case study contributed the following for the national model for biodiversity loss (Figure 13.4):

- The plantation economy elite dominated Negros and also wielded influence in national politics. The concentration of land and wealth in the hands of a few individuals gave them tremendous power.
- A politically powerful group of landowners resisted popular calls for agrarian reform.
- The fluctuations in the fortunes of the sugar industry resulted in higher poverty incidence in Negros, which induced migration to the uplands.
- The US sugar quota resulted in loss of forest.
- Strong international demand for timber also influenced the loss of forest cover.

LOCAL CONTEXT: PALAWAN

In Palawan, forests still cover 54 per cent of the total land area and, as a result, it is one of the most important regions for conservation of biodiversity. There are a variety of reasons why Palawan survived the spasm of deforestation in the Philippines. First, the Spanish influence in Palawan was minimal compared to other parts of the Philippines. Spanish rule did not go much beyond the islands of Northern Palawan. Palawan was never reached by the *encomienda* (land grant) system of the Spanish colonial period and has had no large plantations. An economically and politically powerful landed gentry did not take root in the island in any significant way.

Second, Palawan did not attract migrants until the first half of the 20th century. The location of the national penitentiary and the leper colony on the island, coupled with the prevalence of malaria, were some of the reasons for the lack of population 'pull' in Palawan. In 1990 the province's population density was 35 persons per km^2, compared to the national average of 202. Today, however, Palawan has the highest rate of immigration in the country. It was one of the chosen sites for settlement of the excess populations of the other islands. The population of Palawan increased from 35,000 in 1903 to 627,000 in 1995.

Third, environmentalism overtook the development process and settlement of Palawan. After the revolution of 1986, civil society became a significant force in Philippine politics. Conservation investments have given priority to Palawan, and the island has become the primary target of tourism investments. With tourism, concern about the environment of Palawan was heightened, and advocacy for its conservation increased. However, the reckless development of resorts, together with the exploitation of mineral resources and the high rate of immigration, endanger the island's natural wealth and beauty. Intense awareness of these threats led to the formulation of the SEP and to the organization of a multi-agency Palawan Council for Sustainable Development.

The Legacy of Spanish and American Rule

When the Spaniards began their colonization of the Philippine archipelago in 1565, indigenous groups – the Tagbanua, Batak and Palawan – and Muslim settlers inhabited the islands. These people lived by shifting cultivation, raising animals and gathering wild tubers, fruits, honey, birds' nests, molluscs and numerous other forest and sea products. By the 1570s the Spaniards were collecting tribute in the Calamianes and the Cuyo islands of Palawan. Efforts to relocate the natives to towns were not initially successful and, while the number of converts to Christianity seemed to indicate effective colonization, the Spaniards did not really change the natives of Palawan.

Before the Spaniards came, and throughout most of the period of Spanish occupation, the territories of Palawan were under the influence of Muslim peoples from Borneo and Sulu. This influence persisted in south and central Palawan into the second half of the 19th century. Muslim attacks continued until 1886. The Spaniards saw Palawan as the key to the Philippine archipelago and quite suitable as a military port. They established their capital at Puerto Princesa which, by 1883, had developed into a small colonial town with over 1000 inhabitants, primarily local soldiers and deportees and migrants from other islands. Migrants came from all over the archipelago and established such cash crops as sugar cane and coconut, as well as fruit trees and cattle. The Spaniards held the most land. With the outbreak of the country's revolution against Spain in 1896, Palawan became a place of exile and captured revolutionaries increased the ranks of the deportees. These same deportees then successfully revolted against the Spanish on Palawan.

During the period of American occupation, Palawan's largest exports were timber and secondary forest products, including rattan, tanbark, nigue, almaciga and beeswax. Planting of coconuts and abaca continued and new crops, including maguey and rubber, were tried. While it was reported in 1907 that there was a satisfactory increase in the amount of land cultivated over the previous years, there was also a regret that 'many thousands of acres of rich level land in Palawan are lying idle for lack of inhabitants to occupy and cultivate them'. Such regrets consistently failed to mention the fact of long-standing tribal habitation.

Palawan's frontier character influenced the design of American resettlement policies. The Americans established sites for a leper colony in 1902 and a penal colony in 1904. They established a reservation, with an industrial school, for the Tagbanua at Aborlan, encouraging them to settle nearby. The Palawan were to be persuaded to come down to the coast by the establishment of government trading posts. Puerto Princesa continued to function as a military garrison. The Muslim residents, seen as a problem, were resettled in the south-eastern coast by force.

Migration played a big role in the development of Palawan. Before 1900, people from Cuyo and other islands migrated to Palawan island. Migration started as a seasonal farming activity, but as opportunities in Cuyo became scarcer, population density increased and more attractive farming opportunities were perceived in Palawan, families settled on the Palawan mainland. The Cuyunons were shifting-cultivators. Migrants of more recent times also came in search of agricultural land and the opportunities offered by Palawan's natural resources.

Independence

Starting 40 years ago, migrants from all other regions in the country seeking better livelihood opportunities headed for Palawan. After the Second World War, migrants streamed into Palawan. A settlement area in south-central Palawan covering 24,000 ha was established in 1950 to accommodate settlers from Central Luzon, who were displaced by insurgency or were leaving other densely populated areas of the country. The Cuyunon, Agutaya, Cagayanon and Muslims were the first to be resettled. These populations were then pushed further up the mountain slopes. The experience of the Tagbanua displacement from 1900 to 1980 by various government projects and corporate activities is illustrative; the results have been disastrous to human life, cultural traditions and the environment (Fernandez, 1997). People also came with the logging and mining companies in the 1960s and 1970s and, more recently, with the tourism industry. Migration has accounted for about half of the population growth. Population increased from 106,000 in 1948 to 320,000 in 1980. By 1995, it had reached 627,000.

In the 1960s and the 1970s, there was a heavy influx of development corporations and agribusiness companies into Palawan, each staking claim to large areas. American, Japanese and, later, multinational companies engaged in logging and mining. Claims for logging, mining, pasture, fishing and corporate farming rights, if plotted out on a map, would indicate that corporations have claimed the island of Palawan twice over. In the 1970s and 1980s, politically influential individuals were able to obtain concessions to large tracts of forest in Palawan. However, successful advocacy by environmental groups led to a total ban on logging on the island. In fact, environmentalism has overtaken the development process and settlement of Palawan.

Palawan prides itself on being the only province with a SEP enacted into law. The SEP has been adopted as a comprehensive framework to guide local governments and national government agencies involved in development. The SEP calls for the sustainable development of Palawan through improvement in the quality of life of present and future generations. Development will be characterized by ecological viability; social acceptability and an integrated approach.

The main strategy of the SEP is the establishment of an Environmentally Critical Areas Network (ECAN). ECAN is a graduated system of protection and development control over the whole of Palawan, including tribal lands, forests, mines, agricultural areas, settlement areas, small islands, mangroves, coral reefs, seagrass beds and the surrounding sea. The SEP will also provide for the management of resources outside ECAN, including coastal resources, catchment areas, timber and mines, lowland development, settlement areas and tourism. In addition, a total commercial logging moratorium was declared in Palawan in 1992. All timber licence agreements are suspended and other private permits are disallowed until ECAN has been fully delineated. With all these policy safeguards, the island of Palawan should have a much better chance of conserving its biodiversity. Environmental awareness has risen dramatically, with substantial impacts on policy:

> *A principal reason for changing local attitudes and practices in Palawan is the increasing vigor with which international and Philippine non-government organizations (NGOs), environmental and socially conscious in orientation, are attempting to nudge government development planning and everyday economic behavior in the direction of greater ecological sustainability. An impressive array of international NGOs and other funding agencies concerned with environmental protection and the well-being of local peoples, often indigenous peoples, is today represented in Palawan. More impressive still is the coterie of local NGOs that have grown up in the last ten years...By some counts more than one hundred NGOs now operate in Palawan.*
>
> *...In particular, these initiatives seek to turn over to the indigenous people themselves the legal management of the concessionary rights to these resources [copal and rattan] – rights that heretofore have been in the hands of outside financiers, who presumably had less interest than local residents in exploiting these resources in sustainable fashion...At a more general level... NGOs have also had significant impacts on government policy. Their efforts, for example, led to a recent total commercial logging moratorium in the province, a recent ban on the live fish trade, and the formation of...a civilian watchdog group funded by the provincial government to monitor and report illegal logging, illegal wildlife trading, and the like. There is already local talk about Palawan's environmental movement being a model for the Asian region...* (Eder and Fernandez, 1996).

Current Conditions

Palawan remains predominantly an agricultural province, producing rice, corn, copra and cashew in surplus. About three quarters of its annual fish production, or 72,000 tonnes, supplies Metro-Manila. More than 36,000 farmers, 11,000 municipal fishermen and 440 commercial fishing operators make their living on Palawan. Exports include marine and aquaculture products, gifts and toys, houseware, furniture and wood products, oil, chrome, nickel and silica sand. Its natural parks – St Paul Subterranean River, El Nido Marine Park and Tubbataha Reef – attract a growing number of local and foreign tourists.

In 1966 agricultural land occupied barely 5 per cent of the total land area. By 1995 it accounted for 16 per cent of the total land area – about 245,400 ha. Palawan's medium-term development plan (1996–2000) identified 455,000 ha (30 per cent of total land area) as potential agricultural land. Between 1991 and 1995 virgin forests were disappearing at an average rate of over 10,000 ha annually, primarily because of agricultural development and land settlement. Cultivated areas and pasture areas grew at an average of 2,750 ha per year. Most of these were cleared from the forests in small patches, except for the government land settlement projects and penal colonies. The increasing conversion of forest to agriculture could also have been due to the unsuitability of the lowlands for agriculture and to the fact that the indigenous communities were displaced by the lowland migrants.

Although called dipterocarp forests, Palawan forests do not have the usual species composition of such forests. Apitong (*Dipterocarpus grandiflorus*) is practically the only dipterocarp species present. Together with narra (*Pterocarpus indicus*) and ipil (*Intsia bijuga*) it is used for local and export furniture markets. Moreover, most of the apitong-rich forests in Palawan have already been logged over (Zamora, 1980). The remaining old-growth dipterocarp forests are rather heterogeneous, and the majority of commercial species are non-dipterocarp hardwoods (DENR, 1990). Commercial logging in Palawan started in the 1960s. Products were used locally as well as exported to Japan. Timber licence agreements issued for commercial logging limit the area and the volume that can be logged by the licence holder. In the 1970s, licences could be cancelled if production fell below 50 per cent of the annual allowable cut. The policy clearly encouraged cutting of trees, especially when the allowable cut was set at a relatively high level. Other important Palawan forest products with world markets are Manila copal, used in the manufacture of varnish, and various kinds of rattan used in the manufacture of furniture.

In the 1960s and 1970s government policies encouraged the expansion of aquaculture. In the 1980s, however, a ban on further conversion of mangroves to fish ponds was imposed. Yet some mangroves are still being converted into fish ponds, despite the ban. At the national level, mangrove area decreased by 3000 ha per year from 1918 to 1970 and by 3700 ha from 1980 to 1991, a decline that parallels the increase in the fish pond area (White, 1987). However, an aerial survey of mangroves in Palawan showed very little degradation in comparison with other islands.

The Philippines still has the most extensive coral reef system in the world – an area of 27,000 km^2. The largest area, about 10,200 km^2, is located in Palawan (Fernandez, 1997). Concerns have been raised about the degradation of coral reefs. Dynamite and cyanide fishing are the main causes of coral reef destruction, along with ineffective management for conservation and protection. The local government has undertaken some efforts to prevent further coral loss. In 1993, the Palawan provincial government imposed a five-year ban on coral fishing in the province. Also in 1993 the Puerto Princesa city government prohibited the shipment of live fish and lobster outside the provincial capital. The Supreme Court has upheld both actions, dismissing a suit brought by a group of fishermen.

Palawan is now engaged in mainstream development, and its natural resources are consequently being substantially reduced. The loss of biodiversity as measured by the indicators – forest, mangroves, coral reefs – can be

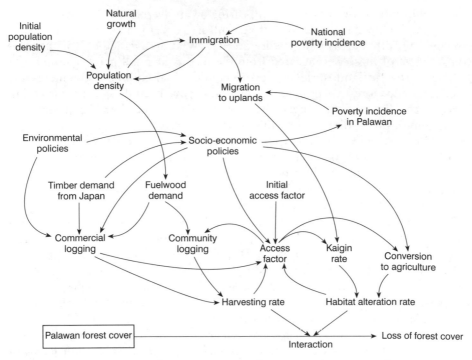

Figure 13.5 *Causal Loop Diagram for Forest Cover in Palawan*

traced mainly to the increase in population. The causal loop for the loss of forest cover in Palawan (Figure 13.5) identifies crucial variables, namely the low initial population density and access factor, immigration and environmental and socioeconomic policies. Low population density and the low population pull of Palawan are the reasons why a significant fraction of its forest cover is still intact. Conspicuous by their absence are variables related to the role of the elite. Spanish influence in Palawan was minimal compared to the other parts of the Philippines. Constantly under threat of invasion by the Muslims, Palawan was a place of exile for criminals and political prisoners. Over the years, various government regimes and private companies in mining, logging and tourism built ports, airports and roads, contributing significantly to access to the biodiversity-rich areas and making immigration to the island easier. Today Palawan has the highest rate of immigration in the country.

Settlements on the island have brought a slow conversion of forests to agricultural land. People came to Palawan for the same reasons people migrated to other frontier areas in the country at earlier times. However,

> *'seen more critically, Philippine land frontiers have historically served as politically convenient "safety valves" to relieve some of the pressures caused by government inability or unwillingness to control population growth or to resolve agrarian problems in the densely populated lowlands'* (Eder and Fernandez, 1996).

As in past decades, the larger share of migrants to Palawan have been farmers. The activities of these farmers and those of the loggers are responsible for the conversion of Palawan's one-time tropical forest landscape into an agricultural one.

The Palawan case study provided the following insights for the national biodiversity loss model:

- Civil society can challenge the power of the elite. In Palawan, NGOs were able to convince the government to impose a total ban on logging.
- Under the right circumstances, an ecologically sound development plan can attract political support.
- Population growth induces migration to areas with rich biodiversity and low population densities.

NATIONAL AND INTERNATIONAL CONTEXT

At the national level, rapid population growth, in conjunction with economic policies favouring exploitation of natural resources by a wealthy minority and continued control of government policy and relations with international markets by that minority, has been the root cause of destructive use of natural resources. Current patterns of resource use are deeply rooted in the history of Spanish and American colonial rule in the Philippines.

Population

The best estimate of the population of the Philippines at the beginning of the Spanish colonial period in 1565 is 1–1.25 million. In the census of 1903, the population was recorded at 7.6 million. Today, the population is 70 million. The loss of forest cover is significantly correlated with population size, and shows a decline from 70 per cent of total land area to 20 per cent during the last century, with the most significant loss occurring between 1960 and 1990.

Policy failures in the population programme have contributed to population growth, while policy failures in resettlement and land distribution programmes for the landless have increased the environmental impacts of population growth. Land availability is affected principally by population density and agrarian reform policies. In the American period and during the first five years of the Philippine Republic, the response to high population density, poverty and landlessness in some areas was resettlement to Palawan and Mindanao. The government has never fully appreciated the seriousness of the high growth and the Catholic Church has successfully blunted efforts to establish an effective population programme. Until the administration of President Ramos, who is a Protestant, politicians did not have the resolve to oppose the Catholic Church. By the time the population issue entered the public policy arena, population growth had already gained momentum. High population densities push landless farmers to frontier areas such as the lowland forests, the coastal areas and the uplands, where they can eke out a living. These are often biodiversity-rich areas and the consequences for biodiversity of migration to these areas is serious.

Economic Factors

Commercial logging, community logging, shifting cultivation and the conversion of forest lands to agriculture are all influenced by economic policies which have penalized the rural population in the post-war period. The government overtly encouraged public and private monopolies in the major export crops, leading to the growth of landlessness and rural poverty. This naturally led to migration to frontier areas and the cities. Policies have also favoured investments in urban areas at the expense of the rural sector because of the political clout of urban areas. These urban investments attract the rural poor, which contributes further to the relative political power of urban communities. While migration to the cities reduces the flow of new migrants to the uplands, the persistence of rural poverty contributes heavily to illegal logging and timber poaching as well as opening of new frontier areas.

Economic policies from the 1960s to the 1980s contributed indirectly to biodiversity loss because they did not generate significant non-agricultural employment. Investment policy took the form of heavy implicit subsidies and market protection. Tax and tariff incentives favoured large, capital-intensive enterprises. Trade policy included a system of import licensing that bestowed lucrative profits on a few 'crony' entities. Financial policy also favoured big operations. Interest rate ceilings on loans and deposits forced banks to ration credit, which meant lending to a few trusted clients. Economic policies therefore failed to reduce poverty.

Other economic policies have contributed directly to forest cover loss, including low stumpage fees common before the 1990s. This allowed loggers huge profits that not only encouraged them to accelerate cutting but also gave them the financial clout to bribe officials to relax some conservation regulations. As world demand for timber and agricultural commodities increased in the 1970s and 1980s, the Philippines, under the corrupt martial law regime, offered large tracts of forest land under concessions without regard to environmental impact. At about the same time, the pace of corporate farming expanded and more forests were converted to agriculture. Since commercial logging and the conversion of forest land to agriculture provided increased access to the public forests, they facilitated upland migration. Commercial logging and agriculture thus served as major forces driving the rapid decline of forest cover.

From the mid-1980s to the early 1990s, foreign debt service consumed some 40 per cent of the national budget. Debt repayment is often blamed for provoking environmental degradation insofar as policies encourage the exploitation of natural resources to meet debt payments. In the Philippines, however, data do not show any correlation between the foreign debt and increased logging or agriculture. Agriculture has maintained its relative share in

GDP while forestry declined continually in importance in the 1980s and 1990s, although the latter decade was the period of ballooning debt payments. From the 100-year perspective of this study, the debt problems of the 1980s are a transient phenomenon that occurred when most of the country's forests were already degraded and so did not play an important role in biodiversity loss.

Political Factors

'Oligarchic politics' and 'feudal society' are phrases that describe the Philippines during the century under study. The elite was created by the Spanish colonial *encomienda* policy, which distributed land to those who helped conquer the country. At the beginning of the 20th century, the elite class of land-owning families was well entrenched. In fact, the elite is so deeply entrenched that, even after several wars and numerous agrarian rebellions, it still wields major influence in state policy-making. With political control in its hands, the oligarchy has pre-empted any major structural reforms. The landed elite dominated the emergent manufacturing sector, stunted the industrialization potential of the import-substitution industrialization phase in the 1950s and 1960s, and blocked the shift to export-oriented industrialization in the 1970s. They railroaded attempts at land redistribution, thus stunting the development of a domestic market needed to absorb local production. They also used their influence to divert massive state resources to traditional sectors, including sugar and coconut milling. Moreover, rather than invest in industrialization, this class was predisposed to use its agricultural surpluses for real estate speculation and consumption of luxury goods.

Despite numerous attempts since the turn of the century, particularly since 1960, agrarian reform has not had substantial success in providing land for the rural poor. The elite has maintained its hold on prime agricultural land through various loopholes in agrarian legislation, which they themselves formulated. The target set by the agrarian reform programme of 1987 is only 41 per cent accomplished after ten years. Plantation owners continue to hold on to their property, but with the threat of reform, tenure has become uncertain. The consequence is a general slow-down in investments in agriculture and the movement of underemployed farmers to the uplands in search of subsistence. In view of the rapidly increasing population, agrarian reform has had no significant impact on land availability for farmers, and it lowers the productivity of agricultural land by discouraging investments. The two principal results of agrarian policies are continuous migration to the uplands and conversion of forest to agricultural use.

The greater the share of wealth held by the elite, the more they are able to capture elective posts and hence political power. Political influence has also enabled the elite to obtain highly profitable forest concessions, enhancing their political power as well as bolstering their ability to corrupt government officials. Thus, commercial logging expanded beyond the regulatory control of government. Political factors working in synergy with the huge demand for timber from Japan were the principal drivers of commercial logging (legal and illegal) and were the main reason for the rapid decline in forest cover from the 1970s to the 1980s. The concessionaires effectively dictated forest policy.

CONCLUSIONS

For the Philippines, the very high population density of 202 persons per km^2 is undoubtedly the single most important contributor to the loss of forest and biodiversity in general. The immensity of this number becomes apparent when compared to the world average of 59 persons per km^2. Migration has been one important consequence of high population density. The movement of people is a natural response to population pressures. Areas of low density attract migrants and high densities push them away. Biodiversity-rich areas, such as lowland forest and mangrove areas, are easy targets for immigration. When these areas became unavailable, the stream of landless and unemployed sought refuge in shifting cultivation in the highlands. Within the study period, Cebu and Negros have lost their forests, whereas Palawan sustained a minimal loss, retaining 54 per cent forest cover in 1990.

The feudal political economy of the Philippines is responsible for the persistence of poverty that causes deforestation. The system was started by the Spanish colonization of the country when the *encomienda* system, which created an enduring elite class, was imposed. The American occupation of the Philippines supported the elite and did not attempt to redistribute land to landless farmers. With their wealth and education, the elite maintained their hold on political power, and with it they gained a relatively large share of land and other natural resources. This class dominated the agrarian and socio-economic policies, with the expected result of increasing their share in the national wealth while increasing the poverty of the masses.

It is interesting to note that in the provinces influenced more strongly by colonial policies, landlords are successfully resisting agrarian reform. In contrast, Palawan, which was not touched by the *encomienda* system, has already met 88 per cent of its target (Table 13.1). In Negros Occidental, which has most of the sugar plantations, agrarian reform is not proceeding as fast as in Negros Oriental. These figures provide further support to the observation that the landed rich wield tremendous political influence. With a corrupt bureaucracy it is not difficult for those with the means to flout the law. Because agrarian reform has been ineffective, the requirements of a growing population for food are met more by agricultural expansion than by increasing efficiency or by the introduction of new technologies.

Some issues arise from a comparison of the three island cases. First, we know that some islands were already severely deforested before the beginning of the study period. For instance, in Cebu, the early Spanish conquerors already noted that there were not many trees on the island. A detailed study of Cebu could yield insight into forces other than the current political economy that could lead to total deforestation. Cebu also presents an interesting case of the urbanization process. Second, because of the significance that we have ascribed to the political economy, Negros is a good case study for this feature

Table 13.1 *Lands Distributed through Agrarian Reform, 1986–96*

	Target, 1987 (hectares)	Accomplished, 1996 (%)	Balance (%)
Phillippines	4,428,357	59	41
Palawan	39,666	88	12
Negros Occidental	272,356	26	74
Negros Oriental	118,934	40	60
Cebu	22,905	39	61

Source: Planning Service, Department of Agrarian Reforms

of the model. An elite has emerged out of a single industry – sugar. The conversion of public forests into sugar lands, and the increasing demand for sugar at the beginning of the 20th century, made the elite of Negros very wealthy and politically powerful. It is also interesting that the industry is linked not only to national politics but also to US colonial and trade policies. Negros is also a good place to look at massive land conversion to support a monocrop economy. Third, environmental activism has been on the rise in the Philippines since the early 1980s. As demonstrated in Palawan, environmental activism can play a role in changing policies when the environmental lobby acts as a counter-force to the elite. As result of the work of various organizations, logging was banned in Palawan. Furthermore, Palawan is the only province with national legislation for a strategic environmental plan. Yet even with strong clamour from planners and environmentalists, there is no specific law on land use for the Philippines.

Economic policies that promote logging; conversion of forest land to agriculture; high poverty incidence in the rural areas; under-valuation of forest resources; and migration to upland and rural areas, are all important to the loss of forest cover. Although logging has diminished in importance since the 1970s, its effects on the remaining forest cover continue to snowball because of the access factor. Similarly, the failure of economic policy to reduce the absolute number of the rural poor encourages shifting cultivation. Even if commercial logging were to stop today, the loss of forest cover will continue until most of it is removed, since the large number of rural poor and access to the remaining forests also drive deforestation.

RECOMMENDATIONS

- Population Growth. The burgeoning population of the Philippines results in the invasion of biodiversity-rich areas. The slow decline in Philippine fertility levels compared to those of its neighbours can be traced to low levels of contraceptive use. The Catholic Church continues to be vigilant in its fight against artificial birth control. Thus, despite the strong latent demand for family planning services, access to such services remains a problem because both the national and local leadership are afraid to incur the ire of the Church. Under the Ramos government, the population programme is addressing such issues as universal access to family planning information and services, especially for poor families and marginalized communities; community-managed services for family planning; closer linkage and broad participation of non-governmental, private and government organizations; and more sustainable and effective programmes run by local governments. These efforts need to be strengthened.

- Land Distribution. Localized pressure on biodiversity will continue unless land distribution issues, as well as population growth, are addressed. A more even distribution of land would be supportive of biodiversity objectives as well as socioeconomic and equity objectives. An ambitious land reform programme was launched in 1988 but has encountereed problems. This land reform should be completed swiftly, since slow implementation creates uncertainty of tenure and leads to faster degradation.

- Poverty and Inequality. Poverty and inequality are important national concerns, independent of their negative effects on biodiversity. Studies of Philippine poverty show that policies and programmes that support overall growth, such as improvements in rural infrastructure, reduce poverty more than those that try to tilt market forces in favour of the poor, such as by price controls and food subsidies. There is room, however, for using market-based incentives to induce the upland poor to support environmental objectives. A new social forestry programme, for example, has the potential to involve upland communities in forestry conservation, and a community-based resource management programme, if properly designed, also has great potential. Careful design, decentralization and devolution of such programmes will enhance their chances of success.

- Market and Policy Failures. The government has failed to apply sufficient charges on logging activities – it has not been 'setting the prices right'. Huge surpluses accruing to private loggers have encouraged them to cut timber at rates higher than the social optimum, a problem exacerbated by uncertainty in tenure. The logger who expects to lose his concession in a few years is apt to cut the trees faster and is discouraged from engaging in reforestation. Stumpage fees and other forest charges were raised in the early 1990s, but the change may have come too late. Initiatives for eco-labelling could help, since under such schemes importing countries would become partners in directly monitoring the Philippine environment.

    One pricing issue seldom mentioned in the literature on deforestation is the high discount rate applied to public investments, which places environmental projects with long gestation periods at a disadvantage. Different criteria should be developed for such environmental projects to make them financially viable.

- Political Economy. The increasing political influence of civil society is a potential counterforce to neutralize the political power of the elite. Civil society should go beyond environmental advocacy and attempt to capture elective posts.

Chapter 14

Tanzania: Rufiji, Ruvu and Wami Mangroves

Research team: The research team was composed of the team leader
and overall research coordinator *Dr K A Kulindwa*, *Dr H Sosovele*
(sociologist) and *Dr Y D Mgaya* (marine biologist). *Mr A S Kapele*,
Ms Merenciana Taratibu, *Mr Mathew Mwamsamali*, *Mr Jonathan
Kabigumila* and *Mr Henry Ndangalasi* (University of Dar es Salaam)
were assistants

Summary: **In the mangrove forests of Tanzania's river deltas, poverty
and isolation drive degradation of the local natural resources.
Persistent conflicts among government policies, failure to enforce
environmental laws and centralization of decision-making about
resource management aggravate the impacts of poverty.**

The mangrove forests of Tanzania (Figure 14.1) face immense pressure from both development policies oriented toward economic growth and from the subsistence needs of local people. In Bagamoyo, where the Ruvu and Wami deltas are found, tourism is taking its toll through clearing for hotel construction and opening of beaches, while illegal charcoal making and salt making also threaten the mangroves. In the Rufiji delta, home to the largest mangrove forest in the whole of East Africa, threats to biodiversity come from as far away as New York: the government has accepted a proposed multimillion-dollar private prawn farming project to be located in the delta area. Subsistence farming and private trading of mangrove poles, mostly illegal, are currently causing considerable damage and decline of mangrove forest in the delta.

In their heyday during the colonial era, Bagamoyo and Rufiji were centres of civilization in the coastal areas of Tanzania. Then bustling towns, they were points of trade between the Arab and Far East countries. Major commodities traded included mangrove poles, logs and tree bark, which were exported to those countries for use in house construction and boat building and for making tanning material. These trade links have since disappeared and the traditional uses of these products changed, overtaken by technological advances. Today, poor management of mangrove resources is leading to biodiversity loss in these deltas. Numerous national policies are either being enacted or reviewed to address needs for sustainable development. However, conflicts often occur among government ministries, departments and individuals. These may be administrative, political, or even social, all pertaining to the use of mangrove resources or mangrove areas.

The Rufiji, Ruvu and Wami deltas provide diverse natural resources and food for human beings and other species. Environmental decline in these deltas, however, is also high, resulting in economic, social, ecological and cultural impacts. The livelihood and culture of the local people will be endangered if mangrove resources are further depleted. The level of destruction is high in Ruvu delta compared to the Rufiji and Wami deltas, and is attributable to differences in enforcement practices and the size of the mangrove forests. However, the driving forces that threaten biodiversity in the three deltas are similar.

DESCRIPTION OF THE STUDY AREAS

The study area has a hot and humid coastal climate with temperatures ranging between 25°C and 35°C. Temperatures are highest between December and April. Two monsoon winds, the north-east and south-east monsoons, affect the climate. The rainy season is from March to May, with short intermittent rains between October and December. Annual rainfall exceeds 1000 mm.

The coastal region falls within the coastal forest and thicket zone, one of six major ecological zones of Tanzania (Stuart et al, 1990; Mwalyosi and Kayera, 1995). The total forest area in the region is about 2.5 million ha, of which about 370,000 ha are protected and the rest are open public forest

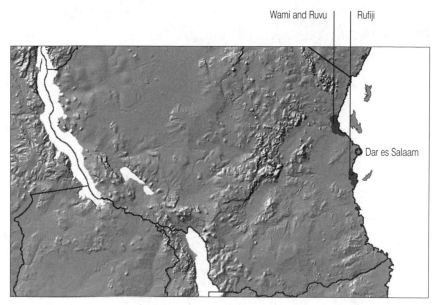

Figure 14.1 *Map of Tanzania Showing Location of the Study Areas*

(United Republic of Tanzania, 1997b). The soils in this ecological zone have poor moisture-holding capacity, which results in high runoff. There are a number of endemic species, including the blue dwarf gecko (*Lygodactylus williamsi*) (Mwalyosi and Kayera, 1995).

The Ruvu delta is located about 67 km north-east of Dar es Salaam, with its catchment area in the Uluguru Mountains in Morogoro Region. The Wami delta, about 90 km from Dar es Salaam, has its sources in the Kaguru Mountains and flows to the south-east across the Mkata Plains to the Indian Ocean. The Rufiji delta is located about 200 km south of Dar es Salaam. Nine major tributaries drain its basin, which extends for about 177,000 km^2 and covers roughly 20 per cent of Tanzania (Semesi, 1991; Rufiji Basin Development Authority, 1981). There are some 43 islands in the delta (Figures 14.2 and 14.3).

The three deltas are rich in biological diversity. Most notable are the mangrove forests, macro-invertebrates and fish. An inventory carried out in 1989 shows that the mangroves of mainland Tanzania cover about 115,500 ha (Semesi, 1991). The Rufiji delta alone covers about 53,000 ha (40 per cent of total). Eight species of mangroves are found in these deltas: *Avicennia marina, Bruguiera gymnorrhiza, Heritiera littoralis, Ceriops tagal, Lumnitzera racemosa, Rhizophora mucronata, Sonneratia alba* and *Xylocarpus granatum*. Mangroves protect the coastline against destructive waves and enhance water quality in coastal streams and estuaries. They also retain sediments and nutrients, provide habitat for fish and supply forest and wildlife resources (Mwalyosi and Kayera, 1995).

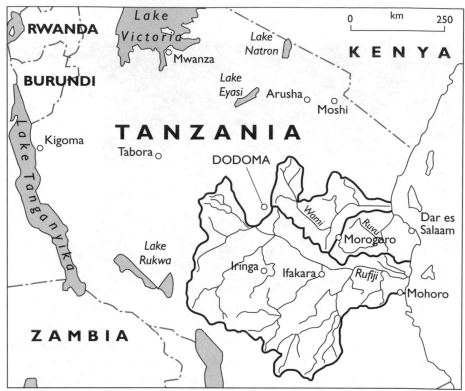

Figure 14.2 *Catchment Areas of the Wami, Ruvu and Rufiji Rivers*

Crocodiles, hippopotamuses, monkeys and many birds, such as kingfishers, herons, egrets and waders, live in the deltas. The most common fish species include *Hilsa kelee*, *Liza macrolepis*, *Chanos chanos* and *Thryssa spp*. Crustaceans include *Scylla serrata*, hermit crabs and prawns. The Rufiji delta is an important prawn-fishing ground for Tanzania. Molluscs include *Saccostrea cucullata*, *Terebralia palustris*, *Cerithidea decollata* and *Strombus spp*. Insects such as wasps, spiders, mosquitoes and ants are also abundant in the mangrove forest. *Lepidochelys olivacea*, a rare turtle species, nests near large river mouths in the south of Tanzania, and both it and other types of turtles visit mangroves (Mwalyosi and Kayera, 1995).

The land in the deltas is largely used for farming, as forest reserve, for harvesting of forest products (for charcoal, poles and timber), for prawn farming, fishing and salt making. More people live in the Rufiji delta than in the other deltas; seasonal settlements are used by charcoal makers in the Ruvu delta.

Fishermen complain that fish catches are declining sharply and that they have to go further out to the deep waters; they further complain that catches now consist of juvenile fish, a further indication of over-fishing and habitat degradation.

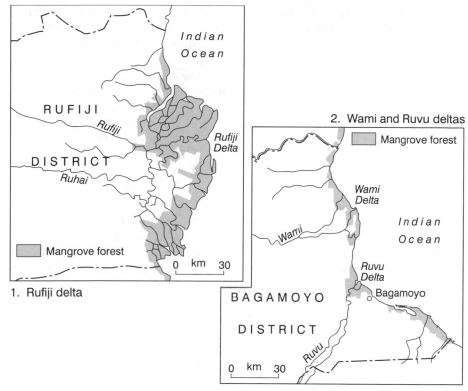

Figure 14.3 *The Wami, Ruvu and Rufiji Deltas*

Over-harvesting of construction poles, firewood, charcoal and timber for furniture and boat-building threaten the mangrove ecosystem. Products from the mangroves such as poles and thick logs for boat making are no longer easily available. Other threats include clear cutting for agricultural expansion, salt making, urban development, construction of tourist hotels, creation of prawn farms, siltation from upper catchment areas and poor fishing techniques, such as the use of dynamite and poison. In addition, the burning of coral for the production of lime, which is very common in Bagamoyo, threatens the stability of the shoreline. This practice destroys the reef and the protective belt of mangrove forests (Bryceson, 1981; Mitzlaff, 1989; UNEP, 1989).

RESEARCH METHODOLOGY

In this study we hypothesize that biodiversity loss is a result of direct, or local, and indirect driving forces working together in complex combinations. The loss of biodiversity in mangrove forests occurs due to actions and activities triggered by social, political and economic factors at the national level. The social factors include social policies, class structure, social participation in decision-making and implementation, societal values and norms, poverty, ignorance and greed. Political and institutional factors also play an important role in the management of resources. Coordination among different sectors using common resources, and conflict resolution, are major issues. Economic factors include adjustment policies such as market liberalization, privatization and fiscal and monetary policies. The effects of these policies filter down to the local level through economic instruments such as taxation, subsidy removal, commodity prices and exchange rates. The national level factors are in turn influenced by external global factors, which put pressure on local situations economically, socially and politically. These factors include world commodity markets and international financial institutions.

Direct causes of biodiversity loss are those associated with the use of natural resources at the local level. These include settlements, smallholder agriculture, harvesting of fuelwood and building materials, salt making, aquaculture and fishing, all of which may have direct ecological impacts on terrestrial and aquatic environments. Local people interfere with natural processes in the mangrove forests through fishing and farming. Pressure on these resources may be exacerbated by local population increase and by migration. To understand the dynamics of these interactions, questions were asked concerning the motives for use of the natural resources, resource-use practices and the enabling and inhibiting factors.

The indirect causes are identified as the cultural, economic, ecological, political and legal factors found at the national and global levels. These play a major role in shaping the local environment or context in which various motives for resource use develop.

The mangrove areas were chosen for this study because of their rich biodiversity. The three deltas provide a good case for comparison, since they have significant differences in terms of their use and hence in the driving forces of biodiversity loss. The Rufiji delta site was also chosen because of the unfolding of a proposed large-scale prawn farming project. This project illustrates the complexity of the interplay among various actors with conflicting motives and objectives.

The study made use of both primary and secondary data sources. Primary data were collected from field surveys in villages in the Rufiji and Bagamoyo Districts near the mangrove areas. These villages were chosen with the assistance of district government officers. A representative sample of respondents was chosen through random sampling. In addition to the interviews and the observations of the research team, physical surveys of the activities taking place in the study area were conducted to facilitate understanding of the situation and also to cross-check the information provided by the respondents. Data collection techniques included structured questionnaires, interviews using a list of leading questions, focus group discussions, physical surveys and the use of informants, especially old people who have a historical perspective.

Secondary data were obtained from institutions such as the University of Dar es Salaam, Bureau of Statistics, Ministry of Natural Resources and Tourism (MNRT), Rufiji Basin Development Authority (RUBADA), National

Environmental Management Council (NEMC) and the Department of Environment in the Vice President's Office. More ecological data are needed to ascertain the trends. Some of the information obtained from the field interviews could not be cross-checked, particularly that pertaining to management and use of mangrove resources from the colonial era through the 1980s, due to lack of records.

Findings from this study open up many interesting questions and should stimulate further inquiry into the complex processes involved in biodiversity loss. Apart from natural processes in the deltas, such as rivers changing courses, more complex relationships among individuals, institutions and government ministries pose a formidable challenge to researchers to understand and resolve.

LOCAL CONTEXT

Population and Settlement

Several theories have emerged that explain the impact of population on the use of natural resources.[1] Local population growth may directly affect use of resources and influence the rate of habitat change. Although the relationship between population and biodiversity loss is complicated, the use of a variety of indicators makes it possible to explain the effect of population growth on natural resources. For example, it is evident that countries with high population densities have converted relatively more land to agricultural use.

It is tempting to follow this line of argument to explain biodiversity loss in the deltas. However, due to the paucity of data on population trends, one must be careful with the conclusions. Data collected from the study area suggest different population dynamics for Rufiji and Bagamoyo Districts: rapid growth for Bagamoyo and slower growth for Rufiji. The population of Bagamoyo increased from 136,000 in 1978 to 174,000 in 1988, an annual growth rate of 2.4 per cent; similarly, the population of Rufiji District grew from 135,000 in 1978 to 152,000 in 1988, an annual growth rate of 1.3 per cent (United Republic of Tanzania, 1997a). In 1988 the population in the delta area alone was 33,000 (Semesi, 1994; Fottland and Sorensen, 1996; Rufiji District Administration, 1998). Immigration is likely to cause an increase of Rufiji's population if the Rufiji prawn farming project takes off. The project proposes to employ about 7750 people when fully operational (National Environmental Management Council, 1997).[2]

However, a careful analysis of events in the study area shows that local population may have fallen over the last few decades. Many elders in the Rufiji delta remember that, between the 1950s and 1970s, the area bustled with people who flocked there to trade in mangrove poles, logs and bark, fish, cashew nuts, prawns, cotton, rice and coconut. Rufiji was one of the major outlets to Arab and Far East countries for mangrove products and timber. This market was central in linking the delta islands, including Mafia Island, and the other parts of the coastal area. Coconut and other products from Mafia passed through this market. The delta's history of interaction with various traders included Arabs, Portuguese, Germans, English and Indians who visited the East African coast. Arabs did most of the trade with the local people. Over 60 dhows docked in the delta each season to buy mangrove products for export when trade was strong. This situation began to change in 1974 when traders stopped coming from the Arab countries. Several factors contributed to the decline in trade, but the local people attribute it to political interference.[3] On the basis of this history, there is little evidence to suggest that current population pressure has been a direct cause of the loss of biodiversity in the Rufiji Delta.

Rather, what emerges is that poor management has contributed to increased depletion of mangroves. In Rufiji, the mangrove forest has passed under public, private and cooperative management. In the 1940s the Rufiji mangrove was under the management of two foreign businessmen. The forests were leased to private dealers for harvesting and management. Harvested areas were replanted and the mangrove forests flourished during that time, despite the great demand, due to good management, monitoring and control.

The system continued until 1965, when these businessmen closed the operation. From 1965 to 1987, the Department of Forestry managed the forests but various local cooperative unions and individuals harvested them haphazardly. Because management was so weak, unsustainable harvesting was common. In 1987, the government instituted a ban on mangrove harvesting that lasted until 1991, when a management plan was put in place. Therefore, it was not population pressure, but rather a management vacuum created by the departure of the two businessmen that led to over-harvesting.

The physical characteristics of the Ruvu and Wami deltas render them uninhabitable. However, access to the area is an important variable for understanding the process of biodiversity loss. Although isolated by distance and the poor quality of the roads, these deltas have been suffering pressure from the town of Bagamoyo and beyond. As noted above, the population of Bagamoyo increased at a rate of 2.4 per cent annually between 1978 and 1988. This increase is reflected in household sizes. Households in Bagamoyo average more than six people.[4] Because families are big, they exert great pressure on natural resources in providing for basic needs.

Social Dynamics

There are no distinct social classes in Bagamoyo and the Rufiji delta. Rather, groups with diverse interests, such as farmers, fishermen, wage earners and entrepreneurs, characterize the community. Most people fish, farm and harvest mangrove products for subsistence and cash needs. Both farmers and fishermen are small-scale producers, using simple tools. Women fish for small pelagic shrimp, known locally as *udavi*, near the seashore, while men fish for larger prawns and fish in deep waters. In the delta, both men and women cut and dry Phoenix palm (*ukindu*) for mat making and for sale.

While the social structure in the study area is strongly influenced by the main economic activities, religion and culture also play an important role in shaping social behaviour. Over 70 per cent of the inhabitants of Bagamoyo and the Rufiji delta are Muslims, who maintain close family ties. Other instruments for social control are statutory rules and regulations. Each village has its own government, which is responsible for the day-to-day matters of peace and order.

Despite this seemingly peaceful situation, social tension is common. In Kaole village, historical animosity, brought about by the 'master-slave' relationship between former landlords (the Arabs) and the local people, has engendered mistrust between the two groups of people. This has split the village into those who support the village government, largely made up of local inhabitants, and a splinter opposition group, which is made up of the descendants of former rulers and landlords. It is alleged that the Kaole village government has not accounted for proceeds obtained from harvested mangrove poles. Furthermore, the leadership, which is composed of many members of the same clan, is said to have overstayed their time, having been in office for the past 15 years. This leadership crisis has adversely affected the participation of the local people in protection of mangrove forest resources, as well as their day-to-day life. For example, although almost the entire population is Muslim, each of the two groups has its own mosque.

In the Rufiji delta, social divisions recently became sharper when the proposed prawn farming project was introduced to the people, dividing them into those who support it and those who are against it. Although social divisions have yet to become very serious, some collective social functions have already been affected. For example, some villagers in Mfisini and Salale villages no longer participate together in weddings or funerals because of the animosity which has been created.

This social tension in the Rufiji delta was heightened when several villagers decided to go to the High Court to sue the government over its decision to allow development of prawn farming in the delta, and in order to protect their environment and their rights. This will obviously increase animosity within the village between contending groups, as well as heighten tension between the government and the villagers. A confrontation between the government and the villagers is imminent. As a farmer in Salale village pointed out, 'The government resettled us during the seventies. We lost many of our possessions. This project intends to resettle us again. This time we are not ready to move out' (NEMC, 1997).

Socially, communities in Bagamoyo and the Rufiji deltas have changed in recent years. Formerly, girls were not given the same opportunities as boys. Now, many girls in Rufiji are reported to be attending schools and doing better than in the past. However, schools are in such bad condition that they discourage many pupils and parents alike (Box 14.1). On the economic front, a few entrepreneurs in retail trade and transportation are emerging. For example, there are an average of about six to eight dhows in each village in the Rufiji delta. Their owners trade in mangrove poles and the dhows are available for hire. However, unemployment and idleness, especially among the youth in Bagamoyo, is rampant.

Most of the people are poor. They cannot meet basic needs or improve their welfare. Incomes obtained from fishing are modest. For example, in Bagamoyo, an ordinary fisherman earns the equivalent of about US$300 per year from fishing. In the Rufiji delta average income from fishing is about US$160 per year.[5] Village governments have few sources of revenue. Most of the village leaders complain that the central government has allocated to itself all the important sources of revenue. Currently, village governments retain only about 10 per cent of all revenue collected for the District Council.

The Dar es Salaam–Kibiti–Nyamisati road in Rufiji is so bad that trade among these areas is affected, and goods from the delta are often stranded. Trade in prawns has been seriously affected, with consequences for the income of the majority of people. Also, markets for agricultural crops are unreliable. Over 70 per cent of all villagers complained about low prices for farm products and fish. Low prices were blamed on high transportation costs (30 per cent), poor transportation (58 per cent) and inadequate markets (46 per cent). Because of the inadequacy of markets and poor transportation, most farmers concentrate on cutting of mangroves for sale.

Similar problems were observed in Bagamoyo. Low prices for fish and farm products is the main complaint (82 per cent), followed by price instability. Poor transport is not such a serious problem in the surveyed villages in Bagamoyo as it is in the Rufiji delta. Bagamoyo is relatively accessible from Dar es Salaam, though during heavy rains the road is difficult. Broadly, however, factors that affect market status in Bagamoyo and Rufiji are the same, namely bad roads and poor transport, delay in receiving payments, expensive transportation, unstable prices and inadequate markets.

Resource Use and Management

In the Bagamoyo and Rufiji deltas, livelihood strategies revolve around three interrelated activities that all have direct implications for the use of natural resources: farming, fishing and cutting of mangrove poles. The usual strategy is not to specialize in any specific activity, thus reducing risk.

Three types of land tenure systems coexist in Rufiji and Bagamoyo. First, the intact mangrove forest areas are held by the government as forest reserves and managed by the Forestry and Bee-Keeping Division of the MNRT. The 'islands' of the Rufiji Delta are also legally governed as forest reserves, despite the fact that some areas are in rice fields rather than mangroves.

The second type is customary land tenure in which the clan has use rights over certain pieces of land and apportions them to clan members. About 40 per cent of the farmers in Bagamoyo and 25 per cent of the farmers in Rufiji obtained land through inheritance. Families allocated land to another 20 per cent of farmers in Rufiji and 10 per cent of farmers in Bagamoyo. Only about 8 per cent of the farmers in Bagamoyo and 3 per cent of farmers in Rufiji have purchased land.

BOX 14.1 POOR EDUCATION DELIVERY: A THREAT TO MANGROVES IN TANZANIA

Mr Muhsin Mohamed Kuchombeka, the chairman of Nyamisati sub-village, tells the story of years of frustrations resulting from poor education delivery in the delta:

'For the past 22 years, our primary schools in this side of the District had never sent any of their pupils to secondary schools. Last year (1997) we decided to set up a camp here in Nyamisati to help our children with their education. All parents contributed money, chicken, fish and everything to our children selected from various schools in the delta so that they can prepare themselves for the final exams. We also paid for the teachers who came from different schools in the delta. After intensive training, six pupils were selected to go to secondary schools. We were very happy indeed. We realized it is possible for our children to go to secondary schools. We will do the same thing this year.'

However, only three of these children were able to go; the other three did not go due to lack of fees. As Kuchombeka points out, this lack of education influences the environment in two possible ways.

'Our children are frustrated, they have resigned and lost interest in schooling because of the dismal performance of our schools in examinations, they have decided instead to cut mangrove poles so as to earn money. The government has decided to abandon us in education; our schools have not enough teachers, not enough materials; we are left like this so that our natural resources can be stolen from us without us questioning.'

The third type is village land. This land can be apportioned to individuals by the village government upon request. Thirty-five per cent of the farmers in Rufiji and 25 per cent of the farmers in Bagamoyo have obtained land in this way. The major issue regarding land in Rufiji and Bagamoyo is not ownership, but rather accessibility and quality. Farmers in Bagamoyo are concerned about the poor fertility of their lands. As regards mangrove areas, the main concern of the people in the Rufiji delta is that these areas are not accessible to them for paddy cultivation, at least not legally.

Agricultural Production

Agriculture is an important activity in both Bagamoyo and Rufiji. About 65 per cent of the people in Bagamoyo and over 70 per cent in the delta consider farming their first priority. Main crops grown include paddy rice, cassava, cashew nut, coconut, maize, banana, simsim, millet, sweet potato, fruits, vegetables and legumes. In the Rufiji delta, cultivation of rice is very important for the survival of the people, to the extent that farmers believe 'without paddy cultivation, many people would have died here'.[6] Rice is harvested twice a year in some of the areas.

Agriculture remains small in scale due to economic, social, ecological and institutional problems. Forty per cent of the farmers cultivate less than 1 ha, about 30 per cent cultivate 1 ha and 30 per cent cultivate up to 2 ha. In the Rufiji delta, farms are much smaller and fragmented. In both Bagamoyo and Rufiji, farmers stated that they expanded their farms because they needed to increase incomes, to get more yields and to be able to support big families. These responses indicate some of the driving forces behind the expansion of farms at the local level. However, in Bagamoyo, only 25 per cent of the people have increased their farm areas by about 1 ha during the last five years. Overall, about 70 per cent of the farmers in Bagamoyo and Rufiji were unable to expand their farms due to shortage of land and farm implements.

Thus, at a local level, expansion of agricultural area is a direct cause of habitat change. New farms are being opened up in the Rufiji delta although such expansion is illegal because the government has prohibited further clearing. Farmers are advised by the government to plant mangroves in their paddy farms and are allowed to cultivate paddy until the mangroves have grown up. Then the farmers must vacate the area. This policy has provoked strong criticism from the farmers. One farmer in Mfisini village said, 'We are really surprised by this government, we do not know what they are thinking about us. We are required to plant mangroves in our paddy farms, will they send us food in future?' Farmers have not been told where to go after the mangroves in their rice fields have grown up.

Some of the most crucial ecological problems for agriculture include inadequate land, inadequate fertility (for Bagamoyo), diseases (for cashew nut and coconut), vermin and pests. Likewise, agriculture causes ecological damage. Crabs found in the sediment affect rice seedlings. Farmers respond by using DDT to kill the crabs (Semesi, 1991), but it also kills other species. Farmers in the Rufiji delta continue to use DDT, perhaps due to lack of alternatives for dealing with the problem or due to ignorance of its effects. Agriculture is also affected by natural processes. For example, the Rufiji changed course some years ago, resulting in changed patterns of erosion, deposition and salt penetration into different parts of the delta. Some rice farmers reacted to these changes by clearing mangroves and introducing rice into areas that now experience less salinity (Sandlund et al, 1997).

Shifting cultivation was a major agricultural system in the Rufiji delta but has become less common as the land shortage has worsened. Under shifting cultivation, yields are initially high in a newly opened rice field in the mangroves, but decline after the third year, and the field is abandoned due to weed invasion by the seventh year (Rufiji District Administration, 1998). This practice led to clearing of mangroves every time a new field was opened. Shifting cultivation is still a threat to the mangroves despite the ban on expansion and opening of new farms in the delta.

Harvesting of Mangrove Products

Harvesting of mangrove products, especially for commercial use, is a major direct cause of biodiversity loss in the deltas because it destroys critical habitat. Mangrove products are important to the people of Rufiji Delta because, as they said, 'about 75 per cent of our life depends on mangrove. The remaining 25 per cent is divided between fishing and farming'.[7] Data on the extent of harvesting of mangrove forest products in the deltas are scanty and inconsistent, but project officials believe legal harvesting is high, and illegal harvesting is even higher. There is a management plan, but it is not followed effectively.

Harvesting of mangrove products for subsistence use is small scale (Semesi, 1991). Mangroves are harvested and used locally for boat making, including dhow ribs, rails and to a lesser extent keels, as firewood and charcoal, and for preparing fish traps. Most of the houses in Rufiji and Bagamoyo are constructed from mangrove poles. In some fish landing areas and rice farms, people live in huts built on platforms supported by mangrove poles (Semesi, 1994).

Mangrove cutting is an economic activity that provides employment for many people. For example, in the Rufiji delta, dhow construction is a thriving business, and between 60 and 100 dhows employ up to ten youths each as seamen.

Harvesting of mangrove products for firewood or charcoal is another important direct cause of the loss of biodiversity in the deltas. While firewood collection is permitted only from dead trees, commercial charcoal production involves felling trees. In Bagamoyo, charcoal makers stay in the mangrove forests temporarily to harvest these resources. Charcoal making is more widely practised in the Ruvu and Wami deltas than in Rufiji. Charcoal and firewood are sold in Zanzibar, Bagamoyo and Dar es Salaam. Charcoal making and firewood selling are also important sources of revenue and employment for most of the people in Bagamoyo.

Fishing

Estimates indicate that over 80 per cent of all prawns caught in Tanzania come from the Rufiji delta and over 90 per cent of all the catch is exported (Mwalyosi, 1990). The biggest cause of biodiversity loss in relation to fishing at a local level is poor fishing gear and practices. For example, local people in Rufiji delta use stake traps (*wando*) made from the roots of *Rhizophora mucronata*. With this technique, fishermen block the large part of a small channel by planting wooden stakes in a V-shape so that fish are stranded during low tide. This process is destructive because it affects the roots of the plant and may kill the entire plant. Also, these traps are woven together so tightly that even juvenile fish are trapped. Apart from traps, the use of fishnets with small meshes causes similar problems. This is also common in Ruvu and Wami deltas. Most fishnets available in the country are imported. Besides being of low quality, they are also prohibitively expensive for most of the fishermen who, as a result, resort to more destructive methods. These practices and technologies are not sustainable and it appears that most fishermen are not aware of the dangers of using them. A final major direct cause of the loss of fish at the local level is the involvement of big trawlers that operate where artisanal fishermen do their fishing.

Salt Making

Salt making is another important economic activity in the deltas that has direct implications for biodiversity. Mangrove areas have been cleared and replaced with solar evaporation pans for the production of salt. The size of the cleared area is not known, but in total there are more than 30 salt works in Bagamoyo. In some areas of the Rufiji delta, mangrove is used for fuelwood in the salt production process (Semesi, 1991).

NATIONAL CONTEXT

The major factor preventing rational use of natural resources in Tanzania has been the lack of integration of environmental concerns into economic policies. Economic policies have aimed at achieving economic growth largely without regard to its implications for the environment. Often, this has resulted in over-exploitation of natural resources and the loss of biodiversity. Conflicting objectives and interests in the use of delta resources among government ministries and departments, be it land for salt making or tourism, forestry or fisheries, have contributed to the loss of biodiversity in the delta areas and continue to pose threats. Bagachwa et al (1995) have indicated the negative effect of structural adjustment programmes on the environment and conclude that, if current programmes continue in the same pattern, more damage will occur to the environment in the years to come. Tanzania's new forestry policy acknowledges the importance of biodiversity conservation, but appreciation of sustainable use and management is only a recent development at the national level and has not been popularized at the local level.

Lack of coordination among various individuals and organizations has led to undesirable outcomes for the environment of the deltas. Among the objectives of the national investment promotion policy of 1992 is the maximum mobilization and use of domestic capacity. The achievement of such a goal poses significant threats to biodiversity in a situation where coordination of activities is lacking among those sharing common resources to achieve their specific goals. While the 1998 forestry policy and hence the forestry department encourage sustainable management of forests, for example, the department of fisheries under the same ministry (MNRT), has approved the prawn farming project in the Rufiji delta. This project is aimed at the economic growth objective, but it conflicts with forestry and social objectives. In some cases, inconsistency and violation of legislation mean that maximization of one objective threatens the mere existence of the other. Another case in point is a proposed shrimp hatchery in the Mafia Island Marine Park.

Land tenure issues are important in that they influence the manner in which land is used. The rules and the underlying principles of the 1923 land ordinance governed Tanzania's land tenure system until 1995.[9] Inadequate capacity to enforce the existing rules and regulations within the relevant government departments, such as the MNRT, allows illegal activities to flourish in the mangrove reserve areas. The government has established grounds for the implementation of various policies and declarations affecting resource use. Among those efforts are a national report on the implementation of Agenda 21, preparation of the National Environmental Action Programme (NEAP) and the formulation of the National Environmental Policy.

Economic and Social Development Policies

In an effort to improve the welfare of its people, the government of Tanzania has experimented with various development strategies. These strategies have frequently alienated people, rather than involving them in the desired development, because they have relied on command-and-control or top-down approaches to economic and resource management. The sustainability of these measures has always fallen short of expectation. A confrontational and patronizing relationship has persisted between the people and their government and, as a result, people have ceased to take responsibility for their own actions. Instead, they look upon the government as their provider.[10] This undesirable attitude has had detrimental effects on the sustainability of numerous projects and programmes initiated by the government.

The Ujamaa strategy (1974–76), which epitomized the Tanzanian brand of socialism, had good intentions of improving the welfare of the people of Tanzania through collectivizing them in Ujamaa villages. However, this type of development could not be sustained for long since it was too heavily dependent on foreign assistance. The strategy was also blamed for contributing to environmental degradation and hence biodiversity loss due to clearing for village settlements and farmland (United Republic of Tanzania, 1997b; Kikula and Mung'ong'o, 1992). Expenditure on social services grew rapidly while production capacity to support the growing social sector grew slowly. This poor growth was primarily due to non-performing parastatals, which turned out to be heavily dependent on government financing rather than generating revenues for the government.

In an attempt to resolve structural problems constraining the productive sector, Tanzania initiated several economic programmes. The National Economic Survival Programme (NESP) of 1981 was the first of what were to become known as Structural Adjustment Programmes (SAPs) or Economic Recovery Programmes (ERPs), which are being implemented in a number of developing countries today. The aim of the NESP was to rehabilitate the ravaged economy and restore balance in the external sector. It lasted only a year and was replaced by a three-year SAP in 1983, with similar objectives of solving structural problems and stabilizing the economy. SAP and NESP were home-grown programmes, as opposed to the subsequent Bretton Woods

Institutions' programmes known as ERP I and ERP II. A primary objective of the SAP was to improve economic performance of the public sector through introduction of incentives for increased production of goods and services for both domestic and export markets. The NESP and SAP programmes could not be fully implemented due to financial constraints arising from the need for external finance, which was not forthcoming.

Soon after the SAP ended, ERP I was introduced in 1986. This three-year programme, whose main objective was similar to the previous programmes, differed in strategies and availability of funds.[11] It aimed to establish market-economy fundamentals through measures that included decontrolling prices, removing subsidies and enhancing labour efficiency and productivity by reforming employment in the public sector. Since these programmes aimed at specific objectives of stimulating economic growth, it was no wonder that, in the course of their implementation, a lot of protests were heard concerning their adverse effects, especially on the social sector and the environment. These effects, though unintended, brought hardships on people through reduction of expenditures on education, health and agricultural and forestry extension services. ERP II (1989–92), alternatively known as the Economic and Social Action Programme (ESAP), aimed at correcting the adverse effects of its predecessor while continuing with the objectives of ERP I.

ERP I and II achieved a positive impact through increased industrial capacity use and output. The value of non-traditional exports increased by 24 per cent per annum between 1986 and 1990, and per capita income increased by 6 per cent in real terms. The objective of moving toward a market economy was slowly being realized. However, dismantling of the state marketing structure resulted in hardships to farmers in areas where private traders were unwilling to go. Trade liberalization increased environmental degradation and biodiversity loss by promoting such crops as tobacco, which result in more land being cleared. Moreover, infrastructure deterioration and poor social services delivery remained problematic (Bagachwa et al, 1995).

One of the effects of these economic programmes on the natural environment, and thus biodiversity, has been the loss of necessary funds for basic environmental services. Natural resource management, especially extension services, monitoring and enforcement of rules and regulation, is a labour-intensive activity. The instruments used by the SAP policies included removal of subsidies from government sectors, reduction of staff in government departments and freezing of employment. These measures have affected the delivery of services in the department of Forestry and Bee-Keeping in the MNRT, among others. Despite the existence of a mangrove management project, funded by the Norwegian Agency for Development Cooperation (NORAD), there are severe shortages of manpower and of funds for recurrent expenditures for daily monitoring and enforcement activities in the project area, including funds for boat fuel. This creates an environment conducive to the illegal harvesting of mangroves for charcoal making in Bagamoyo and poles in Rufiji.

Legal Issues and Enforcement

Tanzania has legal provisions for the management of almost every natural resource and several institutional authorities responsible for the implementation and enforcement of the rules. Main issues include lack of effective enforcement, low penalties for offences and a long and cumbersome procedure to enact and pass bye-laws relevant in local areas. At present, some of the penalties are low compared to the cost of the damage to the environment, and magistrates use their discretionary powers to reduce sentences further. For instance, the Fisheries Act directs that any person who possesses or uses explosives or electrical devices for the purpose of fishing will be penalized by a fine not exceeding Tshs 500,000 (US$757) or imprisonment for not less than three years. Available records from the Bagamoyo District Natural Resources Office show that, of the six fishermen arrested in 1990 in connection with dynamite fishing, two were convicted and each paid a fine of Tshs 2000 (US$3.50). It is apparent in this case that the law is loose and allows culprits to continue their illegal activities. To change this situation, the environmental awareness of magistrates must be raised. They should be made to understand and appreciate not only the value of these resources but also the importance of their ecological functions.

Due to increased control of dynamite fishing in the area, more young men and women seeking employment have moved into the lime-making business, using coral dislodged from coral reefs. Political leaders in the region applaud these young people for their creativeness and initiative in being self-reliant. To the leaders, this phenomenon diffuses the unemployment time-bomb, which the government has failed to disarm. What emerges is a serious situation that calls for immediate awareness-building for the politicians and government leaders in order to protect the environment and biodiversity

Conflicting Interests and Institutional Coordination

The study areas are characterized by dynamic and extremely complex ecosystems with a variety of natural resources. Although several institutions have been established to deal with these resources, management has been poor. A key issue is the lack of effective coordination among the various institutions involved. No authority exists to reconcile conflicting interests among government institutions, such as the issue of licences for fishing, harvesting mangroves and salt making, or land titles. These may concern the Division of Forestry, the Division of Lands, the Division of Fisheries, the Ministry of Water and the Ministry of Energy and Minerals simultaneously. In the mangrove area, there are institutions responsible for mining (mineral prospecting and salt making), land use (Ministry of Lands), forestry (MNRT), environment (Vice President's Office), and under local governments (represented by the newly reestablished Ministry of Local Government). The activities guided by policies and regulations from these institutions have often conflicted with each other due to different immediate objectives and lack of harmonization or coordination of policies needed to achieve the much wider objective of sustainability. To take another example, the Forest Ordinance of 1957 has governed all forest-related matters. However, despite the ban on cutting of mangroves in Bagamoyo, licences for the establishment of salt pans continue to be issued. During the 1994–97 period of implementation of the mangrove project, it is reported that the land and mineral authorities continued issuing permits for salt production that involved clearing of mangroves, especially in Bagamoyo District (Ministry of Natural Resources and Tourism, 1998). The construction of tourist hotels on the beaches of Bagamoyo has contributed to clearing mangrove areas between hotels and the sea in order to improve beach access. Construction of tourist hotels in Bagamoyo is authorized by the Ministry of Lands in Dar es Salaam, while the district offices do not even collect levies for business conducted in their jurisdiction.

In Rufiji, these contradictions are even more glaring. As well as being a forest reserve, the mangrove forests of the delta are under a management project supported by substantial donor assistance (NEMC, 1997). Yet, according to the law, permits may be granted in such areas for exploration of subsurface resources such as oil. Thus, a production-sharing agreement for exploration was issued in June 1997 to an Irish company looking for oil in the delta. A second oil prospecting company, from Canada, also has a licence for prospecting in the Rufiji delta. The prawn farm is another activity granted permission to operate in the delta against technical advice and social protests. Approval of the prawn farm violates the land policy, which does not allow large tracts of land to be allocated to a single investor, and reveals the conflict between the forest and fisheries departments, both under the MNRT. Other conflicts arise between the oil prospecting companies and the prawn farming project since the oil companies expect that the prawn farming project will deny them access and possibly claim compensation if they are granted access. The impending disturbance and possible government displacement of people living in some parts of the delta is another issue that has resulted in a court case against the government. Over the long term, these contradictions may lead to loss of mangroves as the delta people lose faith and trust in the government. These people were once convinced to stop cutting down the mangroves for rice cultivation in order to conserve mangroves for their important ecological functions. Seeing the same government now supporting activities that lead to clearing of mangroves may reduce commitment to conservation activities.

Forest Policy and Management of Mangrove Forests

A new forest policy, created in 1998, goes a long way toward meeting the present challenge facing the local and global environments. Environmental protection and biodiversity conservation have received their due recognition, unlike in the previous policy, last reviewed in 1963. One of the main objectives of the new policy is to ensure ecosystem stability through conservation of forest biodiversity, water catchments and soil fertility. The policy states that new forest reserves for conservation will be established in areas of high biodiversity value and that biodiversity conservation and management will be included in the management plans for all protected forests. Involvement of communities and other stakeholders will be encouraged through joint management agreements. Biodiversity research and information dissemination will be strengthened. This policy is a great departure from the traditional forestry approach of command-and-control. In the wake of failed policing and in the face of a shortage of funds to deal with mounting challenges, people's participation in conservation is clearly seen as the most effective way to achieve the policy's goals.

The lack of capacity to enforce rules and regulations is a major issue for biodiversity conservation. Most resource-use policies have over-emphasized control and prohibitions without the means or capacity for enforcement and inadequately addressed traditional interests of the people or their involvement in the management of natural resources. The mangrove management project, which was initiated with the objective of maintaining the integrity of the mangrove ecosystem, is one example. Phase I of the project, begun in 1994–95, aimed at increasing the contribution of the mangrove ecosystem to the local and national economy through rational, sustainable use of mangrove ecosystems. In Bagamoyo, the district forestry department has a shortage of working facilities and funds for boat fuel. Yet, the project requires the officers to visit the mangrove forests frequently to monitor and enforce regulation. Due to manpower and financial shortfalls, illegal and indiscriminate harvesting is rampant in both the Ruvu and Rufiji deltas.

The district officials in Bagamoyo pointed to some factors that they thought contributed to the shortage of funds and to frustrations in monitoring and enforcement of conservation. First, frequent changes in the administrative set-up disrupt the continuity and institutional memory in natural resource management. Until 1972, natural resource management was under the department of forestry, in the central ministry. During the decentralization era, 1972 to 1984, these activities were put under the stewardship of the regional development director's office. Since 1984, the activities have been conducted under the district executive director. It is alleged that, throughout those transitions, the priority of the administration was to extract revenues from forestry resources rather than to manage them.

Second, the distribution of revenues from natural resources between the central government and the districts where the resources are found was uneven and highly unfair. The distribution of revenues is as follows: 30 per cent is taken by the treasury, the remaining 70 per cent is then distributed to all the ministry, regional and district departments. As an example, revenue between 1985 to 1995 was Tshs 70 million, while retention by the district, according to the district forest officer, was a mere Tshs 200,000 – barely 0.3 per cent of the total. Third, the much publicized decentralization has not been put into practice. Policies remain centrally planned and directed, thus complicating implementation of projects and plans at the local level. Bureaucratic procedures also frustrate management efforts. Finally, political interference in matters that are purely technical is also a problem.

In fisheries too, implementation of policy guidelines is a problem. One case, pointed out by local fishermen in the study areas, was the violation of the guidelines for prawn fishing. Legal conditions include the following: big vessels for prawn fishing are supposed to fish in deep waters, and the number of these vessels is determined for each season in accordance with the capacity of prawn-breeding areas. The trawlers violate these conditions. They sometimes enter the delta area, where they come into conflict with artisanal fishermen, cutting their nets and denying them their catch. More devastating for the marine ecosystem is the fact that the trawling technique damages plants on the ocean floor and other marine creatures. This destruction changes the nature and character of the area disturbed, exacerbating biodiversity loss.

Land Tenure

Land tenure is another policy issue related to biodiversity loss. It is generally believed that lack of tenure security discourages long-term investment in land. However, security of tenure is not a guarantee that long-term investment will be undertaken or that such an investment will not cause biodiversity loss. Various development policies and programmes in the country concentrated on methods of production rather than forms of land ownership (United Republic of Tanzania, 1994). This has resulted in acute land problems and conflicts. The new land policy contains some passages that may lead to the conservation of biodiversity.[12] It states that, 'a mechanism for protecting sensitive areas will be created. Sensitive areas include water catchment areas, small islands, border areas, beaches, mountains, forests, national parks, rivers, river basins and banks, seasonal migration routes of wildlife, national heritage and areas of biodiversity'. Of particular interest is the concern raised in the policy regarding areas of multiple land uses. The Rufiji delta is such an area. Currently, there are many land users in the delta. However, no multiple land-use management system is in place. The Rufiji Environment Management Project (REMP), an IUCN-supported project, intends to work on this aspect. It is important for the responsible ministry to take a leading position while working with other stakeholders in developing this multiple land-use management system. Alongside REMP, the Tanzania Coastal Management Partnership (TCMP) has just started coordinating various programmes operating along the coastal areas of Tanzania. Together with these efforts to address better coordination and sustainable use of natural resources, a body responsible for resolving conflicts over multiple land uses should be established.

INTERNATIONAL CONTEXT

Foreign Markets and International Trade Conditions

Historically, the Arab countries of Yemen, Oman, Saudi Arabia and the Emirates provided the largest market for mangrove poles, tannin and logs.

From the 1940s, or perhaps earlier, until the early 1970s, trade boomed. During this time, trade and urban life in the deltas flourished. The elderly delta people recall that, in the early 1930s, an English trading company known as the Liverpool Company was stationed in the delta at Nyamisati, where there was a harbour. This company bought mangrove poles, logs, tannin, sisal, cotton and cashew nuts. In those days, Rufiji people had many cash crops, and they used the delta villages to get these commodities to the outside world. By 1974, the last Arab merchants were caught, suspected of trading without licences. That was the end of the 'good old days' for the delta people. Currently, the only commodities still being transported by river from the delta are mangrove poles to Zanzibar and Dar es Salaam, and coconuts and cashew nuts from Mafia Island. Other commodities are transported by road to Dar es Salaam and other markets. Cotton, sisal and cashew-nut growing have declined. Problems associated with marketing of these cash crops are the main reason for the decline.

Currently, most of the charcoal, firewood and mangrove poles harvested in these deltas are transported to Zanzibar for sale. Some mangrove poles that are transported to Zanzibar find their way to the Arab states. Although this was substantiated by several people interviewed in Zanzibar, no data were available to gauge the magnitude and significance of the trade. In Zanzibar mangrove poles are in high demand for house construction. The tourism industry is picking up and many hotels are being built on the island. Hotel construction uses a lot of mangrove, the bulk of which comes from the Rufiji delta. This mangrove trade is illegal but no regulations empower the natural resources officers in Zanzibar to seize illegally obtained mangrove poles. What they do, therefore, is to collect from the mangrove traders the duties on imported mangrove products, regardless of whether they were legally obtained or not.

International Financial Institutions

The World Bank and the IMF are among the international financial institutions influencing economic activity in Tanzania. They have facilitated development programmes with unintended adverse effects on the environment. The ERP implemented in Tanzania have aimed at stimulating economic growth through the use of various economic instruments, monetary and fiscal alike. The ERP aimed to stimulate use of the resources at the disposal of the country. What the policy did not consider was the need for a mechanism to ensure that the natural resource base, upon which this economic growth depends, was conserved to ensure sustainability. The inevitable is happening due to this omission. SAPs caused and are still causing social hardships and environmental destruction. ERP II tried to soften the harsh effects of ERP I by supporting the basic social services, but did not address the environment.

Foreign Private Investment Capital

Foreign investment is looked upon as important in facilitating economic growth through transfer of modern technology for efficient production that would not otherwise be available to the country, given the shortage of capital. Today, foreign investors are particularly important for the networking advantage they have in the world market, which is critical in Tanzania. Its position in the world market has, like most developing countries, been chronically weak because the prices of its primary products are dictated by buyers and characterized by instability and stiff competition. Tanzania has few industrial exports. In 1996, the value of industrial exports was only 16 per cent of total exports compared to 55 per cent for agricultural products, including coffee, cotton, cashew nuts, tobacco, sisal and tea. Mineral exports are rising and promise to do so for a long time. In 1996, mineral exports constituted 7 per cent of total exports, but had risen to 13 per cent by 1997, almost double the previous year. The important point is that economic growth is desirable for the betterment of the country's population. However, we have to be careful about the nature of the development for which we strive. We must avoid development that provides short-term benefits but diminishes long-term sustainability, as well as development that benefits a few but leaves the majority bearing the cost of environmental degradation.

The tourism industry is expanding rapidly in Bagamoyo. With the promised construction of a tarmac road from Dar es Salaam to Bagamoyo, a distance of about 65 km, more investment and therefore growth is expected. This expansion in Bagamoyo promises the government substantial revenue. However, it should be done in a sustainable way so as to benefit all the people concerned while maintaining the ecological balance which, to a large extent, provides the tourism value of Bagamoyo. Investors who clear mangroves to create sandy beaches and pour untreated effluent from their hotels into the ocean destabilize the ecological balance and endanger the sustainability of their businesses and development of the country in general. Likewise, the prawn farming project in Rufiji poses the same potential benefits and costs for various actors and stakeholders.

These costs and benefits should be balanced through a well-rounded analysis that integrates all sectors and stakeholders to determine the social, economic and environmental costs and benefits before any major decision is made. Environmental policy states the need for environmental impact assessments (EIAs), but the relevant act is currently being rewritten and EIA guidelines are in the process of being formulated. A few organizations insist on an EIA as a condition for engaging in activities in their areas. The Tanzania National Parks Authority, the Tanzania Electric Company and the Ngorongoro Conservation Area Authority all impose such conditions on investors. Also, some big investors are forced to undertake EIAs when they are looking for project funds.

AID, UN Agencies and Other International Organizations

The role played by international organizations in Tanzania and elsewhere in the world is well-appreciated. Their assistance serves mostly to fill the gap in terms of expertise, financial inputs and providing a wider audience for important humanitarian, conservation and developmental issues by linking the local scene with the outside world.[13] Some international bodies such as the UN organizations provide leadership in various spheres of interest to the world community. Several international organizations and agencies in Tanzania work in humanitarian assistance, development projects, capacity building and environmental matters such as biodiversity conservation.

When the government approved the prawn farming project against the advice of the NEMC, international experts and institutions such as IUCN, as well as local people, lodged numerous protests and pleas with the government. Most organizations, both local and foreign alike, opposed the size and especially the manner in which the project was to be implemented. The projected adverse effects included the loss of biodiversity through the cutting down of mangroves, ecological disturbance due to diseases and pollution, social displacement and loss of livelihoods.

The above-mentioned international institutions are financing many projects for the protection of Tanzania's natural environment. The mangrove forest management project, which is financed by NORAD, covers all the mangroves in the country and aims at maintaining ecosystem integrity and enhancing sustainable use. Other international organizations such as Irish Aid are involved in coastal zone conservation and development specifically for the Tanga region. USAID, in collaboration with the Center for Coastal Resources of the University of Rhode Island, is working with NEMC in a coordination project for integrated coastal management (TCMP). The REMP, a relatively new initiative sponsored by IUCN, has just begun work in Rufiji. A site-based project with headquarters in the Rufiji district, one of its objectives is to assess the biodiversity of the delta mangrove areas and plan for their conservation. All the above efforts and others, added to local initiatives, create a large collective effort.

Tanzania is also a signatory to the CBD, among other conventions and treaties. This convention gives Tanzania the opportunity to contribute to global initiatives for the conservation of biodiversity and makes it eligible to benefit from technology transfer, financial assistance, scientific and research cooperation and capacity building.

CONCLUSIONS

The loss of biodiversity, a loss that is both quantitative and qualitative, in the Rufiji delta and Bagamoyo is driven by strong local dependence on natural resources, particularly for cash needs. This study was unable to gauge the actual quantitative extent of biodiversity loss because of the lack of baseline

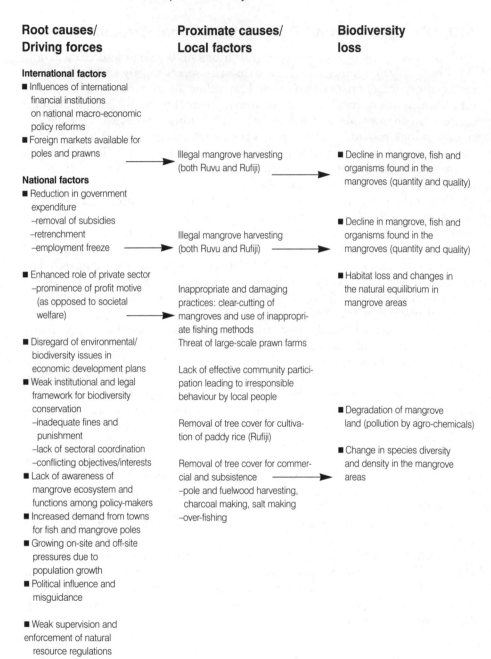

Figure 14.4 *Conceptual Model for Mangrove Biodiversity Loss in Tanzania*

data. Extinction was not observed. However, certain sizes of mangrove trees and fish are not easily available. Major direct causes such as commercial harvesting of mangroves for poles, charcoal and firewood lie behind this perceived loss of biodiversity. Expansion of rice farms is another direct cause. Similarly, salt making and construction of ponds for prawn farming in Bagamoyo leads to habitat loss in deltas (Figure 14.4)

The main influencing factors or root causes that trigger biodiversity loss in the Ruvu, Wami and Rufiji deltas can be traced to national and international policies and programmes. Commercial harvesting of mangrove poles, which is prompted by lack of alternatives and opportunities, accounts for most of the loss occurring in the deltas. Many people are involved in commercial harvesting of mangroves as a means of livelihood because other sources, such as agriculture and fishing, are inadequate and are affected by poor roads, unreliable markets and inefficient supply of equipment.

Issues related to legal and institutional frameworks as well as institutional functions constitute formidable problems. For example, the participation of local governments and the local people in the management of the mangrove forests is inadequate. Only a few villages have formed village natural resources committees, charged with sustainable management of mangroves, under the auspices of the mangrove project. Laws regarding management of forest reserves were enacted in 1957 and revised in 1997. Most of them were inadequate and outdated, and penalties did not reflect the actual value of the degraded areas. Although revised, the laws still give judges the freedom to issue lower penalties. Conflicting government policies also contribute to the loss of biodiversity in the deltas.

Increasing world demand for prawns, and liberalization of the fishing sector, have brought private fishing vessels to Tanzania's waters. International trawlers draw close to the inshore waters where small fishermen fish, denying them their opportunity to fish freely and affecting the nets they set: trawling also damages the seabed and marine organisms.

These processes are not taking place in isolation from international influences. Since 1986, Tanzania has been implementing macroeconomic policy reforms. These reforms are influenced by international financial institutions. One of the key features of the reform programmes is reduction of government expenditure and an increased role for the private sector. These policies have had the effect of diminishing the enforcement capability of the regulatory agencies. Monitoring and patrol against illegal harvesting have been critically affected. The vast mangrove area of the Rufiji delta has only three staff and one boat and often funds are lacking to buy fuel. In Ruvu delta, likewise, patrols are rare.

International influence is also seen in the role of the international private sector. The proposed Rufiji prawn farm is a case in point. This aquaculture project is likely to lead to the extensive felling of mangrove trees during the construction phase, and pose further threats of pollution and increased demand for food and poles in future as the workers begin to arrive in the delta. Increased private investment may push the destruction of the mangrove forests even further because of inappropriate government policies, which would allow large-scale prawn farming to take place in an ecologically sensitive area, and because of weak monitoring, management and law enforcement.

The future of these deltas is precarious. Assuming that the current situation and weaknesses continue, the loss of biodiversity will probably be high. Current harvesting trends are likely to continue or even increase as long as new alternatives and opportunities are not found, and as far as ineffective management regimes are still in place. New threats such as large-scale prawn farming, salt making, population growth and expanding tourism will pose further challenges in future. However if sustainable approaches are adopted, such as the Integrated Coastal Zone Management Project, then the situation will improve.

RECOMMENDATIONS

This study has identified several key factors that threaten or cause the loss of biodiversity in the Rufiji, Wami and Ruvu deltas. The following are some of the recommendations that address those key issues:

- In order to reduce biodiversity loss in the deltas, it is necessary to focus not only on management but also to provide economic alternatives and opportunities to the local communities that will discourage them from over-harvesting natural resources. This will require immediate action from the central government, because some of the alternatives, including farming and fishing, demand improvements in infrastructure. Negotiations between the central government, local authorities and the people must be undertaken to identify suitable areas for farming.

- Since fishing is affected not only by lack of fishing gear, but also by the activities of large commercial fishing vessels, the government should reassess its policies regarding permits to international fishing companies and commit itself to ensuring that all parties respect procedures.

- Not all the farmers in the deltas have access to alternative areas for farming. Therefore, farmers in some villages in the Rufiji delta should be allowed to continue to use their existing land for farming and the decision to plant mangrove trees on the farms should be reconsidered. Alternatively, if these people have to be moved, plans need to be openly discussed and known beforehand.

Although this is an issue that requires immediate attention, negotiation must be carried out among the MNRT, villagers, the Rufiji District Council and NORAD, which supports the mangrove project. These negotiations are important because the MNRT has already prohibited further expansion of farms and demands that existing farms be planted with mangrove trees.

- An inter-ministerial committee should be set up to look into all policies in order to remove overlaps and conflicting goals. While the formation of such an inter-ministerial committee will require prior approval of the government, it requires immediate attention because the damage in the deltas is already great.

- Harmonization of policies is crucial, but not sufficient, to redress the problem. Effective coordination is also required. Therefore, there should be a body responsible for coordination of activities along the coast. In the absence of such a body, and in order to avoid further costs, TCMP should coordinate resource use in the coastal areas. TCMP should be strengthened and should recommend ways of ensuring continuing sustainable use of natural resources at the end of the project life.

The framework envisaged here is that of integrated coastal zone management. Currently, several donor-funded projects operate in the coastal zone but they are not necessarily coordinated.[14] The newly formed TCMP is best placed to facilitate a cross-sectoral integration. This assessment is based on the fact that TCMP aims at supporting the efforts of the government of Tanzania in partnership with ongoing coastal management programmes working at regional and district levels, to establish an effective coastal governance system. However, since TCMP is a donor-funded project with a set life span, sustainability issues should be carefully considered and, if possible, built into the project implementation mechanism. TCMP should also look at the possibility of developing multiple land-use plans for the deltas.

Furthermore, it has been observed that many of the villagers and land users in the deltas are not fully aware of the interdependence between their activities, such as harvesting of mangrove poles, and the health of the marine environment. In many cases, people are concerned with their survival needs, and strive to meet them at any cost.

- The NEMC should take the lead in organizing awareness-raising programmes for the people of the Rufiji delta and Bagamoyo with respect to sustainable use of natural resources. This is not something new; NEMC's portfolio includes training programmes on matters of environmental conservation and sustainable resource use.

The government established the mangrove management project in the coastal areas of Tanzania without adequate consultation with the local communities. Many people in Rufiji and Bagamoyo still question the sustainability of the project and the role of bodies such as the village natural resources committees.

- The mangrove management project should foster greater participation of all those involved at the local level. However, it is also important to ensure that the sustainability of the project is considered, especially by linking the central with the local government in the project administration.
- Since this study was unable to quantify the extent of degradation or loss taking place in the deltas due to lack of baseline information, it is recom-

mended that further long-term studies be carried out in the deltas to estab-
lish baseline environmental data upon which monitoring can be based.
Follow-up studies must be carried out to establish the extent of loss.
Scientists from the University of Dar es Salaam in collaboration with the
MNRT can undertake such studies. Negotiations must be carried out with
the government in order to enlist their support for this study.

Chapter 15

Vietnam: North and Central Highlands

Research team: This case study was carried out by the Center for
Natural Resources and Environmental Studies of the Vietnam
National University, Hanoi, and coordinated by WWF.
Prof Dr Pham Binh Quyen was the project coordinator and
Prof Dr Truong Quang Hoc was the project secretary. Team
members were *Vu Minh Hoa, Dr Nguyen Van San, Vo Thanh Son,
Pham Viet Hung, Prof Dr Le Vu Khoi, Prof Dr Le Dien Duc,
Hoang Van Thang, Chad Ovel, Dr Hoang Minh Khien, Dr Do Minh
Duc, Dr Truong Quang Hai, Nguyen Van Quyet* and *Dr Nguyen
Duc Thinh.* Members of the advisory committee were *Prof Dr Vo
Quy, Prof Dr Le Thac Can* and *Prof Dr Dang Huy Huynh*

Summary: **This study of three protected areas in Vietnam illustrates how
the impact of population pressures and poverty on forests and biodiversity is shaped by international conflicts, national policies and ideologies.**

Rapid population growth and the compelling requirements of economic growth threaten biodiversity in most regions of the world; these threats are particularly pronounced in the tropics. A number of the direct or proximate processes with immediate impacts on biodiversity, such as deforestation, are driven by human activities: agricultural encroachment, fuelwood collection, hunting and logging. Underlying root causes fuelled by social or economic factors at the protected area, local, national and international scales often lie behind these direct or proximate causes of biodiversity loss. Intermediate and distant determinants of biodiversity loss, such as timber exports, international demand for endangered species, or planned migrations are rarely evaluated for their impact on a country's biodiversity. Most studies of the protected areas of Vietnam, including the most pivotal works (Mackinnon et al, 1989; World Bank, 1994b and 1995b; Dang Huy Huynh et al, 1996; Vo Quy, 1987) did not consider the underlying root causes of biodiversity loss.

Stretching from 8°30N to 23°N (Figure 15.1), Vietnam's climate varies from humid tropical in the southern lowlands to temperate in the northern highlands. Consequently, the country enjoys a diversity of natural environments and a high level of biodiversity in its forests, waterways and seas. Vietnam has been rated as the sixteenth most biologically diverse country in the world, with an estimated 12,000 species of plants. About 33 per cent of the flora of northern Vietnam are endemic, and nationally the percentage of endemism could be as high as 50 per cent. Vietnam also has a wealth of fauna: 276 mammals, 828 birds, 180 reptiles, 80 amphibians, 472 freshwater fish and many thousands of invertebrate species have been identified (Vo Quy, 1987). These groups show a high degree of local distinctiveness, with many endemic species of great scientific and economic significance. Of the 34 globally threatened birds identified as occurring in Vietnam, ten are restricted-range endemic forest species. Sixty fish and four primates are also endemic to Vietnam.

Perhaps Vietnam's greatest claim to biodiversity fame is the discovery within the past few years of three new mammal species. The most recent discovery, the truong son muntjac, was found during a survey of western Quang Nam Province during early 1997. Research in Vu Quang Nature Reserve, located on the Lao border, led to the discovery of the saola and the giant muntjac. In addition, a new species of fish, two new bird species and a new tortoise have been found in Vu Quang.

However, biodiversity is rapidly declining throughout the country as a result of habitat loss. While marine fauna and flora are important, this study focused on terrestrial biodiversity loss, given that man has had a relatively larger impact on Vietnam's forests. Originally, forest covered the entire country, but over the past few decades the forests have suffered serious depletion. Between 1943 and 1991, forest cover decreased from 67 to 29 per cent of Vietnam's total area. At least 12.6 million ha of forest, including 8 million ha in southern Vietnam, have been lost. The northern mountains experienced the greatest decline, with forest cover dropping from 95 per cent to 17 per cent in only 48 years. A total of 13 million ha or 40 per cent of the country is currently classified as unproductive, barren land. The remaining forests are degraded, poorly stocked and badly fragmented. Apart from habitat loss, many species are endangered or have been lost as a result of over-use. Collection of rare medicinal plants and rare timbers and over-hunting and collecting for the wildlife trade have had a significant impact. Many species are confined to small geographical ranges and occur at low individual densities, which render them highly vulnerable as the forests are cut into smaller patches and eventually completely cleared.

During this century, the Sumatran rhinoceros, sika deer, Eld's deer, kouprey, wild buffalo, Edwards' pheasant and probably the Malayan tapir have become locally extinct. Without urgent conservation action, the following animals are facing certain extinction in Vietnam: banteng, Javan rhinoceros, tiger, Asian elephant and the saola. Among the resident forest birds most prone to extinction are large waterbirds and galliformes, including the white-shouldered ibis, imperial pheasant, Vietnamese pheasant, green peafowl and orange-necked partridge. Many valuable plants are becoming scarce and some are in danger of extinction. Of species endemic to Vietnam, 28 per cent of the mammals, 10 per cent of the birds and 21 per cent of the amphibians and reptiles are currently listed as endangered species. The total of threatened species is high for a single country, reflecting the seriousness of the threats to wild habitats in Vietnam (Vo Quy, 1987; Ministry of Science, Technology and Environment, 1992; World Bank, 1995b).

This study looks at three sites: the Ba Be National Park, the Na Hang Nature Reserve and the Yok Don National Park. Yok Don and the Ba Be/Na Hang areas are ideal for studying root causes as they represent two distinct but prevalent biome types in Vietnam. Ba Be and Na Hang are nearly identical in biodiversity composition, given their proximity. Yet they provide some useful comparisons since the area is located at the junction of three provincial administrations. The difficulties of cross-provincial coordination and planning in Vietnam create an interesting issue in the study of socioeconomic root causes.

Ba Be National Park and Na Hang Nature Reserve are located in the mountainous northern region of Vietnam where ethnic minority groups practising traditional agriculture outnumber the lowland Kinh Vietnamese. The forests are best described as limestone forest or tropical semi-evergreen forest. Population pressures, seasonal agriculture on sloping lands, breakdown of the traditional land tenure systems, as the government presses for settled agriculture, and forest fragmentation, drive biodiversity losses in the region.

Yok Don National Park lies in a completely different biogeographical zone with lowland dry dipterocarp forests, which provide habitats for bovids and other large grazing animals such as elephants. The forests are good for timber production, and the national park is almost completely surrounded by state forest enterprises. The original inhabitants of Yok Don, mostly Ede, Lao and Mnong ethnic groups, practised traditional agriculture, hunting and collection of forest products. The government has encouraged these groups to settle into permanent villages, but they still make extensive use of nearby forests. The government sees Dak Lak Province, the location of Yok Don, as a 'new frontier'. The forest areas are extensive and much of the flat plateau area is suitable for

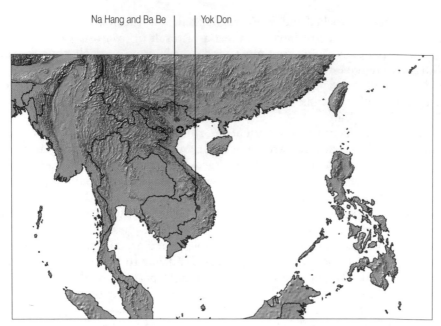

Figure 15.1 *Map of Vietnam Showing Location of the Study Sites*

cash crops such as coffee and cashew nuts. Incentives are provided to ethnic Vietnamese, mostly recent immigrants, to start plantations of cash crops.

DESCRIPTION OF THE STUDY AREAS

Ba Be National Park

Ba Be National Park is situated in the Ba Be District of Bac Kan Province, about 250 km north of Hanoi, in northern Vietnam. Established as a Natural Preserve Zone in 1977, it became a National Park in 1992. The commune of Nam Mau lies within the park, and Na Hang lies to the west. The park has a total area of about 7100 ha, with a core zone of about 4000 ha. The northern buffer zone is about 1100 ha; and that in the south about 1900 ha.

Ba Be Lake lies at the centre of the park. Steep mountains ranging from 500 to 1100 m in altitude surround the lake. Much of the park has steep slopes and is still largely forested. The only flat land (less than 10 per cent of the total park area) occurs on the river plains and flood plains around the lake, all of which have been converted to agriculture. On steep slopes, soil is shallow, and in some very steep areas and on the tops of peaks there is little or no soil. In flatter areas, soil has been able to accumulate and supports quite different fauna and flora. During the rainy season, the inflow to the lake from rivers draining three basins exceeds the outflow, causing the water level to rise as much as 2.8 m. When water levels rise, local rice fields are flooded.

Tropical moist evergreen forest and tropical evergreen limestone forest dominate. Although much of this forest is disturbed to some extent, it still plays an important role in supporting fauna. Wildlife is present in all areas, and regenerating forests are showing encouraging signs of recovery. The rarity of most species indicates the complexity of the local ecosystems. Among the species encountered, four are listed for strict protection by the government and three species of medicinal plants are threatened with extinction due to human exploitation. The estimated forest area lost annually is 100,000 ha, of which about 50 per cent may be due to shifting cultivation (Ministry of Forestry, 1991). The analysis in this study, based on observations and data collected in the park, suggests rather lower deforestation rates from shifting cultivation. However, it is likely that the natural resources of Ba Be are being depleted at an increasing rate by illegal logging, cutting, shifting cultivation and tourism. In a 16-month period in 1996 and 1997, about 80 ha of primary forest were cut and burned for shifting cultivation.

Na Hang Nature Reserve

The Na Hang Nature Reserve is located in Na Hang district, Tuyen Quang Province, about 300 km north of Hanoi. Comprised of five communes, the reserve is bordered to the north and east by three more communes. The reserve covers about 42,000 ha, with a core zone of 27,500 ha and a buffer zone of 14,400 ha. It is situated between the Nang and Gam River watersheds. The Nang River connects with Ba Be lake and plays a role in regulating the water level in the lake. Hills and mountains cover most of Na Hang district. The highest mountain, Thuong Yen, is 1398 m above sea level The region has two distinct seasons. The dry season lasts from October to March, with cold winds from the north, and the rainy season from April to September. Annual rainfall is about 1800 mm. The Na Hang Nature Reserve was created in 1994 but, with only eight staff, management is poor and infrastructure is inadequate.

There are three main types of forest in the Na Hang area. Tropical moist evergreen closed forest consists of *Lauraceae*, *Fabaceae* and *Meliaceae*. These families commonly grow in the valleys of the Gam river. Tropical monsoon closed and semi-deciduous forest consists of *Fabaceae*, *Lauraceae* and *Fagaceae*. Most of this has been destroyed and replaced by secondary forest of bamboo and other species. Limestone tropical forest contains *Burretio dendronhsienmu* and *Garrcinia fagracoides* in the unexploited areas. This forest type does not regenerate easily. Where the forest has been badly degraded, only shrubs and bushes remain. Of the vertebrates present, the endemic Tonkin snub-nosed monkey is of interest. It is now found only in the Na Hang/Ba Be region, with a population estimated at less than 200 individuals. Other threatened mammals living in Na Hang reserve include nine species of primates, the Asiatic black bear, sun bear, clouded leopard and tiger.

The human population in the reserve is about 10,500, and population density is 25 per km^2. The current population growth rate is high, at about 2.4 per cent per year. Most of the local population has lived in the area for a long time. Four major ethnic groups live in the reserve, including Tay (56 per cent) and Dao (22 per cent). Most Tay people live at relatively low altitudes in the valley and flat areas. They generally practise paddy rice cultivation, or shifting cultivation when rice paddies are not available.

Due to destruction of forest and extensive hunting in Tuyen Quang province over the long term, wildlife habitats, especially those of the endangered species, are restricted to the Na Hang Nature Reserve. Many mammals once distributed widely in the province can be found only in the reserve (Dang Huy Huynh et al, 1996). In 1943, forest covered nearly all of the province, but by 1975 forest cover was only 28 per cent and by 1992 only 17 per cent. The rapidly growing population's demand for forest products and agricultural land caused the decrease in the region's forest.

Yok Don National Park

Yok Don National Park is situated in Krong Na Commune in the Buon Don District of Dak Lak province, in the centre of the Srepok River basin, which forms the right branch of the lower Mekong basin. The park's core area is 58,200 ha. The buffer zone overlaps with three communes, Krong Na and two newly established communes, Ea-Huar and Ea-Wel. The western boundary of Yok Don lies along the Cambodian border. The northern and eastern boundary follows the Srepok River. Yok Don was declared a Reserve in 1986 and became a National Park in 1991.

Yok Don includes many kinds of terrain with an average elevation of 100 to 500 m. It is divided into the following subzones: complete preservation for wet deciduous dipterocarp forest on the left bank of the Daken River (31,000 ha); ecological regeneration on the right bank of the Daken River (23,000 ha); and experimental management and animal reproduction on the left bank of the Srepok River (5100 ha). The vegetation of Yok Don can be classified as: dry dipterocarp forest (57 per cent); riverine evergreen forest (8 per cent); hill evergreen forest (12 per cent); mixed deciduous forest (13 per cent); and grasslands (13 per cent). A total of over 56,000 ha is forested. Yok Don has a tropical monsoon climate, with a well-defined dry season from October to April. Mean annual rainfall is 1540 mm.

Yok Don is the only park in Vietnam protecting dry dipterocarp forest. One important feature of the vegetative cover is the grass under the forest canopy. A total of 61 species of grass serve as food for animals, perhaps the most important being those available in the dry season and other times of food scarcity. A total of 62 mammals, 196 birds, 40 reptiles and 13 amphibians have been recorded in the park. Notable mammals include large ungulates: kouprey, banteng, gour, feral/wild buffalo, Eld's deer, hog deer and elephant. Carnivores include tiger, leopard, golden cat, leopard cat, sun bear and black bear. At least 455 plant species have been recorded. Many of the tree species have value as timber or for turpentine resin. The park is also rich in orchids. Yok Don National Park may contain the most numerous species of rare, valuable animals at the highest density in Vietnam.

There are no villages or state enterprises in the core area of Yok Don National Park. The population in the three communes of the buffer zone is 7700. Population density is eight people per km². There are ten ethnic minorities in Krong Na, five in Ea-Huar and ten in Ea-Wel. Ede, M'nong, Giarai and Lao are all native minorities of Yok Don and comprise 71 per cent of the population. Other ethnic groups are generally migrants from other provinces, particularly from North Vietnam. Isolation from inhabited areas facilitates management and control of the park. Between 1978 and 1991, however, 9000 ha of natural forest were lost yearly in Dak Lak. Between 1991 and 1996, 3000 to 3500 ha were lost yearly.

RESEARCH METHODOLOGY

Attempting to determine the underlying motivations for actions that directly cause biodiversity loss is a complex process. This case study is an interdisciplinary work combining social and natural sciences: understanding the larger picture requires interdisciplinary flexibility. The research team began the investigation by examining the mechanisms by which local populations affect biodiversity – the proximate causes of biodiversity loss – at each of the three case study sites. The next step was to conduct further analysis, asking what motivates the local resource users to take such actions as hunting and expansion of agricultural land. After working up to national and international scales on the chain of causes, hypotheses were formulated about the root causes of biodiversity loss in Vietnam (Figure 15.2) A return journey down this chain was taken to confirm those hypotheses, concluding with household interviews.

The collected data cover environmental and socioeconomic conditions, enforcement of government sectoral policies, local policies and biodiversity resources. The data are both quantitative and qualitative. Quantitative data were collected on changes in land use, population, agriculture production and income sources. Qualitative data track changes in the resources and their degradation. Biodiversity loss often had to be inferred from surrogate or proxy measures, such as loss of forest cover or decreases in the population of indicator species.

Data were collected at four levels: commune, district, provincial and central. At the commune, level data were collected from annual socioeconomic statistical reports; formal interviews with commune leaders using questionnaires; informal interviews with village elders; participatory rural appraisal in meetings of village people; and other anecdotal material. At the district level, data collected included annual reports of District's People Committees and Party's Committees; statistical data from the Agricultural and Rural Development Unit, Statistic Unit, Planning Unit, Population and Family Planning Unit and Forest Protection Unit; as well as formal interviews and discussions with the district leaders. At the provincial level, data were collected from annual reports of the Provincial People Committees; formal interviews with provincial leaders; and statistical data from the provincial department. At

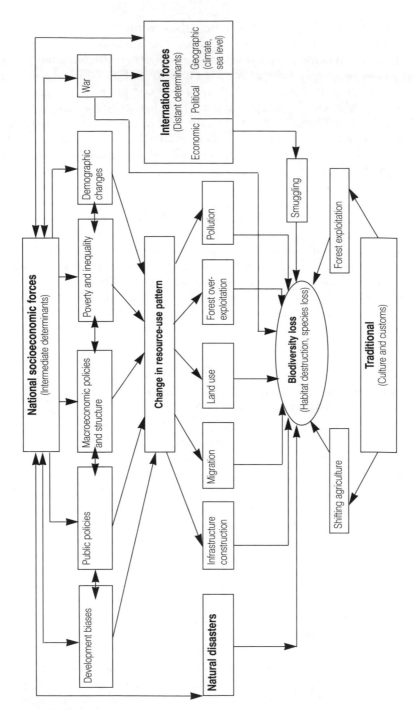

Figure 15.2 *Root and Direct Causes of Biodiversity Loss*

the central or national level, data collected included legal documents related to policies, laws and regulations from the Prime Minister's Office, ministries and government departments; reports of research projects and national and international cooperative systems; and documents issued by international organizations. Formal interviews and invited reports were also solicited from directors of research institutes and government departments.

Publications and research project reports also provided data on biodiversity. These data were compiled from existing field surveys focusing on species diversity, abundance and distribution within habitats or ecosystems, and rapid/participatory biodiversity inventories using a variety of methods.

Information management and storage systems in the provinces and districts are very poor. In general, the older the data, the more difficult they are to obtain. Some data were collected by informal means, including interviews with elders and former leaders. Other data are practically impossible to find, particularly maps. Furthermore, the data are often in incompatible formats as they were collected or generated by different methods and for different purposes. The preciseness and accuracy of different types of data are difficult to evaluate. These problems all limited analysis of collected data.

DIRECT CAUSES OF BIODIVERSITY LOSS

Forest degradation and loss are the most important contributors to the loss of biodiversity in Vietnam. Direct causes of habitat and biodiversity loss in Vietnam are summarized here. Specific local patterns of habitat destruction and biodiversity loss in the case study sites are examined in the following section.

Arable Land Expansion

Expansion of cultivated areas has resulted in the loss of more forest area than any other proximate cause. Shifting cultivation alone has transformed 13 million ha of previously forest-covered land to bare hills (Box 15.1). In the densely populated northern upland areas, the loss of natural forest was largely due to the expansion of annual crops such as hill rice. In the Central Highlands and along the south-central coast, lands were opened for industrial crops such as coffee, tea and rubber. The cleared land, made accessible to farmers as a result of logging, is cultivated until soil fertility is exhausted. The land is then abandoned to extended fallow periods, interrupted by occasional grazing and fuelwood collection. These extensive activities, in a fire-prone region, prevent forest regeneration. Soil erosion and weed invasion are part of the process of land degradation. Most logging and subsequent agricultural production, especially in recent years, is on steep slopes that are highly susceptible to erosion once the protective vegetative cover has been removed. In this way, barren land is created.

Logging

Between 1986 and 1991, State Forest Enterprises (SFE) harvested 3.5 million m³ of wood annually; an additional 1–2 million m³ were logged illegally. Converting this volume to area equivalents, SFE logging accounted for the loss of perhaps 80,000 ha of forest per year during this time period (Ministry of Forestry, 1991). While all SFE logging of primary forests has since been halted, illegal logging by small operations is still prevalent. Rare hardwood species such as rosewood face extinction as people selectively harvest and hand-carry logs out of the forest.

Fuelwood Collection

Nationally, more than 90 per cent of domestic energy consumption is fuelled by biomass. Approximately 21 million tons of fuelwood are burned annually for household cooking and heating, preparation of pigfeed and processing of agricultural products such as sugar cane. In most regions of the country, fuelwood collection is outpacing the forest's regenerative capacity. Conversion of total weight of fuelwood exploitation to area equivalents shows that fuelwood collection accounts for six times as much forest loss as commercial logging (World Bank, 1993 and 1995b).

Hunting and Collection of Other Forest Products

A large share of species loss in Vietnam is due to hunting and collection of forest products both for household use and sale. These products are an important source of income. Nearly 2300 different plant species are affected. Fruit, flowers, bark, roots, stems and resins are harvested for purposes ranging from food and medicine to construction and textile production. Fauna diversity has also suffered. Hunting has reduced wildlife in most forests, including those in protected areas. An increasing volume of these products is now bartered and traded to neighbouring countries, especially China and Thailand.

Fire

Of the 9 million ha of forest remaining in Vietnam, 56 per cent is fire-prone in the dry season. On average, 25,000 ha of forest area are lost to fire each year; up to 100,000 ha are lost in particularly dry years. In the Central Highlands, where the natural cover is dry dipterocarp forest, annual fires gradually degrade the quality of forest by repeatedly eliminating saplings and some large trees. Before planting each crop, shifting cultivators use fire as a tool for clearing land, controlling weeds and insects and producing ash for fertilizer. Since uncontrolled fires often burn 10 to 20 times the intended area, the result is not only the localized destruction of protective vegetative cover but also the extensive loss of soil organic matter and associated soil structure.

Box 15.1 Traditional Shifting Cultivation

Shifting cultivation is the traditional form of agricultural production for most of Vietnam's ethnic minorities. About nine million people from 50 ethnic minorities practise shifting cultivation. There are two basic types:

1. itinerant cultivation; and
2. sedentary cultivation.

About 120,000 households are itinerant cultivators, primarily from such ethnic minority groups as the H'Mong and Dao. Itinerant cultivators fully exhaust soil fertility and then abandon the land without plans for further use. To find new lands to practise this pioneer shifting cultivation, people usually have to travel great distances. For example, over 200 households in Ba Be National Park have migrated from Cao Bang and Ha Giang provinces. In 1990 the cultivated holdings of itinerant cultivators were estimated at about 180,000 ha, primarily in the Central Highlands and the northern mountains.

The sedentary shifting cultivators include most of the rural population outside of the deltas, about 15 to 16 million people. They have fixed households but shift cultivation sites. Sedentary shifting cultivation is estimated to cover as much as one million hectares every year.

In general, shifting cultivation is sustainable only when the population density is low. The threshold depends on factors such as the susceptibility of land to deterioration, previous farming history, and crop viability. Because of high population growth, shifting cultivation has become the main factor causing serious land degradation, and has been a primary cause of deforestation and formation of barren lands in Vietnam.

War

Often merely a consequence of war, environmental degradation was an important tactic during the Second Indochina War. In addition to the impact of 13 million tons of bombs, 72 million litres of defoliants and herbicides destroyed 4.5 million ha of forest between 1961 and 1975 (World Bank, 1994b).

LOCAL CONTEXT

Ba Be National Park

The population of Ba Be District was over 37,000 in 1975 and doubled to over 65,000 in 1995. Population growth is between 3.5 and 5 per cent per year in some villages. The majority of the population is Tay, Dao and H'Mong. The nine villages in the core and buffer zones of the park have an approximate population of 1500, a lower density than outside the park. Many villages also surround the park. Most Tay villages have been established in the area for a long time, but the Dao and H'Mong have moved in since 1979 in search of new agricultural lands. Shifting agriculture is the traditional land use of ethnic minorities in Ba Be district. In a number of places, Tay, Nung and Kinh have adopted fixed cultivation, but traditional methods of farming are still used. Animals such as buffalo, cows, pigs and goats are kept in every village on grazing land or fallow fields. Surplus crops or animals are sold.

The people of Ba Be are living at a subsistence level. Because agriculture often cannot meet all their needs, they have little alternative but to exploit forest products. All minorities in the area of Ba Be use many forest products: timber and bamboo for construction of housing, animal stalls and boats; fuelwood; palms for roofing material; rattans and other weaving materials; fruits, mushrooms and bamboo shoots; and grazing for animals. Some products, especially bamboo shoots, birds and snakes, are collected for sale in the market. Most Tay fish in the lake and rivers using traditional tackle, nets and traps or illegal dynamite. Although hunting within park boundaries is prohibited, it is still very widespread.

Population growth is clearly one of the factors contributing to poverty. The number of landless and land-poor rural households is increasing. In the whole Ba Be district, 30 per cent of the population suffers from food shortages all year round and 40 per cent for three to six months of the year. As more people become dependent on the same agricultural resources, those resources are used more intensively. Inputs required are high, and yields are declining from year to year. The migration of H'Mong and Dao people from Cao Bang and Tuyen Quang province and other parts of Bac Kan province to Ba Be has led to further forest clearing for shifting cultivation. Between 1992 and 1997, 100 households with 800 people migrated to Ba Be, of which 70 households with 550 people went to the core zone.

Shifting cultivators remain poor, in part because hill rice productivity is very low. However, the problem is compounded by their inability to speak Vietnamese, very high illiteracy and population growth rates and their agricultural techniques. In north Vietnam, the area under natural forest cover in the places where the ethnic groups practise shifting cultivation has drastically decreased. In the north-west, where many H'Mong live, less than 13 per cent of the land area is under natural forest cover and forest plantation; in the north-east the figure is 15 per cent. The cold, humid winter and very uneven temperatures and distribution of rainfall and humidity lead to low yields and frequent crop failures. In Ba Be a total of 32,000 ha of forest land are classed as barren land due to shifting agriculture. Often the most feasible strategy for the minorities in upland Ba Be is to consume less, eat less nutritious foods such as cassava and gather food in the forest.

The Bac Kan provincial and Ba Be district institutions and agencies have implemented large programmes for infrastructure development, flooded rice fields, forest rehabilitation, agroforestry models, fruit trees, special crops and livestock breeding, as well as providing subsidies, occasional free rice and loans. The government's current aim is to end forest clearing and burning for shifting cultivation. Although fixed cultivation programmes have been implemented in Ba Be district for over 25 years, the results are still limited. These programmes, which were implemented in combination with the establishment of cooperatives in Ba Be, were ineffective because of lack of analysis of the needs of the various ethnic groups and the lack of coordination between agencies. Infrastructure is poor and the sustainability of land-use alternatives is not ensured. Markets are unstable. Many people consider that they have the right to clear the forests to practise shifting cultivation.

The government has not invested in extension services for crop varieties or livestock husbandry. Productivity and yields are low. There is growing evidence that public funds were mainly invested in buildings and infrastructure for the government, rather than transfer of knowledge, assistance in increasing production, or protection of the environment. Management is poor and the staff of cooperatives and forest protection authorities have limited knowledge of land or forest management, policy implementation or biological resources, causing local farmers to lose faith in them.

With the development of the private sector, people in Ba Be have opportunities to develop commodity production, but markets are not yet stable. Due to the harsh topography, and difficulties in transport and communication that hamper marketing of commodities, people continue to practise shifting cultivation, log and hunt for subsistence. In some communes the people have even destroyed commercial product trees, since there are no markets for the products, and have returned to shifting cultivation. However, cultivation of cash crops, such as Chinese plum and tea, and forest exploitation for export earnings, is increasing. Recently, with the opening of the Chinese market, a number of forest products including tortoise, scaly anteater, turtle, snake, squirrel, flying fox, monkey and medicinal plants have found new export outlets. As a result, the number of forestry law violations in Ba Be increases every year.

Na Hang Nature Reserve

In the Na Hang district, the main proximate causes of deforestation are agricultural expansion and shifting cultivation for food security, forest product consumption, wildlife collection and poaching, and the legacy of the war. Agricultural production is the major source of food and income for probably 90 per cent of households living inside the reserve. Many households raise poultry and pigs and keep a small number of cows and water buffalo. Cultivated land is very scarce and people frequently have to clear new land for shifting cultivation. Agricultural practices vary among ethnic minorities, but the main activities of shifting cultivation are similar. Various crops are cultivated, such as dry rice, cassava and maize. After several years of cultivation, the land becomes eroded and the soil infertile. Plots are then left fallow for 10 to 15 years.

Poverty and food shortages directly affect biodiversity loss in the district by forcing local people to clear forested land for agriculture. Poor households make up about 43 per cent of the population living inside the reserve (Tuyen Quang Department of Statistics). Food crops for local consumption account for over 90 per cent of agricultural land in the district. According to people in

Na Hang, the food shortages of the late 1970s and early 1980s led to serious forest destruction. Over the last decades, agricultural lands have increased significantly to meet the food needs of the growing population.

Food production has been increased mostly by agricultural expansion, particularly by creation of more hill fields. Average food production per capita rose from 180 kg in 1981 to 280 kg in 1986. This amount of food is insufficient for the district. Particularly between 1986 and 1992, agricultural production was so low that people had to rely on food from other natural resources. Since 1992, with intensive cultivation and new rice and maize species, the district has been able to produce more food. Average food per capita rose to 340 kg by 1996, reaching the average food product per capita in Vietnam. Pressure on the forest as an additional source of income has been significantly decreased. However, this situation may be reversed due to rapid increase in population.

Local people harvest forest resources for food, shelter, traditional medicines, oils, fuel, beverages, tools and cash income. The extraction of products such as fuelwood by rural communities, perhaps once within the carrying capacity of surrounding forests, has now crossed the limits of sustainability. In Na Hang district, wood provides 50 per cent of cooking fuel. If the present population of Na Hang district is about 60,000, annual fuelwood consumption is probably 30,000 m^3 per year. Commercial wood exploitation was very high in the 1960s. In the following years, forest production fell steadily while the range of products expanded. By 1990, forest-based production in Tuyen Quang was quite low because of over-exploitation of the resources. In the Na Hang district, between 1973 and 1993, the SFE officially exploited 80,000 m^3 of logs, in addition to extensive extraction of bamboo. Illegal logging is probably much more serious, but has become less common since 1992, perhaps because of improvements in local food production.

Various other forest resources are legally collected, but only in small quantities, including bamboo shoot and ear fungus, used as food; palm leaves, used for construction; and the bark of the gio tree, used as medicine. Limits on collection are intended to protect the forest from extensive disturbance. Wildlife hunting and collection are traditional local practices. Traditional targets are pig, tiger, leopard, bear, deer, monkey, varran, fresh water turtle and tortoises. Because of extensive hunting of these animals over a long period of time, their numbers are decreasing dramatically. With the new market orientation of the economy, pressures on wildlife are rapidly increasing. The extensive wildlife trade with China encourages hunting and collecting of a much wider range of wildlife species.

The population living inside the reserve is the main pressure on local biodiversity. This population has been increasing rapidly for many years. Over just the last eight years, the population increased by 1.4 times. Population growth affects biodiversity directly through increased resource consumption and indirectly by fuelling the processes of poverty and migration. Over a period of 50 years, the movement of migrants to Tuyen Quang, and in particular to Na

Hang district, has contributed significantly to population growth. Many factors forced people from other regions to migrate to Tuyen Quang. In the 1960s, the government implemented a campaign of land colonization and established a new economic zone to achieve economic development of the mountainous region. At the same time, the government set up state-owned forestry and agriculture enterprises as well as agricultural cooperatives in the mountains. This campaign encouraged approximately 1 million people to migrate from the Red River delta to the northern midlands and highlands. Bombing during the Second Indochina War forced the evacuation of many people from the Red River delta to the mountains; Tuyen Quang province willingly received tens of thousands of people in this period. In 1979 border conflicts with China forced many H'Mong, Dao and Nung minorities to evacuate from border areas to Tuyen Quang. With the food shortages in the late 1970s and early 1980s, large areas of forest were cleared for shifting cultivation. In the 1990s, because the district still has some relatively fertile lands under forest cover, people from land-poor neighbouring provinces have migrated to Na Hang. The Da Vi commune, bordering the reserve, has been a 'hot spot' for spontaneous migration to Tuyen Quang.

In the Na Hang district, forests were intensively cleared in two periods, both closely linked with the policies of the cooperative movement. Between 1975 and 1983, when this movement was seriously curtailed, living conditions became very bad and people were forced to clear the forest for agricultural land and to exploit forest resources as an additional source of income. Between 1989 and 1993, food self-sufficiency policies were issued that engaged people from all sectors in clearing the forest in order to expand food crops.

Local authorities in the Na Hang district carried out work under the government's fixed cultivation programme for about 29 years, but the number of shifting cultivators was not much reduced, for several possible reasons. First, the living conditions of these former shifting cultivators did not improve much, so they went back to their traditional practices. Second, the construction of infrastructure for the new settlements was insufficient. Third, authorities sometimes forced the programme on people, regardless of their wishes and knowledge.

Beginning in 1992, Tuyen Quang was one of the first provinces in Vietnam to enforce a policy of closing natural forests. In 1997 Na Hang district created a new organization to prevent deforestation and wildlife hunting, a group consisting of staff from the Na Hang Forest Protection Unit, the police, army and local authorities. Also in 1997, the People's Committee of Tuyen Quang province officially recognized the urgency of strengthening measures for forest protection and development. However, for the Na Hang Reserve, poor management and facilities, including human resources and material infrastructure, in combination with the large population living inside the reserve, make it extremely difficult to preserve biological resources.

Yok Don

People have lived in Yok Don for a long time, following traditional agricultural practices, collecting forest products and hunting. In 1975 the population of Dak Lak Province was 36,000. It is now 1.6 million. Natural growth contributes 3 per cent yearly to population growth, with the remainder a result of planned and spontaneous immigration from the North, a particularly strong factor in the mid-1990s. With high population growth, demands on land for cultivation, food, wood and construction materials have increased.

Shifting cultivation is the traditional land use practised not only by local ethnic minorities but also by migrants from the North. Local infrastructure is very poor and living standards are low. The obligations and rights of local ethnic minorities and migrants are unequal, creating a growing gap between rich and poor, making the poor more dependent on forest products and forest clearing to earn a living. Agriculture is the main source of income for all villages within the buffer zone. Ninety per cent of workers are in agriculture. Rice is the main crop, and productivity is low at 270–460 kg per capita per year – sufficient food for only part of the year. Many families raise poultry, pigs and a small number of cows, water buffalo and elephants. Cattle and elephants are raised mainly for farming and transport. The government has had a policy of encouraging ethnic groups to settle down in permanent villages since 1984. However, they continue to collect vegetables, wild animals and other products for food from nearby forests.

The main commercial crops are coffee and rubber. Ethnic immigrants maintain plantations of these and other perennial crops. Three SFEs together exploit about 11,200 m^3 of timber per year. Timber exploitation occurred intensively from 1990 to 1993 for export to the South and to the former Soviet Union and the Czech Republic. Some forestry enterprises paid no attention to reforestation. Forest quality and quantity has decreased significantly as a result. Border trade, particularly trade with China since 1992, has led to over-exploitation of natural resources, including timber, other forest products and animals, in Dak Lak province and the Buon Don district. In Ea-Tul, even domestic elephants have been illegally shot for their tusks. The Yok Don area has great tourism potential. One major attraction of the area are the Ban Don elephants, many of which are kept by private households and can be rented to tourists.

Hunting was traditionally done with crossbows from the backs of elephants. Since the war, there has been an abundance of automatic weapons in the area, and hunting is now far more lethal for wildlife. In the dry season, hunters set fires in the park and animals are later attracted by the new grass shoots. Ede people catch wild animals including elephants for domestication. In addition, resin collectors make fires to start the resin flowing from dipterocarp trees. Within the borders of the National Park, 10 tons of *Strychnos nux-vomica* seeds, ten tons of *Kaempferia galanga*, five tons of honey, 50 tons of *shorea vulgaris pierre*, 20 tons of *Dipterocarp alatus roxb* and 1 ton of dried bamboo shoots are collected each year.

The central plan for socioeconomic development of Tay Nguyen plateau in general and Dak Lak province in particular led to forest clearing for coffee, rubber, tea, cashew and pepper plantations, as well as hydroelectric stations. The agricultural cooperative movement began in Dak Lak province in 1976, but was in operation for only five years before it was dissolved. Policies for the economic and cultural development of Tay Nguyen after liberation, with planned migration from the North, have resulted in a population increase. A total of nine planned migrations from Thai Binh province to the buffer zone of Yok Don National Park were carried out from 1978 to 1995. Each newly established household gets a permit from the local people's committee to cut 10 m³ of wood for house-building. People often use the permit to cut more than this.

Based on a government decision to reorganize SFE, Dak Lak province has reorganized forestry management by separating the forest industry from the forest planting sector. Although the basis of this decision was logical, there have been big gaps in the implementation. Some enterprises, individuals and officers took advantage of these gaps to exploit forest resources and capital through smuggling, illegal transport and price manipulation. A programme under which forestry land is allocated to farm households for protection and reforestation, known as the 327 Programme, has been implemented in Dak Lak since 1985. Due to mistakes in policy implementation and organization of forestry management by the forestry department and local authorities, people did not actively take part in forest protection for a long time.

NATIONAL AND INTERNATIONAL CONTEXT

To effectively decipher the root causes of biodiversity loss, a country's national socioeconomic context must be clearly understood. Thus, this section provides a brief presentation of Vietnam's history since 1945, which can be divided into five distinct periods.

1945–54: Establishment of Democratic Republic of Vietnam and the First Indochina War

In 1945 Vietnam's economy was overwhelmingly based on agriculture, employing over 90 per cent of the labour force and generating over 60 per cent of national income. Agriculture was plagued by outdated cultivation techniques and low productivity. Additionally, land distribution was skewed, as 2 per cent of the country's population controlled 51 per cent of the country's land. In rural areas, 60 per cent of farming households were landless and worked as tenants. Beginning with Ho Chi Minh's declaration of national independence, this decade was fraught with hardship as the country struggled to end nearly a century of French occupation. In July 1954 the First Indochina War ended as the North was liberated from French occupation.

Table 15.1 *Direct Causes of Biodiversity Loss*

	Ba Be	Na Hang	Yok Don
Agriculture expansion			
Annual crops	+++	++	++
Cash crops	–	–	+++
Logging			
Legal	+	++	+++
Illegal	+++	++	+++
Fuel-wood consumption	+++	+++	+++
Non-timber product collection	++	++	+
Fire damage	+	+	+++
Hunting	+++	+++	+++
War damage	–	–	++

Key: – Weak   + Medium   ++ Strong   +++ Very Strong

1954–60: Building the Foundations of Socialism and the Struggle for Reunification

The signing of the Geneva Accords resulted in the separation of Vietnam into two zones divided at the 17th parallel. During the following 20-year period, two separate economies developed. In the South, the Saigon administration set up a free market economy which received considerable support from foreign countries, primarily the US. In the North, the major development steps were further improvement of democratic revolution, economic reforms and build-up of the initial physical and technical foundation for socialism. Throughout this period, the struggle for national unification was regarded as the foremost priority.

The severe aftermath of the First Indochina War hobbled the North's economy. The first three-year plan (1955–57) aimed at economic rehabilitation through completing the land reform and creating a solid foundation to bring the North to socialism. By 1957 the land reform was complete, with the early formation of rural agricultural cooperatives. The second three-year plan aimed at turning the multi-sector economy into a socialist ones based on state and collective ownership. Collectivization of land and other means of production was completed by 1960. The second stage of the formation of agricultural cooperatives was also developed. The seeds of weakness leading to eventual collapse of these cooperatives were sown from their inception. Major problems included the fact that their speed of development outpaced the establishment of a supporting framework; poor and landless farmers with little production experience were selected for leadership positions, while rich and experienced older farmers were prohibited from leadership positions; and a contradiction existed between the proclaimed liberation of the labour force and the constraints of highly collectivized production units. The establishment of these Agricultural Protection Cooperatives (APC) led to labour and land depredation in rural areas. Due to blind optimism, these mistakes and contradictions in establishing the cooperatives were ignored, leading eventually to their collapse in the 1980s.

1961–75: The Second Indochina War

The Communist Party's first five-year plan (1960–65), calling for completion of socialist reform in the North, was interrupted by the Second Indochina War that began in 1964 and lasted until 1975. The North's economic construction and development efforts were redirected toward the war, but the formation of agricultural cooperatives still held an important position.

During this period a campaign to improve cooperative management and cultivation technology began. Enlargements of APC from hamlet to commune and even inter-commune scale were conducted hastily. Embezzlement and mismanagement of cooperatives' assets occurred everywhere. Investigation showed that between 20 and 30 per cent of APC capital and fixed assets were lost and approximately three-quarters of all machines were damaged, resulting in a 50 per cent increase in production costs by 1975. Massive upgrading of APC and collectivization of farmers' land and other productive assets, particularly in mountain regions, deepened the inherent contradictions of the APC model. Difficulties caused by the war and problems with the APC model brought agriculture and the economy as a whole into a recessionary crisis in the North. Food production failed to meet domestic demand, and the state had to import increasing amounts of cereals.

1976–85: Reconstruction of a Unified Nation

After formal reunification of the North and South in 1976, harmonization of the South's economy with that of the North became an immediate priority. The 1976–80 plan reemphasized the traditional socialist model and large-scale socialist production. Consequently numerous state and local enterprises were established. For instance, 50 forest enterprises were established in Dak Lak Province alone. Meanwhile the agricultural cooperative movement was in turmoil. Despite growing evidence of problems, further collectivization was carried out. By 1979 the Communist Party recognized emerging weaknesses in the economy and consequently decentralized economic decision-making: state enterprises were placed on a self-accounting and self-financing basis; the private sector, until then officially non-existent, was sanctioned by the government; and responsibility for managing agricultural production was transferred from the cooperatives to individual farming families, creating a contract-output system.

Under the new agricultural system, the cooperative allotted land to the farm which, under the contract, was responsible for providing a predetermined output to the cooperative. Any surplus produced over the contracted output would remain with the family for its own consumption or sale. The cooperative, however, remained the owner of the land and major capital equipment. It also remained responsible for the provision of agricultural inputs and service, the collection of taxes and fees, and the sale of the contract output at a price fixed by the government. Initially, this contract-output system had a significant positive impact on the growth of paddy production. Rice distribution to consumers, however, still remained the sole responsibility of the government, which used a rationing system and subsidized prices well below those in 'parallel' retail markets. This heavy subsidization led to an increase in the budget deficit and, coupled with simultaneous increases in wages and money supply, to accelerating inflation, which reached as high as 775 per cent in 1986. Once again, agricultural output slowed.

1986–present: Doi moi, an Economic Renovation

Under the pressure of an increasingly serious economic crisis and in the context of new economic thinking, the Sixth Congress of the Vietnam Communist Party, held in 1986, made the pivotal decision to initiate *doi moi*, a national economic reform with the following key aims:

- Adjust the investment and production structure, with shift in emphasis to such priority objectives as food and foodstuffs, consumer goods and goods for export;
- Adopt a multi-sectoral economic policy for the long term;
- Replace the bureaucratic central-planning mechanism with a management mechanism better suited to a market economy; and
- Expand and upgrade foreign economic cooperation.

The first five years of *doi moi*, 1986–90, saw the transition to a new management mechanism. By the second five-year period, 1991–95, the change had a significant impact on economic performance. Average annual GDP soared to 7 per cent and export earnings increased 30 per cent yearly between 1989 and 1992, while inflation dropped from 400 per cent in 1988 to 4.5 per cent in 1996.

Of direct pertinence to biodiversity loss, *doi moi* reforms facilitated phenomenal agricultural growth. Communist Party decisions in 1988 designated the farming household as an autonomous economic unit, and allowed farmers to retain up to 40 per cent of contracted output. Most importantly, the national assembly adopted a new land law in 1993 that allowed farmers to transfer, exchange, lease, mortgage and inherit land-use rights. The tenure period was extended to 20 years for annual cropland and 50 years for perennial cropland, to be renewed as long as the allocated lands are lawfully used. This law provides the necessary incentive for farmers to make long-term investments. Thus, land-use rights in Vietnam are now little different from private land rights in modern market economies, even though state ownership of land is maintained. This has encouraged farmers to invest more labour and capital into production on their land. As a direct consequence of these reforms, food production increased from 18 million tons in 1987 to over 24 million tons in 1992.

ROOT CAUSES OF BIODIVERSITY LOSS

The causes of biodiversity loss discussed below are closely interlinked, and the relationships among them are complex. Moreover, they tend to reinforce each other. Intensity of the impact of these causes is different across the studied areas. The research determined the following to be the most critical root causes of biodiversity loss in Vietnam at the national and international levels:

War

During the 45-year period from 1945 to 1990, Vietnam was a battleground for two major wars and two border conflicts. Both the First and Second Indochina Wars had a large direct impact on biodiversity loss. Indirectly, war increased the amount of land cleared for agriculture. To feed the rapidly growing population and grow foodstuffs to feed the armies, large new areas of forest were cleared for agricultural expansion. The areas cleared were larger than normal because so much food was lost to air attacks on the supply columns, aerial spraying of crops and bombing of dikes and irrigation channels.

War also affected biodiversity by causing large migrations of people. For instance, during the Northern Border War with China (1979–80), many households of ethnic minorities migrated away from the border provinces to the uncultivated forest lands of Tuyen Quang (Na Hang), Bac Kan (Ba Be) and Thai Nguyen provinces. After the war ended, most of these households remained in these provinces illegally, carrying out shifting cultivation in upland areas. This immigration of war refugees significantly increased the population density in Ba Be, Na Hang and surrounding areas. After these initial pioneers migrated at the height of the fighting, many relatives followed in the next few years, increasing the size and impact of the new settlements.

Moreover, at the end of the Second Indochina War in 1975, which was fought mainly in the Central Highlands, many automatic guns remained in the hands of local villagers, greatly increasing the efficiency with which hunting of large mammals could be carried out. Fauna populations have since declined rapidly in the Central Highlands.

Demographic Change

Demographic change in Vietnam is a main root cause of biodiversity loss. A growing national population demands more resources from an unchanging amount of land, thus forcing expansion of arable land to meet increasing food demand. Vietnam is the second most populous nation in South-East Asia and the twelfth in the world, creating great pressures on limited land resources. The population has grown quickly, from 35 million in 1945 to 75 million in 1995, with predictions of 158 million by the year 2050. Consequently, the arable area per capita is sharply reduced. From 1940 to 1990, a period of just 50 years, the average arable area per capita fell 50 per cent, from 0.26 to 0.12 ha (Khong Dien, 1995).

The population of Vietnam is not equally distributed among different areas of the country. Delta regions cover only one-quarter of total area but are home to three-quarters of the population. In 1995 the countrywide average population density was 220 people per km², but the density in the Red River delta was over 1100 people per km². The population density in the northern mountainous and upland regions was only 120 people per km², and in the Central Highlands just 55 people per km² (Khong Dien, 1996). In mountainous areas, where ethnic minorities predominate, the natural population growth rate is usually higher than in lowland regions. For example, in Na Hang Nature Reserve, the population increased from almost 2000 in 1950 to over 10,500 in 1997, with annual growth rates of 2.8 to 3.6 per cent. The rates in Ba Be National Park are even higher, at 3.5 to 5 per cent per year.

The dramatic difference in population densities between the highlands and the more densely populated lowlands continues to lead some analysts to believe that the distribution of population and human resources has not been in line with that of natural resources. However, it can be argued that the uplands are already relatively more overpopulated than the lowlands. The irrigated wet rice systems of the Red River delta are among the most robust and sustainable systems known in the world. They have been able to support extremely high human densities for centuries. Calculated in terms of agricultural productivity, population densities are as high or higher in the mountains than in the deltas. In general, the mountains, except in those limited areas where irrigated terraces can be constructed, have a much lower carrying capacity and respond to intensification with rapid declines or even total collapse of productivity. This is especially true under traditional systems of shifting cultivation. Growth in population densities, combined with deforestation and environmental degradation, has created a crisis in upland agriculture. Unfavourable shifts in the people-to-land ratio have forced a dramatic shortening of the fallow cycle so that fields that formerly were cropped for one year and then fallowed for 20 are now cropped for two or three years and then fallowed for no more than four years, a cycle that has occurred in most parts of the northern mountain region, resulting in greatly reduced yields and permanent environmental degradation.

Planned and Spontaneous Migrations

Migration, both legal and illegal, has been an important cause of population growth in the Central Highlands. Starting in the 1960s, the government encouraged approximately 1 million people to migrate from the Red River delta to the northern midlands and highlands. The migration movement was on such a large scale that it fundamentally altered the demographic balance of the uplands. In the 30 years between 1960 and 1989, the Kinh population (ethnic Vietnamese) in the midlands and highlands increased at astronomical rates, rising from 640,000 in 1960 to almost 2.6 million in 1989 (Be Viet Dang, 1996).

After reunification in 1975, and until 1989, the government sponsored all migration. Of the 2.4 million people who were officially resettled between 1981 and 1990, about 75 per cent moved within their own provinces. Of the

0.6 million people who moved outside their provinces between 1981 and 1989, 75 per cent moved from the North to the South, primarily from the Red River delta and the north-central coastal region to the low-density Central Highlands. In addition to the planned migrations, many households illegally followed relatives or friends to the relocation areas. Thus, between 1976 and 1988, 3.6 million people migrated to establish 'new economic zones'. The case of the Krong Na commune, in the buffer zone of Yok Don National Park, illustrates the migration pattern. In 1975, Krong Na's population consisted of 2,700 people of eight ethnic minorities. The population increased quickly, reaching 7700 in 1995, including 17 ethnic minorities.

Attempts at Settlement

After 30 years of the government's sedentary cultivation programme, 65 per cent (1.9 million people) of the original resettlement target (2.9 million) have adopted permanent settlement. Of these, 30 per cent (nearly 600,000) may be considered to be successful in that they are settled and cultivating permanent cash crops with relatively stable income and little need for government support. Some 40 per cent (about 800,000) may be considered to be marginally successful in that government support for production activities is still needed. The remainder have proved to be unsustainable even with government support. They continue to practise shifting cultivation. The unsustainable producers are generally in the northern midlands and mountain region, while the successful ones are in the Central Highlands, where production conditions are more favourable (Be Viet Dang, 1996). Although the sedentary cultivation programme has been in place for 30 years, people are still poor, and shifting cultivation is still popular.

Poverty and Inequality

Vietnam remains one of the poorest countries in the world. With nearly 80 per cent of its population living in rural areas, Vietnam depends on its agricultural and natural resources. Poverty varies greatly throughout the country, with the northern uplands and the Central Highlands remaining the poorest regions. In each of the protected areas studied, 90 per cent of the population depends on agricultural production.

Poverty in Vietnam is rooted in a number of factors. For the mountainous areas, the most important factors are very poor material and technical infrastructure; a seriously damaged environment; a poorly developed economy; rapid population increase; unemployment; and poor education and training. As a rule, poor people are either landless or have been pushed to areas of low agricultural potential, including steep slopes and infertile lands, where high population densities or poor land-use practices lead to further impoverishment and declining social wellbeing. Poverty prevents people from taking a long-term economic or environmental view. Poor farmers extract what they can from the environment to support themselves, and have little time or resources left to invest in resource conservation or management. Marginal resources, which are often all that are available to the poor, are used intensively. Moreover, poor farmers often lack the resources or skills needed for restorative or protective works. These communities are often faced with a shortage of agricultural land. As a result, arable land is more intensively exploited and forests are cleared more aggressively for agriculture production. Degradation due to excessive or inappropriate use creates a dangerous cycle.

Macroeconomic Policies and Structures

Dividing Vietnam's recent macroeconomic history into pre-*doi moi* and *doi moi*, this section attempts to determine the importance of the *doi moi* macroeconomic reform to the country's biodiversity loss. The main question is: how have economic policy changes altered resource use patterns in Vietnam? Until 1975, the Vietnam economy was a war economy. The nature and demands of the war economy played an important role in shaping the exploitation of natural resources, especially forest resources. After reunification in 1976, Vietnam began to turn to peaceful economic development, based on state planning. Despite this planning, the country's economy suffered many difficulties and entered a period of serious inflation and economic crisis in the mid-1980s.

No one doubts that *doi moi* has brought a new prosperous face to Vietnam's economy. Nevertheless, current environmental studies have shown an alarming degradation of the country's natural resources over the past few years. This research project has perceived a direct link between some *doi moi* policies and accelerated biodiversity loss in Vietnam. These problems are discussed below.

Cash Crop Export Promotion

Export promotion of agricultural products of high value, one of the primary goals of *doi moi*, has caused significant biodiversity loss since 1986. Thanks to liberalization of the domestic market, decentralization and simplification of controls on exports and imports and an increase in the exchange rate to market level, the export of agricultural products has increased dramatically over the past ten years. Profits from the export of agricultural products have encouraged both state and private investors to expand plantations of export crops. As a consequence, forests are cleared and the biodiversity of forest ecosystems is threatened. Most development of cash crops is occurring in the Central Highlands. Much of the new agricultural land in Dak Lak, opened up from tropical forests, is planted with high-value export crops such as coffee, rubber, cashew and fruits. Intensive and uncontrolled clearing of forest to obtain land for export crops in Dak Lak is a visible cause of biodiversity loss.

Lack of Market Accessibility and Information

As domestic prices for primary export products fluctuate with international market prices, lack of information on prices and potential markets affects farmers' income as well as national foreign exchange income. For instance, the

Table 15.2 *Export of Agricultural Products after* Doi Moi *(US$ millions)*

	1985	1990	1995
Total export value of agricultural products	396	1,148	2,703
Agriculture	274	783	2,005
Forestry	40	126	98
Fisheries	82	239	600

Source: Cao Duc Phat, 1997

farm-gate price for coffee in Dak Lak was less than US$1 per kg for the first five months of 1997. In June, the price reached $1.5 per kg, but most of the harvest had already been sold (Vietnam Economic Times, 1997). The income from coffee sold at the lower price was hardly sufficient to cover farmers' costs. An unstable market for both domestically consumed and export products has driven local people into remaining forests to look for alternative income sources, until other cultivated crops or the next harvest season can provide them with badly needed income.

Timber Export Promotion

Intensive logging by SFE, in order to meet both domestic demand for industrialization and export targets set by the government, resulted in a large loss of forest after reunification. Yet, this period of timber exploitation pales in comparison to the years immediately after the introduction of *doi moi*. Exploitation of timber was emphasized at the beginning of *doi moi* for the sake of earning hard currency. The total export volume of roundwood for the pre-*doi moi* period (1976–80) was 11,700 m³, increasing to 277,100 m³ for the period 1986–90 (Ministry of Forestry, 1991). By 1990, the value of exports of forest products was US$126.5 million, which put trade in forest products in third place after agricultural and light industry products. Moreover, these figures are underestimates, because considerable difference exists between officially reported volumes of wood exported and the real volumes exported. In 1995, due to the government's export ban on raw logs, the export value of forest products declined to about US$98 million (Cao Duc Phat, 1997). This policy has put greater emphasis on exporting processed timber products in order to retain a greater share of the added value from these resources and to preserve remaining forests.

Regional Demand for Other Forest Products

Export booms have not been limited to coffee and logs. Wildlife exportation has also increased significantly, especially after the reopening of the Chinese border in the early 1990s. While *doi moi* does not explicitly promote the export of wildlife, the associated trade liberalization has facilitated growth of this illicit activity. Vietnam also serves as a conduit for the transport of wildlife from Laos and Cambodia being transported to China and elsewhere. The

Table 15.3 *Timber Export Boom After 1986*

Item:	Export volume:					
	1986	1988	1990	1991	1993	1995
Roundwood (m³)	22,000	17,000	124,000	240,000	23,200	
Floorwood (m³)	69,000	54,000	43,000	36,000	40,700	4,000

Source: General Statistical Office, 1996

Forest Protection Department has determined that Dak Lak Province has the greatest activity of wildlife hunting and trade in the country.

Other Public Policies

Land-Use Policies

Land-use policies play a decisive role in socioeconomic development, particularly in agricultural countries such as Vietnam. Since peasants make up about 80 per cent of the population, the success or failure of land-use policies and the cooperative movement had strong impacts on the economic condition of the whole country. After liberation in 1954, collectivization of agricultural land began. As discussed above, inefficiency of the APCs led to an agricultural crisis. As their productivity declined, many farmers took to the forests to set up private plots, hunt, and collect forest products to supplement their dwindling income. For example, in the Ba Be district during the 1965–70 period, wildlife was very abundant. Today, the buffer zones are grasslands or completely barren hills. In Na Hang district, forests were intensively cleared in two periods. From 1975 to 1983, APC productivity dropped, as in other locations in the North. From 1989 to 1992, food self-sufficiency policies were implemented. Under these policies, everyone, including administrators and factory workers, had to work in clearing forest land for expansion of food crops.

From the early 1960s to 1990, the government sponsored population redistribution programmes with the following objectives:

- Match human resources with agricultural resources;
- Develop the agricultural sector of the economy;
- Create opportunities for employment in the agricultural sector; and
- Strengthen national defence.

Among the programmes in support of the government's resettlement policy, the one with the largest implications for forest degradation and soil erosion was the sedentary cultivation programme. Its main objective was to stabilize the agricultural land use of ethnic minorities, such as the H'Mong and Dao who have a long tradition of shifting cultivation, and encourage socioeconomic development for about 3 million shifting cultivators. This programme established 445 projects in 34 provinces.

After 1991, when the state-farm concept fell out of favour, two programmes played key roles in the provision of capital for agricultural and rural development. The 327 Programme, a source of investment credit for individual farmers, also provided funding for forest protection activities. Rural credit systems extended by the Vietnam Bank for Agriculture provided credit to rural public institutions and individual farmers. The issue of investment credit for poor farm households is receiving great attention from the Vietnamese government and foreign organizations. Nevertheless, the effectiveness of the government's effort to grant credit to poor households in remote areas is limited. Surveys in the buffer zone of Yok Don National Park found that the low amount of borrowing allowed, and the poor terms of credit, do not meet households' capital demands nor allow them to make investments to improve the sustainability of cultivation.

Forestry Policy

Among the most important policies related to biodiversity loss are forestry policies. The Ministry of Agriculture and Rural Development (formerly the Ministry of Forestry) manages forest lands. Following liberation in 1954, forest enterprises were established in almost all mountainous districts to manage, protect, exploit and develop forest resources. By 1991 there were 412 forest enterprises. Dak Lak province alone has 50 forestry enterprises, including 30 managed by the state. One of the main tasks of forest enterprises is to exploit forest products, mainly wood, necessary for reconstruction of the country and for export. As a result, legal logging has caused degradation of about 70,000 ha of forest per year, and an absolute loss of about 30,000 ha per year (World Bank, 1995b).

Government Conservation Efforts

Vietnam's first protected area was established in 1962. More recently, the government has enacted a substantial body of domestic legislation aimed at the protection of biodiversity. One of Vietnam's largest achievements in biodiversity conservation has been the establishment of a protected area system that is representative of most of the major habitat types in the country. The protected area system now includes ten national parks, covering over 252,000 ha, and 61 nature reserves with a total of almost 1.7 million ha.

To date, the government has established management boards in each of the national parks and 35 of the nature reserves. Besides serving management and organizational functions, these management boards also carry out scientific research in protected areas. Forest protection units and forest protection and management stations have also been set up in some major parks and reserves. However, despite these protective entities, weak management, poor cooperation among government sectors, weak law enforcement and lack of facilities, infrastructure and investment, have caused both quantitative and qualitative degradation to protected forests (Ministry of Agriculture and Rural Development, 1996). Shifting cultivation and forest clearance for agriculture, as well as poaching of wood and animals, still occurs. The presence of settlements of local people near or within the protected areas poses the most difficult challenge to Vietnam's protected areas. There are some 250,000 people living inside protected forests. As a result, many important ecosystems and endangered species are inadequately protected.

Effectiveness of Policy Implementation in Vietnam

From 1954 until 1986, the long period prior to *doi moi*, Vietnam developed under a central planning mechanism. As a rule, the Party Congress issued the key policies of the three- and five-year plans, which were put into practice through a series of government policies and regulations. An administrative system subdivided into provinces or municipalities, districts and communes has implemented policies. At all levels of this governmental structure, there is a parallel hierarchy within the Communist Party organization concerned with the policy-making and implementation effected by the government. After a state policy is issued by the national government, administrative systems at all levels (ministries, provinces and districts and then communes) translate the policy into practice by designing particular measures to implement the policy in ways appropriate to local circumstances. The same policy, therefore, may produce very different effects in different localities depending on many factors, including capacity, responsibility, knowledge and quality of the leaders. Additionally, at the local level, provincial and district People's Committees, entities of the parallel Party hierarchy, can issue their own policies or regulations to better implement the government's policies.

A socioeconomic development policy may have an adverse impact on the environment, or on biodiversity in particular, due to one or more of the following problems with policy design and implementation:

Limited knowledge of policy-makers

An issued policy may be either inappropriate in practice. An example is a policy promoting the development of certain cash crops in mountainous areas. Due to lack of necessary processing facilities or transportation, sale of surplus crops was often poorly timed. This clear lack of communication, which is needed to synchronize policies, is repeatedly harmful to farmers.

Mistakes or shortcomings in the process of policy implementation at different administrative levels

Many irresponsible leaders have taken advantage of policy gaps either to advance themselves in the administrative system or to engage in corruption and smuggling. Violation of state laws and corruption have threatened to distort numerous economic activities. Personality power politics – individuals vying for personal promotion within a department or ministry – often result in irrational decision-making for the sake of personal gain.

An unclear division of the managing responsibilities of different administrative systems

Several management organizations may control one entity while others do not belong to any management line. Unclear delineation of management authority within a national park is a strong example. National park management is principally under the direct management of the Ministry of Agriculture and Rural Development, located in Hanoi. Yet the communities within a park, both in core zones and buffer zones, are under the local district administrative system. Hence, even if a park's management board has enacted a policy to stop new migrants settling in the park, local authorities can still allow registration of new migrants.

Inaccurate reports

In order to appease superiors and managers, progress reports are often camouflaged to hide many alarming but true figures, situations and phenomena. As a result, policy-makers are not properly informed of the actual situation and develop inappropriate or insufficient policies.

Table 15.4 *Root Causes of Biodiversity Loss*

	Ba Be	Na Hang	Yok Don
War demands	+++	+++	−
Demographic change			
Natural growth	+++	+++	+
Migration	+	+	+++
Poverty	+++	+++	+++
Policies on:			
Export			
Legal	−	+	+++
Illegal	++	+	+++
Land tenure	+++	+++	−
Forestry (state sector)	+	++	+++
Policy and law enforcement	+++	+	++
Traditional shifting cultivation	+++	++	+

Key: − Weak   + Medium   ++ Strong   +++ Very Strong

CONCLUSIONS

Biodiversity loss is occurring throughout the country, particularly in mountainous regions. In all three protected areas studied, biodiversity is rapidly declining and forests have been reduced alarmingly by human activities. Among the three protected areas, there are clear differences across time as well as in quantity and quality of the proximate and root causes of biodiversity loss. In the subtropical forests of the Ba Be National Park and the Na Hang

Nature Reserve, biodiversity loss grew substantially prior to the *doi moi* reform. The socioeconomic root causes of biodiversity loss in these mountainous areas of northern Vietnam consist primarily of high natural population growth rates, traditional agricultural and hunting practices and the inefficiency of the APC, all causes which had their impact on biodiversity before the mid-1980s. In the dry tropical forest of the Yok Don National Park, biodiversity loss occurred most intensely during the *doi moi* renovation, with the exception of the effects of hunting by automatic guns left over from the Second Indochina War. Economic development of the late 1980s brought planned migrations, arable land expansion for cash-crop export earnings and extensive logging.

There are important differences between Ba Be, Na Hang and Yok Don related to socioeconomic conditions. In Ba Be and Na Hang, natural forests were still abundant in the 1960s. The largest biodiversity losses occurred from 1970 to 1983 and from 1989 to 1992. The first peak of biodiversity loss was partly due to a disintegration of the cooperative movement. The second peak occurred as a result of the government's policy on food self-sufficiency. Both these peaks of forest degradation were due to food shortages and poverty. Poverty promoted population growth on the one hand and environmental degradation on the other. Forests were extensively exploited, first for food security, then for expansion of agricultural production. Illegal migration due to the Northern Border War (1979–80) contributed to population growth in the Ba Be area. In turn, population growth increased poverty and environmental degradation, including the formation of huge areas of barren hills and decreases in wildlife populations. Illegal hunting has compounded the loss of wildlife.

Although Na Hang Nature Reserve and Ba Be National Park are close to each other, there are differences between the two areas, first in administrative management and second in conservation. In Tuyen Quang province, where Na Hang is located, the administrative system is active and flexible. Administrators have understood the significance of environmental protection. They therefore not only implement state policies strictly, but also have promulgated regulations to protect and develop forests. Forestry protection units are active and effective. Authorities have been introducing new agricultural techniques to raise the local standard of living. The 327 Programme has been widely implemented and violations of forest protection laws are recognized in time, so that forests have been protected.

In Ba Be, the situation is different because of frequent reorganization of the administrative system. Originally a district of Bac Kan province, it became a district of Bac Thai province in 1964, then a district of Ca Bang province in 1978 and again a district of Bac Kan province in 1997. Consequently the current situation of both administrative activities and conservation work in Ba Be is worse than that in Na Hang. There is some conflict between the Ba Be National Park directorate and Ba Be district authorities in management of the park. Violations of the forest protection law still occur, including illegal logging, hunting, collecting forest products and clearing forest land for agriculture. Results of the 327 Programme are rather limited.

Yok Don presents a different situation. In the early 1970s, the population was still small. Indigenous people followed traditional agricultural practices, collected products from forests, and hunted. Under the government policy to encourage ethnic people to settle in permanent villages, initiated in the early 1980s, they made extensive use of forest products for subsistence. However, the impact of these indigenous people on the forest, natural resources and environment was not significant. After national reunification, and especially since 1980, many changes occurred in the Yok Don area, resulting in heavy forest degradation and deforestation. Logging by many state and local forest enterprises for domestic needs and for export, as well as illegal logging by state enterprises and smugglers, contributed to deforestation. The forest protection agency is understaffed and underfinanced, and thus is unable to control poaching of forest products. Government-sponsored and spontaneous migrants from other provinces, especially from the Red River delta and the northern highlands, have contributed to the high population growth of the area. Population growth, in turn, has led to over-exploitation of natural resources for food security. Illegal hunting with automatic weapons and illegal wildlife trade with China, Thailand and Singapore are causing wildlife loss. Recent arable land expansion for cash and export crops – cashew, pepper, fruits and especially coffee and rubber – adds to deforestation.

Under the *doi moi* renovation, the government enacted a series of resolutions, policies and strategies for conservation of environment and biodiversity. However, for many reasons, biodiversity of the country in general and of protected areas in particular is still being degraded in both quantitative and qualitative terms. For biodiversity conservation to be effective, it should be linked to sustainable development. Thus, it is essential to address the root causes of biodiversity loss by integrating conservation into economic development plans. Conservation efforts must combine upgraded protected area management with concrete strategies to provide livelihood opportunities for communities living adjacent to, or in enclaves within, the protected areas.

RECOMMENDATIONS

Knowledge of the proximate and root causes of biodiversity loss in Vietnam reveals which aspects of policy and administration are in need of improvement to slow the degradation of Vietnam's terrestrial ecosystems, providing the foundation for recommending realistic and achievable changes.

First, recommendations are presented for administrators who can effect change at the level of the protected area, including protected area management and district- and provincial-level authorities. Specific recommendations are made for each of the three protected areas examined by this project. Second, more general recommendations are made for the audience of national-level long-term planners who work on a much larger scale. Appropriately, it is at this level that the potential solutions to the root causes emerge. Finally, some brief recommendations are made for addressing the international pressures that lead to biodiversity loss within Vietnam.

Proximate and Intermediate Scales

These recommendations are applicable to the protected area, district and provincial scales:

- Halt any further immigration of people into protected areas.

- Relocate households settled inside protected areas to outside areas in order to reduce human population densities to sustainable levels. Households should be moved outside the protected area boundaries but not to other areas of remaining high biodiversity.

- Reform settlement programmes to increase their effectiveness. Provide settlement assistance to households in areas of remaining high biodiversity.

- Improve policy coordination among protected area, district and provincial authorities. Make attempts to eliminate jurisdictional ambiguities through regular forums with participation of district and provincial People's Committees, district and provincial department heads and protected area management.

- Firmly enforce laws prohibiting forest exploitation. To do so, the capacity of forest protection units must be increased substantially. Enforcement needs to occur not only at the forest level, but also at the market level in district and provincial collection centres.

- Clearly demarcate protected area boundaries and zones.

- Design tourist revenue redistribution systems that benefit the protection of biodiversity.

- Use an integrated conservation and development approach when addressing needs of households in the buffer zones of protected areas. Improve the living standard of local people living near the forest by introducing alternative employment and upgrading infrastructure.

- Integrate education on family planning and environmental awareness with traditional customs.

Ba Be National Park
- Clearly demarcate the boundaries of the park and its different zones. The communities living within park boundaries need a clear idea of which activities are allowed before stricter enforcement can ensue.

- The population density of the core zone is currently considered to be beyond carrying capacity and should be lessened through assisted relocation.

- Address the controversial migration of H'Mong people between Bac Kan and Tuyen Quang Provinces with inter-provincial meetings. The division of authority and obligations to address the impacts of the shifting cultivators living in the provincial border region must be effectively delegated between these two provinces that have a common interest in the resolution of the situation.

- Strengthen the capacity of the forest protection units to prevent any new immigration or further forest clearance for agricultural expansion.

Na Hang Nature Reserve
- Limit the population living inside the reserve by disallowing any further immigration.

- Address the controversial migration of H'Mong people between Bac Kan and Tuyen Quang Provinces with inter-provincial meetings. The division of authority and obligations to address the impacts of the shifting cultivators living in the provincial border region must be effectively delegated between these two provinces that have a common interest in the resolution of the situation.

- Strengthen the organization and capacity of the reserve management board.

Yok Don National Park
- Prevent any further migration to the areas surrounding the park, reconsider current provincial plans for planned migrations into the relatively uncultivated but potentially fertile areas north of the park and seek alternative relocation sites for planned migrations.

- Enlarge the current boundaries of the park to encompass adjacent areas not yet settled and cultivated.

- Strengthen the forest protection unit to enable it to assess the impact of hunting.

National Scale

These recommendations have been kept as realistic as possible given the difficulty of incorporating environmental considerations into national-level policy-making:

- Revise the protected area system to introduce more clearly delineated jurisdictional authority over the land, resources and people located within the boundaries of protected areas.

- Collaborate and cooperate across ministries and departments and develop appropriate government mechanisms to facilitate effective collaboration and information sharing. Policies should be a product of interdisciplinary review and impact assessment.

- Designate land-use categories in national-level planning, including areas suitable for the expansion for cash crops.

- Harmonize regulations and enforcement for natural resources throughout the country.

- Consider the future impact of households moved to previously unculti-vated areas when conducting planned migrations. Opening new frontiers is no longer a desirable alternative.

- Give the forest protection department stronger authority.

- Improve working facilities and pay, professionalism and relationships with villagers.

- Shift investment focus to mountainous areas that have been neglected thus far in reforms, giving priority to assistance in agroforestry.

- Build sufficient flexibility into policies so that they can be tailored for each region, area and minority.

- Assist provinces in halting free migration. Government-sponsored migra-tion and fixed cultivation and settlement programmes should be implemented carefully, especially with respect to the selection of relocation sites.

International Level

- Initiate a dialogue with bordering countries on limiting the cross-border trade of endangered species and strengthen CITES enforcement, also in cooperation with bordering countries.

- Maintain new legislation banning the export of logs, timber and processed wood products and introduce an exception to the ban for wood products from sustainably managed forests.

- Welcome new technologies for processing agricultural products more effec-tively.

Notes

CHAPTER 1 AN EMERGING CONSENSUS ON BIODIVERSITY LOSS

1   WWF (1999). This report is based on the Living Planet Index, which aggregates a number of key indicators relating to the state of the world's environment (for example forests, freshwater and marine) to produce an index of how fast nature is disappearing from the Earth.
2   There are many voices, especially from the developing world, that believe that the choice and definition of those problems reflect Northern, and not Southern, interests.
3   See Sjoberg (1994); Benedick (1991) and Swanson (1997)
4   Wolf (1995).
5   For discussion of some of these approaches, see Brandon et al (1998), Swanson (1997) and Hanna (1996).
6   For seminal works see Pearce, Barbier and Markandya (1990); Pearce and Warford (1993) and Repetto (1985).
7   Cruz and Repetto (1992) and Reed ed (1992 and 1996).

CHAPTER 2 A FRAMEWORK FOR ANALYSING BIODIVERSITY LOSS

1   For good reviews of the proximate causes, see McNeeley et al (1990), Barbier et al (1994), Perrings et al (1995) and ESD (1995).
2   See, for example, Barbier et al (1994),WRI, IUCN, and UNEP (1992), McNeeley et al (1990) and Asian Development Bank (1990).
3   Work on analysis at the global level includes Meyer and Turner eds (1994), Stern et al (1992), Robinson (1991) and Gallopin (1991).
4   The background paper prepared for these case studies (Stedman-Edwards 1998) provides a more comprehensive literature review.
5   The background paper prepared for these case studies (Stedman-Edwards 1998) provides a more detailed rationale for the development of this approach and a more detailed description of the approach.
6   Useful references on this topic include Barbier et al (1994), Bilsborrow and Okoth-Ogendo (1992), Blaikie and Brookfield (1987), Dasgupta (1992), Erlich and Erlich (1990), Jepma (1995), Leonard (1989), Meyer and Turner (1992) and Sage (1994).
7   Useful references on this topic include Boyce (1994), Dasgupta (1992), Kates and Haarman (1992), Leonard (1989), Sage (1994) and Serageldin (1996).

8   Useful references on this topic include Barbier et al (1994), Mahar (1989), McNeely (1988), Perrings et al (1995), Repetto and Gillis (1988), Sanderson (1994), Schiff and Valdes (1992), Sedjo and Simpson (1995), Southgate (1988), Swanson (1995) and World Bank (1994).

9   Useful references on this topic include Anderson and Blackhurst (1992), Bhagwati (1993), Capistrano and Kiker (1995), Daly (1993), Dean (1992), Lutz (1990), Maler and Munasinghe (1996), Redclift (1987), Reed (1992 and 1996), Røpke (1994), Sanderson (1994), Serageldin (1996), Swanson (1995) and World Bank (1994).

10 Useful references on this topic include Blaikie and Brookfield (1987), Browder (1989), Gadgil et al (1993), Painter (1995), Redford and Mansour (1996), Rockwell (1994), Schumann and Partridge (1989), Serageldin (1996), Uquillas (1989), Vincent and Panayotou (1997) and Western and Wright (1994).

11 Most proposals for research agendas in the field stress the need for interdisciplinary work. See Robinson (1991), Machlis and Forester (1996), Stern et al, eds (1992) and Meyer and Turner (1992 and 1994).

12 The best examples of these are Stonich (1995), Blaikie and Brookfield (1987), Painter and Durham, eds (1995), Little and Horowitz, eds (1987) and Schmink and Wood (1987).

13 For definitions of political ecology, see Blaikie and Brookfield (1987), Stonich (1995) and Schmink and Wood (1987).

14 Machlis and Forester (1996) provide the most explicit and pertinent review and discussion of the utility of various types of models of causes of biodiversity loss.

15 See, for example, Machlis and Forester (1996), Robinson (1991), Meyer and Turner (1994) and Stern et al (1992).

16 This literature is reviewed in Stedman-Edwards (1998).

CHAPTER 4 MAIN FINDINGS AND CONCLUSIONS OF THE ROOT CAUSES PROJECT

1   See for example, Barbier et al (1994), WRI, IUCN and UNEP (1992), McNeely et al (1990) and Asian Development Bank (1990).

2   See Repetto and Gillis (1988), Mahar (1989), McNeely (1988) and World Bank (1994).

3   Similar conclusions are reached by Brandon et al (1998), drawing on case studies of protected areas in Latin America.

CHAPTER 5 RECOMMENDATIONS ON ADDRESSING THE ROOT CAUSES OF BIODIVERSITY LOSS

1   For a more detailed description of what such an assessment might involve, see WWF (1999).

CHAPTER 6 BRAZIL: CERRADO

1 Mantovani and Pereira (1998). Unfortunately the limits of the area studied by these authors coincides with the limits of 'savanna' in the Brazilian Vegetation Map (IBGE 1993), which includes the Pantanal wetland that we are not considering as part of the Cerrado biome. The numbers for the Cerrado biome alone would be slightly different, probably showing a lower percentage of intact area.

2 This figure is for federal indirect-use conservation areas (parks and reserves). We do not have data for state, municipal, or private reserves.

3 In simplest terms, this refers to differences in the density of trees and shrubs.

4 Note that the term Cerrado can denote one of these vegetation types (*sensu stricto*) or the entire complex (Cerrado biome). Due to the lack of English equivalents, the Portuguese terms for the vegetation types within the Cerrado biome are used (Coutinho, 1978).

5 This includes 38 per cent of family establishments that are considered marginal or practically inactive in terms of agriculture, which occupy about five per cent of the area of family establishments, serving primarily as residences and averaging two hectares.

6 Patronal sector establishments average 600 ha, while the consolidated family sector establishments (excluding the marginal establishments described in the previous note) average 50 ha.

7 The agriculture traditionally practised in the Cerrado was shifting cultivation, which moved to a new area of cultivation every five years, due to low soil fertility. This practice was common in Goiás at least until the 1930s when land tenure regularization and demographic growth made it unviable. Extensive ranching in natural areas of the Cerrado also requires large areas and is still practised today, interspersed with planted pastures.

8 In Rio Verde, Perdigão is installing a $550 million project involving the integration of farmers, ranchers, production of breeding stock, slaughterhouses and packing plants. The project is expected to absorb all the county's production of corn, sorghum, and soybean meal

9 According to Brazilian legislation, the use and occupation of the buffer zone (considered to be a minimum of ten km from the border of the protected area) should be regulated by the management agency, in this case IBAMA.

10 We worked with relative values due to the changes in municipal boundaries.

11 Brazilian Agricultural Extension Agency and Support Centre for Mini, Small, and Medium Producers

12 The Buriti Alto Project involved an area of 15,600 ha and 40 producers in four counties. Storage space was created and seed improvement activities were implemented.

13 It is worth mentioning, since it is frequently cited, that some groups believe the economic stagnation of Alto Paraíso is due to the action of extra-terrestrials or spirits determined to preserve the region.

CHAPTER 8 CHINA: SOUTH-WESTERN FORESTS

1 Current exchange rate is about 1 US dollar = 8.3 Chinese yuan.

2 This decrease includes 24 animals shipped out of the county to zoos.

CHAPTER 11 MEXICO: CALAKMUL BIOSPHERE RESERVE

1   About half the reserve is medium tropical semi-evergreen forest; 35 per cent is low tropical semi-evergreen forest; five per cent is high tropical semi-evergreen forest; the remainder is primarily grasslands and wetlands. See INE and CONABIO (1995).

2   A 1986 satellite image shows about five per cent of the reserve lands in agriculture or noticeably disturbed, and 29 per cent of the surrounding area in agriculture or noticeably disturbed (Ecosur).

3   For a detailed explanation of this methodology, see Stedman-Edwards (1998).

4   See references to Tavera, Boege, Galleti, Murphy, Galindo-Leal, March, and Haenn.

5   See Pronatura (1997a,b and c)

6   This is the population of the newly formed Calakmul Municipality, of which the CBR forms over 40 per cent (Government of Campeche, 1997a). The most recent population census of the buffer zone and area of influence was carried out in 1995 (INEGI, 1995). Population data were also collected from a number of *ejidos* around Calakmul by Ericson (1996).

7   This description is based on documents from Pronatura, Boege, and Ericson (various dates).

8   Chicle is the resin of the chico zapote tree, used for making chewing gum.

9   See Haenn (1996), Richardson (1995) and Pronatura (1997a and 1997b).

10 The information on agricultural and extractive activities presented here is based primarily on a field study by Ericson (1996) of four local *ejidos*, Galleti (nd), Boege and Murguia (1989), Boege (1993 and 1995) and interviews carried out for this study (Tavera, 1997).

11 Educational and health care services in the area are poor. Illiteracy levels are high, commonly 25 per cent or more. *Campesinos*, on average, spend 60 per cent of their income on food (Ericson, 1996).

12 See Boege (1995), Haenn (1996), Richardson (1995) and Ericson (1997).

13 Ericson (1996). Data from PROCAMPO confirm this estimate.

14 This figure is based on figures from PROCAMPO, a government agriculture programme, for 44 *ejidos* in the area of the CBR, plus an estimate from PROCAMPO of the agricultural area not covered by its programme (Tavera, 1997). Other information suggests that PROCAMPO is underestimating the area outside the programme. We estimate, given productive use of three years and fallow periods of five to ten years, that the area affected by agriculture may be from 23,000 to 40,000 ha in a five-year period alone.

15 The highly valued woods, namely mahogany and Spanish cedar, in the area are reputed to have been largely exhausted, but their exploitation continues. Other species commonly harvested include *Lonchocarpus castilloi*, *Platymiscium yucatanum*, *Cordia dodecandra*, *Bursera simaruba*, *Pseudobombax ellipticum*, and *Metopium brownii*.

16 A study is now being conducted to determine the impact of bee-keeping on other species in the forest (Galindo-Leal, nd). This impact may prove to be substantial.

17 Africanization of bees in recent years has diminished enthusiasm for beekeeping, but new efforts are underway to boost participation and production.

18 See Aranda (nd), March (1991a and 1991b) and Weber (1997).

19 This conclusion is based on figures from Ericson (1996) and from INEGI (1995). The decision to plant corn reflects its traditional role as a the staple of life in Mexico, as well as the scarcity of other, more secure, sources of income.

20 Murphy (1990) found, in a study of a Mayan region in the neighbouring state of Quintana Roo, that a 'successful' sustainable forestry programme ignored the importance of subsistence agriculture, both economically and socially. Rather than slowing the expansion of agricultural land, improved incomes from forestry may have had the perverse impact of providing the capital needed to expand agricultural land.

21 About 30 per cent of Mexico's population lives in rural areas, producing only seven per cent of GDP. Seventy per cent of Mexicans living in poverty live in rural areas, despite the distribution of about 42 million ha of *ejidal* lands since the Revolution (DeWalt and Rees, 1994).

22 Under self-sufficiency policies, rates of deforestation were high, and the agricultural frontier expanded rapidly. From the late 1940s to the mid-1960s, the agricultural sector grew by more than four per cent a year, boosted by a variety of subsidies (World Bank, 1995a). Most growth was achieved through expansion of land area in agriculture rather than increases in productivity. Agricultural expansion reached Calakmul as new *ejidos* were allotted to accommodate migrants in search of land.

23 Morett (1992), DeWalt and Rees (1994). In order to make a reasonable living, most *ejidatarios* throughout the country combine agriculture with other activities, including work outside the community, day labour and small commercial activities.

24 Levy and van Wijnbergen (1992). For example, in 1995, when hurricanes affected crops, a survey of four families in the region found that 36 to 61 per cent of their income came from government subsidies (Haenn, 1996).

25 About 42 per cent of Mexican land is held by *ejidos*, including about 15 million ha of forests (DeWalt and Rees, 1994). There are about 9000 forest *ejidos* in Mexico (World Bank, 1997).

26 See, for example, World Bank (1995a) and Reed (1992).

27 At the time of the NAFTA agreement, Mexican wood was 10 to 30 per cent more expensive than US or Canadian wood (World Bank, 1995a).

28 Estimates of rural use of local timber for firewood suggest that as many as 90 per cent of rural households burn wood, accounting for five times the legal annual extraction of timber (World Bank, 1995a).

29 The area has a 20-year history of grassroots organization, which began in response to perceived abuses by the timber companies; this history is responsible for some of the government interest in the area: Boege and Murguia (1989), Boege (1997) and Ericson (1996).

30 See Haenn (1997), Pronatura (1997a and 1997b) and Acopa et al (1996).

31 Pronatura is sponsoring a new population-environment initiative which will include a reproductive health programme and community land-use planning: Freudenberger and Boege (1995) and Ericson et al (1998).

CHAPTER 13 PHILIPPINES: CEBU, NEGROS, AND PALAWAN

1   Unlike forest cover and mangroves, natural infestation, such as that of the crown-of-thorns starfish, is a substantial cause of loss of coral. However, some experts argue that this is also caused by environmental disturbances.

2   For example, differences in ease of access explain why beach forests have been logged completely, while areas such as the northern Sierra Madre, which is relatively inaccessible, remain forested.

3   The Philippines has a total land area of about 300,000 km^2.

4   Barrera (1963) estimated that an average of 17 cm of topsoil had been removed from 400,000 ha of land that was prone to erosion.

5   While probably the most important case of this type, Cebu also provides a model of the lesser plantation economies that evolved in different parts of the Philippine archipelago, namely in central Luzon and, in later periods, in Mindanao.

6   Mount Canlaon is among the most degraded natural parks in the country. Wildlife hunting and military shelling have driven away wildlife and devastated large areas of forest. It is still a biodiversity-rich area and is listed among the 18 centres of plant diversity in the Philippines. Five of the rarest birds in the country are found in the area. Due to continued deforestation, several species of plants and animals have been declared endangered.

7   However, in the early 1970s, Palawan had about 92 per cent of its land covered with forest (Bureau of Forestry).

8   Specific direct causes under these categories depend on the particular biodiversity loss indicator under consideration. For instance, examining forest cover loss, the direct causes under the category of over-harvesting could be commercial logging, firewood gathering and community forestry.

9   One such zone is the Mactan Export Processing Zone (MEPZ), which is being developed in three phases. MEPZ I houses more than 100 companies, employing about 32,700 workers. MEPZA II has a total area of 63 ha, of which 42.5 ha are classified as industrial.

10   In 1990, 360,000 out of the 506,000 households used firewood.

11   Reported in *The Freeman*, a Cebu newspaper.

12   Many Cebu establishments have resorted to desalinization, and the Metro-Cebu water district is now building a dam in the Mananga watershed to increase Cebu's water supply.

13   The Philippines was given a US quota of 980,000 to 1.5 million tonnes, bought at prices 35 per cent higher than the world market rate.

14   In 1959, 193,000 ha of sugar lands produced 112 *piculs* per ha. By 1972, cultivated areas jumped to 424,000 ha but yielded only 68 *piculs* per ha (*Sugarland Bacolod*, 11, no 4, cited in McCoy and de Jesus, 1982).

CHAPTER 14 TANZANIA: RUFIJI, RUVU, AND WAMI

1   For details see Stedman-Edwards (1998).

2   NEMC's review of the environmental impact statement for the prawn-farming project put the employment generation capacity at around 3000 people.

3   One version of the story is that some Arab merchants were apprehended by the police in 1974, allegedly for trading without a licence.

4   Over 30 per cent of the respondents in Bagamoyo said they had over six people in their households who depend on them for the provision of their basic needs.

5   These are estimates reported by the respondents; they may be grossly understated.

6   Comments made by several farmers in the Rufiji delta.

7   Similar views on the importance of mangroves to local welfare were also expressed in Bagamoyo District.

8   Mangroves for the purpose of making keels are rarely found. Mango tree trunks have largely replaced them.

9   After a court finding in 1995 that the land tenure policy was unconstitutional because it conflicted with customary law, the policy has been under review. Two land bills will be put before the parliament soon.

10   The Ujamaa policy, which seemed to embody popular participation, was in practice an attempt to bring development to the people, hence the resulting dependency. The nationalization of the foremost enterprises was intended to put the major means of production under the control of the people through public enterprises. Although well-intentioned, the state usurped too much power and allowed too little popular participation, killing self initiative. People were wary of being branded capitalists and seeing their legally acquired wealth confiscated or nationalized.

11   Being a programme initiated by the twin Bretton Woods Institutions, it had the support of donor countries, which financed the programme. So, unlike the preceding programmes, this one enjoyed the availability of funds for implementation as long as the stated conditions were met.

12   This new policy incorporates the findings of a report of the presidential commission of inquiry into land matters and the recommendations and observations of the national workshop on land policy.

13   The politics of such organizations in developing countries is well-acknowledged but will not be discussed here.

14   These projects include the Mangrove Management Project (national project), Tanga Coastal Zone Conservation and Development Project (Tanga region), Rural Integrated Project Support (Lindi and Mtwara regions), Mafia Island Marine Park, and Rufiji Environmental Management Project (REMP).

References

Acopa, M (1996) *Self-Evaluation Calakmul Model Forest Campeche, Mexico*

AIDEnvironment (1997) *Strategic Environmental Analysis*, SNV/AIDEnvironment, Amsterdam

AIDEnvironment (1998) *Examination of the Root Causes of Biodiversity Decline in Central and Eastern Europe, by Two Case Studies of Wetlands in the Danube River Basin*. Proposal to WWF Danube-Carpathian Programme, AIDEnvironment, Vienna

Ambrose OB et al (1988) *Analysis of the MCP-GEF Socio-Economic Survey Data for the West Coast and Bomana Corridor Area*, Mount Cameroon Project, Limbe

Anderson, K and Blackhurst, R eds (1992) *The Greening of World Trade Issues*, University of Michigan Press, Ann Arbor

Andreasson-Gren, IM and Groth KH (1995) *Economic Evaluation of Danube Floodplains*, WWF International discussion paper, WWF, Gland

Annandale, N (1915) Fauna of the Chilika Lake-Mammals, Reptiles and Batrachians, *Memoirs of the Indian Museum* 5(2), pp 163–174

Annandale, N and Kemp, S (1915) Introduction to the Fauna of the Chilika Lake, *Memoirs of the Indian Museum* 5, pp 1–20

Aranda, M. (nd) *Mamíferos de Calakmul*, Pronatura Península de Yucatán

Asian Development Bank (1990), *Economic Policies for Sustainable Development*, ADB, Manila

Asthana, V (1979) Limnological Studies of Lake Chilika, Orissa, *Final Project Report, Indian Programme on Man and Biosphere*, Project No 112, Department of Science and Technology, Government of India, New Delhi

Baer, W (1995) *A Economia Brasileira*, Editora Nobel, São Paulo

Bagachwa, MSD, Shechambo, FC, Sosovele, H, Kulindwa, KA, Naho, AA and Cromwell, E (1995) *Structural Adjustment and Sustainable Development in Tanzania*, Dar es Salaam University Press, Dar es Salaam

Baillon, I (1995), unpublished data, WWF Cameroon Programme Office, Yaoundé

Baimaxueshan Nature Reserve (1997) Yearly Work Summary of Baimaxueshan Nature Reserve, 1987–92, 1996–97

Barbier EB, Acreman, M and Knowler, D (1997) *Economic Valuation of Wetlands: A Guide for Policy Makers and Planners*, Ramsar Bureau, Gland

Barbier, E, Burgess JC and Folke, C (1994) *Paradise Lost? The Ecological Economics of Biodiversity*, Earthscan Publications, London

Barrera, A (1963) Soils and Natural Vegetation, in Huke, RE, *Shadows on the Land: An Economic Geography of the Philippines*, Bookmark, Manila

Barrera, A (1956) Soils and Natural Vegetation of the Philippines, *Philippine Geographical Journal* 4, pp 2–3

Be, VD (1996) *Ethnic Minorities in Socio-economic Development in Mountainous Regions*, National Politic Publishing House, Hanoi

Benedick, R (1991) *Ozone Diplomacy: New Directions in Safeguarding the Planet*, Harvard University Press

Berlanga, M and Wood, P (1991) *Estudios Base de Comunidades de Aves en la Reserva de la Biósfera Calakmul*, Pronatura Península de Yucatán, Mérida

Bhagwati, J (1993)The Case for Free Trade, *Scientific American* 269, 5, pp 42–47

Bilsborrow, RE and Okoth-Ogendo, HWO (1992) Population-driven Changes in Land-Use in Developing Countries, *Ambio* 21/1

Biodiversity Support Programme (1994) *Conserving Biological Diversity in Bulgaria: The National Biological Diversity Conservation Strategy*, WWF, Nature Conservancy, WRI, USAID and Government of Bulgaria

Blaikie, P and Brookfield, H (1987) *Land Degradation and Society*, Methuen, New York

Boege, E (1993) El Desarrollo Sustentable y la Reserva de la Biósfera de Calakmul, Campeche, México, *Boletín de Antropología Americana*

Boege, E (1995) *The Calakmul Biosphere Reserve, Mexico*, UNESCO South-South Cooperation Working Paper No 13, UNESCO, Paris

Boege, E (1997) Algunos Apuntes Para Analizar las Causas Socioeconómicas de la Pérdida de Biodiversidad en Calakmul Campeche

Boege, E and Murguia, R (1989) *Diagnostico de las Actividades Humanas que se Realizan en la Reserva de la Biósfera de Calakmul*, Pronatura Península de Yucatán, Mérida

Borges, HC (1981) *História de Silvânia*, Cerne, Goiânia

Bowles, I and Prickett, G (1994) *Reframing the Green Window: An Analysis of the GEF Pilot Phase Approach to Biodiversity and Global Warming and Recommendations for the Operational Phase*, Conservation International and Natural Resources Defense Council

Boyce, JK (1994) Inequality as a Cause of Environmental Degradation, *Ecological Economics* 11/ 3, pp 169–178

Brandon, K, Redford, K and Sanderson, S eds (1998) *Parks in Peril*, p13, Island Press, Washington DC

Browder, JO (1989) *Fragile Lands of Latin America: Strategies for Sustainable Development*, Westview Press, Boulder

Bryceson, I (1981) A Review of Some Problems of Tropical Marine Conservation with Particular Reference to the Tanzanian Coast, *Biological Conservation* 20, pp163–171

Bulgarian Institute of Statistics (1998) Socioeconomic Data on the Danube Region, 1989–1996, unpublished, Sofia

Cao, DP (1997) Implications of Foreign Trade on Vietnam's Agriculture, in *Vietnam's Socio-economic Development: A Quarterly Review*, 11, pp30–36

Capistrano, AD and Kiker, C (1995) Macro-scale Economic Influences on Tropical Forest Depletion, *Ecological Economics* 14/1, pp21–30

Carey, G ed (1996) *A Biodiversity Review of China*, WWF China Programme, Hong Kong

Cavassan, O (1990) *Florística e Fitossociologia da Vegetação Lenhosa em um Hectare de Cerrado no Parque Ecológico Municipal de Baurú*, University of Campesinas, São Paulo

Coutinho, LM (1978) O Conceito de Cerrado, *Revista*, Brasil, Bot 1, pp17–24

Cruz, W and Repetto, R (1992) *The Environmental Effects of Stabilization and Structural Adjustment Programs: The Philippines Case*, WRI, Washington, DC

Daly, H (1993) The Perils of Free Trade, *Scientific American* 269/ 5, pp50–55

Dang, HH (1996) Assessment of Status and Variation of Biological Resources of Tuyen Quang Province, in *The Forest Challenge in Vietnam*, unpublished

Daphne Foundation (1996) *Framework for the National Biodiversity Strategy in the Slovak Republic*, Bratislava

Das, BB (nd) *Chilika: The Nature's Treasure: Will It Be Allowed to Die?* Krushak Unnayan Trust, Orissa Krushak Mahasangh

Das, GS (1993) *The Report of the Fact Finding Committee on Chilika Fisheries*, submitted to the Honourable High Court, Orissa

Das, TK (1997) *Environmental Monitoring of Chilika Lake Region, Orissa: Using Integrated Remote Sensing and GIS*, Indian Institute of Technology, Kanpur

Das, NK and Samal, RC (1988) Environmental Survey of Chilika, in Patro, SN ed *Chilika–The Pride of Our Wetland Heritage*, Bhubaneshwar, Orissa Environmental Society

Dasgupta, P (1992) Population, Resources, and Poverty, *Ambio* 21/ 1, pp95–101

Davies, J et al *A Directory of Philippine Wetlands,* vol II, Asian Wetland Bureau Philippine Foundation, Cebu City

Dean, J (1992) Trade and the Environment: A Survey of the Literature, in Low, P ed *International Trade and the Environment*, World Bank Discussion Paper 159, World Bank, Washington, DC

Department of Agriculture and Natural Resources (various years) *Annual Report*, Manila

Department of Environment and Natural Resources (1990) *Integrated Research and Development Plans and Programs 1989–93*, Quezon City

Department of Natural Resources, Bureau of Forestry Development (various years) *Philippine Forestry Statistics*, Quezon City

Deqin County Forestry Bureau (1992) *Statistical Forms on Resources Depletion by Forest Logging*, Deqin

Deqin County Forestry Bureau (nd) *Explanations on the Preparation of Allowable Logging Quota*, Dequin

Deqin County Poverty Alleviation Office (1997) *Baseline Data Statistics for the 73 Poverty-Combating Counties in Yunnan Province*, Deqin

Deqin County Statistical Bureau (1998) *Deqin Statistics Reports (1993–97)*, Dequin

DeWalt, BR and Rees, MW (1994) *The End of Agrarian Reform in Mexico: Past Lessons, Future Prospects*, Center for US–Mexican Studies, University of California at San Diego

Dias, BFS (1990) Conservação da Natureza no Cerrado, in Novaes-Pinto, M *Cerrado: Caracterização, Ocupação e Perspectivas*, University of Brasília Press, Secretaria de Meio Ambiente, Ciência e Tecnologia do Distrito Federal

Diqing Tibetan Autonomous Prefecture Editorial Office of Farming Zoning Project at the Agricultural and Animal Husbandry Bureau (1984) *Zoning of the Planting Industry in Diqing*, Zhongdian

Diqing Tibetan Autonomous Prefecture Statistics Bureau (1949–96) *Statistics Yearbook*, Zhongdian

Diqing Tibetan Autonomous Prefecture Statistics Bureau (various dates) *Collections of Diqing Prefecture Population Census*, Zhongdian

Economist (1993) *Special Report on Mexico*, February 13, S1–22

Eder, JF and Fernandez, JO eds (1996) *Palawan at the Crossroads: Development and the Environment on a Philippine Frontier*, Ateneo de Manila University, Quezon City

Editorial Office of Deqin Annals (1998) *Deqin Annals*, Deqin

Editorial Office of Pingwu County Annals (1995) *Pingwu County Annals Section Eleven–Forestry*, Pingwu

Environment Management Bureau (1990) *Philippine Environmental Quality Report 1990–95*, Department of Environment and Natural Resources, Quezon City

Environmental Resources Management (1998) *Environmental Impact Assessment of Plantation Expansion in Forested Lowlands of the Mount Cameroon Region*, Department of International Development, London

Ericson, J (1996) 'Conservation and Development on the Border of the Calakmul Biosphere Reserve, Campeche, Mexico', MSc thesis, Environmental Systems, Humbolt State University, California

Ericson, J (1997) 'Regional Assessment: Calakmul Population–Environment Initiative', unpublished article

Ericson, J, Boege, E and Freudenberger, M (1998) *La Dínamica Poblacional, Migración y el Futuro de la Reserva de la Biósfera de Calakmul*, Pronatura Península de Yucatán, World Wildlife Fund and Population–Environment Fellows Program, University of Michigan, Mexico City

Ericson, J, Maas Rodriguez, R (1998) 'La Dínamica Poblacional en los Ejidos Alrededor de la Reserva de la Biósfera de Calakmul', Pronatura Península de Yucatán, World Wildlife Fund and Population–Environment Fellows Program, University of Michigan, unpublished article

Erlich, P and Erlich, A (1990) *The Population Explosion*, Simon and Schuster, New York

FAO/Instituto Nacional de Colonização e Reforma Agrária (1995) *Diretrizes de Política Agrária e Desenvolvimento Sustentável. Resumo do Relatório Final do Projeto UTF/BRA/036*, Brasília

Fisher, AC and Krutilla, JV (1974) Valuing Long Run Ecological Consequences and Irreversibilities, *Journal of Environmental Economics and Management* 1

Felfilli, JM, Silva, Jr, MC, Rezende, AV, Machado, JWB, Walter, BMT and Hay, JD (1993) Análise Comparativa da Florística e Fitossociologia da Vegetação Arbórea do Cerrado *sensu stricto* na Chapada Pratinha, DF-Brasil, *Acta Botânica Brasileira* 6/2, pp27–45

Fernandez, RA (1997) Almost All of RP's Coral Reeds Gone, No Thanks to Greed, *Philippine Star* 11(299),pp1,12

Fleiger, W (1994) *Cebu: A Demographic and Socioeconomic Profile Based on the 1990 Census*, Manila

Fottland, H and Sorensen, C (1996) Issues Related to the Establishment of Prawn Farms in Tanzania with an Example from the Rufiji Delta, *Catchment Forestry Report* 96/4, The Mangrove Management Project and Institute of Resource Assessment

Franceville, A (1984) *Yaoundé: Construire une Capitale*, ORSTOM, Paris

Freudenberger, M and Boege, E (1995) *Iniciative par la Población y el Medio Ambiente en la Reserva de Calakmul: Documento Conceptual*, World Wildlife Fund, Washington, DC

Gadgil, M, Berkes, F and Folke, C (1993) Indigenous Knowledge for Biodiversity Conservation, *Ambio* 22, 2–3, pp151–156

Galindo-Leal, Carlos (nd) 'Diseno de Reservas: El "Mal" Congénito de Calakmul', unpublished article

Galleti, HA (nd) 'Bases para la Implementación de una Politica Regional de Desarrollo en la Región de Xpujil, Campeche', unpublished article

Gallopin, GC (1991) Human Dimensions of Global Change: Linking the Global and the Local Processes, *International Social Science Journal* 43/4, pp707–718

Garcia, R (1984) *Food Systems and Society: A Conceptual and Methodological Challenge*, UNRISD, Geneva

GEF (1996) *Operational Strategy of the Global Environment Facility*, GEF, Washington, DC

Government of Bulgaria (nd) *National Action Plan for The Conservation of the Most Important Wetlands in Bulgaria*, report prepared by the Ministry of Environment, Sofia

Government of Pakistan (1996) *Agricultural Statistics*, Ministry of Food and Agriculture

Government of Pakistan and IUCN (1991) *National Conservation Strategy*

Government of the Slovak Republic (1995) *Act of the National Council of the Slovak Republic No 287/1994 on Nature and Landscape Protection*, Translation of the Act, Spisska Nova Ves

Gwekok, SH (1937) *The Golden Book of Cebu*, JS Leyson, Cebu City

Haenn, N (1996) *Who is this Person in my House? Community Based Conservation in the Calakmul Biosphere Reserve*, The Nature Conservancy

Haenn, N (1997) Creating Communities through Acceptance/Rejection of Migrants in Frontier Campeche, paper prepared for the Latin American Studies Association meeting, Guadalajara

Hall, CAS and Day, JW eds (1977) *Ecosystem Modelling in Theory and Practice: An Introduction with Case Histories*, University of Colorado Press, Niwot, Colorado

Hanna, SS, Folke, C and Maler, K-G eds (1996) *Rights to Nature: Ecological, Economic, Cultural, and Political Principles of Institutions for the Environment*, Island Press, Washington DC

Holling, CS (1995) Biodiversity in the Functioning of Ecosystems: An Ecological Synthesis, in Perrings C et al (1995) *Biodiversity Loss: Economic and Ecological Issues*, Cambridge University Press, Cambridge

INE and CONABIO (1995) *Reservas de la Biósfera y otras Áreas Naturales Protegidas de México*, Mexico

Instituto Brasileiro de Geografia e Estatística (1998) *Censo Agropecuário 1991–1996: Goiás, Número 25*, Rio de Janeiro

Instituto Brasileiro de Geografia e Estatística (1997) *Contagem da População - Resultados Relativos a Sexo da População e Situação da Unidade Domiciliar*, vol 1, Rio de Janeiro

Instituto Brasileiro de Geografia e Estatística (1993) Brazil Vegetation Map, Rio de Janeiro

Instituto Nacional de Estadística, Geográfica e Informática (1995) *Estadísticas del Medio Ambiente: México 1994*, Mexico

International Institute for Sustainable Development (1996) *The World Trade Organization and Sustainable Development: An Independent Assessment*, IISD, Winnipeg

IUCN (1993) *Hydrology and the Environment*

IUCN (1996) in Sikod, F, *Interlinkages Between Trade and the Environment: a Case Study in Cameroon*, UNCTAD report

IUCN (1998) *Biodiversity Action Plan*

Jepma, CJ (1995) *Tropical Deforestation: A Socio-Economic Approach*, Earthscan Publications, London

Jhingran, VG (1963) *Report on Fisheries of Chilika Lake 1995–1960*, Bulletin, Central Inland Fisheries Research Institute, Barrackpore

Jhingran, VG and Natarajan, AV (1966) *Final Report on the Fisheries of the Chilika Lake 1957–65*, Bulletin, Central Inland Fisheries Research Institute, Barrackpore

Jorgenson, AB (1993) *Chicle Extraction and Forest Conservation in Quintana Roo, Mexico*, University of Florida

Kates, R and Haarman, V (1992) Where the Poor Live: Are the Assumptions Correct? *Environment* 34/ 4, pp 4–11, 25–28

Khong, D (1995) *Population and Ethnic Population in Vietnam*, Social Publishing House, Hanoi

Khong, D (1996) *Socio-economic Future of Ethnic Minorities in Northern Mountainous Region*, Social Publishing House, Hanoi

Kikula, IS and Mung'ong'o, CG (1992) Environmental Problems of Natural Resources: A Case Study of HADO Project, EIA seminar, NEMC, Dar es Salaam

Klarer, J and Moldan, B eds (1997) *The Environmental Challenge for Central and Eastern European Economies in Transition*, John Wiley & Sons, Chichester

Klink, CA, Moreira, AG and Solbrig, OT (1993) Ecological Impacts of Agricultural Development in the Brazilian Cerrados, in Young, MD and Solbrig, OT eds *The World's Savannas – Economic Driving Forces, Ecological Constraints and Policy Options for Sustainable Land Use*, MAB vol 12, UNESCO, Paris

Larson, PS, Freudenberger, M and Wyckoff-Baird, B (1998) *WWF Integrated Conservation and Development Projects: Ten Lessons from the Field 1985–1996*, WWF

Leonard, HJ ed (1989) *Environment and the Poor: Development Strategies for a Common Agenda*, Transaction Books, New Brunswick

Levy, D and van Wijnbergen, S (1992) *Transition Problems in Economic Reform: Agriculture in the Mexico-US Free Trade Agreement*, Policy Research Working Paper 967, World Bank, Washington, DC

Li, Z, ed (1993) *Pingwu County Natural Geography*, Pingwu People's Government, Pingwu

Little, PD and Horowitz, MM eds (1987) *Lands at Risk in the Third World: Local-Level Perspectives*, Westview Press, Boulder

Long, Y, Kirkpatrick, C, Tai, Z and Li, X (1996) Status and Conservation – Strategy for the Yunnan Snub-nosed Monkey, *Chinese Biodiversity* 4(3), pp145–152

Low, S (1956) *The Effect of Colonial Rule on Population Distribution in the Philippines, 1898–1941*, Fletcher School of Law and Diplomacy

Lu, Z et al [37] (1998) *Socioeconomic Investigation Report on the Integrated Conservation and Development Project of the Giant Panda Habitats in Pingwu*

Lutz, E (1990a) Agricultural Trade Liberalization: Price Changes and Environmental Effects, World Bank Environment Department Working Paper 16, World Bank, Washington, DC

Lutz, E (1990b) *Environmental and Resource Economics 2*, pp79–89, World Bank, Washington, DC

Machlis, G and Forester, D (1996) The Relationship between Socioeconomic Factors and the Loss of Biodiversity: First Efforts at Theoretical and Quantitative Models, in Szaro, R and Johnston, D eds *Biodiversity in Managed Landscapes: Theory and Practice*, Oxford University Press, New York

Mackinnon, J et al (1989) *Draft Management Plan for Yok Don Nature Reserve, Easup District, Dak Lak Province, Vietnam*, unpublished

Magsalay, PM. (1993) Rediscovery of Four Cebu Endemic Birds (Philippines), *Asia Life Sciences* 2(2), pp141–148

Mahar, D (1989) *Government Policies and Deforestation in Brazil's Amazon Region*, World Bank, Washington, DC

Maler, K-G and Munasinghe, M (1996) Macroeconomic Policies, Second-Best Theory and the Environment, *Environment and Development Economics* 1, pp149–163. Also Beijer Reprint Series No 71

Mantovani, JE and Pereira, A (1998) *Estimativa da Integridade da Cobertura Vegetal de Cerrado Através de Dados TM/Landsat*, Instituto Nacional de Pesquisas Espaciais, São José dos Campos, Brazil

March, I (1991a) Estudio sobre Cacería de Subsistencia en la Reserva de la Biósfera Calakmul: Informe parcial, Pronatura Península de Yucatán, Mérida

March, I (1991b) Estudio para la Auto-Regulación de la Cacería de Subsistencia en la Reserva de la Biósfera de Calakmul: Segundo informe de actividades, Pronatura Península de Yucatán, Mérida

McCoy, AW and de Jesus, EC eds (1982) *Philippine Social History: Global Trade and Local Transformations*, Asian Studies Association of Australia, Southeast Asia Publications Series, no 7, Manila University Press, Quezon City

McNeely, J (1988) *Economics and Biodiversity: Developing and Using Economic Incentives to Conserve Biological Resources*, IUCN, Gland

McNeely, J et al (1990) *Conserving the World's Biodiversity*, IUCN, Gland

Meyer, WB and Turner, BL (1992) Human Population Growth and Global Land-Use/Cover Change, *Annual Review of Ecology and Sytematics* 23, pp39–62

Meyer, WB and Turner BL, eds (1994) *Changes in Land Use and Land Cover: A Global Perspective*, Cambridge University Press, New York

Mgaya, YD (1998) Biodiversity and Conservation of the Marine Environment, *Kakakuona* 10, pp58–61

Ministry of Agriculture and Rural Development (1996) *Summary Report on Forestry Development Plan in Period 1996–2000 and to 2010*, unpublished

Ministry of Forestry (1991) *Vietnam Forestry Sector Review: Tropical Forestry Action Programme*, unpublished

Ministry of Forestry and WWF (1989) *National Conservation Management Plan for the Giant Panda and its Habitat–Sichuan, Gansu and Shaanxi Provinces, the People's Republic of China*, Hongkong

Ministry of Natural Resources and Tourism (1998) The Mangrove Management Project: Phase II Sector Agreement between Ministry of Natural Resources and Tourism and Norwegian Agency for Development Co-operation, Dar es Salaam

Ministry of Science, Technology and Environment (1992) *Red Data Book of Vietnam*, vol I and II, Science Publishing House, Hanoi

Mishra, PM (1988) Fishery Development of Chilika Lake, in Patro SN ed *Chilika – The Pride of Our Wetland Heritage*, Orissa Environmental Society, Bhubaneshwar

Mitra, GN (1946) *Development of the Chilika Lake*, Orissa Government Press, Cuttack

Mitzlaff, UV (1989)Coastal Communities in Tanzania and Their Mangrove Environment (Appendix 4 to Semesi, 1991), The Catchment Forestry Project. Dar es Salaam

Model Forest Network and SAHR (1994) *Bosque Modelo para Calakmul: Ecología Productiva Propuesta*

Mohanty, RC (1998) *A Report on the Present Status of Weeds in Chilika Lagoon*, Chilika Development Authority Project, Utkal University, Bhubaneshwar

Mohanty, SK (1975) The Breeding of Economic Fishes of the Chilika Lake – A Review, *Bulletin, Department of Marine Sciences*, University of Cochin, 7(3), pp543–559

Mohapatra, LK (1973) Fishing and Fishermen on the Chilika Lake in Orissa, *India Museum Bulletin* 8(1)

Mohapatra, P, Samant Singh, NC, Mohanty, DC and Bhatta, KS (1988) A Study of Physico-Chemical Observation of Three Stations in Chilika Lagoon During the Years 1985–87, *National Seminar on Conservation and Management of Chilika*, Bhubaneshwar: Department of Science, Technology and Environment, Government of Orissa

Mohapatra, SN (1988) *Scope for Development of Chilika Lake*, Bhubaneshwar: Department of Science, Technology and Environment, Government of Orissa

Morett, S and Jesus, C (1992) *Alternativas de Modernización del Ejido*, Editorial Diana, Mexico

Murphy, J (1990) Indigenous Forest Use and Development in the 'Maya Zone' of Quintana Roo, Mexico, Graduate Program in Environmental Studies, York University, Ontario

Murphy, J (1992) Interacción de la Explotación Forestal Comercial a la Agricultura Milpera en la Zona Maya de Quintana Roo, in Daniel Zizumbo Villareal et al, eds *La Modernización de la Milpa en Yucatán: Utopia o Realidad*, Centro de Investigación Científica de Yucatán, Mérida

Muuchal, PK and Ngandjui, G (1997) *Impact of Village Hunting on Wildlife Populations in the Western Dja Reserve*, Ecofac, Yaoundé

Mwalyosi, RBB (1990) Resource Potentials of the Rufiji River Basin, Tanzania, *Ambio* 19(1), pp16–20

Mwalyosi, RBB and Kayara, J (1995) Biodiversity Conservation and Management: A Contribution to the National Biodiversity Country Study, report for the NEMC

National Research Council (1992) *Conserving Biodiversity: A Research Agenda for Development Agencies*, National Academy Press

NEMC (1997) Technical Review of an Environmental Impact Assessment for an Environmentally Responsible Prawn Farming Project in the Rufiji Delta, Tanzania, Government of Tanzania

Orissa Environmental Society (1997) *Workshop on the Participation of the Local Communities for the Protection of Natural Resources – The Wetland of Chilika*

Orissa Remote Sensing Application Centre (1988) *Interim Report on Study of Chilika Lake Resources and Environment*, Bhubaneshwar

Painter, M (1995) Anthropological Perspectives on Environmental Destruction, in Painter, M and Durham, W eds *The Social Causes of Environmental Destruction in Latin America*, University of Michigan Press, Ann Arbor

Painter, M and Durham, W eds (1995) *The Social Causes of Environmental Destruction in Latin America*, University of Michigan Press, Ann Arbor

Patnaik, S (1971) Seasonal Abundance and Distribution of Bottom Fauna of the Chilika Lake, *Journal of the Marine Biological Association of India*, (13)1, pp106–125

Patro, SN (1988) *Chilika – The Pride of Our Wetland Heritage*, Orissa Environmental Society, Bhubaneshwar

Pearce, D, Barbier, E and Markandya, A (1990) *Sustainable Development: Economics and Environment in the Third World*, Edward Elgar, London

Pearce, D and Warford, J (1993) *World Without End*, World Bank, Washington, DC

Pearce, D and Moran, D (1994) *The Economic Value of Biodiversity*, Earthscan Publications, London

Pelzer, KJ (1948) *Pioneer Settlement in the Asiatic Tropics*, American Geographical Society, New York

Perrings, C et al eds (1995) *Biodiversity Loss: Economic and Ecological Issues*, Cambridge University Press, New York

Pingwu County Finance Bureau (1997) *County Status Briefing*, Pingwu

Pingwu County Statistical Bureau (1990–95) *Pingwu Statistics Yearbook*, Pingwu

Presidency of the Republic of Brazil (1970) *Metas e Bases para a Ação do Governo, 1970/74*, Brasília

Pronatura Península de Yucatán (1997a) *Estudio Rural Participativo, Población y Medio Ambiente, Ejido: Conhuas, Calakmul, Campeche*, Mérida

Pronatura Península de Yucatán (1997b) *Estudio Rural Participativo, Población y Medio Ambiente, Ejido: 11 de Mayo, Calakmul, Campeche*, Mérida

Pronatura Península de Yucatán (1997c) *Estrategía para la Conservación y Ecodesarrollo en la Reserva de la Biósfera de Calakmul, Campeche, México*, Jan 1998–Dec 2002

Pufal, DVL (in press) *Atividades Agropecuárias no Cerrado e Desenvolvimento Sustentável*, Projeto Conservação e Manejo da Biodiversidade do Bioma Cerrado, Componente Socioeconomia, Subprojeto Atividades Agropecuárias no Cerrado; Institute for Society, Population and Nature, Brasília

Qureshi, T (1989)Rehabilitation and Development of Indus Delta Mangroves Forest, in Tirmizi, NM and Kazi, QB eds *Study and Management in Coastal Zones in Pakistan*, Proceedings of National Sciences

Rajyalakshmi, T (1983) Application of Pen and Cage Culture Technology in Certain Brackishwater Lagoons and Lakes in India, *Proceedings of the National Seminar on Cage Pen Culture*

Rath, A (1997) *Preservation Value of a Wetland Ecosystem: A Case Study of Chilika*, unpublished, University of Delhi

Redclift, M (1987) *Sustainable Development: Exploring the Contradictions*, Methuen, New York

Redford, KH and Mansour, J eds (1996) *Traditional Peoples and Biodiversity Conservation in Large Tropical Landscapes*,The Nature Conservancy, Rosslyn

Reed, D, ed (1992) *Structural Adjustment and the Environment*, Earthscan Publications, London

Reed, D, ed (1993) *The Global Environment Facility: Sharing Responsibility for the Biosphere, Volume II*, WWF International Institutions Policy Programme

Reed, D, ed (1996) *Structural Adjustment, the Environment, and Sustainable Development*, Earthscan Publications, London

Repetto, R (1985) *The Global Possible: Resources, Development, and the New Century*, Yale University Press

Repetto, R and Gillis, M eds (1988) *Public Policies and the Misuse of Forest Resources*, Cambridge University Press, New York

Richardson, L (1995) *Análisis de Agroecosistemas en Narciso Mendoza, Campeche, México*, Colegio de Postgraduados Institución de Enseñanza e Investigación en Ciencias Agricolos, Montecillas, Mexico

Robinson, JB (1991) Modelling the Interactions between Human and Natural Systems, *International Social Science Journal* 43/4, pp629–648

Robinson, N, ed (1993) *Agenda 21: Earth's Action Plan*, Oceana Publications

Rockwell, RC (1994) Culture and Cultural Change, in Meyer, WB and Turner BL, eds *Changes in Land Use and Land Cover: A Global Perspective*, Cambridge University Press, New York

Ropke, I (1994) Trade, Development and Sustainability, *Ecological Economics* 9, pp13–22

Roque, C (1997) Comparative Study of Biodiversity Loss in Three Island Ecosystems of the Philippines: Inception Report

Rufiji Basin Development Authority (1981) *Study of the Impact of the Stiegler's Gorge Multipurpose Project on Fisheries in the Rufiji Delta and Mafia Channel*, Adkins Land and Water Management, Cambridge, England

Rufiji District Administration (1998) *The Rufiji Delta and Floodplain: Environmental Management and Biodiversity Conservation of Forests, Woodlands and Wetland Project*

Ruitenbeek, HJ and Cartier, C (1998) *Rational Exploitations: Economic Criteria and Indicators for Sustainable Management of Tropical Forests*, CIFOR

Sage, C (1994) Population and Income, in Meyer, WB and Turner, BL, eds *Changes in Land Use and Land Cover: A Global Perspective*, Cambridge University Press, New York

Sahu, BN (1988) The Chilika Lake is in Danger, in Patro, SN ed *Chilika–The Pride of Our Wetland Heritage*, Orissa Environmental Society, Bhubaneshwar

Salim, CA (1986) As Políticas Econômicas e Tecnológicas para o Desenvolvimento Agrário das Áreas de Cerrados no Brasil: Avaliação e Perspectivas, *Cad Dif Tecnol* 3(2),pp297–342

Sanderson, S (1994) Political-Economic Institutions, in Meyer, WB and Turner, BL, eds *Changes in Land Use and Land Cover: A Global Perspective*, Cambridge University Press, New York

Sandlund, OT, Bryceson, I, Larsen, K, Maro, W and Kulindwa, K (1997) *NORAD Funded Programmes for Management of Natural Resources and Environmental Planning in Tanzania*, Norwegian Consortium for Development and Environment and the Economic Research Bureau, University of Dar es Salaam

Schiff, MW and Valdes, A (1992) *The Plundering of Agriculture in Developing Countries*, World Bank, Washington, DC

Schmink, M and Wood, CH (1987) The Political Ecology of Amazonia, in Little, PD and Horowitz, MM eds *Lands at Risk in the Third World: Local-Level Perspectives*, Westview Press, Boulder

Schumann, DA and Partridge, WL eds (1989) *The Human Ecology of Tropical Land Settlement in Latin America*,Westview Press, Boulder

Secretaria de Estado de Agricultura e Abastecimento (1997) *Informações Estatísticas Agropecuárias*, Safras (harvests) 1994/95 and 1995/96, Goiás

Sedjo, R and Simpson, D (1995) Property Rights, Externalities and Biodiversity, in Swanson, TM ed *The Economics and Ecology of Biodiversity Decline: The Forces Driving Global Change*, Cambridge University Press, New York

Seffer, J et al (1996) *Wetlands for Life*, Daphne Foundation, Bratislava

Semesi, AK (1991) Management Plan for the Mangrove Ecosystem of Mainland Tanzania in *Mangrove Management Plan of All Coastal Districts* vol 11, Ministry of Tourism, Natural Resources and Environment, Forest and Bee-Keeping Division, Dar es Salaam

Semesi, AK (1994) Coastal Communities in Tanzania and their Mangrove Environment: A Case of Communities Living in Rufiji Delta Mangroves, *Mangrove Ecosystems Proceedings* 3, pp63–76, Okinawa, Japan

Serageldin, I (1996) *Sustainability and the Wealth of Nations: First Steps in an Ongoing Journey*, Environmentally Sustainable Development Studies and Monographs Series no 5, World Bank, Washington, DC

Sinha, BN (nd) Impact of Large Scale Commercial Prawn Cultivation in the S.E. Sector of Lake Chilika on its Ecosystem

Sjoberg, H (1994) *From Idea to Reality: the Creation of the Global Environment Facility*, GEF working paper 10, Washington, DC

Snook, LK and Jorgenson, AB eds (1994) *Madera, Chicle, Caza y Milpa*, Memorias del Taller, July 1992, Chetumal, Mexico: PROAFT, Instituto Nacional de Investiaciones Forestales, Agricolas y Pecuarias, USAID and WWF-US

Southgate, D (1988) *The Economics of Land Degradation in the Third World*, World Bank Environment Department working paper 2, World Bank, Washington, DC

Sperrer, S et al (1997) *A Organização dos Pequenos Agricultores de Silvânia – Goiânia: Origem, Estrutura e Impactos Sociais*, Empresa Brasileira de Pesquisa Agropecuaria, Série Documentos, no 68, DF, Planaltina

Stanova, V et al (1997) *Strategy for Sustainable Agriculture in the Lower Part of the Zahorie Region*, Daphne Foundation, Bratislava

Stedman-Edwards, P (1997) *Socioeconomic Root Causes of Biodiversity Loss: An Approach Paper*, WWF MPO, Washington, DC

Stedman-Edwards, P (1998) *Root Causes of Biodiversity Loss: An Analytical Approach*, WWF MPO, Washington, DC

Stern, P, Young, O and Druckman, D eds (1992) *Global Environmental Change: Understanding the Human Dimensions*, National Academy Press, Washington, DC

Stonich, SC (1995) Development, Rural Impoverishment, and Environmental Destruction in Honduras, in Painter, M and Durham, W eds *The Social Causes of Environmental Destruction in Latin America*, University of Michigan Press, Ann Arbor

Stuart, SN et al (1990) Biodiversity in Sub-Saharan Africa and Its Islands: Conservation, Management, and Sustainable Use. A Contribution to the Biodiversity Conservation Strategy Programme; IUCN Species Survival Commission no 6, Gland

Swanson, T (1997) *Global Action for Biodiversity*, Earthscan Publications, London

Swanson, TM ed (1995) *The Economics and Ecology of Biodiversity Decline: The Forces Driving Global Change*, Cambridge University Press, New York

Tavera, G (1997) Calakmul: Productos de la Selva

Thompson, M F and Tirmizi, NM (1995) *The Arabian Sea Killing Marine Resources and the Environment*

Tierra y Libertad, Bufete Jurídico (1997) Análisis Jurídico del Nuevo Marco Legal para el Campo

UNEP (1989) Coastal and marine environmental problems of the United Republic of Tanzania, *UNEP Regional Seas Reports and Studies* 106

UNEP (1992) Convention on Biological Diversity

United Republic of Tanzania (1994) Report of the Presidential Commission of Inquiry into Land Matters, *Land Policy and Land Tenure Structure*, vol 1, Government of the United Republic of Tanzania and Scandinavian Institute of African Studies, Uppsala, Sweden

United Republic of Tanzania (1997a) *Coast Region Socio-Economic Profile*, The Planning Commission and Regional Commissioner's Office, Coast Region

United Republic of Tanzania (1997b) *National Biodiversity Country Study Report*, UNEP, Nairobi, Kenya

Uquillas, J (1989) Social Impacts of Modernization and Public Policy, and Prospects for Indigenous Development in Ecuador's Amazonia, in Schumann, DA and Partridge, WL eds *The Human Ecology of Tropical Land Settlement in Latin America*, Westview, Boulder

Varshney, CK (1993) Integrated Shrimp Farming Project at Chilika Lake; Ecological

Implications and Critique of Environmental Management Plan, monograph, WWF India

Venkataratnam, K (1965) *Studies on Some Aspects of the Sediments of Chilika Lake*, unpublished, Department of Geology, Andhra University, India

Vettivel, S (1992) Managing Chilika Lake Environment, Orissa Environmental Society, Bhubaneshwar

Vietnam Economic Times (1997) Sept 13, p74

Vincent, JR and Panayotou, T (1997) Consumption: Challenge to Sustainable Development or Distraction? *Science* 276, pp53–57

Vo, Q (1987) *Endangered and Rare Species in Vietnam*, Garrulax 2, UK

Weber, M (1997) Evaluación Rápida de la Cacería de Subsistencia en la Región de Calakmul, Campeche, Pronatura Península de Yucatán

Wells, M (1994) The Global Environment Facility and Prospects for Biodiversity Conservation, *International Environmental Affairs* 6(1)

Western, D and Wright, RM eds (1994) *Natural Connections: Perspectives in Community-based Conservation*, Island Press, Washington, DC

White, AT (1987) *Coral Reefs: Valuable Resources of Southeast Asia*, ICLARAM Educational Series, Manila

Wolf, A (1995) *Incremental Cost Analysis in Addressing Global Environmental Problems*, WWF International Institutions Policy Programme

World Bank (1993) *Vietnam: Transition to the Market: An Economic Report*, Washington, DC

World Bank (1994a) *Economywide Policies and the Environment: Emerging Lessons from Experience*, Washington, DC

World Bank (1994b) *Vietnam: Environmental Program and Policy Priorities for a Socialist Economy in Transition*, Washington, DC

World Bank (1995a) *Mexico: Resource Conservation and Forest Sector Review*, report 13114-ME, Washington, DC

World Bank (1995b) *Vietnam: Environmental Programs and Policy Priorities for a Socialist Economy in Transition*, Washington, DC

World Bank (1995c) *Monitoring Environmental Progress: A Report on Work in Progress*, World Bank, Washington, DC

World Bank (1997) *Mexico: Community Forestry Project*, report 16134-ME, Washington, DC

World Commission on Environment and Development (1987) *Our Common Future*, Oxford University Press

WRI, IUCN and UNEP (1992) *Global Biodiversity Strategy*, WRI, Washington, DC

WRI, IUCN and UNEP (1992) *Global Biodiversity Strategy: Guidelines for Action to Save, Study, and Use Earth's Biotic Wealth Sustainably and Equitably*, WRI, IUCN and UNEP

WWF (1994) *Ramsar Sites of India: Chilika Lake*, New Delhi

WWF (1999) *Living Planet Report – 1999*, WWF

WWF (1999) Initiating an Environmental Assessment of Trade Liberalization in the WTO, discussion paper, [86]

Yunnan Provincial No 4 Forestry Survey Team (1981) *Field Survey and Planning in Baimaxueshan Nature Reserve, Kunming*

Zamora, PM (1980) Philippine Mangroves: Assessment of Status, Environmental Problems, Conservation and Management Strategies, *Bakawan* 1(1), p2

Zouya-Mimbang, L (1998) *Les Circuits de Commercialisation des Chasses dans le Sud-Est Cameroun*, GTZ, Yokadouma

Index